An Archaeology of Identity

PUBLICATIONS OF THE INSTITUTE OF ARCHAEOLOGY, UNIVERSITY COLLEGE LONDON

Director of the Institute: Stephen Shennan
Publications Series Editor: Peter J. Ucko

The Institute of Archaeology of University College London is one of the oldest, largest and most prestigious archaeology research facilities in the world. Its extensive publications programme includes the best theory, research, pedagogy and reference materials in archaeology and cognate disciplines, through publishing exemplary work of scholars worldwide. Through its publications, the Institute brings together key areas of theoretical and substantive knowledge, improves archaeological practice and brings archaeological findings to the general public, researchers and practitioners. It also publishes staff research projects, site and survey reports, and conference proceedings. The publications programme, formerly developed in-house or in conjunction with UCL Press, is now produced in partnership with Left Coast Press, Inc. The Institute can be accessed online at http://www.ucl.ac.uk/archaeology.

ENCOUNTERS WITH ANCIENT EGYPT
Subseries, Peter J. Ucko, (ed.)

Jean-Marcel Humbert and Clifford Price (eds.), *Imhotep Today* (2003)
David Jeffreys (ed.), *Views of Ancient Egypt since Napoleon Bonaparte: Imperialism, Colonialism, and Modern Appropriations* (2003)
Sally MacDonald and Michael Rice (eds.), *Consuming Ancient Egypt* (2003)
Roger Matthews and Cornelia Roemer (eds.), *Ancient Perspectives on Egypt* (2003)
David O'Connor and Andrew Reid (eds.), *Ancient Egypt in Africa* (2003)
John Tait (ed.), *'Never had the like occurred': Egypt's View of its Past* (2003)
David O'Connor and Stephen Quirke (eds.), *Mysterious Lands* (2003)
Peter Ucko and Timothy Champion (eds.), *The Wisdom of Egypt: Changing Visions Through the Ages* (2003)

Andrew Gardner (ed.), *Agency Uncovered: Archaeological Perspectives on Social Agency, Power, and Being Human* (2004)
Okasha El-Daly, *Egyptology, The Missing Millennium: Ancient Egypt in Medieval Arabic Writing* (2005)
Ruth Mace, Clare J. Holden, and Stephen Shennan (eds.), *Evolution of Cultural Diversity: A Phylogenetic Approach* (2005)
Arkadiusz Marciniak, *Placing Animals in the Neolithic: Social Zooarchaeology of Prehistoric Farming* (2005)
Robert Layton, Stephen Shennan, and Peter Stone (eds.), *A Future for Archaeology* (2006)
Joost Fontein, *The Silence of Great Zimbabwe: Contested Landscapes and the Power of Heritage* (2006)
Gabriele Puschnigg, *Ceramics of the Merv Oasis: Recycling the City* (2006)
James Graham-Campbell and Gareth Williams (eds.), *Silver Economy in the Viking Age* (2007)
Barbara Bender, Sue Hamilton, and Chris Tilley, *Stone Worlds: Narrative and Reflexivity in Landscape Archaeology* (2007)
Andrew Gardner, *An Archaeology of Identity: Soldiers and Society in Late Roman Britain* (2007)
Sue Hamilton, Ruth D. Whitehouse, Katherine I. Wright (eds.), *Archaeology and Women: Ancient and Modern Issues* (2007)

An Archaeology of Identity

Soldiers and Society in Late Roman Britain

Andrew Gardner

Left Coast Press Inc.

Walnut Creek, California

LEFT COAST PRESS, INC.
1630 North Main Street, #400
Walnut Creek, CA 94596
http://www.LCoastPress.com

Copyright © 2007 by Left Coast Press, Inc.

All rights reserved. No part of this publication may be reproduced, stored in a retrieval system, or transmitted in any form or by any means, electronic, mechanical, photocopying, recording, or otherwise, without the prior permission of the publisher.

ISBN 978-1-59874-226-8 hardcover
ISBN 978-1-59874-227-5 paperback

Library of Congress Cataloging-in-Publication Data:

Gardner, Andrew, 1973–
An archaeology of identity : soldiers and society in late Roman Britain / Andrew Gardner.
p. cm. — (Publications of the Institute of Archaeology, University College London)
Includes bibliographical references and index.
ISBN-13: 978-1-59874-226-8 (hardcover : alk. paper)
ISBN-10: 1-59874-226-4 (hardcover : alk. paper)
ISBN-13: 978-1-59874-227-5 (pbk. : alk. paper)
ISBN-10: 1-59874-227-2 (pbk. : alk. paper)
1. Great Britain—History—Roman period, 55 B.C.–449 A.D. 2. Great Britain—Social life and customs—To 1066. 3. Great Britain—Antiquities, Roman. 4. Romans—Great Britain. I. Title.
DA145.G37 2007
936.2'04—dc22

2006035674

Printed in the United States of America

⊖™ The paper used in this publication meets the minimum requirements of American National Standard for Information Sciences—Permanence of Paper for Printed Library Materials, ANSI/NISO Z39.48–1992.

07 08 09 10 11   5 4 3 2 1

Dedicated to the memory of Bill and Marjorie Slater

CONTENTS

List of Illustrations		9
Preface		13
Acknowledgements		14

1. Introduction: the Roman Empire in the 21st century — **15**
- An archaeology of identity — 15
- Particular studies and general problems — 20
- The development of Roman studies — 24
- 21st century agendas — 31

2. The practice of identity — **35**
- Texts and theory in a historical discipline — 35
- Agency, structure, and practice — 39
- 4th century problems — 51

3. The material dimensions of 4th century life: objects and spaces — **63**
- Studying materiality — 63
- Portable material culture — 67
- Architectural material culture — 97
- Texts as objects — 122
- Material practices and identity — 128

4. The temporal dimensions of 4th century life: traditions and change — **133**
- Studying temporality — 133
- Biographies of assemblages — 139
- Biographies of places — 166
- Writing Roman history — 186
- Tradition, transformation, and structuration — 191

5. The social dimensions of 4th century life: interactions and identities   **197**

    Studying sociality   197

    From practices to identities   203

    The social world in late Roman Britain   217

    A topography of 4th century identities   239

6. Conclusion: Roman Britain in the 4th century   **243**

    The dynamics of identification in late Roman Britain   243

    Late Roman Britain and the late Roman Empire   258

    The archaeology of complex identities   261

    An empire for the 21st century?   264

Bibliography   267

Index   303

About the Author   312

LIST OF ILLUSTRATIONS

Figure 2.1.	A suggested theoretical synthesis for historical archaeologies.	39
Figure 2.2.	A visualisation of the duality of structure, using Giddens's terminology.	44
Figure 2.3.	Dimensions (temporality, materiality, sociality) of human life that connect agency and structure.	52
Figure 2.4.	Map of Roman Britain, showing major administrative boundaries of the 4th century and the locations of sites mentioned in the text.	54
Figure 3.1.	Photograph of the southwestern corner of Caernarfon.	70
Figure 3.2.	Plans of coin deposition at Caernarfon.	71
Figure 3.3.	Photograph of the western gate area at Birdoswald.	72
Figure 3.4.	Plans of coin deposition at Birdoswald.	72
Figure 3.5.	Photograph of the reconstructed southwestern gate at South Shields, on the site of the Roman portal.	74
Figure 3.6.	Plans of coin deposition at South Shields.	75
Figure 3.7.	Plans of coin deposition at York.	77
Figure 3.8.	The British Mean for coin loss.	79
Figure 3.9.	Overview of small finds categories at selected sites.	81
Figure 3.10.	Examples of significant later Roman small find types.	82
Figure 3.11.	Plans of small find deposition at Caernarfon.	83
Figure 3.12.	Plans of small find deposition at Birdoswald.	84
Figure 3.13.	Plans of small find deposition at South Shields.	86
Figure 3.14.	Plans of small find deposition at York.	87
Figure 3.15.	Examples of the range of pottery supplied to different sites in the 4th century.	93
Figure 3.16.	Examples of the range of animal species consumed on different sites in the 4th century.	96
Figure 3.17.	Plan of Caernarfon.	100
Figure 3.18.	Plan of Birdoswald.	101
Figure 3.19.	Plan of Housesteads.	102

Figure 3.20. Plan of South Shields. 103

Figure 3.21. Plans of Portchester Castle and Richborough. 104

Figure 3.22. Plan of Caerleon. 105

Figure 3.23. Plan of Chester. 106

Figure 3.24. Plans of Forden Gaer and Leintwardine. 108

Figure 3.25. Plan of Caerwent. 109

Figure 3.26. Plan of Canterbury. 110

Figure 3.27. Plan of Lincoln. 111

Figure 3.28. Plan of Cirencester. 112

Figure 3.29. Plan of Wroxeter. 113

Figure 4.1. An example of the type of 'time-space map' generated by time-geographical studies. 135

Figure 4.2. Caerleon coins/1000 and the British Mean. 141

Figure 4.3. Western sites coins/1000 minus the British Mean, noncumulative. 142

Figure 4.4. Western sites coins/1000 minus the British Mean, cumulative. 142

Figure 4.5. Coin deposition at selected sites in Wales. 144

Figure 4.6. Coin deposition at selected sites in northern England. 144

Figure 4.7. Coin deposition at selected sites in central and southern England. 146

Figure 4.8. Coin deposition at selected fort and fortress sites. 146

Figure 4.9. Coin deposition at selected *civitas* capitals. 148

Figure 4.10. Coin deposition at selected other towns and settlements. 148

Figure 4.11. Coin deposition at selected villas and farms. 149

Figure 4.12. Coin deposition at selected temple sites. 149

Figure 4.13. Small finds patterns through time: Caernarfon. 152

Figure 4.14. Small finds patterns through time: Caerleon. 153

Figure 4.15. Small finds patterns through time: Carlisle. 154

Figure 4.16. Small finds patterns through time: Orton Hall Farm. 155

Figure 4.17. Table of coin deposition through time at Orton Hall Farm. 155

Figure 4.18. Pottery supply through time: Birdoswald. 158

Figure 4.19. Pottery supply through time: Llandough. 159

Figure 4.20. Pottery supply through time: Cirencester. 159

Figure 4.21. Animal bone patterns through time: Caerleon. 161

Figure 4.22. Animal bone patterns through time: Caernarfon. 162

Figure 4.23. Animal bone patterns through time: Lincoln. 162

Figure 4.24. Animal bone patterns through time:
Orton Hall Farm. 163

Figure 4.25. Plan of Caerleon: activity density. 177

Figure 4.26. Plan of Chester: activity density. 178

Figure 4.27. Plan of Housesteads: activity density. 179

Figure 4.28. Plan of Portchester: pits and rubbish. 180

Figure 4.29. Plan of Canterbury: activity density. 180

Figure 4.30. Plan of Cirencester: activity density. 181

Figure 5.1. Photograph of the interior of the reconstructed
4th century officer's house at South Shields. 221

Figure 5.2. Photograph of one of the 'chalet' barrack rooms
at Housesteads. 222

Figure 5.3. A stratified model of identification in later
Roman Britain. 240

PREFACE

The origins of the research on which this book is based can be traced to an evening spent in the small town of Caerleon in Gwent, in September 1996. On this particular occasion, Richard Reece delivered the 10th Annual Caerleon Lecture, entitled 'The Future of Roman Military Archaeology' (published as Reece 1997). Characteristically controversial, this lecture planted the notion that there are many different ways of thinking about the subject with which I was primarily engaged at that point—the Roman military. That this notion took hold is thanks also to the long-standing encouragement and open-minded tolerance of my supervisor Mark Hassall; to Peter Guest for facilitating my initial phase of research on Caerleon's Roman fortress; and to Cyprian Broodbank and Stephen Shennan, whose teaching in the 'Themes, Thought and Theory in World Archaeology' course that same year was responsible for what can only be described as a theoretical epiphany. It is upon these specific foundations that my subsequent research into the Roman army in Britain (Gardner 2001a) was built.

The goal of this book is to present, among other things, a different way of looking at the archaeology of the Roman military. As much as anything, this is about using this particular—and often very narrowly studied—subject as a springboard for tackling much wider questions. The topics dealt with in the book can thus be seen as operating at a range of nested scales: the Roman military within late Roman Britain; late Roman Britain within the Roman Empire; and the Roman Empire within the spectrum of human societies. More will be said on the relationship between particular and general knowledge in Chapter 1; here, I wish only to state my firm conviction that studies focused on a context as specific as the Roman military still have much to contribute to the understanding of past social dynamics, and indeed must do so to avoid marginalisation within archaeology. Indeed, academic ghettoisation is not the only issue. The wider public outside of this discipline remains keenly interested in the Roman period, which is frequently represented by the Roman army in the form of re-enactment groups. If we accept that interpretations of the past play an important role in structuring the present, then continual re-invigoration of these interpretations is vital if archaeologists are to make responsible, relevant contributions to the societies in which they live and work.

ACKNOWLEDGEMENTS

My acknowledgements must begin with those who were instrumental in the completion of my doctoral studies. Mark Hassall, Stephen Shennan, Richard Reece, and Jeremy Tanner (all of the Institute of Archaeology, UCL) were involved in its supervision, while Matthew Johnson (University of Southampton) and Simon James (University of Leicester) were my examiners. In addition, a number of other people who are or have been based at the Institute of Archaeology offered practical, moral, or intellectual support during this and subsequent periods of research. These include Andrew Bevan, Cyprian Broodbank, James Conolly, Gwyn Davies, Jo Dullaghan, Stuart Laidlaw, Kris Lockyear, Sven van Lokeren, Judy Medrington, Katie Meheux, Koji Mizoguchi, Kathryn Piquette, Laura Preston, Ash Rennie, Joanne Rowland, Aaron Shugar, Steve Townend, Todd Whitelaw, and John Wilkes. I am especially grateful to Peter Ucko for his continued assistance and encouragement, without which I would not have had the opportunity to complete this book.

Those in other institutions who have been helpful in providing access to material or ideas include Lindsay Allason-Jones (University of Newcastle upon Tyne); Edward Besly, Richard Brewer, and Susan Fox (National Museums and Galleries of Wales); Paul Bidwell, Bill Griffiths, Nick Hodgson, and Graeme Stobbs (Tyne and Wear Museums); Richard Brickstock (University of Leeds) and John Casey (UCL); Edith Evans (Gwent-Glamorgan Archaeological Trust); Garrick Fincham (University of East Anglia); Peter Guest and Peter Webster (University of Cardiff); Simon Esmonde Cleary (University of Birmingham); Guy Halsall (University of York) and Ian Haynes (Birkbeck College, University of London); Robert Ireland (Department of Classics, UCL); Stephanie Koerner (University of Manchester); Martin Millett (University of Cambridge); John Miles Paddock (Corinium Museum); Ellen Swift (University of Kent at Canterbury); Colin Wallace (National Museum of Scotland); and Diane Williams (Cadw). I would also like to acknowledge the financial support of the AHRB and the Institute of Archaeology.

For their assistance in the later stages of the development of this book, I would like to thank my colleagues at Reading, Leicester, and Cardiff and the anonymous referees for their constructive criticism. While this volume began its life at UCL Press, it has been brought to completion under the auspices of Left Coast Press, and I am deeply indebted to Mitch Allen, Eliot Werner, and Andrew Brozyna for their vital roles in this process. Above all, I would like to express my deep gratitude to my partner Kathryn Piquette and to my family for their support in all things.

Chapter 1

INTRODUCTION: THE ROMAN EMPIRE IN THE 21ST CENTURY

An archaeology of identity

This book is about the lives and experiences of human beings in a different world from our own—the Roman world. As such it attempts to strike a delicate balance between the uniqueness of that world and the more general commonalities to being human that allow us to comprehend it in this, present, world. There are many ways in which people in the present, and in the more recent past, have identified with Roman culture, whether as a source of politics or entertainment. This has had both positive and negative consequences. It means that most people know something about the Romans, but—quite apart from the very serious part that Roman role-models have played in imperialist and fascist ideologies—it has also made the Roman world seem perhaps a bit too easily comprehensible. This impression is far from groundless, given that many elements of modern Western culture, consciously or not, draw upon Roman technologies or institutions. However, it is at best only half of the story, and at worst distorts the diversity of social processes in the past into the perceived unity of what resulted from them. It also leads to a certain degree of public apathy towards the Roman past, at least in Britain, which some other periods or cultures—such as that of ancient Egypt—manage to avoid thanks to their stimulating degree of exotic mystery. One of the main aims of this book is to challenge this familiarity by highlighting the many gaps in our understanding of what life was like in a Roman province, as well as offering some novel ways of closing them.

The part of the Roman world that the book has at its core is, at first sight, one of the most prosaic and close to home. The reason I began the research upon which it is based was because I had questions about the Roman army, particularly in Britain in the later part of the Roman occupation. I was puzzled about what became of Roman soldiers in

16 ■ An Archaeology of Identity

Britain (were they all withdrawn, or did they 'go native'?) and how this related to the so-called 'collapse' of Roman Britain at the beginning of the 5th century AD. Both of these topics—Roman Britain and the Roman army—are indeed amongst the most familiar parts of the Roman period to modern audiences. This is for the simple reason that they are the most fully studied. A combination of perceived connections between the Roman and British empires, and in more recent years a high level of professional archaeological organisation in the UK, have ensured that Britain is one of the most explored parts of the Roman world. Meanwhile, across the countries now inhabiting that world, the military has always been a focus of attention as one of the most obvious and dramatic elements in Roman imperial culture, particularly in what were frontier areas.

Nonetheless, this impression of comfortable familiarity begins to break down when one starts asking questions that have no easy answers within the established story. These questions can start from the smallest problems. At the end of the 3rd century, for instance, the fortress at Caerleon in southern Wales was supposedly abandoned by the legion based there, with 'squatters' subsequently moving in (Boon 1972: 66–70). This fits the idea that the Roman Empire was increasingly under pressure in this period, as well as the idea that the locals were quite keen to benefit even from the leftovers of civilised living. But what is the real difference between the artefacts, and assemblages of artefacts, in these 'military' and 'civilian' phases? After all, there are no texts telling us that this is what happened. As subsequent chapters of this book will demonstrate, the answer is that there is not much difference at all, and the same goes for many sites in this period, and indeed earlier too. From this small question, then, other questions spring, and soon the whole narrative we have constructed about the 'Romanisation' of Britain, or the 'professionalism' of the Roman army, begins to unravel. If people were using similar things whether they were 'soldiers' or 'squatters', how do we tell them apart? More importantly, how did *they* tell each other apart? And, going deeper, how did Roman soldiers in this period—and earlier ones too—think of or define themselves as soldiers through the objects they used and their behaviour? What about the significance of other aspects of their lives—their families or where they came from? How were their interactions with local people actually structured, in material and social terms, and what impact did this have on the history of 'Roman' Britain as part of the Roman Empire? How did the history of this one area, in turn, shape or reflect the history of the empire as seen from the perspective of the emperors?

It soon becomes clear, once these questions are asked, that the Roman army is not what we think it is (James 2002; Reece 1997), and the same is true for Roman Britain (Hingley 2000). This is partly because the narratives we use (which are explored in detail below) have been so heavily shaped by more modern concerns, such as the need to find lessons from the Roman Empire for the people running the British Empire. It is also because Roman culture is not our culture, but is different. To confront this difference, we have to re-examine in considerable detail the material culture used by the people about whom we are asking questions, with a full appreciation of its context. In other words, we need to particularise our study and focus on what the patterns in this material culture can tell us about the day-to-day life of those people. This entails multilevel comparison within and between parts of the Roman world. Thus, from their small beginnings at Caerleon, my efforts to understand the nature of 4th century military culture have expanded to encompass aspects of the interaction between Roman and local identities across the whole span of the history of Roman Britain, from the 1st century AD onwards, as well as drawing upon material from other parts of the empire. This comparative scope is fully reflected in this book, though my aim is less to produce another grand narrative of Roman Britain and more to highlight a range of diverse narratives.

At the same time, however, to produce any narratives of Roman Britain at all, we need to generalise and introduce perspectives and even languages from other disciplines that study human culture. This is because the quest for a *different* Roman past still depends upon finding those *common* features of the human experience that provide a starting point for the investigation of a vanished culture. Without such common features, the stories one might tell about that past would be meaningless and irrelevant rather than surprising or enlightening, if they could even be told at all. Archaeological interpretation has been likened to translation (e.g., Shanks and Tilley 1987: 115–7; cf. Thomas 2004: 243), and though such an analogy is not without controversy (e.g., Hodder 1999: 63), it does seem appropriate. We have to explore past worlds in our present, converting them into something that we can understand. This presumes that they can be converted—that they are *human* pasts, with which we share many features—but at the same time that our own terms of reference will be stretched in the dialogue, as we encounter unfamiliar ways of life that do not have an exact parallel today. This can then form the basis for contributions from archaeology to the wider social sciences, and to society at large. While for Roman culture, some of the necessary common ground is furnished by specific historical processes that connect it to the modern West, at a more general level, it is charted in this book through the concepts of agency and identity.

These words are used with increasing frequency in the literature of the social sciences, but that should not be taken as a sign that they have lost their power through overexposure. On the contrary, they refer, in my view, to fundamental elements of the human condition. Another aim of this book, then, is to offer a demonstration of their value, at the same time as refining their meaning, by putting them to work in the case at hand. 'Agency' is probably the more nebulous of the two terms. Confusion over its definition—in archaeology and elsewhere (Dobres and Robb 2000: 4–6; Gardner 2004a)—is commonplace, and has arisen partly because it has been used in a number of ways in philosophy, social theory, and everyday language. It can be said that agency is something that people 'have'—a capacity for acting in a particular, self-conscious way (Giddens 1984: 9). It can also be said that agency is what people 'do'—the particular way they engage in the world through a flow of interactive practices (Giddens 1979: 55). Both of these senses can be accommodated if we define agency as 'active involvement' (Elliott 2001: 2), which means that an individual capacity for action only develops through an ongoing relationship with the wider world.

This wider physical and social world can be described by the vital companion term to agency, 'structure', and the significance of this relationship is encapsulated by Anthony Giddens' formulation of the 'duality of structure' (1984: 25–7; cf. Wenger 1998: 65–71). This holds that agency and structure are mutually constitutive, in that agents affect and shape the world, and yet at the same time are constructed by it. Identity comes into this—more straightforwardly—as a key symbolic medium through which agency and structure interrelate (Jenkins 2004: 23–5; Woodward 2002: 4; cf. Gardner 2002: 345–6). Actors deal with the world in terms of classifications of similarity and difference—which are what identities reduce to—and it is primarily in these same terms that structure 'acts back' on them. Connecting agency and structure through identity, as part of a broader concept of 'sociality' and in conjunction with concepts of 'materiality' and 'temporality', provides a powerful theoretical framework for interpreting past social life, as will be explored further in Chapter 2. In particular, it allows us to appreciate how the small-scale actions that are overwhelmingly represented in the archaeological record were shaped by the concerns of the people doing them, and at the same time to consider what effects they had in creating the broader trajectory of a society through time.

The role of identities in shaping different kinds of agents and, through them, different kinds of structures will thus be explored through an archaeology of actions or practices—that is, what people *do*. An emphasis on practice follows from the relational model of agency outlined above, and is based on the idea that it is possible to understand what people are from what they do, not just what they think (Thomas 2004: 191). It is also a convenient approach given the 'action-packed' nature of archaeological material. In later chapters, I also develop a distinction between different attitudes or qualities of practice that together characterise the embodied awareness that humans possess: habitual, reflective, and affective. While these overlap strongly and really describe phases or even layers of action, they are useful inasmuch as they relate to the ways in which particular practices are associated with particular identities at different points in time. A certain way of doing something—eating, for example—may pass from a reflective mode as it is learned to a habitual mode as it becomes routine. It may then be drawn back into a reflective mode again when comparison with a different way of eating highlights it *as* particular and therefore as an identifying characteristic of a person's repertoire of practices. At such a time, the feelings that this comparison engenders (of happiness or disaffection) add an affective dimension to the practice. This approach to the modes of engagement that agency entails allows us to think about patterns of practice (i.e., archaeological material) in a way that relates directly to the generation, reinforcement, and transformation of identities.

And what sort of picture does this kind of interpretation produce? Primarily, it is a multifaceted one. My aim is to capture the complex lives of people in Roman Britain, particularly in the 4th century, and to tell stories about their involvement in a dynamic world. These are stories of how soldiers, for example, are not simply cogs in a 'war machine' (*contra* Peddie 1994), but individuals bound into an organisation that simultaneously affords them great mobility and yet structures their lives—sometimes deliberately, sometimes not—through a range of traditions. These are people who can move around Britain and, indeed, the empire, shifting as they go from father, lover, local boy, or comrade to bully, foreigner, administrator, or statistic. They embody the traditions of their class, their unit, and their home, in different mixes and in different degrees as they move or as they stay put. Their lives as soldiers are similar when compared to merchants or farmers, but are very different depending on whether they are based in the north or the south. And, increasingly as our period proceeds, they are less tied to the structures of the empire and more to the concerns of their local communities. In short, they are people whose lives are very different from ours, but who—like us—cannot be reduced to a single category without doing violence to important dimensions of their being. By applying this approach to broader processes, we will also see how, for example, the 4th century in Britain can be characterised *both* as a 'golden age' (Bédoyère 1999a) and as a time of 'decline and fall' (Faulkner 2000), depending on which stories one chooses to tell.

This is the consequence of taking agency and identity seriously in the writing of archaeology. In terms of the structure of this book, it is reflected throughout in the inter-relation of 'theories' and 'data', with each being used to inform and develop the other. In Chapter 2, I will pursue a more overtly theoretical agenda, but also aim to show how the approaches to agency and practice already introduced above capture important aspects of lived human experience in the 4th century, and to highlight their implications for archaeological methods. Chapters 3–5 constitute the heart of the particular study, but they are structured to demonstrate clearly the benefits of focusing on practices for archaeological interpretation more broadly. In each of these chapters, the exposition of material patterns and contexts will be interwoven with consideration of the material, temporal, and social dimensions of life in this period. Finally, in Chapter 6, the implications of the perspectives developed throughout the book for our understanding of the late Roman period, and its relationship to the present, will be considered. Before setting about this task, though, I want to expand upon two areas that have already emerged as significant contexts for this book: the goals of archaeology as a discipline, and the agendas of Roman studies within that discipline.

Particular studies and general problems

Concern about whether general or particular interpretations should be the proper domain of archaeology—and the connected problem of the relationship between archaeologists and the pasts they claim to study—has been commonplace since at least the 1960s (Trigger 1989: 19–25). Cycles of changing fashions in the level at which archaeological interpretations have been directed do, however, go back rather further than this. It is possible to paint, with the broadest of brushes, a picture of oscillation between generalist—and also evolutionary— ideals (in the mid- to late 19th century and the corresponding period in the 20th) and more particularist and contextual approaches in the early 20th century and the 1980s and 1990s, at least within Anglo-American archaeology. The connections between these cycles and the changing economic and political fortunes of Western nations have been well established, as have some differences between the perceived relationships of past and present in Europe and North America (Trigger 1984, 1989: 119–29, 148–9, 186–95, 289). In short, while global dominance and/or detachment from the people being studied produce generalising approaches (as in imperial Britain and 1960s America), concern with internal national problems and origins (as in many parts of early 20th century Europe) effect the reverse.

These kinds of factors can thus be held at least partly accountable for the differences between the rhetoric of Lewis Binford and Ian Hodder at early points in their respective careers. Binford expressed the agenda of the 'New Archaeology' (later to become 'processual archaeology') in the early 1960s in no uncertain terms: "Until the tremenendous quantities of data which the archaeologist controls are used in the solution of problems dealing with cultural evolution or systemic change, we are not only failing to contribute to the further-ance of the aims of anthropology but retarding the accomplishment of these aims" (Binford 1962: 224). Hodder, 20 years later and at the beginning of an explicitly 'post-processual' archaeology, was equally unambiguous: "Man's actions and his [sic] intelligent adaptation must be understood as historically and contextually specific, and the unique-ness of cultural forms must be explained" (Hodder 1982a: 13). These two positions exemplify the different possibilities that archaeologists have envisaged for themselves in terms of the creation of knowledge or understanding. More recently, though, it seems as if some kind of rapprochement has been reached between them, insofar as different scales of the problem have been argued to be equally valid and simply requiring different kinds of approach (Preucel 1991: 28–9). Thus clas-sically 'processual' methods are useful for answering general questions about past populations, while 'post-processual' approaches are rele-vant for thinking about individual action at interactional scales and in specific contexts.

This kind of methodological dualism seems both politically healthy and common-sensically valid. However, there is a danger that if too much distance is created between different scales of social life, or dif-ferent kinds of analytical objective, we will be unable to make much progress in either direction. Indeed, I would argue that we still need to look for ways of integrating or mediating such multiscalar studies within some kind of coherent theoretical perspective, if we are to avoid the perpetuation of the dichotomous models of reality which have pervaded the human sciences for at least five centuries (Koerner 2001, 2004). One such perspective is developed in this book, based on a persistent tradition of antidualist thought that has developed since the end of the 19th century, finding its most developed recent expression in the work of Giddens mentioned above. The main argument for an approach that can tie particular and general questions together is that these seemingly separate objectives are actually intimately entwined (Latour 1999: 69–72). One way of conceiving this intimacy is through a 'hermeneutic' model, based on a philosophical approach with its roots in biblical scholarship (Hodder 1999: 32–3), in which interpretation proceeds by connecting parts to wider wholes, with small-scale and large-scale analytical units providing contexts for each other.

Recognition of this kind of relationship between seemingly different epistemological agendas has led to the processual/post-processual lines not just being respected, but in some cases crossed. While some in the processual tradition have remained firmly attached to very generalising studies (e.g., Binford 2001; cf. Renfrew 1994), others have tried to use robust general approaches to illuminate specific contexts (e.g., Marcus and Flannery 1994). Equally, in arguing for the understanding of a past society in its own terms, Hodder (1982a, 1991a, 1991b) has acknowledged that he must not only rely on certain rules of interpretation which are applicable in different situations, but also assume that there are some grounds which make such an exercise possible and worthwhile—i.e., a connecting thread of common humanity. The more polemically post-processual, and profoundly inspirational, work of Michael Shanks and Christopher Tilley did take a harder line, as they were more keen to stress the limitations imposed on such communication by a truly particularistic perspective (1987: 102–17, 1992: 7–28, 48–64, 107–15; cf. Hodder 1999: 63). They stopped short, however, of totally undermining the aim of discovering something in the past that was different to the present. Such discovery—which presupposes the ability to *talk* with the past if one is to *translate* it—remained, for them, vital to any self-consciously political use of archaeology in the present (Tilley 1989a; cf. Hodder 1991a; Wylie 1992). More recently, though, Julian Thomas has offered a serious criticism of the retention of any communication with the past on the basis of human *similarity*. He sees this as part of a persistent tendency towards humanism—a belief in certain essential and immutable attributes of human experience—in archaeological theory (2000, 2004). His conclusion is that we must take the category of 'humanity' itself as a problem, and look for *difference*.

There are indeed different ways of 'being human' in terms of how individuals and persons are defined, for example, but it seems to me that exploration of these is hampered if we pretend that humanity is not still some kind of valid category, which is indeed the focus of our interest. The theoretical approach that I have outlined briefly above relies on a range of social theories that explore interaction and process in human life. Can such an approach evade the trap of humanism? In one sense I believe that it does, as the recursive relationship of agency and structure allows for variation in how each is specifically constituted in societies with different attitudes to materiality, temporality, and sociality. However, this variation is still within a category that, for want of any other name, is called 'human'. Insofar as these dimensions of variation have specific characteristics for us, which are distinct from those of other species (Mead 1934: 236–7; Thomas 2000: 145), we are confined by our 'species-being' to humanism on some level. Within this perspective, then, general theories about humanity are both means towards and ends of ongoing research into particular societies (Barnes 2000: 134). Only by relating generalities and specificities in such a fashion can we try to achieve the fullest interpretation of the remains of a dead culture, like that of Roman Britain, while being aware of what we bring to the attempt and what we hope to carry away from it.

Learning to mediate between the particular and the general in this way is profoundly important in the context of Roman archaeology. It has long been recognised that Roman studies, and cognate disciplines like medieval studies, Egyptology, or others dealing with historical, old-world cultures, have tended to remain oblivious to the kinds of discussion aired above, sticking obstinately to a narrowly particularist approach. In contrast, even highly contextual prehistories have more often engaged with general theories of culture (Andrén 1998; Balbaligo 2006; Johnson 1999a). It is no accident that this division relates to a difference between the study of cultures with writing as against those without. It would seem that the appearance of having access to the recorded thoughts of past people is taken as a sufficient reason to disregard explicitly general theories about human action, whether as ends or means, as part of interpretation—except, of course, this is not really the case, both because those written records are themselves products of action that should be taken to be problematic (Moreland 2001: 119), and because archaeologists in such disciplines routinely and implicitly make assumptions about the workings of the minds of the people they study, above and beyond the words of the texts.

In Roman studies, at least, things have been changing, and the last decade or so—since the establishment of the Theoretical Roman Archaeology Conference by Eleanor Scott in 1991—has seen both greater acknowledgement of these assumptions and much greater awareness and importation of ideas from outside the discipline (Scott

24 ■ An Archaeology of Identity

1993a; see esp. Hodder 1993a). Yet still the emphasis has remained upon using this greater range of general perspectives as a means of addressing the particularities of the Roman world. Not much has been given back in the other direction, towards the end of understanding the problem of 'humanity' by broadening the range of comparisons available to social science. A key goal of this book is to contribute to this greater process of exchange and dialogue, and in the last part of this chapter I will endeavour to explain how. Before reaching that point, however, it is necessary to explore in more detail the potential of Roman studies for achieving such aims, and the problems that have inhibited the discipline so far, in relation to those familiar topics of Roman Britain and the Roman army.

The development of Roman studies

Since its inception in the Renaissance, a defining characteristic of academic study of the Roman world, including its material cultures, has been the strong influence of the 'classical sources'. Often treating ancient Rome as a cultural ideal, like ancient Greece, but also a political one for European nation and empire builders, much scholarship of the period at least up until the Second World War was constrained by the conceptual limits of ancient written material. This does not necessarily mean that early archaeologists of the Roman period, including local antiquarians interested in provincial artefacts, never questioned literary assertions on the basis of their material (Andrén 1998: 9–25; Trigger 1989: 46–7). Nonetheless, it is clear that the research agendas of much Roman archaeology, particularly a focus on military conquest and administration, have been dictated by the 'dominant discourses' of the literary texts (e.g., Hogarth 1899; cf. Potter 1999: 152–5). Restricted as these are to the views of the male politico-military elite of the Roman Empire, they constitute very particular attitudes towards gender roles, cultural identity, and achievement, and the importance of state authority (as enforced by the military). Such views were not entirely out of tune with scholars occupying similar intellectual territory in the early centuries of Roman scholarship, whose writings also had somewhat similar cultural goals (e.g., Mommsen 1958 [1854–6]: 548–50; see Comber 1997: 47; cf. Lucy 1998: 18–19, 107). The influence of this framework was not confined to the production of new Roman histories, largely concerned with state affairs and 'high culture' (e.g., Grant 1968), but also affected Roman archaeology. This much is clear from the focus on villas, towns and particularly forts in, for instance, 19th and early 20th century excavations in Britain (Hingley 2000: 150) and Germany.

While this narrowness of perspective may have been recognised in the past, it is only really in the generations of scholars emerging after the Second World War that it has been actively questioned and criticised, in keeping with wider social trends (Andrén 1998: 20–5; Storey 1999: 203–6). Although some scholars remain rooted in the traditions of 'classical archaeology', many others have succeeded in breaking out of this mould. Much effort in the last two decades has exposed the gender and cultural biases of previous research, and attempting to explore the infinitely more complex range of past perspectives that this opens up, using a wide range of theoretical tools. Such approaches relate to the processual and post-processual movements in the broader archaeological discipline, albeit lagging at least a decade behind them (e.g., Barrett 1997; Dyson 1989; Scott 1993b, 1995; Wells 1999; Woolf 1998). Similar transformations have occurred in the field of history, based partly on effective source criticism (e.g., Comber 1997; Potter 1999). However, the study of the Roman military, which plays a significant part in this book, has been marginalised in this process of transformation precisely because of its central place in the traditional research paradigm (James 2002: 5).

Study of the later part of Roman imperial history has undergone similar changes as the broader field of Roman studies, even though it has frequently been treated as a discrete subject. Indeed, another of the goals of this book is to reintegrate later Roman archaeology in Britain into its historical context. This separation began at an early stage in the development of Roman studies. The cultural ideals that made the Republic and early empire appealing exemplars for European scholars led the later empire of the 3rd, 4th, and 5th centuries, with its supposed shift to 'oriental' despotism, to be viewed in terms of 'decline and fall' (e.g., Gibbon 1994 [1776–1788]), again following the judgements of some ancient writers (e.g., Zosimus). The influence of this approach lasted well into the second half of the 20th century, with the period generally either being ignored altogether (e.g., Grant 1960: 19) or examined for causes of 'decay' and 'collapse', ranging from 'racial admixture' and lead poisoning (Frank 1970; Gilfillan 1970) to military problems (Ferrill 1986). In exception to these trends stands a small number of detailed studies of the period, principally Bury (1923) and Jones (1964), which are less explicitly partisan on the relative 'merits' of the late empire but remain firmly situated within the traditional approach to Roman historical research, centred on the state affairs that also preoccupied the 4th century writer Ammianus Marcellinus (Wallace-Hadrill 1986: 23).

More recently, as changes have been taking place in Roman studies as a whole, the discourse of 'decline and fall' has been replaced with the idea of 'Late Antiquity'. Work within this framework generally stresses continuities between the 'Roman' and 'early medieval' periods, rather than major disruptions (e.g., Bintliff and Hamerow 1995a; Cameron 1993a, 1993b), and a major current theme is ethnicity. This interest has produced sophisticated re-interpretations of the use of ethnic labels in written texts, and of the role of material culture in expressing ethnic identity, which overturn pre-existing normative understandings of 'Romans' and 'Barbarians' (e.g., Geary 1983; papers in Mathisen and Sivan 1996, Webster and Brown 1997). It has yet, however, to make a significant impact on discussion of these issues in the wider archaeological community (though see Jones 1999), partly because the focus has remained parochial and the use of theory rather unambitious (see e.g., Lavan and Bowden 2003). The time for 'catching up' on theoretical developments in other parts of the discipline is past, and circumstances are ripe for a more radical setting of agendas from areas such as Late Antique studies (cf. Gardner 2003a). Among European 'historical' subdisciplines, a very similar situation prevails in medieval archaeology (e.g., Arnold 1997; Gerrard 2003), but has been increasingly challenged in post-medieval archaeology in a fashion that Roman archaeology in its broadest sense might successfully emulate (e.g., Buchli and Lucas 2001; Tarlow and West 1999).

All of these general trends can be seen in still sharper focus if we turn to the study of Roman Britain. The imperialist sociopolitical context of the late 19th/early 20th century origins of interest in the Roman occupation of Britain is increasingly evident (Hingley 1996, 1999). Even if the degree to which Francis Haverfield—the subject's founding figure—was conscious of this is controversial (Freeman 1996), one quotation seems to confirm Richard Hingley's view (1996: 37–8) that there was a shift from Anglo-Saxon to Roman antecedents for the British state at this time, in keeping with the changing relationship with Germany. In the latter part of the First World War, in which many of his students were killed, Haverfield wrote of the Roman period, "We may reflect, not without satisfaction, that Britain was then in touch with the predecessors of our French allies, and that there then was—if one may say so—a West-European culture which differed widely from that of 'Mittel-Europa'" (Haverfield 1918a: 162). In addition to the need for origin myths for modern Britain, connections with Rome were also established because it served as a paragon of empire at a time when the British Empire was becoming increasingly difficult to maintain (Hingley 2000). As a result, the cultural and military forces successfully brought to bear upon conquered peoples by the earlier imperial power were central to the interests of the nascent discipline. Chief among those cultural forces, as Haverfield in particular argued, was active 'Romanisation'.

In its favour, the concept of Romanisation was phrased in the language of 'cultural fusion' (Haverfield 1923: 11–22) and it represented an advance on previous notions that the 'Romans' in Britain remained largely separate from the 'Britons'. Nonetheless, it tended to both simplify and reify the ideas of 'Roman' and 'Native', even as these groups supposedly 'interacted' (Jones 1997: 33). It also perpetuated a sense of the inherent superiority of Roman civilisation. The army was treated as a relatively unproblematic part of this process, spreading the benefits of Roman culture. There was little room within the Romanisation discourse, therefore, for multiple perspectives on cultural identity—whether on the part of indigenous farmers, or of soldiers and administrators in different parts of Britain (and indeed the empire). This paradigm effectively remained dominant from the time of Haverfield to the beginning of the 1990s (though queried in Hingley 1989; Reece 1988), with Martin Millett's *The Romanization of Britain* (1990) representing its most sophisticated expression. This did significantly shift attention to the 'Native' side of the Romanisation equation, and—as an implicitly 'processual' work—focused more on socioeconomic aspects of the period than had many previous 'standard' accounts (e.g., Frere's *Britannia* [1987]), with their emphasis on military history. Nonetheless, the homogenisation of categories like 'Roman', which had served the interests of many writers of both the Roman and British empires, remained a problem (Freeman 1993: 443–4). It is only with the introduction of post-colonial critiques in the 1990s that the essentialism of these identity categories as commonly used has really been attacked (e.g., Barrett 1997; Fincham 2002; Freeman 1993; Hingley 1999; Webster and Cooper 1996). This is the immediate present-day context for the issues considered in this book.

However, since the later part of the Roman occupation of Britain will receive most emphasis, it is worth also going into some further detail about the study of a period that has always held an ambiguous position. To a considerable extent, the 3rd and particularly the 4th centuries have been detached from the 1st and 2nd centuries and discussed rather differently, in keeping with the 'decline and fall' motif discussed above. Again, this can be related to the cultural values of many Romanist scholars as well as to changes in the number and

28 ■ An Archaeology of Identity

nature of Roman-period writings. In many of the straightforwardly historical 'textbooks' on Roman Britain, the later period plays a minor role, relegated to a concluding chapter or two (e.g., Frere 1987; Todd 1981). Military affairs figure even more prominently in such accounts than for earlier periods, thanks largely to the restricted concerns of the major written sources of the time (Ammianus and the *Notitia Dignitatum*) in their references to Britain and a decline in the availability of epigraphic material.

Meanwhile, across an unfortunate disciplinary divide, many of the numerous studies of the 'sub-Roman' and early Anglo-Saxon periods use the 4th century as little more than a preface (e.g., Dark 1994a; Higham 1992; Jones 1996; Snyder 1998). It is testimony to the persistence of this divide that, while ethnicity has always been a central theme in discussions of the 5th century, many of these studies seem to have largely ignored the recent theoretical discussions of identity categories in Roman Britain mentioned above, which have usually focused on the 1st and 2nd centuries rather than the 4th (one exception being Pohl 1997). Within 'sub-Roman studies', therefore, the 4th century is often approached rather traditionally. It is only in work more exclusively focused on early Anglo-Saxon archaeology that similar theoretical themes of identity appear (Arnold 1997: 1–32, 176–210; Lucy 1997, 1998), though by then entirely detached from issues such as Romanisation.

Between these approaches, which place the 4th century in particular at one or other chronological pole (as 'end' or 'background'), there are some studies, of a fairly eclectic character, that make this century the central focus. These include general histories (Esmonde Cleary 1989; Johnson 1980) and more thematic studies, focusing on aspects such as the archaeology of late Roman towns (Reece 1980) or the rural elite (Bédoyère 1999a). There is also of course a considerable body of work on the specific circumstances of the 'end' of the Roman occupation, within which the military plays an important part (e.g., Casey 1992; Dark 1992; Evans 1990; Welsby 1982). It is difficult to pinpoint a consensus on late Roman Britain. While there has been considerable detailed work, as a whole the period has remained insulated from some of the wider debates that have focused either on earlier phases of Roman-period Britain (though see Cooper, N.J. 1996; Hines 1996; Reece 1989) or indeed on other parts of the 'Late Antique' world. Where specific interpretative perspectives have been taken (e.g., a Marxist one in Faulkner 2000), these are rarely made explicit. The result is a lack of any coherent narrative for the period. While this represents a de facto state of 'multi-vocality' (cf. Reece

1993a: 38), it has not really engendered any of the fruitful debate that multi-vocality should produce.

Finally, as the focal point for my consideration of Roman-period identities will be the military, it is worth briefly considering the position of Roman army studies within these Roman and Romano-British contexts. Indeed, as has been noted above, military institutions have occupied a central place in the majority of traditional histories of the Roman world and its provinces. This alone makes critical analysis of views of the Roman military essential—particularly as this identity group now needs rehabilitation back into the wider study of the Roman past, having fallen out of favour in the last 15 years. The military has also, of course, been the focus of numerous specialised studies, within which can be discerned two dominant themes: military history (dealing with campaigns, organisation and 'operations') and military equipment. While the scope of individual works can obviously range from the chronologically or thematically general (e.g., Connolly 1998) to the particular (e.g., Dixon and Southern 1992; Johnson 1983), there is a significant fracture along the now-familiar chronological line between the early and later empires. The former period has been dealt with in a greater number of devoted studies (e.g., Alston 1995; Watson 1969; Webster 1985) than the latter (e.g., Southern and Dixon 1996), partly because it is perceived to be the more 'professional' phase in the army's history. In the same vein, what work there has been on the later Roman military has largely focused on whether it was an institution in terminal decline (e.g., Elton 1996a; Nicasie 1998).

Across this spectrum of Roman army studies, concentration on the themes of military history and equipment has, until recently, marginalised more 'social' dimensions (except in the most structural sense— e.g., rank hierarchies). The traditional approach to the military has remained deeply entrenched, partly because of the armed service background of some of the specialists in the field (cf. Scott 1993b: 7–8) and partly because of the associated belief that 'military science' is a cross-cultural universal: that warfare is such a basic element of human existence that it can always be comprehended in the same terms (the experience of battle, the importance of discipline, etc.) regardless of the past cultural context (e.g., Godsal 1909: 70–3; Goldsworthy 1996: vii; Peddie 1987: xiii–xvi, 1994: ix–xiii). I would certainly accept that a comparative study of warfare can offer insights into Roman military culture and practice (e.g., Randsborg 1995; Treherne 1995), and equally that (as someone who has never been in a military organisation) my own perspective on such matters is as partial as that

30 ■ AN ARCHAEOLOGY OF IDENTITY

of someone with a 'military' background. However, the manifest-ations of comparison in many studies of the Roman military tend to be normative and functionalist, stressing similarity rather than difference, and often remaining implicitly 'common sensical' rather than being explicit and analytical. Insights that might be drawn from a background of 'soldiering' are often compromised by the cultural preconceptions that are deeply embedded in such personal experiences. Indeed, this kind of problem besets many broader studies of Roman culture in its technological aspects (e.g., Wilkinson 2001), which reduce material culture to 'engineering'.

This does not mean, of course, that much valuable material work has not been done on understanding the technical aspects of Roman weapons, fortifications, and so forth—far from it. However, I would argue that by largely ignoring the social context of these themes, Roman army studies has both limited what it can say about the lives of 'Roman soldiers' and failed to offer the contribution it might to debates in the wider discipline (cf. James 2002). Furthermore, although archaeo-logical material is frequently used to illustrate such accounts, rarely has the full potential of this material been explored from a more holistic perspective that is not text determined (for some exceptions see Bidwell 1997; Bishop 2002; Blagg and King 1984). Thus, works of military history such as Webster's *Roman Imperial Army* (1985) tend to confine any discussion of broad social themes to a minor chapter (pp. 269–85; which includes topics like 'civilising influences'). Equally, studies of equipment often confine issues of identity to a conclusion (Bishop and Coulston 1993: 196–205) or ignore them entirely (e.g., Russell Robinson 1975; Stephenson 1999; Stephenson and Dixon 2003). In most cases, such works do achieve what they have set out to do, and there are exceptions to this trend (e.g., Bishop 1989; le Bohec 1994: 205–59), but it is the dominance of this descriptive and func-tional approach that needs to be challenged.

Frontier studies and 'social histories', which are increasingly suc-cessful in broadening the scope of military-based research, offer hope for a more diverse and exciting future. Although once very much part of the same traditional paradigm as 'army studies' in general (Scott 1993b: 6–7), considerable advance has been made in debates surround-ing the nature of frontiers. Partly sparked by the Cold War-influenced analysis of Edward Luttwak (1976), a number of works have addressed the character of Roman frontiers and of interactions across them, often drawing upon comparative cases like the Americas (e.g., Elton 1996(b); Isaac 1992; Wells 1999; Whittaker 1994). Other, more particularistic studies have focused on similar themes in specific areas (e.g., papers in Brandt and Slofstra 1983; Groenman-van Waateringe et al. 1997; Maxfield and Dobson 1991). At the same time, a number of specifically social histories of the military have been produced, some rather limited by the written sources (e.g., Watson 1969), others with a more broadly based approach or more penetrating analysis (Alston 1995, 1998; Haynes 1999a, 1999b; James 1999a; MacMullen 1963, 1984; Pollard 2000). There has also been some important work on diet (King 1984, 1999a). These have shown that there was no such thing as the 'Roman army' as a homogenous institution, and that the military was a much more complex and interesting part of Roman culture than has generally been suspected, with a great deal of evidential potential. They have also demonstrated that, on this basis, the time is ripe for the military to be reintegrated into broader accounts of the Roman world, which also address theoretical issues of concern to archaeologists in all specialisms. That, in a nutshell, is what this book hopes to achieve.

21st century agendas

Having set out the main aims of this book in the context of past approaches to the Roman world, I want to conclude this introduction by taking a wider view of how it fits into agendas of the future. Roman archaeology has had something of a crisis of conscience of late (Gardner 2003a; James 2003), and yet in many ways the discipline is better equipped than ever to make real contributions to archaeology and to interdisciplinary debates in the social sciences, as I have already indicated. Obviously, this book is only one small step in this direction, but for this very reason I want to offer some suggestions for how Roman studies more broadly might start to look in the future, if the momentum that is building in recent work is maintained. There is still an 'image problem' for Roman archaeology in the wider field of academic, and indeed public, archaeology, and it is worth highlighting some of the reasons that this need not be the case in the future (cf. James and Millett 2001a; Woolf 2004). I will do this by focusing on four key themes that are emerging as 21st century agendas for Roman archaeology: identity, materiality, transformation, and reflexivity.

Identity is of course at the heart of this book, and much more will be said on the theme at a later stage. At this point, then, it is sufficient to note that identity has always been a central theme in Roman studies— Haverfield's Romanisation theory, for instance, is fundamentally a theory of identity—but that this has usually been implicit and has frequently been oversimplified. While this situation has changed in the last decade or so, most critical attention has still been directed at the prominent categories of 'Roman' and 'Native', rather than turning to no less important areas such as gender, age, status, occupation, religion, and community (Hill 2001; cf. Baker 2003). Some of these themes have been profitably explored in classics (e.g., Harlow and Laurence 2001), but there needs to be much wider consideration of them in archaeological work, where only a small number of finds studies (see below) have been leading the way. Along with giving attention to hitherto neglected kinds of identity, new studies of this rich topic need to be theoretically sophisticated. The detailed criticism of the 'Romanisation' paradigm, discussed above, has been based upon a post-colonial understanding of identity as a more flexible concept than it has been represented as in the past (Koerner 2003). Nonetheless, this approach needs to be taken further in the direction of constructing coherent theoretical frameworks for future study, and not just for critique. Having deconstructed the identity of the Roman Empire (Barrett 1997), we now need to rebuild it, or rather them—identit*ies*—from the ground up.

This requires not only new concepts to replace Romanisation (Mattingly 2002, 2004), but also a new fabric of explicit social theories within which these concepts work and make sense. At the same time, bold theoretical development can be grounded in another key theme of Roman archaeology, past and future—materiality. As with identity, the object world of the Roman Empire has not so much been ignored, as mis-represented. In spite of the many surveys and excavations of Roman sites over recent centuries, and the compilation of numerous catalogues of finds, all of which give Roman archaeology an aura of data richness, it is only really in the last 20 years that this material has begun to be aggressively interrogated (e.g., Allason-Jones 2001; Cooper 2000; Crummy and Eckardt 2003; Evans 2001). This is partly the result of new questions being asked, but it is also due to the impact of computers in enabling large samples of finds data to be manipulated statistically, or plotted in relation to contexts in a Geographical Information System. Again, though, there is still much to do. Many new methods need to be tried on larger or more comparative datasets, and the problems created by diverse classification conventions—which can inhibit this kind of work—need to be addressed.

More fundamentally, the materiality of Roman culture needs to be built into our social theories of how that culture worked. One of the seemingly familiar aspects of the Roman Empire is its vast array of artefacts, which appear to have been 'consumed' in deliberate ways (Cooper, N.J. 1996; Woolf 1998: 169–205). We should not underestimate the profound impact that this materiality must have had on people's lives in parts of the empire with different pre-conquest traditions of engaging with the material world. Nor should we necessarily try to reduce this diversity to a model that fits our own visions—or nightmares—of modern consumerism and globalisation (particularly as there is still lively debate about how *this* works [Koerner 2004; cf. Hingley 2005]). Comparisons between the materialities of different colonial societies are still worthwhile (Gosden 2004), but they always also need to be contextualised at the level of the various specific episodes of cultural contact through any history of imperial expansion. Thus, questions about the acceptance and development of new technologies, or about the new ways in which meaningful things (including writing) mediated power relationships between people, must play a major role in our new theories of the Roman Empire.

This leads into my third theme: transformation. The key issues here are process and scale. 'Romanisation', as a catch-all paradigm for understanding a transformative cultural process across the empire, has collapsed. It may still have applicability to particular areas at particular times (Woolf 1995; cf. James 2001; Mattingly 2002), but this is precisely the kind of problem we now need to examine: at what spatial and temporal scales are different explanations or models valid? In this book, I will explore this issue with reference to theories of agency and structure, but the field is really wide open, even after over a century of professional academic attention to mechanisms of change in the Roman Empire. In addition to the stifling weight of the Romanisation paradigm, a major reason for this lack of progressive debate has been the compartmentalisation of the past into hard-edged 'prehistoric', 'Roman', and 'early medieval' periods. Some of the consequences of this have already been noted with respect to the 'end' of Roman Britain. While it is increasingly recognised that this is a problem, with a corresponding shift in emphasis to the interstices or 'transitions' between periods (James and Millett 2001b: 2), we need to accept that any slice of time we choose to study will encompass *both* continuity *and* change. An appreciation of which areas of life are changing, and which are being sustained, in any particular 'snapshot' will allow us to produce much more nuanced accounts of Roman culture and specify relevant processes at relevant scales. Combining synchrony and diachrony in this way will also require that we take seriously the differences between *our* understandings of time, and those of the people we are trying to engage with in the past.

Such reflexivity is the final major theme I wish to highlight, but it applies to a much broader range of issues than temporality. Attention to the cultural and political forces that have shaped the study of the Roman world has certainly been increasing, again in the last 10–20 years, with particular reference to the 19th and earlier 20th century phases of our disciplinary history (e.g., Hingley 2001). This work has been one of the vital forces in freeing up the intellectual gridlock imposed by the 'Romanisation' paradigm (Hill 2001: 13). While I have suggested above that we also need to turn our deconstructive theories into constructive ones, in reality this is a cyclical process, as those new approaches must also be debated in their turn. Such debate is healthy as long as it addresses the relationships between four spheres—the past, an alien culture in that past, our discipline, and the contemporary society of which we should be an active part (Shanks and Tilley 1992: 108). Maintaining reflexivity means working at all of these relationships, thus invigorating the present as we reinvigorate the past.

In this book, I will be dealing with identity, materiality, and transformation, and I hope to do so reflexively. More specifically, the various aims for the book that have been mentioned during the course of this introduction can be summarised by saying that the book is about the relationships among three sets of contexts. The first of these is a specific identity group—the military—and how it was constituted in Romano-British society, particularly after the 'conquest' period. The second is that wider society, as a heterogeneous network of identity groups, with different local and global connections. The third is the much broader experience of being part of a human society, which can be compared from one time or culture to another, and through such comparison understood in terms of common principles or frameworks. Each context is closely related and serves as a 'way in' to the others. The process of interpretation has to start somewhere, however, and rather than follow the well-worn path of attempting a 'neutral' description of Roman Britain, we begin with the framework of theoretical preconceptions and points of departure that will be used and developed in that context.

Chapter 2

THE PRACTICE OF IDENTITY

Texts and theory in a historical discipline

Any discussion of theory in relation to a context for which there are written sources of evidence available must address, at the outset, two closely related problems: how do these texts relate to the theoretical framework adopted, and how are they to be used in conjunction with other, nontextual forms of material culture? In the preceding chapter, I indicated that texts have proved as much of a hindrance to Roman archaeology as a boon, but that this situation has begun to change. This process of change requires some attention, however, in the sense of constructively building written sources into theoretical development, rather than simply trying to jettison them altogether. The latter is not really an option, since our very terms of reference—'Roman', for instance—are defined by the existence of written material that gives us this name. Roman archaeology is emphatically a historical archaeology, but what exactly this means is an open question. In this section, I will explore some of the relationships between archaeology and history in an attempt to answer this question. I will argue that 'historical archaeology' should not mean an archaeology that supplements or fills the gaps of a narrative described by texts, but rather an archaeology of both artefacts and texts considered within a broader interpretive framework.

That this framework is not provided by the texts themselves requires some stressing. The idea that texts might be an alternative to theory has already been mentioned, and a good example of this view is provided by the author of one of the standard textbooks on Roman Britain, Sheppard Frere.

> But above all, we need to teach the new generations of archaeologists the virtues of clear selective reporting, and to show them that Roman Britain was an outpost of the classical world where wild anthropological or sociological theories and their accompanying jargon, introduced from

36 ■ AN ARCHAEOLOGY OF IDENTITY

> the shadowy and depersonalized world of prehistory, have little place—at least until tested against the great body of knowledge which survives from that classical world (Frere 1988: 36).

In one sense, the spirit behind this statement, that broad theories need to be worked through in relation to specific data without obscuring their particularity, is quite acceptable. However, in his implication that the classical sources are the only data that count in this regard, and that they are somehow 'outside' of theory, Frere is surely mistaken (cf. Scott 1993b: 6, 19). Among a range of broad theoretical suppositions expressed in this quote (the need for 'selective' reporting, for instance, or the view that Roman Britain was home to a fundamentally 'classical' culture), Frere assumes that the interpretation of historical texts is itself not problematic. While a common assumption in traditional historical archaeology (Andrén 1998: 3–4; Moreland 2001: 33–4; Morris 1997: 4–5), this view is well out of step with recent developments in history.

Indeed, some of these developments are actually not so recent. The great philosopher of history (and sometime Roman archaeologist) R.G. Collingwood noted in the 1940s that "strictly speaking, all history is prehistory, since all historical sources are mere matter, and none are ready-made history; all require to be converted into history by the thought of the historian" (1993 [1946]: 372). This perspective did not have a wide impact in history until the 1970s as part of the wider postmodern movement, which also of course was to affect archaeology later in the form of post-processualism. One of the key figures in history is Hayden White, whose 1973 book *Metahistory* effectively initiated a 'linguistic turn' in the discipline, marking a shift to the study of how historical narratives are constructed by the historian. In exploring the ways in which historians use language when creating histories, the question is begged of how (or indeed if) 'facts' really exist outside of these linguistic constructs (Munslow 2000: 88–9, 97–100, 151–3, 184–6; White 1973: 5–7). Therefore, in addition to the traditional epistemological concerns of historical theory— how can we come to know the past?—ontological issues are raised: what is 'the past' and how do historians stand in relation to it? As has subsequently been the case with post-processual archaeology, the assertions of postmodern history have been far from universally accepted (e.g., Elton 1991; cf. Moreland 2001: 111–9). Many have attacked, from various standpoints, any undermining of objectivity as a movement towards a false and dangerous relativism.

However, in constructing a new kind of historical archaeology, some of these postmodern insights into how texts should be viewed can be profitably linked to recent approaches in archaeology. While influenced by many of the same intellectual sources as those in history, these have tackled the problem of relativism in distinctive ways. There have been earlier attempts within historical archaeologies to break away from the 'tyranny of texts' described above, particularly under the influence of processual archaeology and more socioeconomic forms of history. Thus, the recognition that archaeological and historical data have different degrees of resolution (Millett 1981), or can be related to different sectors of society (Arnold 1984: 163), has been used to construct a kind of complementary approach—for instance, in addressing long-term landscape change (e.g. Barker 1991; cf. Storey 1999: 209–12). Such an approach, however, still tends to pay insufficient attention to written texts themselves as centres of meaning production in specific contexts. This is the role for texts that postmodern history has highlighted, albeit mainly with a focus on the work of contemporary historians. Addressing this issue with texts from past contexts requires not only effective source criticism (Barnes 1998; Potter 1999), but also a broadly post-processual perspective on how those contexts can be interpreted. Ian Hodder has done most to set out such a perspective, referred to already in Chapter 1. Inspired partly by Collingwood, Hodder has advocated a hermeneutic approach to interpretation in which theory and data are inter-related, and understanding proceeds from continual question-and-answer and from the connecting of different scales of context (1991b, 1993b, 1995a, 1999). This process involves a mediation between objectivity and subjectivity, where one recognises that the past is only brought to life in the present by a situated interpreter, but that this is happening in engagement with a range of material data that relate to the different experiences—in a sense, the different realities—of past people.

While this approach therefore accepts that we are dealing with a diversity of pasts, it also diminishes the threat of total relativism by acknowledging that, through the empirical patterns in the data we have, we can successfully represent some of those pasts today by choosing the most encompassing interpretations. As Julian Thomas has put it, "It is of the utmost importance to overcome the perceived dichotomy between 'social constructionism' and out-and-out empiricism. It is possible to assert that there is a real material world, and yet recognise that the way we come to understand it is problematic and unstable" (1996: x; cf. Derrida 1988: 148–9; James 1995 [1907]: 76–91; Wylie 1992). This perspective thus combines some of the deconstructive insights of postmodernism with a more constructive archaeological emphasis on the interpretive possibilities of context in establishing meanings. As such, it offers a fruitful way forward with all remnants of past practices, including those that bear writing, when these are treated as meaningful cultural products rather than simply as 'sources'. Just as interpretations of artefacts can only be developed by relating them to different contexts, so written materials must be positioned within theirs, as one perspective on a past world (Berkhofer 1995: 170–201; Hodder and Hutson 2003: 187–91). In this sense texts are like other material culture products, because they were *written on* something and had a particular mode of use and circulation (Andrén 1998: 147–8; Johnson 1999a: 31–2), and because they were *written for* something—serving particular purposes, perpetuating memories, or negotiating power or identities.

Such features are de-emphasised in traditional historical archaeologies, which tend to treat documents very simplistically (Johnson 1999a: 29), but they explain why documents cannot be dealt with independently of theory and used as a control upon it. Rather, they are *theorised*, as they express intentions of the author that we can at least partly translate into our own terms by the application of theories of interpretation and, indeed, of what kind of being that author was (Jenkins 1991: 5–13; Munslow 2000: 11–18). Written texts were authored by individuals who had their own theories of these kinds. They were written with a wide variety of intents and could be read (and can be read) in a variety of different ways, but they are also tangible things created and used in specific contexts. Texts, therefore, are both discursive and material entities. Again, this means that they are, in very broad terms, just like all other kinds of objects. Of course, the idea that material culture that does not bear writing itself has some 'language-like' meanings is another important strand of post-processual archaeology and has been influenced by elements of postmodernism, but discussion of this will be deferred to the next chapter. My main aim in this section has been to show that texts need to be treated differently within historical archaeologies if these disciplines are to progress, and that the combined insights of postmodern history and post-processual archaeology offer a way forward (see Fig. 2.1).

By bringing texts and artefacts within a broadly hermeneutic approach to past meanings, in which different kinds of material can be related and treated as each having some of the characteristics of the other (Johnson 1999a: 27–8, 31–2), an integrated interpretation of a specific past context can be developed. This makes 'archaeology' (as the study of past things) 'historical', not just by the inclusion of written things, but by allowing for the fullest possible understanding of complex processes of change in a particular cultural space. In this sense, 'history' is also about more than texts and concerns narratives of human life and experience. It thus also has much to offer the study of 'prehistory'. The focus of such an approach in this book will be the

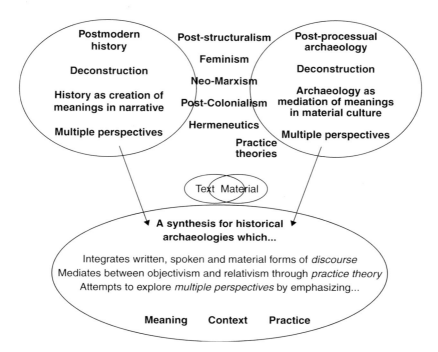

Figure 2.1. A suggested theoretical synthesis for historical archaeologies. While postmodern history and post-processual archaeology share many characteristics and intellectual sources, the distinctive emphasis on practice and context in archaeology provides a positive balance to postmodern relativism.

treatment of both material and written artefacts as media involved in the construction of identities. By situating these artefacts, as far as possible, within the contexts of their production and use—that is, within the context of practices—it is possible to retain a sensitivity to the plurality of past meanings, at the same time as actually saying something about what these meanings were. Rather than a material/text division which seeks independent evidence for writing the same story (Dymond 1974; Kosso 1995), I will try to pursue an integrated approach to writing different stories.

Agency, structure, and practice

The problem of agency and structure

This approach needs more than just a theory of how its evidence will be considered, however. The view of 'meaningful cultural products' outlined above must also be embedded in a view of how these artefacts,

40 ■ An Archaeology of Identity

with or without writing on them, are involved in people's relationships with each other. This is vital if we are to address the problems of identity introduced in Chapter 1, and elaborated upon further below. The particular framework for understanding social life that I intend to use is based squarely in the work of Anthony Giddens, and while this is hardly a new name to appear in the archaeological literature, there has been a sustained critique of Giddens's ideas in both social theory and archaeology. My main goal in this section, therefore, is to address this critique and to defend Giddens's basic position—the 'theory of structuration'—on the basis that answers to many of the more serious criticisms can be found in Giddens's own writings. His work emerges as profoundly useful in grounding the interpretation of past identities in an understanding of social practice—much more so, I think, than that of Bourdieu, who is equally often cited but whose ideas remain constrained by a latent structuralism (Jenkins 1992: 91–8). This does not mean, though, that Giddens's theory is flawless. Indeed, various sections in the rest of the book will address these flaws in relation to three themes that I have already referred to—materiality, temporality, and sociality—with reference to both specific theoretical points and to concrete examples from later Roman Britain.

The main problem to which structuration theory is directed is the relationship between agency and structure. There are many subtle variations in how these terms are defined (e.g., Mouzelis 1995: 100; cf. Gardner forthcoming), but essentially—and rightly or wrongly—they deal with our experience of a distinction between individual lives and the larger society of which those lives are a part. Understanding the relationship between these scales, levels, or entities has been arguably *the* defining problem of sociology—not to mention an important concern in philosophy, economics, political theory, anthropology, and increasingly in archaeology (Archer 2000: 17; Jenkins 2002: 46; Parker 2000: 9–10). Whether this is only a problem in modern Western cultures is a matter for debate, as we will see later on, but it is certainly the case that many of the approaches to this issue in Western academic discourse have been characteristically 'dualist'—that is, treating these two concepts as fundamentally opposed (Giddens 1979: 49). Interestingly as with other dualisms in Western thinking (e.g., nature/culture, subject/object [Koerner 2004: 213–20; Thomas 2004: 131]), this has not led to them being explored equally, but rather to one pole being emphasised over the other—and even treated as the only 'real' aspect of social life—in different schools of thought.

Thus, on the one hand, there are strongly individualist approaches such as rational choice theory. This holds that human society is simply composed of autonomous, rational individuals, going about their lives in accordance with goal-oriented decisions, and that everything else about human behaviour can be explained from this starting point (Barnes 2000: 50–62; Bell 1992: 38–53). On the other hand, there are major paradigms such as functionalism and structuralism that tend to subordinate individuals to their roles in functioning, pseudo-organic systems, or to deeply seated cognitive rules (Morris 1991: 232–9, 402–9). Unfortunately, and in spite of their significant impact on a great deal of research, neither of these types of approach really provides a satisfactory account of how people—in the West or else-where—actually experience their lives, which is a much more complex mixture of freedom and constraint (Barnes 2000: 3–15; Bauman 1990: 20–36). Moreover, in both of these models, individuals are actually treated in a similarly abstract and standardised way, rather than as situated in real contexts of interaction, where they may behave more or less individually depending upon circumstances.

Indeed, this has long been recognised, and for at least the last century, there have been a range of attempts to reconfigure or transcend this dualism. Karl Marx, for instance, is often quoted as providing a neat encapsulation of the interaction between these supposedly dichotomous concepts of agency and structure: "Men [sic] make their own history, but not spontaneously, under conditions they have chosen for themselves; rather, on terms immediately existing, given and handed down to them" (1983 [1852]: 287). Despite the way in which some later forms of Marxism have erred towards a strongly structure-determined view of history, Marx's own views included a much more recursive relationship between individual self-consciousness and the social and material world, as well as an acceptance of both general and particular forms of 'human nature' (Fromm 1998 [1966]: 24–43; McGuire 2002 [1992]: 28–30, 41–3). The abiding lesson of Marxism is that the dialectical relationship between human actions and structures is based on power—both 'power to' shape the social world and 'power over' parts of that world (McGuire 2002 [1992]: 131–4). This has been influential in Giddens's development of structuration theory, as has Marx's 'dialectical' view of agency and structure. This is a subtle step beyond dualism, with the two concepts still being treated as potentially contradictory, but no longer as independent and mutually *exclusive* phenomena (Parker 2000: 9; cf. Giddens 1984: 139), but rather as mutually *constitutive*.

A second tradition that has tried to transcend dualisms, and has also been important in Giddens's work, is phenomenology. Loosely definable as 'describing the world as it is experienced', this is an eclectic

42 ■ An Archaeology of Identity

branch of philosophy that includes the influential figures of Martin Heidegger and Maurice Merleau-Ponty. Though each has distinctive ideas, not to mention ways of expressing them, both are concerned with humans as fundamentally embedded or 'dwelling' in the world and as inseparable from it; an emphasis on human embodiment is a key aspect of this approach, as is the idea that people are constantly engaged in interpreting things in their specific contexts as they go about their daily lives (Moran 2000: 4–7; 238–9; 391; Thomas 2004: 185–9, 216–20). For Heidegger, humans are characterised by a sense of practical self-awareness—as beings for whom being is an issue—in a relationship of 'caring' for other beings and things in the world (1962 [1927]: 67–8, 78–86; Moran 2000: 238). Although phrased in idiosyncratic language, this is an excellent account of how agency and structure inter-penetrate (cf. Giddens 1984: xxii). Merleau-Ponty, in a similar vein, has offered an account of experience as 'being-in-the-world', with the addition of a much fuller account of the body's role in perception (2002 [1962]: 171–7; Moran 2000: 403–4, 417–27). Again, the focus on the situated human being—situated in relations with others— is effectively a focus on how agency and structure intertwine in the ongoing flow of activity on the interactional scale. Although correspondingly there is less attention to the larger institutional scales of the social world in the work of Heidegger and Merleau-Ponty, this is a theme of concern to some other phenomenologists, particularly Alfred Schutz (1967) and his followers.

The third and final significant antidualist tradition that I want to draw attention to is pragmatism. In its own way as diverse as Marxism or phenomenology, pragmatism is an American tradition that, among other tenets, asserts that meaning (as symbolic 'structure') is only made real in action (James 1995 [1907]: 1–32; Thayer 1981: 424–31). Although this principle underlies the important school of 'symbolic interactionist' social psychology, pragmatism has been neglected as a broader tradition of thought in comparison with continental philosophy, at least until quite recently—and this in spite of clear trans-Atlantic connections between these movements (see, e.g., Rosenthal and Bourgeois 1991). This is partly because it is unfairly regarded as a stereotypically American form of utilitarianism (Thayer 1981: 5–7). Only the work of Erving Goffman, a peerless analyst of small-scale interaction loosely attached to the pragmatist tradition, has been more widely influential in the work of Giddens and others (esp. Goffman 1959; cf. Giddens 1984: 68–73; Musolf 2003: 121–2). However, the leading thinkers in classical (i.e., late 19th/early 20th century) pragmatism—William James, John Dewey, and George Herbert Mead—produced extremely useful accounts of the nature of action, of the social formation of the individual 'self', and of symbolic communication, some of which will be referred to in Chapter 5 in connection with the theme of self-identity (e.g., James 2001 [1892]; Dewey 2002 [1922]; Mead 1934). The Giddensian solution to the problem of dualism, however, is our main focus here. While he has drawn to greater or lesser extents upon each of these three traditions, his arguments are uniquely clear and explicit. The importance of achieving a workable solution to this problem is simply that in interpreting the material culture of a context like late Roman Britain in terms of concepts like identity, we are very much dealing with the problem of relating specific actions to broad social categories.

Outline of a theory of structuration

Giddens's approach to transcending the dualism between agency and structure is set out in three major works (1979, 1984, 1993) and has already been introduced in Chapter 1. The definition of agency put forward there—as 'active involvement'—draws on the two senses in which Giddens uses the term, as something people 'have' and as something they 'do' (1979: 55, 1984: 9; cf. Elliott 2001: 2; Jones 2002: 176–7). For Giddens, agency is united with structure in the context of specific activities or practices, which are the crucible of the 'duality of structure' (see Fig. 2.2). This is the seemingly paradoxical principle that "the structural properties of social systems are *both medium and outcome* of the practices they recursively organize" (1984: 25, emphasis added). Giddens's choice of the term 'duality' here is meant to imply that the relationship between agency and structure is mutually constitutive, as distinct from the separate poles of a 'dualism'; this is similar to Marx's dialectical view (albeit with less emphasis on possible contradictions of power and interest and more upon complementarity). The concept of 'structuration' specifies more closely how the duality of structure works over time, referring to the ways in which social structures and systems are continually created and maintained through people's interactions (1984: 25). The key elements of structure, for Giddens, are 'rules and resources', which both constrain and enable the practices of human agents or 'actors'. While these rules and resources can coalesce into institutions over time, within which roles might be created that transcend individual people's lifespans, at a fundamental level the duality of structure means that social structures are dependent upon human agents (1979: 65–81; 1984: 1–37). This means that in some senses they only exist in the practices of

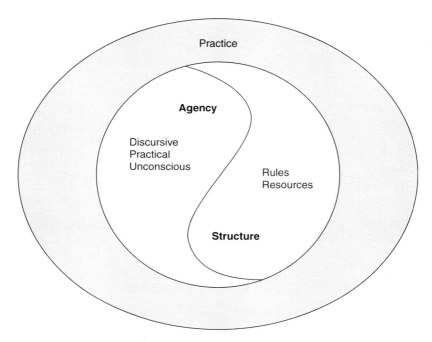

Figure 2.2. A visualisation of the duality of structure, using Giddens's terminology.

agents, and not independently of them. The reverse is also true, however: actors are always part of structural networks that shape their activities in predictable ways.

Relating structure and agency this intimately requires a detailed treatment of how practices unfold in contexts of interaction, particularly at the face-to-face level (which I will discuss in more depth in Chapter 3), and depends upon a sophisticated model of the way people think and act. The latter is necessary to allow for both the repetitive character of much social life and for some level of 'free will' in individual action. Taking inspiration from Freud, but deploying his own terminology, Giddens distinguishes between discursive consciousness, practical consciousness, and the unconscious (1984: 4–7). The knowledge that actors have of their actions and the rules involved in them—which is considerable—is partly open for evaluation and potentially, therefore, transformation. More often, though, it is thoroughly routinised by repetition and thus part of practical consciousness. Both forms of consciousness are involved as embodied actors act in the world, engaging in encounters and monitoring their competence at doing so. Moreover, there can be interchange between these facets of consciousness as different ways of doing things are learned, habituated, and questioned. However, the unconscious is contained by repression and is largely inaccessible, though it underpins embodiment and a basic sense of 'ontological security' (this is the most Freudian, and least satisfactory, part of Giddens's model). Overall, though, it is the routinisation of rules and resources in practical consciousness which is the key to their (re)production as structural properties through the unintended consequences of practices (Giddens 1984: xxii–xxv, 1–28, 35–83). This creates a model of human life that emphasises *doing things* at every level, and not simply individual intentionality.

Defending structuration theory

As a theory of the relationship between agency and structure, Giddens's approach is highly sophisticated. While it is impossible to do full justice to structuration theory here (although further elements will be introduced in later chapters), its hugely ambitious scope should be clear. This ambition is one of the factors behind the criticisms that have been directed at Giddens's work; another is the sheer density of his theoretical apparatus. These account for some of the more easily rebuffed critical commentaries, but other points of contention deserve to be taken more seriously. To begin with the former, a major axis of critique in social theory has been the 'analytical dualist' position championed by Margaret Archer (1995, 1996, 2000) and supported by some others (e.g., Parker 2000). Archer defines Giddens's approach as 'conflationary' or 'elisionist', and is aggressively critical of it in staking out her claim that agency and structure must be firmly separated if one is to properly understand the relationship between them. She argues that Giddens cannot do this, nor indeed give a proper account of agency or structure in their own right, because of his emphasis on the 'duality of structure' (cf. also Mouzelis 1995: 121–6), which allegedly collapses the two concepts into each other.

The concepts of agency and structure can be elaborated beyond the (actually quite extensive) accounts that Giddens gives, but much of this argument is being conducted at cross-purposes. In spite of her direct attack on Giddens's account of agency and structure as being ontologically inseparable (1995: 93), Archer herself admits that her insistence on dualism is only 'analytical', not philosophical: "There is no suggestion that we are dealing with separate entities" (1996: xvi; cf. Parker 2000: 72). While Giddens emphasises this ontological unity, he is equally not opposed to methodological or 'analytical' bracketing of one or the other term (1979: 95). In other words, the differences

46 ■ An Archaeology of Identity

between these positions are significantly overstated, and Archer must take responsibility for this (cf. Barnes 2000: 154–5). It is also worth noting that Archer's detailed study of agency (2000), in which she tries to elaborate upon how it is separate from structure, depends upon a bizarre assertion that practice is an 'asocial' form of behaviour (e.g., 2000: 255; cf. Benton 2001). This is highly problematic, as we will see, and does nothing to support the idea that 'analytical dualism' is a helpful or valid position.

Other criticisms of the theory of structuration that can be relatively easily dismissed include the contention by Nicos Mouzelis that the intimate relationship that Giddens posits between agency and structure prevents his actors from being able to take a detached or questioning attitude to social rules of conduct (1995: 119–24). This totally neglects Giddens's provision of discursive consciousness in his model of agency and the role this can play in challenging institutionalised ideology (e.g., 1979: 5, 208, 1984: 375). A more genuine problem has been raised with regard to Giddens's implication that social structure is not 'real' except in its manifestation in practices, which seems rather reductive (e.g., 1979: 64; Loyal 2003: 71–92; Thompson 1989; cf. Bryant and Jary 2001: 16). Nonetheless, account needs to be taken of the complex network of terms that Giddens uses for the more 'objective' elements of social life—structure, structures, structural properties, systems—that address this issue in a subtle and admittedly somewhat ambiguous fashion. Giddens himself seems confident that the apparatus is there to deal with both the way that actors make institutions 'real' in discourse (1984: 25–6, 179–80), and the way that collectivities at the systems level develop an integrated 'reality' of their own kind (1979: 73–81, 1984: 25). This is a more difficult area of Giddens's work, which I will address by developing a more powerful theory of identity.

Another area of criticism that has spread beyond the social science literature into archaeological accounts of structuration theory has to do with the nature of Giddens's individuals. On the one hand, he has been accused of making individual actors too dependent upon practical consciousness, and thus of casting them as unmotivated, uncreative, and unfree (e.g., Cohen 1994: 21–2; Meskell 1999: 25). On the other hand, his agents have been said to be too individual*ist*—that is, too powerful, autonomous, and framed in the mould of the idealised modern, Western male (Gero 2000; Loyal 2003: 183–6; MacGregor 1994; McGuire 2002 [1992]: 134). This seems a bit unfair, and I think derives partly from the persistence of dualist thinking in the minds of Giddens's critics—the need to view either agency or structure as more singularly important than Giddens's 'duality' allows. Certainly, he is explicit in his desire to avoid portraying actors as 'cultural dopes' (e.g., 1979: 71), slavishly following routines; at the same time, however, he has developed the idea of constraint in his later writings (1984: 169–80; cf. Cohen 1989: 207–31), as well as giving some attention to the nature of roles and identities in affecting interaction (1979: 115–20, 1984: 83–92, 282–3). There is no doubt, though, that the issue of identity is capable of much further development than Giddens has himself worked through, and again this kind of refinement is one of the key aims of this book.

Other worthwhile archaeological critiques have drawn attention to the lack of a theory of materiality or embodiment in Giddens's work (e.g., Barrett and Fewster 2000; Berggren 2000; Meskell 1999: 25–6). This is a sin of brevity rather than omission, at least with regard to embodiment. Giddens is clearly very concerned with the 'social physics' of face-to-face interaction, even if the specific theories of spatial and temporal structure that he uses need to be modified (e.g., 1984: 64–83; Adam 1990: 25–30; Gregory 1989; cf. Barnes 2000: 138). Material culture does not really figure in structuration theory—except as resources or constraints—but given the focus on contexts of interaction, it can certainly be made more central to it in a number of ways (as we will see in Chapter 3). Another important issue, related to the 'reality' of structure, is whether there is a possibility of group or collective agency (e.g., Dobres and Robb 2000: 11; Parker 2000: 106). Giddens is fairly unambiguous on this point, accepting collective *action* but not collective agency, given that—as we have seen—a full definition of agency requires not just a process of 'active involvement' but also a capacity for it, which is confined to "beings which have a corporeal existence" (1984: 220–1, cf. 1979: 55–6). In this sense, agency is certainly social, but is still contingent upon the presence of individual human beings with their specific properties and powers. This seems an entirely reasonable position. Finally, a major point on which Giddens can be taken to task is his "temporal chauvinism" (Meskell 1999: 26; cf. Barnes 2000: 90–8): his account of premodern societies as much more tradition bound than those of modernity (1984: 181–2, 194–9). This is a legacy of Giddens's interest in both Marx and Lévi-Strauss, with their particular views of the classification of societies, and is thankfully easy to address with contextual archaeological studies.

Theories and methods

All of these critical points having been taken on board, I believe that Giddens's structuration theory remains the strongest foundation of social ontology upon which to build. As one of the critics mentioned above puts it, "It is my opinion that Giddens has done more than any other contemporary thinker to advance our understanding of the complex ways in which action and structure intersect in the routine activities of everyday life" (Thompson 1989: 75–6). The extended exposition of this theory has been necessary here because explicit theories about how societies work are as vital to the continued development of historical archaeologies as theories about how our evidence is to be connected. The latter provide firm foundations for the investigation of the problems associated with the transformation of identity in contexts like the late Roman period, which are fundamentally problems of how individual people dealt with both social categories (e.g., ethnicity and gender) and social institutions (e.g., the military). Understanding the routine activities of those people, how they changed, and what those changes meant, is vital if we are to separate study of this period from simplistic grand narratives like 'the collapse of civilisation' and produce more diverse and sensitive interpretations. Ideally, though, our theories about the workings of past societies will not be separate from our methods of working with archaeological material, and it should already be apparent that key terms like practice and context have appeared in both my discussions of structuration and of integrating different kinds of data. In this section, I will address some of the more methodological implications of integrating the ideas about the nature of our evidence developed in the first part of this chapter with Giddens's ideas about the nature of people and societies.

It is worth noting here that Giddens himself has made a link between hermeneutics and archaeology, as he has been sensitive to some of the implications of the 'linguistic turn' (Giddens 1984: xx–xxi) and thus to the problematic nature of interpretation. This is very clearly expressed in the following quotation from *The Constitution of Society* (1984: 357), which serves as a counterpoint to that with which this chapter began.

> If there are two disciplines, then, whose intersection concerns the limits of presence, they are surely those of archaeology and hermeneutics: archaeology, because this is the subject *par excellence* which is concerned with relics or remains, the bric-à-brac washed up on the shore of modern times and left there as the social currents within which it was created have drained away; hermeneutics, because all survivals of a 'conserved past' have to be interpreted, regardless of whether they are pots or texts, and because this task of recovering the past is conceptually and methodologically indistinguishable from mediating the frames of meaning found in coexisting cultures.

This strongly underscores the view expressed above that all kinds of archaeological data need to be interpreted, but also that this act of interpretation is very much a part of all human experience. In this sense, archaeological practice is much the same as any other kind of practice, involving both routinised, 'practical' activity (whether this be trowelling or writing) and discursive, 'theoretical' activity (whether this be considering the merits of different pottery quantification methods or of different explanations for a particular distribution of data). For the archaeologist, as for the late Roman soldier, the specific context of activity determines the range of 'rules and resources' that are drawn upon routinely, and therefore reproduced, as well as those that are considered problematic and questioned. It follows, therefore, that the key to interpreting the meaning of actions—present or past—is an understanding of context.

The emphasis on contextual interpretation outlined in my earlier discussion of historical archaeology is thus very much in sympathy with the model of human action provided by structuration theory. This emphasis has important methodological implications. Foremost among these is the need to appreciate the range of possible meanings of the term 'context', and following from that the range of possible contexts that must be considered in investigating the particular case at hand. In considering the relationships between Roman Britain and the Roman Empire, for example, the data considered must come from different sites in different areas, and different temporal phases. Moving further down the scale of archaeological resolution, individual sites are situated within a cultural and physical landscape, while the settlement itself is a context for the structures or groups of structures excavated in a typical archaeological intervention. Then, within this excavated site, there is a series of depositional contexts, which might include features comprising a structure or several fills of a pit. Such units usually form the immediate contexts for artefacts, which also have other artefactual contexts—typologies—based upon formal qualities compared across time and space (Hodder 1991b: 135–6). 'Context', even in these relatively strict archaeological senses, is thus an ever-shifting term, referring to "sets of relationships which bestow meaning" (Shanks and Tilley 1992: xix), which are chosen purely on the basis of the level of interpretative focus in which the analyst is interested at a particular moment. Another definition might be "the totality of the relevant environment" necessary to give meaning to something (Hodder 1991b: 143), the concept of relevance again opening up flexible chains of association and multiple dimensions of comparison.

50 ■ An Archaeology of Identity

This degree of fluidity is equally applicable to the contexts in which material culture was used as part of the structuration of a past social world. How do these contexts relate to those of archaeological method? A classic processual approach to this problem is Schiffer's (1972) distinction between the present 'archaeological'/depositional context and the past 'systemic'/behavioural context. An inferential link between these could be made by 'testable' middle-range theories based primarily on ethnographic or experimental analogies (Hodder 1999: 26–9). While opening up the subject of 'transformation processes' that affect material culture during and after deposition, this approach is flawed in the way that it entirely brackets out the frames of meaning of human agents even within the 'systemic' context (Schiffer 1972: 156–7; cf. Giddens 1984: 327; Shanks and Tilley 1987: 31–6, 114). These were critical to the structuration of the past social world in the form of actors' 'knowledge' or interpretations of how to carry on their lives, and are therefore equally so in the construction of present archaeological interpretations. While Schiffer's goal is to reconstruct the systemic context in a way which will not be "subject to interminable dispute" (1972: 157), the recognition that past practices are meaningful, and that the present social practice of archaeology is an active mediation of those (multiple) meanings, implies that archaeology is a dialogue between past and present, always open to dispute and transformation (Johnsen and Olsen 1992: 428–33; Shanks and Tilley 1987: 103–15, 256–8; Thomas 1996: 55–64; cf. James 1995 [1907]: 23–6; Mead 2002 [1932]: 57–9). The 'truth' of interpretations lies in their success at accounting for patterns as they exist at a particular moment, but this can change.

The archaeological 'record' comprises material traces of past practices, which were meaningfully structured to varying degrees. In the interpretation of these meanings, the archaeologist constructs both the 'archaeological' context and the 'systemic' (or, better, structuration) context in a hermeneutic exercise informed by pre-understanding as well as interaction with the empirical data. This interaction ideally proceeds through a reflexive and multiscalar approach that builds up networked patterns of interpretation based upon networked patterns in the empirical data, relating parts and wholes (i.e., different kinds of contexts) in a spiralling exploration of comparisons, addressing variation and similarity (Hodder 1982b: 185–229, 1991b: 128–46, 1999: 47–9, 76–8, 84–8; Shanks and Tilley 1992: 104–5). This procedure requires the interpreter to consider the data as fully as possible, from a range of scales and perspectives, and thus not be confined to a particular class of site or material. Variables might range from attributes of individual artefacts of metalwork or bone to regional or supra-regional distributions of sites, or from a context of individual action in a single room to the relationship between social institutions across great distances.

In the next three chapters, I will aim to put this procedure into practice by looking in detail at archaeological assemblages and structural sequences from a range of sites across Britain, as well as some from neighbouring parts of northern Gaul and textual material from the wider empire. While the selection of sites discussed is far from comprehensive, there being many hundreds of known Romano-British settlements, the reasons for my focus on particular examples will become clear as we proceed, and I will set each within a more general picture of dominant material patterns. Detailed attention to the quantitative methods used in the handling of particular categories of data will also be given at the appropriate points in subsequent chapters. In pursuing my goal of explicitly integrating 'theory' and 'data', however, these chapters are organised in line with the major themes that I wish to develop in resolving the problems of identity outlined in Chapter 1. These themes are grounded both in the problems of the archaeological record in the 4th century, which I will elaborate upon further below, and the framework of structuration theory. While the latter provides many of the basic tools with which a new interpretation of 4th century life can be developed, in particular the emphasis on contexts of practice as connecting individuals and institutions, this linkage between agency and structure needs to be elaborated along three overlapping dimensions: materiality, temporality, and sociality (see Fig. 2.3). Giddens's work is capable of development in each of these areas, with more attention to the role of material culture, to the human experience of time, and to the importance of identity in social interaction. The latter is my major concern in this book, given the questions with which I began, but consideration of the other two will prove to be vital theoretical and empirical steps towards constructing an archaeology of identity based firmly upon people's experiences in specific material and temporal practice-contexts. Why these are also important steps in shedding new light on current questions surrounding 4th century life will be the subject of the final part of this chapter.

4th century problems

The established narrative

The initial questions about 4th century Britain that are at the heart of this book were outlined in Chapter 1, and in returning to these here

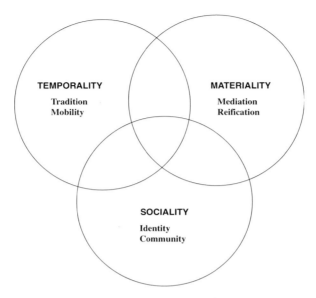

Figure 2.3. Dimensions (temporality, materiality, sociality) of human life that connect agency and structure (cf. Gardner 2004b: 45).

my aim is to both expand upon the background to them and to explain why a new approach—based on the methodological and theoretical perspective set out in this chapter—is needed. I will begin, therefore, with an outline of the established story of Roman Britain, in relation to the wider empire and with a focus on the later period, and then proceed to highlight the gaps in that story that I hope to address.

The bare bones of the chronological framework for Roman Britain can be summarised very briefly. After a period of arm's-length interaction between British tribal communities and the Roman Empire following the expeditions of Julius Caesar in 55 and 54 BC, military conquest began in AD 43 under the emperor Claudius. A protracted series of military campaigns led by a succession of governors followed, with the west and north of Britain proving much more difficult to subdue than the south, where new towns were quickly founded. By the early 80s, the British province had more or less reached the shape it would occupy until the 5th century, with the only major setback within that area being the destructive but ultimately unsuccessful Boudican revolt of AD 60/61. As the development of towns and the emergence of new kinds of rural settlements ('villas') continued into the 2nd century, the military was based mainly in the west and particularly the north. Here the frontier oscillated between the line of the Solway-Tyne, where

Hadrian's Wall was built in the 120s, and further north up to the Clyde-Forth line of the short-lived Antonine Wall. However, by the early 3rd century, Hadrian's Wall defined the limits of a well-garrisoned but prosperous region of the empire, now split into two provinces: Britannia Superior and Britannia Inferior.

What happened to this region in the 3rd century is problematic, and—as we will see later in this book—many of the processes of change that become evident in the 4th century may well have begun then. Suffice it to say for now that, at least from a traditional historical point of view, the middle part of the 3rd century is something of a 'dark age' in Roman Britain. Writers based in other parts of the empire—where a series of political, military, and economic crises were unfolding—were evidently preoccupied with events closer to home. These crises, which involved barbarian invasion, civil war, and currency collapse and which were linked to the cessation of imperial expansion in the 2nd century, do not seem to have had a direct impact on Britain, the economy of which was still apparently successful (Millett 1990: 127–31). Nonetheless, there was political fallout that set the scene more directly for the important developments of the 4th century. In the 260s and 270s, insecurity in the western provinces resulting from external pressure on the frontiers led to the establishment of a breakaway 'Gallic Empire' comprising the provinces of Gaul, Spain, and Britain. Rather than an anti-Roman rebellion in the manner of the Boudican revolt, this was an attempt to force some devolution of imperial power to a local level with more local 'emperors' (Esmonde Cleary 1989: 16–17). Although this region was re-incorporated into the empire proper in 274, similar movements were to follow, most notably the establishment of a 'British Empire' in 286–96 led by Carausius and Allectus. It was during this period of at least perceived insecurity that a new frontier began to be established in Britain, this time on the southern and eastern coasts: the so-called Saxon Shore (Cotterill 1993; Pearson 2002). This was to remain another concentration of military activity into the 5th century.

The Roman Empire that emerged from the period of 3rd century instability was quite a different entity from that of the 1st and 2nd centuries, and more will be said on the key social changes below. On a political level, Britain was now divided again into four provinces (see Fig. 2.4), part of a new administrative hierarchy for an imperial system that was also split into eastern and western halves to an unprecedented degree, within the tetrarchic system of two senior and two junior emperors. At the same time, imperial laws became more restrictive, and power was jealously guarded by the 'official' emperors

54 ■ An Archaeology of Identity

Figure 2.4. Map of Roman Britain, showing major administrative boundaries of the 4th century and the locations of sites mentioned in the text (boundaries after Millett 1990: 134).

(Cameron 1993a: 45). Such an attempt to harness the power of devolved security arrangements within a still centralised ideology of imperial authority was only partially successful, and while some of the local security crises which increasingly dominated the 4th century history of Britain led to visits from central authorities, others generated further local usurpations. One of the former occurred with an expedition by Constantius I, senior western emperor, in 306. His death on this campaign led to the elevation of his son Constantine, who temporarily reunited the empire after a period of civil war but also established a new capital at Constantinople. Later in the century, another high-ranking visitor was Count Theodosius, who apparently dealt with a significant 'conspiracy' of barbarian tribes against Britain in around 367, although it is likely that the damage caused by this has been exaggerated (Millett 1990: 215). Between these events the usurper Magnentius unsuccessfully attempted to use a British power base to establish himself as a western emperor in 350–53, while the same thing occurred in the 380s with Magnus Maximus, and yet again with a succession of commanders in the first decade of the 5th century— Marcus, Gratian, and Constantine III. It was in AD 410, during this latter period of sustained rebellion in Britain, and renewed crisis on the continent (a major invasion of Gaul and the sack of Rome), that the emperor Honorius apparently told the people of Britain to look after themselves. This is the traditional end point for the history of Roman Britain.

Within this narrative framework, which is of course based heavily on the work of Roman writers, a number of other themes can be developed that lead us towards some of the problems with our current understanding of the period. As already noted in Chapter 1, and in line with the majority of events that figure in the historical narrative, the role of the army in Roman Britain is a major feature of the established story. The mobile invasion force and garrison of the 1st century AD has been tracked through timber forts, temporary camps, and epigraphic evidence (see, e.g., Hassall 2000), into the period where it settled down into more permanent installations, increasingly built in stone, in the 2nd century. While again the 3rd century is somewhat problematic, some changes to organisation seem to have begun at this time that are more fully reflected in the 4th century (Hodgson and Bidwell 2004; Southern and Dixon 1996: 4–33). By this time the early imperial organisational/status division between citizen legionaries and noncitizen auxiliaries had been superseded (partly because citizenship was now more universal) by one separating the more mobile field armies, or *comitatenses*, from the static *limitanei* on the frontiers.

In Britain, where most—if not all—of the troops were *limitanei*, the garrison has often been interpreted as becoming a less effective, more militia-like force, closely integrated with the civilian settlements or *vici* surrounding the forts, whose inhabitants may even have joined the soldiers within the walls in the later 4th century. Alternatively, this garrison is believed to have dwindled numerically, as the various usurpers and imperial visitors of the 4th century took troops with them to the continent to fight other Romans or barbarians (leaving 'squatters' to move into abandoned forts), or the units sustained losses during attacks on Britain (see, e.g., Frere 1987: 217–26). The decline of Roman Britain was thus closely linked to the decline of the Roman army.

The problems with which this picture presents us will be discussed further below, but it is worth reiterating here that the general perception of decline in the strength and effectiveness of the late Roman military forces in Britain is in keeping with a widespread view that such decline was consistent across the empire, and a major factor in its collapse (e.g., Ferrill 1986; Nicasie 1998). This view is based on certain phenomena that are evident in different parts of the empire, including reductions in unit sizes, recruitment problems, and the increasing use of 'barbarian' soldiers in 'Roman' armies (Cameron 1993a: 137–50; see, e.g., Bagnall 1993: 175–6, for Egypt). All of these changes were part of broader political developments which are also key parts of the background to life in 4th century Britain. Diocletian, who instituted the tetrarchy and subdivided provincial administrations in the late 3rd century, seems also to have been responsible for creating a larger number of smaller units as part of an army reform that also involved introducing conscription and expanding the overall number of soldiers (Southern and Dixon 1996: 17). In addition, he reorganised the tax system, which throughout Roman imperial history was one of the major functions of the state and intimately connected to the need to pay the soldiers. Currency problems in the 3rd century were partly ameliorated by an introduction of taxation—and pay—in kind, as well as coinage reforms that do not seem to have had much lasting effect (Reece 2002: 26–7). Administering this required further additions to the bureaucratic structure of the state, and in tandem with laws that attempted to keep taxpayers—primarily farmers—in their place and providing revenue, this has created a perception of the later Roman Empire as a parasitic, totalitarian state, which ultimately failed to stem the tide of barbarian attacks because of the disaffection such policies caused (Cameron 1993a: 33–46, 113–24, 132; Faulkner 2000). Internal weakness thus exacerbated the effects of external pressure.

The extent to which these factors may or may not have affected Britain has been addressed not just with regard to the military, but also in connection to the prosperity of towns and farms. The archaeology of towns has obviously been a central part of the study of Roman Britain since its inception, with the 'public towns' in particular being vital to any understanding of the impact of Roman culture. These establishments had a significant administrative role—the *coloniae* established for veteran soldiers, the specially chartered *municipia*, and the centres of the tribal subdistricts of the province, or '*civitas* capitals'. Detailed studies of examples of all of these will follow in later chapters, but here the general trajectory must be noted, though this is not straightforward. While it is broadly agreed that the main towns were established in the later 1st century AD and prospered into the 2nd, with increasing numbers of Britons participating in local administration and mercantile activity, there is disagreement over developments in the later Roman period. Some see them as continuing to be populous centres well into this period, perhaps with a substantial urban proletariat (Faulkner 2000; Frere 1987: 368–9). Others, however, have argued that the economic and social changes of the 3rd century—particularly the development of a new bureaucracy and new tax collection mechanisms—led to a reduced role for the public towns. Production and market activities seem to have shifted to a more dispersed network of small towns and villages that emerged away from the *civitas* centres, while the traditional administrative elites that remained linked to those centres increasingly spent their money on their villas—situated in the rural estates that had always been the basis of their local power—rather than on new public buildings (Bédoyère 1999a; Millett 1990: 127–211; Reece 1980). This privatisation of interest disconnected even powerful individuals from the state, creating the conditions for collapse already referred to above, while paradoxically giving the impression that considerable wealth was still in circulation.

Another major area of social change that has long been a part of the dominant narrative of the transition to Late Antiquity is religion. The widespread adoption of Christianity in the late Roman Empire was identified as a factor in its decline by Gibbon (1994 [1776–1788]), and while this interpretation is debateable, the issue is clearly an important one. Its significance in Britain, however, is less easy to discern, as although there certainly is evidence for the adoption of Christianity (Petts 2003), it is somewhat limited in comparison to the abundant material relating to earlier—and indeed contemporary—pagan practices. It does seem to be the case that while there were more dramatic

58 ■ An Archaeology of Identity

conflicts between faiths in other parts of the empire, the 4th century was generally a period of coexistence and interaction. Thus, while some temples seem to have been destroyed in Britain (e.g., the Mithraeum at Caernarfon), others prospered at the same time that churches were being constructed (Boon 1960; cf. Salzman 1990). What has scarcely been established with reference to Britain is the social changes that these developments brought about, in terms of areas like morality (cf. Cameron 1993a: 125–32). These might be expected to be profound, however, given the degree to which religious and secular life inter-penetrated in the Roman world.

This question of more intangible changes to life brought about by the Roman conquest of Britain brings us, finally, to the dominant narrative of cultural transformation that encompasses all of the above issues: Romanisation. Various problems with this paradigm have already been aired in Chapter 1, and so here it is only necessary to elaborate upon how these relate to the late Roman period. The idea that, during the Roman period, the people of Britain were subject to a gradual process of assimilation to Roman culture—from urban life and use of Latin and decorative mosaics, to ubiquitous pottery types and new modes of religious representation—has always faced a difficulty with the seemingly abrupt end of this 'civilisation' in the early 5th century. The cessation of coin use and pottery production, and apparent desertion of many sites, present real archaeological problems for understanding this period, and real problems for the idea that Romanisation had become deeply rooted throughout society. These have produced a range of alternative theories about what happened. Some stress rapid military or economic collapse, depriving people of the resources of Roman culture and the means to defend it (Esmonde Cleary 1989: 160–1; Frere 1987: 353–75). This may have been followed by some depopulation, at least of the most 'Roman' elites, with their subordinates choosing 'Germanisation' when the Anglo-Saxons arrived a generation later (Millett 1990: 227–30; cf. Higham 1992). Others emphasise the idea that Romanisation was only ever a temporary fashion, which disintegrated slowly over time, or at least easily fell away in the 5th century (Reece 1988: 123–55). More rarely, it has been argued that Romanisation continued to prosper in less archaeologically visible forms well into the early Middle Ages (Dark 1994a). This period, then, is when any 'grand narrative' for the history of Roman Britain seems to break down, and where questions of identity arise. It is in answering these questions, while trying to avoid some of the pitfalls of constructing a new grand narrative, that the approaches outlined earlier in this chapter offer a way forward.

Material, temporal, and social problems—and solutions

This is not to say that there is no truth at all in this grand narrative, but merely that it fails to account satisfactorily for change in Roman Britain because it pays insufficient attention to the details of how particular institutions intersect with the lives of individuals at any point in the region's history. Instead, we see the political and cultural currents of the empire—manifest in organisations such as the military or in more nebulous forces such as Romanisation—wash over the people of Britain, with only celebrated historical characters like Claudius or Agricola, or generalised classes of individuals like the native elites, being ascribed much in the way of situated agency in dealing with these. 'Big pictures' are not intrinsically wrong, but as indicated in my discussion of generalisation in Chapter 1, and in keeping with the spirit of structuration theory (Giddens 1984: 359–63), they need to be married with small-scale accounts of how specific ideas like 'being Roman' were enacted and transformed in specific moments of practice, which will produce much more diverse sets of narratives. It is necessary for Roman archaeology to do this in order to reflect a wider range of the experiences of living in the Roman Empire, and therefore to shed greater light on the complexities of life in the past and in the present. As already discussed in Chapter 1, it is something that Roman archaeology is only just beginning to do, and I hope that this book helps to further that progress.

That the late Roman period should be my focus in pursuing this goal is partly because it has been relatively neglected in the recent critical attention to the earlier phases of Roman Britain, but also because of the major problems thrown up by the narrative of decline and fall outlined above. As I have already noted, these are largely problems of identity. The difficulties in explaining the end of Roman Britain are not only related to the patchiness of the evidence, but are more about what we mean by 'Roman'. They thus cut right back into the heart of how we understand Roman Britain and must be pursued at least through the whole 4th century. The more specific questions that feed into the end of Roman Britain are also primarily related to identity. Who was living in late Roman forts, soldiers or squatters? If they were soldiers, how effective were they? Did they see themselves as Romans, or were they barbarian mercenaries? How did this affect their loyalty to the empire? Who was living in late Roman towns, and how numerous were they? Were they traditional elites, new bureaucrats, or perhaps soldiers? In what ways did they see themselves as Roman, especially if they were ignoring their civic duties to spend more time at their villas? Were the trappings of Roman culture found in those villas compatible with a supposedly increasing disdain for the imperial state? Were other farmers affected by the major political or social changes in anything other than superficial ways, and what did Roman citizenship or identity mean to them? To what extent did all of these different communities, in different places, ultimately constitute a 'Roman' culture that could have a united beginning and end at all?

Such questions of identity, left hanging in the traditional narrative, need to be addressed not just with better evidence, but with a new approach. This is because that narrative lends itself too easily to generalising, black-and-white answers that simply do not account for the variety of the evidence. Such answers obscure the variations in contexts of practice that are brought much more centre stage within a framework like structuration theory. Arguing this point more fully is one of the key tasks to be undertaken in subsequent chapters, in which I will work towards the problems of identity by first discussing the equally essential themes of materiality and temporality. These elements are vital to the understanding of the 4th century insofar as they overlap with the role of identity in shaping the interactions between the individuals who used artefacts and the institutions of which those individuals were part. Many of the questions posed above depend upon how we interpret material culture. What kinds of objects defined particular identities, and what others were mutable in their meanings? What significance should the changes to structures and artefacts in use across the Roman period, and particularly as we approach its end, be accorded? This second question brings in the issue of time, and clearly the whole narrative of Romanisation—and the inadequacies that it has in terms of an overly simplistic appreciation of the link between artefacts and identity—are fundamentally temporal matters. Developing a more thorough theoretical, and more nuanced empirical, picture of the shifting currents of continuity and change in 4th century material culture will thus be essential to understanding the problems of identity that are central to the period.

In trying to develop an approach to these problems that focuses on the contexts of social practice, I have argued in this chapter for the use of specific theoretical tools that address the multiple factors at work in the interpretation of texts and artefacts, and in the interaction of people and social institutions. These will help us to see how some of the factors discussed above in the narrative of 'decline and fall' were experienced in the lives of ordinary people, particularly soldiers, who are at the core of many of the outstanding questions and who are also in a useful position to illuminate the relationships between individuals and broader groups or communities. This perspective will in turn address the root cause of the gaps and inconsistencies in the traditional narrative—the lack of accountability to the diversity of everyday life in the past. That life was rooted in practice, and it is by establishing the material and temporal dimensions of practice in the 4th century that we can move on to consider the social, encompassing the key questions of identity that have been raised here and in Chapter 1. These three overlapping themes, then—materiality, temporality, and sociality—define not just the theoretical linkages between agency and structure that I wish to develop, but also the key problems of evidence and interpretation that need to be addressed in understanding the 4th century. Considering them in turn in the next three chapters will not produce a new grand narrative, but rather a set of contextual studies that complements the strengths of the existing one and makes up for its weaknesses.

Chapter 3

The Material Dimensions of 4th Century Life: Objects and Spaces

Studying materiality

In this chapter, I will set out in a broadly synchronic fashion the dominant material patterns in 4th century Britain, along with some comparative data from the wider empire. I will also begin to link these material patterns into contexts of practice, a process that will be continued from a more temporally dynamic perspective in Chapter 4. The significance of these practices in terms of military and other identities can then be considered in detail in Chapter 5. Since the ways in which material culture has been treated by archaeologists are diverse, some background is necessary to pave the way for a consideration of artefacts as both *meaningful* and *material* in the constitution of human action. Taking a long-term view, the 'culture-historical' approach that characterised archaeology's early days as a coherent discipline in the later 19th and early 20th centuries (and beyond in many historical subdisciplines) depended upon a normative view of material culture. Thus, artefacts were understood as a passive reflection of behavioural norms within a culture (Shanks and Tilley 1987: 79–93). In historical fields like Roman studies, of course, these norms tended to be taken directly from textual sources (see Chapter 1). Advocates of the New Archaeology in the 1960s attempted to move beyond this kind of perspective, which rather limited the role of objects in human life, and were initially optimistic about the dimensions of artefactual significance which could be studied (see esp. Binford 1962: 218–9). However, in stressing the importance of material culture as a way of adapting to environmental conditions, processual archaeology became confined to a rather narrow form of functionalism (Hodder 1982b: 3–7; Shanks and Tilley 1987: 87–92; cf. Renfrew 1994). Only in discussions of artefactual 'style' was this problem partially transcended, and this theme provides something of a link into post-processual approaches to material culture.

In one of Binford's early formulations of the New Archaeology (1962: 220), style was defined in very basic terms as relating to formal artefact characteristics that did not have a clear technological, social, or ideological function. This represented little progress from traditional approaches. Subsequently, style itself was brought into the functional fold, with Martin Wobst (1977) relating the concept to adaptively useful communication and information exchange. This trend culminated in a more nuanced debate over what kinds of information different 'styles' of objects might convey, and therefore what kinds of function they might serve. This was particularly developed in a series of papers by James Sackett (e.g., 1982) and Polly Wiessner (e.g., 1989, 1990). The main types of style proposed here were a basically 'active', deliberately comparative style (which can in turn be 'emblemic' or 'assertive', referring to social groups or to individuals) or a more 'passive' style. The latter is referred to by Sackett as 'isochrestic', a neologism meaning that superficially different objects still serve the same purpose (are 'functionally equivalent'), so the variation is not meaningful (1982: 72–3; cf. Dietler and Herbich 1998: 239–42). These approaches certainly come close to dealing with the complexity of artefactual meaning, but still lack the kind of contextual sensitivity necessary to understand how a wide range of "ideas, beliefs and meanings . . . interpose themselves between people and things" (Hodder 1991b: 3; cf. Shanks and Tilley 1992: 55; cf. Schiffer 1999). Debate over the nature and importance of the concept of 'style' has thus receded.

The range of post-processual perspectives that have since set the agenda for discussion have been united behind one key idea: that "material culture is actively and meaningfully constituted" (Hodder 1993a: xvii). The significance of this has already been examined with reference particularly to textual evidence for past action. In terms of more 'mute' artefacts, the earliest studies looked towards ideas from structuralist anthropology of deep, dichotomous conceptual oppositions as the key to human thinking (e.g., Hodder 1982c; Tilley 1984; cf. Hodder 1991b: 35–56). However, it was quickly realised that there was no way of accounting for how such structures arose or changed, and humans were rendered just as unable to creatively act in the world through their material culture as they had been by normative traditional archaeologies (Dietler and Herbich 1998: 239; Shanks and Tilley 1987: 100–1). Subsequent developments have therefore moved towards post-structuralism and hermeneutics. It is from the former in particular that we get the idea of a 'linguistic turn' in archaeology, already discussed in the context of history. As in that discipline, though perhaps with less overall impact, the focus of post-structuralist archaeology has been on the deconstruction of the written texts that archaeologists produce (e.g., Bapty and Yates 1990; Tilley 1989b) and suggestions for alternative formats of data presentation (e.g., Hamilton 1999). Following more from the hermeneutic strand, there has been a limited move towards explicitly treating material culture as a 'text', in that it is part of a structured system of meaning that can be 'read' (Hodder 1991b: 126–8; Tilley 1991; cf. Johnsen and Olsen 1992).

This idea is perhaps most useful at a general level, in two ways. First, emphasis is placed on context and referentiality (Hodder 1991b: 125–8; Tilley 1991: 16–23, 95–6). Understanding the meanings of words is heavily dependent upon the rest of the sentence, paragraph, chapter, or book; similarly, interpreting artefactual meaning depends upon the ever-widening spatial, temporal, and social context. Whether the specific meanings of objects are purely abstract and arbitrary, as post-structuralism would hold for words, is more debateable given the practical nature of material culture use (Tilley 1999: 265–70). Nonetheless, objects can clearly have multiple meanings in different contexts, in very much the same way as people have varying identities in different contexts. Second, and adding emphasis to the last point, the notion of 'text' is useful in bringing both 'author' and 'reader' to the fore (Johnson 1999b: 105–7; Munslow 2000: 24–30). Material texts can be 'authored'—that is, produced by human agents with meaningful intentions—but they can also have unintended meanings, and in any case (regardless of the author's intent) any material text is capable of diverse 'readings'. The essentialism of 'one story' with 'one reading' (Berkhofer 1995: 47–53; Buchli 1995: 182) can therefore be avoided.

Notably, this approach has been explored most fully in prehistoric rather than historical archaeologies (cf. comments by Matthew Johnson in Hodder et al. 1995: 225–6). Yet it seems vital that such issues be addressed in contexts in which we are required not only to interpret meaning in material culture—'textual' or otherwise—but also to understand written sources as artefacts. Therefore, just as insights can be gained from treating material culture as in some senses 'textual', so the modifications to this idea that have also been developed in archaeology can be extended to ground the interpretation of written texts as *material* products of their (ancient) authors. These modifications temper the concept of textuality with an emphasis upon the involvement of objects in practical, physical action (e.g., Hodder 1991b: 127; Moore 1986: 73–90; Shanks and Tilley 1987: 101–5). In this way, as we saw in Chapter 2, some of the extreme relativism of postmodern history can be counterbalanced. Indeed, to push the textual analogy for material culture beyond the two general points just elucidated is clearly problematic. Different types and levels of meaning can be conveyed in material media, and while these can include written language or language-like symbol systems with a semiotic structure, they very often depend upon nonlinguistic, pragmatic, and evocative meanings. Furthermore, by its very materiality, material culture serves to solidify, reify, and sometimes naturalise what would be transient spoken meanings, being relatively durable and involved in repetitive practices (Hodder 1995b: 201–12; 1999: 74–8; Shanks and Tilley 1987: 102–5). Objects, to paraphrase Tilley (1999: 262–73), can be metaphors, but they are solid ones. The particular meanings they explicitly convey will thus depend heavily on the context in which they are being used, and whether this is routine and unproblematic or unusual and open to discursive attention—thus implicitly involving the ways in which structures impact upon agents, and agents shape structures. Establishing such links between artefacts and practice contexts is a key goal of this chapter.

The most recent work on material culture interpretation attempts to deal both with a plurality of meaning types, and with the ways in which people's actions are both shaped and assisted by tangible but meaningful things linking agency and structure. This perspective is not just confined to archaeology (e.g., Gardner 2003b; Johnson 1999a; Moreland 2001), but has been crucial in the development of a more cross-disciplinary field of 'material culture studies'. Anthropology is well represented in this, with Danny Miller in particular pursuing a number of the implications of taking 'things' seriously in the analysis of globalisation, looking for example at the relationships between categories of objects and people (e.g., 1994, 1998; cf. Attfield 2000; Graves-Brown 2000; Kopytoff 1986). This follows from the idea that the consumption of artefacts can be interpreted 'biographically'— that is, in terms of the artefacts' own 'life-stories' (Appadurai 1986; Gosden and Marshall 1999; see further discussion in Chapter 4). Similar approaches to looking at how artefacts seem to 'act back' on people through the semiotic and tangible meanings they convey have also been adopted in sociology (Dant 1999, 2005; cf. McCarthy 1984), a discipline hitherto very reluctant to give much attention to the artefactual world. This emerging interdisciplinary project is characterised by an interest in the overlapping of spoken, written, and other material forms of meaning communication, especially in relation to the negotiation of identity. It is also drawing upon some long-standing traditions, like phenomenology and pragmatism, to establish how interaction with objects shapes self-awareness—making materiality a key part in the development of agency, as well as of the structures in which agents live.

All of these matters will concern us as we move towards interpreting the archaeology of 4th century Britain in terms of identities, which are a major dimension of artefactual meanings. This process will begin in this chapter with an attempt to describe some of the key characteristics of that archaeology, in terms of the links among artefacts, spaces, and texts and their respective contexts. One more immediate implication of these ideas is that the classification of this material must be carefully considered. Archaeologists are increasingly asking questions about the categories that we adopt in material analysis, and their relationships to the categories that people assigned things to in the past (Allison 1997; Evans 1995). Clearly, taxonomies are situationally specific phenomena, varying not only cross-culturally but also between different contexts within a culture (Hodder 1999: 72–9; Kopytoff 1986: 70; Shanks and Tilley 1987: 79–84). As a result changes are underway in the methods by which Roman artefacts—particularly small finds—are classified, with a shift to the use of functional rather than material categories (e.g., Cool et al. 1995). This is a very positive step, provided that these do not become an end in themselves or are too narrowly defined (thus perpetuating some of the problems of functionalism mentioned above). Rather, they need to be developed as ways into understanding meaningful practice. Ideally more dimensions of comparison will be used in the future, including well-established ones like material types (for instance, there is evidence that pewter was a ritually significant metal in the 4th century [Poulton and Scott 1993; cf. Meskell 2004: 39–46]), to establish all of the possible dimensions of artefact use and meaning. In this chapter, I will try to exploit functional categories of artefacts as a springboard to develop a more socially meaningful typology of practices (including such activities as exchanging, eating, appearing, and dwelling) that can provide the link between objects and identities. To begin, though, we will look at some of the artefactual patterns from the 4th century in terms of the categories into which archaeological practice has typically divided them.

Portable material culture

Coins and small finds

In dealing with artefacts, a broad distinction can be made between the small objects that are normally recorded to a high level of detail—both typologically and locationally—in excavation, and more common or larger-scale 'bulk' finds such as pottery and animal bone. In this section, I will divide the material to be considered along these lines, as different descriptive frameworks and analytical techniques can

68 ■ An Archaeology of Identity

be applied to these groupings. With both of these sets of artefacts, though, I will use examples from key sites to begin to establish the main characteristics of their distribution and deposition in the 4th century, as well as to place them in the context of particular practices. This process will continue with greater attention to continuity and change in the next chapter, where further comparative techniques will be deployed. Similarities and differences between the patterns of practice thus revealed can then be considered in terms of identities in Chapter 5. Coins offer a good type of material with which to begin: they are well recorded and fairly ubiquitous, but are also under-exploited as artefacts that were embedded in the practices of daily life (as opposed to tools for constructing site chronologies). There are various important problems and issues with studying coinage in the late Roman period that need to be discussed in order to provide a backdrop to the more detailed examples that follow.

Numismatic work on the Roman period has traditionally been the-oretically conservative, and one of the major elements of this is the assumption that Roman coins were used in much the same way as modern ones (Guest 1999: 200–2; Ryan 1988: 2–3). While it may be the case that modern monetary coinage has been partly based upon Roman models in one way or another, this clearly does not provide a firm foundation for retrojective analogies of use. The Roman govern-ment's reasons for producing such objects should not be assumed to be the same as those of a modern capitalist nation-state. Furthermore, coins need not have been acquired, perceived, used, or disposed of in a uniform way across the temporal, spatial, and social diversity of the empire. There were wide fluctuations in the quantities and qualities of coins minted centrally, and of local copies, as well as idiosyncratic practices such as the clipping off of the edges of late Roman silver *sil-iquae* in Britain (Bédoyère 1999a: 159–60; Reece 1977, 1987: 42–5). These kinds of phenomena tend to suggest that there were real dif-ferences from modern coin use and that there was variation across the Roman world, as well as through time. From the perspectives of both producers and consumers, then, the nature of coin use becomes a problem rather than something to be taken for granted. We must ask how and why coins were supplied and circulated, and to what extent—if at all—these processes can be described in economic terms. This means, for instance, that the quantity of coins at a site at a par-ticular time cannot simply be equated with its 'level of prosperity' (Reece 1988: 47, 51–2). Rather, alternative reasons at a range of scales (individual, local, regional) must be explored for changing numbers of coins. Some of these will emerge in the next chapter.

Of more immediate concern is a consideration of what archaeological coin assemblages represent. While it has been established that there is a particular pattern of coin supply to Britain, and that this is linked to the tax and pay structures of the late Roman state (Reece 1977, 1988: 51–2), if we are to build this into more local narratives of coin use, we need to begin at the smallest scales and explore how contextual information from particular sites might tell us about the mechanics of loss and discard processes. From this foundation the broader patterns of changing coin numbers occurring on sites or in regions over time can be more fully interpreted in terms of people's engagement with artefacts in practice.

In this section, I will use four examples of sites with good published data to explore those mechanics: Caernarfon, Birdoswald, South Shields, and York Minster. These four sites, all with military associations and central to any understanding of military identity in this period, provide a useful range of different kinds of data with which to work. They are also actually among a very small number of sites where it is possible to make detailed associations between coins and their contexts of discovery (Reece 2002: 142–3; cf. Ryan 1988: 32–5; 143–7). More sites will be included in the broader temporal analysis of coin patterns in the next chapter, where less contextual resolution is required. Some concern with time and dating is also necessary here, actually, as the dates stamped upon coins (in the form of imperial titles) are a fairly major element of their materiality and closely constrain all work upon them. Two main approaches have become established for simplifying the chronology of coin issue in Britain, in both of which imperial reigns are amalgamated or divided to create 'issue periods' that relate more to the changing nature of the coinage itself (such as denominations) and make for easier quantitative analysis. These are the methods of John Casey (1984: 26–48) and Richard Reece (1968, 1991). The former, which comprises 27 periods, has been used in reports on coins from a number of sites, mainly in the north and west (e.g., Brickstock 1994); the latter, with 21 periods, has been employed on various sites in the south and east, and some elsewhere (e.g., Davies 1997). Reece's method owes its wider application to the existence of a useful corpus of comparative data, which he prepared from 140 sites across Britain (Reece 1991), and this will underpin the techniques used here.

To turn to the examples of sites with detailed data that I want to explore here, Caernarfon will crop up again in several other situations. It has been extensively excavated, primarily by Mortimer Wheeler in the 1920s and then by a Cadw (Welsh Historic Monuments) team in the

1970s, and seems to have been continuously occupied through most of the Roman period. The southeastern quadrant of the fort, excavated in the latter campaign, produced a sequence of early barracks, followed by an area of mixed use containing administrative and bath buildings and, later still, light industrial activity (Fig. 3.1 [Casey et al. 1993]). The coins from the site can be plotted on a plan of the main structures, in the area of their context of discovery (not, it should be emphasised, their precise location), and thereby related more closely to the circumstances of their deposition (Fig. 3.2). This shows that the majority of coins were found in four types of context: the fill of a large drainage feature cut across the site in the later 4th century; dumps on the eastern side of the area; various pits; and areas of 'dark soil'. All of these can be regarded as refuse deposits that are likely to contain redeposited material. Very few of the coins occur in other types of contexts that might be more related to the construction (e.g., wall trenches) or use (e.g., floors/surfaces) of buildings. Most of these refuse contexts are 4th century (or later) in date, when the site was used for a range of activities—not just dumping, but also work on the defences and small-scale manufacturing of metal objects. Many of the coins themselves are also 4th century, particularly from Period 17 (AD 330–348). The few 1st to 3rd century coins, as well as the early to mid-4th century coins, are generally found in later contexts. While some of the coins that could not be located on the available plans may come from more contemporary features, the general picture is that coins do not occur in contexts of loss as such, but in rubbish fills/features of rather later date than that of the coins themselves.

Figure 3.1. Photograph of the southwestern corner of Caernarfon (© Gwyn Davies).

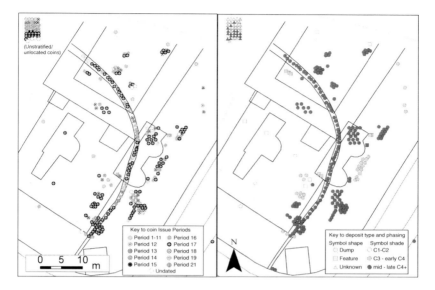

Figure 3.2. Plans of coin deposition at Caernarfon (plan after Casey et al. 1993: 8; Wheeler 1924: f.p. 186; data from Casey 1993).

The most obvious reasons for this are either long circulation, or re-deposition of refuse accumulating over long periods.

A comparable picture comes from Birdoswald, in northern Britain. This fort on Hadrian's Wall was constructed during the early 2nd century development of that frontier system. It was explored in the 1920s and 1930s, but can be analysed in contextual detail thanks to the more recent English Heritage excavations in the vicinity of the west gate and adjoining stores buildings (Fig. 3.3 [Wilmott 1997]), where occupation activity seems to have continued well into the post-Roman period. Although detailed information on the types of contexts in which coins were found is lacking, something of their character can be gleaned from their phasing, which was also based on pottery (Fig. 3.4). Here a clear chronological progression can be seen from the earlier Phase 4 contexts in the gate and workshop structures (late 3rd century); later Phase 4 on the *via principalis* running toward the gate (early 4th century); Phase 5 in the stores buildings (late 4th century); and Phase 6 or later (5th century and beyond) in the general soil covering the site. This can effectively be used to differentiate types of contexts, coinciding with the road surfacing and metalworking activity in Phase 4; rubbish disposal and occupation in Phase 5; renewed construction in Phase 6 (some coins on the *via principalis*); and then medieval use of the site. Very few coins came from contexts

Figure 3.3. Photograph of the western gate area at Birdoswald.

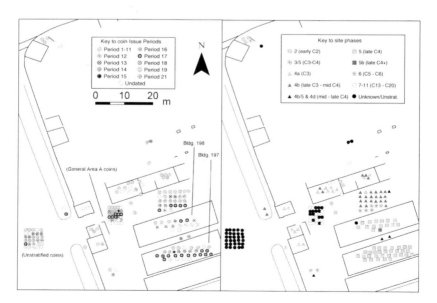

Figure 3.4. Plans of coin deposition at Birdoswald (plan after Biggins et al. 1999: 161; Wilmott 1997: 10–11; data from Davies 1997).

of the 2nd to early 3rd centuries, though coins of these periods were certainly present. Indeed, as at Caernarfon, the later contexts (particularly those associated with rubbish disposal) contained coins of considerably earlier periods.

This association of coins and rubbish is reinforced by the finds from the two stores buildings (*horrea*). The group from the northern building (Building 198) has a later focus than that from the southern one (Building 197), the emphasis shifting from Period 17 (AD 330–348) to Periods 18–19 (AD 348–364; AD 364–378). This relates directly to the sequence of use: in the mid-4th century, Building 197 was resurfaced and reused, while from around the same time Building 198 was primarily a rubbish dump. Furthermore, most of the coins in the Building 197 group came from the backfill used to level the floor, rather than subsequent (apparently domestic, and possibly high-status) occupation surfaces; these produced only one coin later than the date of backfilling (a Theodosian issue of the end of the 4th century), the rest being 3rd or earlier 4th century issues. The implication is that most coins used after the backfilling of 197 ended up in the dumps in 198 (Wilmott 1997: 207–9). This emphasises the point that many 4th century coins were found in rubbish contexts, rather than on occupation surfaces where they might actually have been lost. Interestingly, though, of those that were found on such surfaces, most were quite old.

This also applies to the coins found on the surfaces of the *via sagularis*, the road parallel to the defences. Here, the coins from Phase 4b contexts (early 4th century) included only two coins of the contemporary early Constantinian period, the rest being of late 3rd century date or earlier; the Phase 6 (5th/6th century) coins are mostly Constantinian. In other areas of the site, some coins were found in earlier contexts (Phase 4a, 3rd century), but again tended to be old when those contexts formed. It is easier to posit long-term circulation as an explanation for this phenomenon with early (1st and 2nd century) coins, as these were more intrinsically valuable, than it is for later issues that were increasingly a 'token' currency. The occurrence here, as at Caernarfon, of a majority of late Roman coins in rubbish deposits rather than in use contexts (while the latter still contain early coins) raises the possibility of coins being thrown away (cf. Butcher 2001: 24; Reece 1988: 48–61, 1999a: 129–39; Ryan 1988: 32–6). In addition to length of circulation—or redeposition—as factors relevant to the final location of coins, we must therefore also consider whether 'loss' is always an appropriate concept to deal with the active decisions that people made about the use of coins.

The fort at South Shields was an important, but belated, element in the Hadrian's Wall system, with the extant stone structure begun in the AD 160s (a Hadrianic fort probably preceded it, in a slightly different location). Its life after that point was complex, with the addition of a supply base function at the beginning of the 3rd century, and shifting arrangements for the accommodation of troops. Occupation continued into the 5th century (Bidwell and Speak 1994: 9). Parts of the central headquarters building (*principia*) and southwestern gate areas were excavated in the 1980s, and the stratified coins from these excavations can be plotted in the same way as for Caernarfon and Birdoswald (Figs. 3.5–3.6). This clearly shows that the majority of coinage was found in the southwestern ditches area, where there is also a greater proportion of later (4th century) coins; the *principia* group is weighted more towards coins minted before the late 3rd century. Moreover, the only coins stratified in Phases 4–6 (mid-2nd to late 3rd centuries) are in the *principia* area. The others here, and all of those in the gate area, are from Phases 7–9, covering the 4th century and beyond. Most of these come from 'occupation' or 'disuse' deposits, particularly dumps of rubbish or backfill in the external ditches (not all of which are shown on the plan). In contrast, most of the *principia* coin finds were associated with 'construction' or 'demolition' activities, as were those

Figure 3.5. Photograph of the reconstructed southwestern gate at South Shields, on the site of the Roman portal.

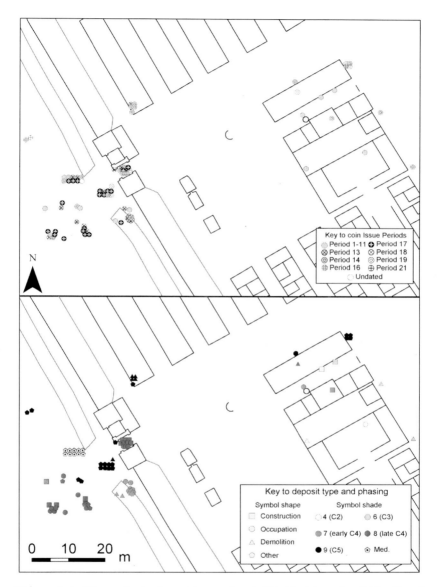

Figure 3.6. Plans of coin deposition at South Shields (plan after Bidwell and Speak 1994: 34; data from Brickstock 1994).

in the *horreum* behind the gate and many of those in the gate itself (from road surfacing).

Once again, then, the coin finds seem to be an indication of the location of rubbish disposal activities as much as anything else (although the ditch-area material did include a small hoard). Some coins were found

76 ■ An Archaeology of Identity

in contexts associated with different kinds of activity, but even if these are treated as relating to primary 'loss', closer examination of their issue periods shows (as observed elsewhere) that such coins could be rather old. In the *principia* area, several of the coins from mid-2nd to 3rd century phases actually date from the 1st or early 2nd centuries. Some of the later deposits relating to building activity here, and in the *horreum* and gateway, also include later 3rd century 'radiate' coins (named after the type of crown borne by the emperors depicted) in later 4th century contexts. Indeed the groups from the filling deposits in the ditch area (Phases 8–9) are more consistently 4th century in composition. This suggests that 4th century coins were more readily deposited in contemporary or near-contemporary contexts than coins of earlier periods, which were available for redeposition for rather longer periods and may well have been in circulation for much of this time.

Finally, York gives a slightly different perspective on these issues. The central area of the legionary fortress here, encompassing parts of barracks and the headquarters building, was excavated under difficult conditions during restoration work to the Minster cathedral in the late 1960s and early 1970s (Phillips and Heywood 1995a, 1995b). Although a detailed exploration of context types is not possible, comparison can be made between the site periods of coin-bearing contexts and the production dates of the coins themselves (Fig. 3.7). This indicates quite clearly that the great majority of coins were found in contexts of Periods 7 (5th to 8th centuries), 8 (9th to 11th centuries), and 9 (unstratified and other post-Roman)—concentrating to some degree in the central barrack (Barrack 2), which was most intensively excavated. Furthermore, the coins in Period 5 or 6 contexts (early and late 4th century respectively) tend to be pre-4th century issues. Very few coins were stratified in contexts of Periods 1 (late 1st century) to 4 (3rd century). Unless Roman coins were being used and lost as late as the 11th century, it would seem that the coinage from the Minster site is overwhelmingly residual. Furthermore, it appears that quite old coins were being deposited late in the Roman period, as we have seen at other sites. A key problem is the nature of the primary depositional contexts for the quantities of coinage found, for instance, in Barrack 2. Since few coins across the site are stratified in 'use' deposits, it is likely that late Roman-period refuse disposal accounts for a large part of the observable patterning. One prosaic point to draw out of this section is, therefore, that coins will rarely provide a reliable date for the contexts in which they are found.

More generally, in trying to treat coins as objects within an initially limited definition of their context, various points have emerged about how they may have been used in the 4th century. While the examples considered obviously constitute only a limited sample, the patterns

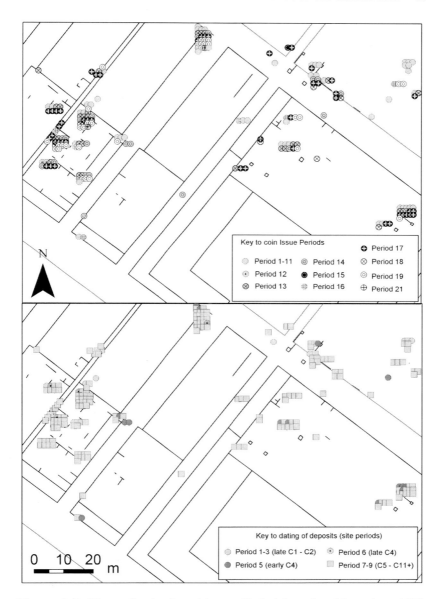

Figure 3.7. Plans of coin deposition at York (plan after Monaghan 1997: Fig. 435; Ottaway 1996: Fig. 186; data from Casey 1995).

observed at each of these four sites indicate a consistent pattern. In each case, coin finds (including those of early issue periods) were most prolific in the 4th century or later deposits. Furthermore, these late Roman deposits were often rubbish dumps and relatively few

78 ■ An Archaeology of Identity

coins were stratified in contexts directly associated with any other kind of activity. This patterning prompts a series of questions. Did early Roman coins circulate for longer periods than later ones, or can their persistence be accounted for purely in terms of post-depositional processes and 'residuality'? Why are few coins found in contexts of immediate 'loss'? How do coins come to be present in refuse deposits? And what are the implications in terms of the cultural significance of coins? Such questions are not new, and have been answered in a number of ways, which lead us into some of the more general characteristics of 4th century coinage. The intrinsic value of coins minted in the 1st, 2nd, and early 3rd centuries AD was both greater and more consistent than that of most late 3rd and 4th century issues, the quality of which—as noted in Chapter 2—was always struggling to recover after the 3rd century currency crisis. As a result, they remained in use for considerably longer periods (a picture supported by hoard evidence). At the same time, and partly because the earlier coinages were too valuable to be of much use in day-to-day transactions, they circulated less widely and so were not as available to be lost or otherwise deposited (Guest 1999: 204–6; Reece 1987: 28–45, 1988: 60–1). Regarding loss itself, it is common-sensically believed that a coin dropped in a visible place—particularly if it is large and/or valuable— will be picked up, and so will rarely enter an archaeological deposit such as a floor surface (Reece 1996: 341–5). If this is the case, however, the question remains of how coins end up in rubbish deposits. A number of factors are important here. Coins may be lost into contexts that are subsequently disturbed and redeposited, becoming mixed with later material, and thus 'residual'. It may simply be stratigraphic accident that these coins commonly end up in 4th century deposits: as the last phases on many sites, these are relatively undisturbed (though certainly at some risk from later ploughing).

These factors are all potentially involved in creating the observed patterning. In addition, there may be changes in the location of refuse disposal in the 4th century (e.g., from extra- to intramural) that affect the quantities of coins found in particular places; such issues will be examined in detail in Chapter 4. For the time being, however, let us assume that while such aspects of general depositional activity may well undergo transformations in the late Roman period, they accompany rather than create a genuine increase in coin deposition. Reece has linked this increased deposition to the supply (whether official or unofficial) of small-value coinage in greater quantities than were hitherto available, facilitating increased use of coinage in daily exchange (Reece 1987: 25–45, 1999a: 134–40 [see Fig. 3.8]). Thus greater numbers of

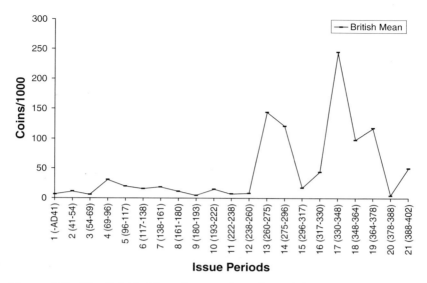

Figure 3.8. The British Mean for coin loss, derived from 140 sites (Reece 1995: 183), showing the trend towards greater loss (and presumably supply) through much of the later Roman period.

coins, increased use in exchange practices, and lower unit value all contributed to a pattern of more loss and less recovery. The common occurrence of coins in 4th century rubbish (rather than 'use' contexts) can be used to support this, but also to suggest a tension between coins being more widely used than they were previously, and at the same time less worthwhile to keep—to the extent that many were thrown away. This tension might be expected to lead to different patterns of coin use in different places, depending both on the frequency with which coins needed to be used and the ways in which their cultural value was perceived. These are all fruitful questions to explore with a longer temporal perspective in the next chapter.

Many of the archaeological issues just considered in relation to the use of coins as objects in the 4th century also relate to the other kind of high-definition data that is available for the period: small finds. This term encompasses objects made in a wide range of materials and with a wide variety of uses. Essentially, it includes all portable artefacts that are not broken pots, animal bones (unless reworked), or coins. This classification is regularly employed in the reporting of finds assemblages, commonly further divided by material but increasingly by functional categories. In looking at this material, I will follow the pattern set out above for coins—examining individual objects in their contexts against

80 ■ An Archaeology of Identity

the general background of the period, deferring further consideration of continuity and change within it until the following chapter.

Before proceeding with this exercise, however, a couple of points need to be made concerning classification to elaborate on the above comments. The first is that in general terms, although the functional aspects of some objects (such as locks and keys) may be taken to be a sufficient account of their meaning, the involvement of these objects in the complex but routine practices of individuals may well entail other kinds of significance—which are no less related to functionality, and in some ways dependent upon it.

Following from this, many objects that are classed as small finds—for instance, dress accessories—may have highly important roles to play in the negotiation of social identities as part of practices relating to appearance. The specific nature of these identities cannot, though, be assumed on a priori grounds. A case in point is the traditional gendering of objects as female (rings, bracelets, pins) and male (weapons, tools) in much Roman archaeology (e.g., Daniels 1980: 189; Wright 1872: 274–304). Such associations are not simply potentially misleading in terms of the uses of the objects themselves (and Allason-Jones [1995] has successfully refuted several of them), but also in terms of the stereotyped gender identities and behaviours implied by them. In the approach developed in this book, it is important to address social identity categories critically and focus not just, for instance, on whether women lived or worked inside forts (cf. Driel-Murray 1995), but also on how gender identities were constructed across Romano-British society. For this reason, while a gendered differentiation of artefacts is employed in the analysis of small finds in succeeding sections, it is really only a starting point to develop ideas about the validity of such schemes.

The categories used in the functional analysis of small finds can best be introduced with examples. The assemblages represented in Figure 3.9 are not chronologically or spatially divided, but still provide food for thought in terms of overall patterns and comparisons between sites of different types. Three sites from western Britain are shown on this graph, Biglis, Caerhun, and Caerleon, and these are all quite different—the first a small farmstead sporadically occupied through the Roman period, the second an early fort (with ambiguous later occupation), and the third a fortress. Nonetheless, the ratios of functional categories contain some interesting similarities. Personal objects, encompassing both those putatively gendered as 'female' (primarily hairpins and bracelets) and 'male/female', are an important presence at all three, as are the categories of 'furniture/fittings' and 'tools', which encompass quite a lot of miscellaneous and amorphous

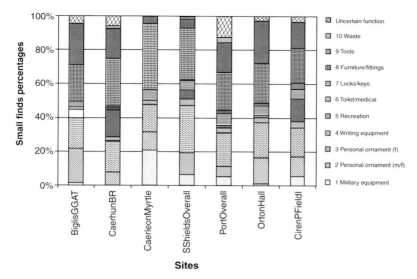

Figure 3.9. Overview of small finds categories at selected sites (data from Brewer 1988; Greep 1988; Parkhouse 1988: 60–3; Webster, J. 1988; Baillie Reynolds 1938; Fox 1940: 127–36; Allason-Jones and Miket 1984; Webster 1975; Mackreth 1996: 92–102; Rennie 1971: 79–84; categories after Cool et al. 1995).

ironwork. Significantly, while Caerleon conforms with expectations that military equipment (weapons, armour fragments, harness fittings) should be present, this is not the case with Caerhun—and yet the farmstead does have one object in this category. This kind of occurrence is not unusual and blurs the boundaries between sites of different kinds.

Such an impression is reinforced by the other four columns on the graph. The South Shields assemblage contains many more personal objects than military ones, and many miscellaneous fittings, and very much the same can be said of the assemblage from Portchester Castle, a later Roman Saxon Shore fort with—in the opinion of the excavator—different degrees of military and civilian occupation at different times (Cunliffe 1975: 422–31). This interpretation will be investigated in more detail later, but whether small finds can be a guide to different kinds of occupation (i.e., the identities of different resident communities) is called in to question by the assemblages from Cirencester and Orton Hall Farm, which show that towns and farms can have quite similar patterns of artefacts to forts or fortresses. There are various potentially distorting factors in these graphs, such as the differences in numbers of objects (as opposed to percentages) and the lack of chronological control, so that certain types of objects might be more important in different phases—military objects in towns, for example, might come from a fort present on the site in its earliest days (as happened at a number of locations). The graphs also obscure the presence or absence of particular types of objects, including some that are generally considered important in marking out late Roman official identities, such as crossbow brooches and certain types of belt fitting (Fig. 3.10). Nonetheless, the general trends illustrated here are interesting in terms of the broad consumption pattern of a wide range of objects at different kinds of site—particularly the emphasis on personalia (gendered or not) and other kinds of functional fittings.

To grasp more firmly the material in use during the later Roman period, we can look in some detail at the sites discussed above with

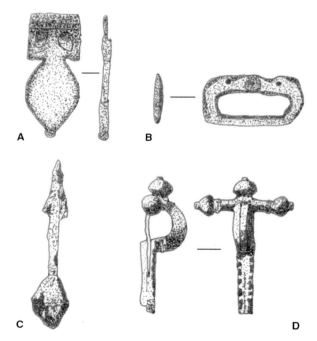

Figure 3.10. Examples of significant later Roman small find types: belt fittings (A and B) from South Shields, and a weighted throwing dart (C) and crossbow brooch (D) from Caernarfon. These types of objects are often taken to be diagnostic of 4th century military presence. (After Allason-Jones and Miket 1984: 191; Allason-Jones 1993: 167, 188; scale approx. 1:1.25, except for brooch, 1:2.5).

respect to coinage: Caernarfon, Birdoswald, South Shields, and York Minster. While it is not always possible to display all categories of small finds on these plans (particularly at Caernarfon there are large numbers of miscellaneous, unidentified pieces of metalwork that would unduly clutter the distribution), we can get more leverage on some of the problems raised in the last section—the indirect relationship between coin finds and practices of exchange—in terms of different sets of material practices. Again although patterns of continuity and change within the late Roman period are not my primary concern in this chapter, some important insights into practices of use can be gained by comparing stratigraphic and typological object chronologies, and Caernarfon is helpful here (Fig. 3.11). While many of the objects are not specifically dated (indicative in itself of the relatively slow rate of stylistic change in many classes of material), there is a spread of artefacts that are, several being made in the 4th century or later—including brooches, weaponry, and bracelets. As with the coins, though, most finds of all periods were stratified in late contexts, almost all of which were associated with refuse disposal.

Clearly, deposition in this part of Caernarfon was at its most intensive in the 4th century and the material deposited was refuse incorporating material of some antiquity, but also a considerable number and variety

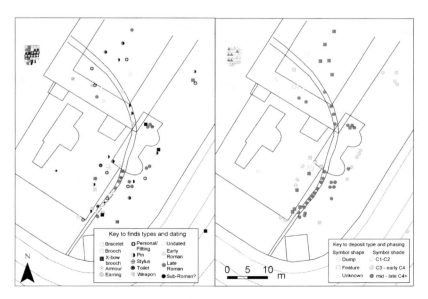

Figure 3.11. Plans of small find deposition at Caernarfon (plan after Casey et al. 1993: 8; Wheeler 1924: f.p. 186; data from Allason-Jones 1993).

of finds of recent date. These finds can themselves be associated with a range of activities by virtue of their function, but even their circumstances of disposal are informative. The numbers of personal objects reflect a concern on the part of the members of this community with practices of 'appearing'. In conjunction with particular forms of clothing, these different objects attest to differentiated identities within the community, whether these were defined by gender, age, status or authority, or wealth. At the same time, since objects of all different kinds were mixed in final disposal (and indeed probably in contexts of initial loss), there clearly were established practices that cut across these embodied differences—not just in refuse dumping, which may have entailed changes in object meanings, but in habitation too.

Similar patterns can be seen in the more comprehensive plan for Birdoswald, showing all stratified and unstratified small finds (Fig. 3.12). Again, many objects are not specifically dated, and this does complicate matters somewhat. However, it is notable that a number of the artefacts in the northern *horreum* (Building 198) are of rather earlier dates than their late phasing might suggest, and this is interesting insofar as much of this dump accumulated during the reuse of the more southerly *horreum* (Building 197) in the mid-4th century. However, material from Building 197 itself that was deposited in this phase does include late

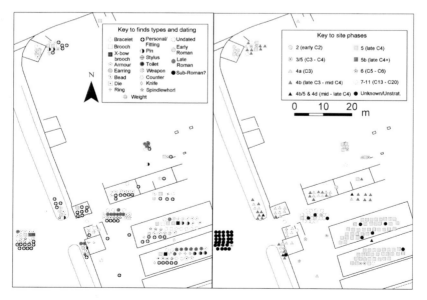

Figure 3.12. Plans of small find deposition at Birdoswald (plan after Biggins et al. 1999: 161; Wilmott 1997: 10–11; data from Summerfield 1997).

beads, pins, and a penannular brooch. Otherwise very few finds occur in contexts preceding Phase 4 (late 3rd/early 4th century). While this would suggest a high rate of residuality or redeposition, the 'old' objects dumped in Building 198 (along with many *contemporary* coins—see above) might be a clue to prolonged use or retention as 'heirlooms' of some kind. This may be an important element in the meaning content of artefacts in use in this period in terms of their temporality. As for the contexts in which they were used, we are again confronted with a dominant proportion of personalia becoming mixed together through depositional practices.

The focus in the South Shields finds plots is more on spatial variation, which gives some clues as to the original situations in which objects were used. All stratified objects are shown here, with their context types and phasing; few of the objects have specific dates (Fig. 3.13). In terms of the distribution of finds types, the majority of those in the *principia* area (which at times actually included *horrea* structures) are miscellaneous fittings ('other'), except for a few counters and a late deposit containing more personalia outside the 'forecourt granary' at the northern end of the site. This later deposit is also unusual in being a late 'disuse' dump; most of the others are construction deposits from the 3rd or 4th century building operations. The southwestern gate area contexts are slightly more varied in finds composition, although unidentified fittings are again dominant, and more of these finds come from Period 9 'disuse' deposits such as upper ditch fills. The deposition of these objects was evidently not a novel feature of the latest occupation: a significant number of artefacts, including a seemingly coherent group of pieces depicting or symbolising heads, were placed in one ditch in period 7 (the early 4th century). Overall, these distributions illustrate the differences in depositional practices between the two areas, and importantly also the different range of activities in the *principia*. As a place with a more specialised range of functions, relating to the ceremonial and bureaucratic aspects of the unit's life, access to this area may have been more restricted than the gateways, roads, and barracks.

This means that, while refuse disposal is the main activity that shapes the finds assemblages being plotted here, that activity appears to bear some relation to the other activities occurring in the areas or buildings concerned. Our final example confirms this (Fig. 3.14). As with the coins, the excavations at York Minster produced a range of objects coming mainly from late or post-Roman deposits. This again would suggest that redeposition ought to be a significant factor, but it is notable that the types of artefacts found within the *principia* is quite limited; many more objects of a personal nature were recovered

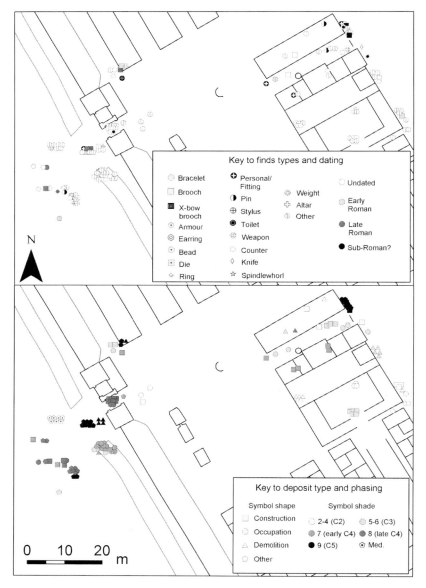

Figure 3.13. Plans of small find deposition at South Shields (plan after Bidwell and Speak 1994: 34; data from Croom et al. 1994).

from the barracks, where people were actually living. Therefore, the importance of refuse disposal and movement to artefact patterning need not obscure the structuring effect of the practices in which those objects were engaged at other times in their lives—and those of the

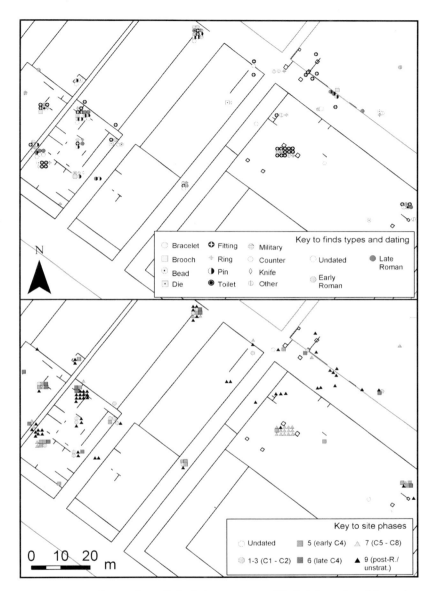

Figure 3.14. Plans of small find deposition at York (plan after Monaghan 1997: Fig. 435; Ottaway 1996: Fig. 186; data from Price et al. 1995).

people who used them. As already suggested for other sites, these practices included quite prominently the presentation of a particular appearance, as well as activities involving the formation of specific social relationships such as gaming. Once we have placed these activities into

88 ■ AN ARCHAEOLOGY OF IDENTITY

a fuller spatial and temporal context, below and in the next chapter, it will be clear that they were important elements in the construction of particular identities.

Before leaving the topic of small finds, however, one specific kind of context in which such things were used has not been considered: burial. In Britain, cemeteries that contain late Roman burials relevant to the problems of the relationship between military and other identities are few and far between, partly because there are simply many more excavations of settlements than of cemeteries (cf. Esmonde Cleary 1993). Lankhills is the most well known and widely discussed of those burial grounds that has been examined and fully published, and does indeed contain a group of burials that seems to include officials or soldiers serving the Roman state, who came to Winchester from Pannonia. This interpretation is based both upon some of the key artefact types mentioned above, such as crossbow brooches, and more definitively upon some of the exotic material found in the female graves that are part of the group (Swift 2000: 69–77). While this sheds important light on the use of 'small finds' in the creation of a range of identities and will be returned to in a later chapter, it has been so widely discussed (see, e.g., Baldwin 1985) that a less well-known— and yet potentially more illuminating—example will be introduced here from the other side of the Saxon Shore. Oudenburg is a fort on the Belgian coast and contemporary with sites like Portchester. The interior of the square enclosure, like its companions on the other side of the Channel, is not well understood.

However, unlike those forts, the associated cemetery has been excavated, providing a tantalising glance at the material culture of the site's inhabitants in a context rather different to those we have been considering so far (Brulet 1990: 118–22, 1991: 161–3; Mertens 1964, 1972, 1977; Mertens and van Impe 1971a, 1971b). Excavated from the late 1950s to the late 1970s, only part of the northern end of the fort enclosure has been revealed, and while timber and stone buildings and roads were uncovered, these related to an early (1st/2nd century) phase that was not contemporary with the later Roman defences and cemetery. The latter is crucial for understanding life at Oudenburg in the late 4th and early 5th centuries. Containing 216 inhumations, it was situated west of the defensive enclosure, overlying an earlier settlement. Orientation of the burials varied, but the majority were arranged east-west and sexing was conducted purely on the basis of grave goods. Out of 133 furnished burials, only 21 were judged on these grounds to be female, and there also seem to have been few children. Although weapons were absent from the 'male' burial suite, crossbow brooches were common (occurring in 32 cases), suggesting to the excavators that these were regular 'Roman' soldiers rather than their 'Germanic' allies (or *foederati*), who were usually buried with their weapons. Even so, two of the 'female' burials contained 'Germanic' brooches. These artefacts, as well as the coins and pottery, were of late 4th/early 5th century date, and occupation apparently ended suddenly in ca. AD 410.

Elements of this interpretation may be questioned, however. Although the excavators have drawn attention to the high number of burials with crossbow brooches (Mertens and van Impe 1971a: 228), this does only constitute a quarter of the 133 accompanied burials. A rather greater number (83, or 38% of the total) had no grave goods at all, while 44 of the furnished burials contained only pottery or glassware (Mertens and van Impe 1971b). Moreover, the crossbow brooches did not uniformly co-occur with belt fittings and knives to form an 'official' suite, despite the emphasis of the excavators upon this combination, which is attested elsewhere—indeed there are only nine instances of this association (cf. Mertens and van Impe 1971a: 230; Reece 1999a: 154–61; Swift 2000: 45–52). Other artefacts occasionally occurring with crossbow brooches include combs, a pair of shears, and a bracelet, albeit of a potentially masculine type (Ellen Swift pers. comm.; Mertens and van Impe 1971a: 225). If the brooches were a mark of distinction—whether military, official, or wealth related—the people who wore them in life were buried with a variety of other people who lacked this distinction (common soldiers or civilians?) and were themselves not buried in a uniform way.

Although coming from outside of Britain, this example complements the others examined in this section to highlight how small objects were used in a wide variety of contexts and by a wide variety of people, even on sites with strong military associations. The resolution of the data studied in this section has allowed an examination not just of the kinds of objects used, but of how they were used in the contexts of life and death. We have looked at some of the general characteristics of coinage and other small objects in the late Roman period, but more importantly explored the practices within which they were embedded—exchange, creating certain appearances, and also discard, rubbish disposal, or burial. Such objects can also be looked at from a broader perspective, to see what patterns can be discerned over time and between different kinds of sites. These aspects will be addressed in the next chapter, but the foundation of material practices that we have begun to establish in this section will be vital in converting those broader patterns into similarities and differences

90 ■ An Archaeology of Identity

that were meaningful in terms of identities. One other major area of practice needs to be considered at this point, though, before looking at the more spatial characteristics of some of the sites we have encountered: the production and consumption of food.

Pottery and animal bone

The food that people eat, and the technologies they use to prepare it, are major aspects of daily life with both implicit and explicit cultural significance. In this section, I will consider some general issues pertaining to the technologies—primarily pottery, in the archaeological record for Roman Britain—before looking at the meat part of the actual diet. In both cases I will also describe the general patterns of use in the 4th century, looking—as with small finds—at more dynamic processes with this evidence in the next chapter. Unfortunately, the detailed studies of deposition and use undertaken above are not possible with this kind of material, given the resolution with which they are normally recorded. It is equally regrettable that pottery and animal bone are really the only kinds of data pertaining to 'eating' practices that can be analysed in a meaningfully quantitative way, given the poor preservation of vessels made of organic materials (and the remains of vegetable/cereal foods), as well as the recycling of metal vessels in antiquity. While environmental sampling is now a routine feature of excavations, producing increasing evidence for the nonmeat elements of diet in Roman Britain, animal bones remain the most consistently quantified resource in earlier excavation reports, and—given their relatively large size—the most potentially informative in terms of preserving visible evidence of preparation methods. Taking pottery and animal bone as indicative of eating practices is therefore an incomplete approach, but by no means an irrelevant one.

To focus for now on pottery, obviously one of the staples of archaeological research in an enormous variety of contexts, a significant issue for debate has been the level on which ceramic production, use, and deposition actually do have social meaning. The broader terms of this debate have been discussed above, but some specific points can be added here, as the study of Roman pottery in Britain provides a good illustration of different approaches to material culture. Having once occupied a central place in the traditional 'Romanisation' paradigm, with wares like Samian furnishing an index of cultural change (e.g., Haverfield 1923: 46–7), the homogenising concept of Roman pottery has recently been questioned from a number of angles, as with 'Romanisation' itself. One of the most successful industries in Roman Britain, for instance, was that making 'Black-Burnished Ware category 1' in direct continuation of a pre-Conquest tradition (Reece 1988: 8, 41–3). Equally, new pottery styles drew upon diverse areas of influence (from Gaul to Africa), while the way in which any of these vessels were used might vary depending upon the localised practices of the 'consumer' (Cool 2004a: 30–2; Freeman 1993: 443–4). It has even been suggested that too much 'cultural baggage' is attached to pottery use by archaeologists (Cooper, N.J. 1996); thus, any changes in patterns of consumption can substantially be reduced to simple changes in the availability of particular goods.

While this point has some definite merit, it is perhaps more appropriate—in keeping with the approach to the variable significance of context outlined in Chapter 2—to say that patterns of pottery distribution were significant at some times and in some contexts, and not in others. They might thus be related to particular identity groups (cf. Reece 1979), providing attention is paid to the occasions when those identities would be discursively marked and noticed, as against those times when social practices were simply 'carried on' as matters of routine without explicit concern for meaning. This is the case for all categories of artefact, and indeed the question of whether pottery *availability* determines 'choices' is equally relevant to other kinds of material, and thus worth some consideration. A great deal of research in Roman archaeology, in both its 'traditional' and 'processual' orientations, has been directed at the issues of pottery production and distribution, partly because of the considerable interest in Roman trade as an aspect of the dynamics of empire, and partly because of the visibility of ceramics compared to other goods (Rush 1997: 55; e.g., Hodder 1974). This has elucidated much of the detail of supply without really addressing the problem of demand: to what extent did the distribution of material culture relate to active choices on the part of their consumers, as opposed to the range of objects available and/or supplied to them?

We know, therefore, a considerable amount about the variability of pottery production across the Roman world, and particularly across Britain. There were different kinds of production context (e.g., workshop, household), mechanisms of distribution (e.g., water borne, road), and technologies of manufacture (e.g., BB1 was hand formed while many other wares were wheel thrown). Some wares (again BB1, for example) travelled far beyond their region of production, while others did not. Furthermore, there is evidence that pottery supplies across Britain fluctuated through time in a consistent manner, creating periods of high and low availability. Such fluctuations are difficult to account for

92 ■ An Archaeology of Identity

but may relate to broader imperial economic cycles (Going 1992; Peacock 1982: 75–151; Tyers 1996). While accepting that the range of available ceramics thus varied for a range of reasons beyond the control of individuals living on a particular site, I would argue that even in extreme situations, this did not entail an absence of meaning content for the artefacts concerned—and therefore of agency for the people using them. Regardless of what limitations on choices existed (both in terms of what vessels to use and how to use them), and also of the extent to which convenience or 'economics' influenced those choices, objects of daily use would have been integrated into the routines of those using them. They therefore had the potential to be engaged in more active negotiations of meaning, including issues of identity. Such negotiations will have involved recognitions of similarity and difference—and the amount of variation in Romano-British pottery certainly allowed for these.

This brings in another familiar theme: classification. The major archaeological categories for the ceramics in use in Roman Britain tend to be fabric groups from particular locations (wares), divided into type series on the basis of form. Alternative classifications might switch the emphasis from fabric to vessel form, whether in specific ('beaker', 'jar') or more general ('storage', 'serving') terms. All such classifications have their problems (Orton et al. 1993: 217–8), not least that use of the same vessels in (meaningfully) different ways may be obscured. Only by comparing them might insights be gained regarding their validity; unfortunately such comparative work is only just beginning to be seriously undertaken with the material currently available in Roman Britain (Evans 2001). Another issue that should be given much greater attention in Roman archaeology in the future is the use lives of vessels, which—like the problem of differential preservation mentioned above—could have a significant but currently invisible effect on our data. This has been explored in other contexts (e.g., Varien and Mills 1997) and is relevant to how pottery is quantified in relation to time. Here only relatively crude measures of pottery use are employed, but they do still produce some interesting results.

More will be said in the next chapter on comparisons across time. At this point, it remains only to summarise the broad range of different pottery supply patterns in later Roman Britain, and as before this can be illustrated with a small number of examples representing a fort, a town, and a farm (Fig. 3.15). Caernarfon, familiar from the discussions of coins and small finds, presents a good example of a western site with a fairly diverse pattern of supply in the 4th century. The assemblage includes a fair quantity of fabrics imported from across

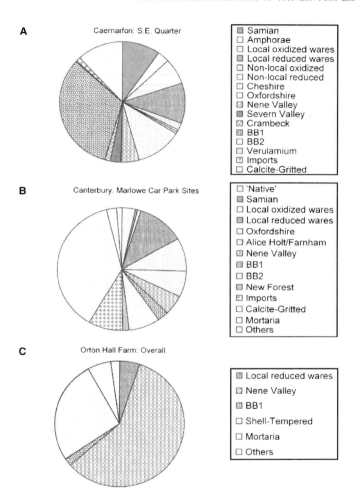

Figure 3.15. Examples of the range of pottery supplied to different sites in the 4th century: Caernarfon, Canterbury, and Orton Hall Farm (data from King and Millett 1993; Webster 1993; Bailey et al. 1995; Perrin 1996).

western Britain, but also some—particularly Nene Valley ware—from further afield, as well as some residual Samian. Particularly dominant, though, is BB1, the hand-formed ware used for both cooking and serving vessels. This reflects the variety of domestic supplies available in 4th century Britain and the limited role of extraprovincial imports (Millett 1990: 163). The Marlowe Car Park site in the large town of Canterbury presents a somewhat similar picture, showing that forts and towns enjoyed a fairly wide range of choices. Here, the dominant

94 ■ AN ARCHAEOLOGY OF IDENTITY

supplier was a more local manufacturer of calcite-gritted ware, which fulfilled many of the same roles as BB1 but was an increasingly popular fabric in the 4th century (cf. Tyers 1996: 77). Finally, Orton Hall Farm in Cambridgeshire, a fairly complex site that was occupied into the post-Roman period, shows the more usual rural pattern of a restricted range of supplies. This assemblage, moreover, is dominated by a particular large local supplier—the Nene Valley industry—that furnished the majority of tablewares here.

These graphs highlight both the considerable number of regional industries working in 4th century Britain, and also some of the variations between rural and other sites that have been confirmed by functional analyses of pottery (Evans 2001). The variations between different kinds of pots that were used on different sites, even just in appearance, offered some possibilities for distinctive practices of cooking in these places. To understand more about what was being cooked, we need to turn to the evidence of meat consumption. Animal bone assemblages do present some good opportunities for comparisons that highlight the particularities of different contexts, but their quantification is difficult—like pottery—because of varying standards of reporting in excavated results. Unlike pottery, though, animal bone has only relatively recently become a focus of archaeological scrutiny. In many site reports until the 1970s, this class of material warranted very little attention (e.g., Wheeler 1924: 170). The increased recognition of the potential importance of faunal (and botanical) assemblages from Roman-period sites can be situated within the incorporation of environmental agendas into mainstream field practice in Britain from the 1970s. Current interpretive concerns with specific regard to animals, however, have moved rather beyond subsistence economics to consider, for instance, the cultural choices and expressions bound up with the consumption of food (e.g., Grant 1989; Hawkes 1999; King 1984; Meadows 1994; Stallibrass 2000). Of course, this kind of approach cannot ignore the environmental background, which favours the exploitation of certain species of animals or plants and which may impose constraints on some aspects of human action. Nonetheless, in keeping with the emphasis on 'meaningful' material culture in the previous chapter, I would argue that concepts like the 'environment' or 'resources' will always be culturally mediated: the relationship between people and the world they live in is mutually constitutive (Gosden 1994: 34–6; cf. Mead 1934: 129) in its physical as well as its social aspects.

This being the case, there are still certain considerations to bear in mind when attempting to build interpretations of this relationship upon archaeological samples of faunal material. Taphonomy—the study of post-depositional processes—has long been strongly associated with the various factors affecting ancient bones (e.g., Binford 1981). Although embodying a divisive approach to 'systemic' and 'archaeological' contexts, already discussed in Chapter 2, such work clearly shows that all of the human practices and other factors that have a bearing on the numbers of coins, for instance, appearing in a published report apply no less to faunal remains. When comparing quantities of different species for information on matters such as animal husbandry or dietary choices, attention should be paid to the excavation strategies employed and to the possible influence of differential preservation according to bone type (e.g., cattle bones may be more robust than those of other species). Care must also be taken to consider the full range of socioeconomic variables that may be of importance, including regionally distinct animal husbandry regimes, exploitation of animals for traction or secondary products prior to consumption, and trade in livestock (Grant 1989: 138–9; Stallibrass 1995: 133–4). Taking such issues on board, however, recent work on animal bone has demonstrated that a wide range of questions can be addressed with such material, particularly in conjunction with other aspects of material culture.

In addition to the straightforward comparison of species representation from different sites, information on the ages of animals when slaughtered, butchery practices (both from marks on the bones and the presence or absence of carcass elements), and patterns of discard within sites can all be deployed to understand dietary choices and a range of other activities (e.g., rubbish disposal, organisation of meat provision [Stallibrass 2000: 65]). The dietary angle can further be expanded to encompass food preparation and serving when ceramic and botanical materials are integrated into any study (Hawkes 1999: 91–2). Although only a limited approach to these questions is possible within the scope of this book, the combination of animal bone evidence with the other artefactual patterns discussed in this chapter clearly offers considerable potential for understanding the relationship between material practices and social identities.

To set the scene for this relationship being developed in later chapters, we need to establish here the main features of the animal diet in the 4th century. As with pottery, this can be done with a few example sites illustrated in Figure 3.16. Here again a fort, town, and farm are contrasted, and a couple of key points emerge. One is that cattle is the dominant species represented at all of these sites, and although this owes something to the relatively high robustness of cattle bones,

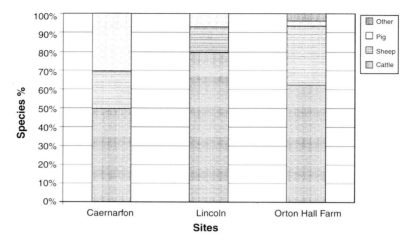

Figure 3.16. Examples of the range of animal species consumed on different sites in the 4th century, based on bone assemblages: Caernarfon, Lincoln, and Orton Hall Farm (data from Casey et al. 1993: 76–8; Noddle 1993; Dobney et al. 1995: 20–61, 132–3; King 1996).

these animals are also high in terms of meat yield and seem to have been preferred across Roman Britain (Grant 1989). More differences are apparent in the secondary species, where pig has a greater presence at the fort and sheep on the farm. These may well relate to specific dietary preferences (with pork being favoured by military communities earlier in the Roman occupation, and sheep belonging to a more indigenous tradition of consumption), perhaps twinned with different economic factors (Grant 1989; King 1999a). As with the ceramic evidence, then, we have some possible grounds for distinctions between different communities along the lines of food eaten, though this does not quite map onto the similarity between forts and towns noted in that context. Both of these points will be important in establishing how different identities might have been negotiated by people living in particular places.

So far in this chapter, I have tried to set out some of the basic problems and possibilities for constructing an archaeology of material practices from different types of evidence available in 4th century Britain. In addition, therefore, to introducing some of the dominant types of things and major large-scale patterns, I have related these objects to particular activities that people undertook in the past. The resolution of different kinds of data provides variable opportunities here. While for pottery and animal bone, it is only possible at this stage to get a rough idea of some of the likely axes of similarity and difference in practices of eating, for coins and small finds, more can be said about the relationship between contexts of use—in practices like exchanging or 'appearing'—and contexts of deposition. These in turn bring in other practices to do with inhabiting or 'dwelling' in a particular space and losing things or dumping things in it. More can be gleaned from these artefactual patterns by putting them in a fuller temporal context, and that will be undertaken in the next chapter. Here, however, we need to further expand on the link between artefacts and spaces and flesh out the picture of the different materialities of the built world in 4th century Britain.

Architectural material culture

Structuration and space

By way of introduction to a survey of this built world, it is useful to return to structuration theory a little more explicitly. While my focus on contexts of material practice in this chapter is designed to take us into the heart of the agency-structure relationship, Giddens has been particularly concerned with how spaces shape these contexts, and as a result has developed particular theoretical concepts in dealing with them. Since a full interpretation of the artefactual patterns explored here and in the next chapter will necessarily involve these spatial contexts, it is worth reviewing Giddens's concepts here. These are very much in tune with the general approach to material culture meanings, as determined by the duality of structure in specific practice contexts, outlined above. Spaces or 'places' (to use a less abstract term) can be regarded as material parts of the social world, which are both invested with and constitutive of meaning. Of course this process is a temporal as well as a material one: people do not engage with places simply by standing still, but by *moving* through and between them (Thomas 1996: 85–91; Urry 2000a: 131–7). This dynamic aspect of use will be more specifically addressed in the next chapter, but the concepts Giddens introduces to define the limits of practice contexts are useful in dealing with both space and time. These are regionalisation, presence-availability, and distanciation (Urry 2000b: 427–8). All are concerned with the small-scale dimensions of social life upon which structural principles are built.

Most important for Giddens is the notion of presence-availability, which can be defined as "the degree to which, and the forms through which, people are co-present within an individual's social milieu" (Urry 1991: 164). The link between agency and structure, between the routine practices of individuals and their social world, is dependent upon the *co-presence* of actors within an area of space referred to

98 ■ An Archaeology of Identity

as a *locale*. A locale is a social space or a 'place' only partly defined by architecture and other forms of material culture. It is also defined by *regionalisation*: the way a space is zoned by the practices that occur within it, as in the specialised uses of particular rooms (Cohen 1989: 96, 110; Giddens 1984: 64–7, 118–22; Urry 1991: 164). While specific places might be understood in such terms, these concepts are not limited to a microscale of analysis. Locales can be state sized, and different transportation or communication technologies can have a significant impact on presence-availability. *Distanciation* refers to the stretching of social life across time and space, facilitated by such technologies and also by institutional structures. As distanciation increases, so a society becomes characterised more by system integration than social integration—the latter referring to interaction developed through face-to-face encounters, the former to more absent exchanges (Cohen 1989: 93–113; Giddens 1984: 28, 34–7, 142–4; Urry 1991: 164–6). Increased distanciation may also be associated with strongly unequal distributions of power.

This battery of time-space concepts, which cut across the material, temporal, and social aspects of life, provides much to work with in this and subsequent chapters. Structures and spaces can be looked at with reference to their potential impact on presence-availability, especially in terms of constraints (Cohen 1989: 97–100) and the ways in which they might be regionalised. A particularly fruitful line of enquiry relating to the manifestations of Roman imperialism in Britain might be the relationship between the mechanisms of institutional distanciation supporting the Roman state and different scales of material culture patterning, and this will be pursued in detail in Chapter 5. It is also useful to add the notion of 'imaginary co-presence'—the influence of spatially or temporally distant others on an individual's actions—something underdeveloped by Giddens (Urry 1991: 170; 2000a: 133–4; cf. Bauman 1990: 26–35). This is of considerable significance in understanding communities of identity (Jenkins 2004: 108–23; cf. James 1999a). Through the use of these conceptual tools, linkages can be made between the dynamics of practices in particular places and identity groups of different social scales.

As always, however, there are caveats and difficulties to be borne in mind as we analyse the uses of space in and around structures; these include the inescapable problems of interpreting archaeological spaces above ground level, and the no less challenging question of how we can understand the purposes for which particular areas of buildings may have been used. However, I will argue in this section that it is possible to comprehend something of the practices that took place in past spaces, and that the spatial elements of structuration theory are helpful in doing so. This represents a different approach to the more recent developments in the archaeology of built spaces, where formal analytical methods of studying space syntax have been deployed (e.g., Grahame 2000). While profitable in well-preserved sites like Pompeii, I feel that a more flexible approach is needed in the rather patchier record of Roman Britain, albeit one which is sympathetic to the same goals—the treatment of the built environment as meaningfully constituted material culture. A large part of the difficulty in Roman Britain is the incompleteness of archaeological plans, and this will require a measure of care in the analysis of past spaces whatever the approach adopted.

Site planning

The first aspect of architectural material culture to consider is the way that larger sites were laid out in later Roman Britain. While the morphology of individual sites is usually taken rather for granted in defining the type of community to which they belong (i.e., military or civilian, urban or rural), relatively little critical attention has been focused on the social consequences of the relationships of different kinds of buildings to each other, and the arrangements of groups of buildings across sites. Later in this section, the internal planning and construction of individual buildings will be looked at in their turn, to complement the artefactual studies above and give a full sense of the material world of 4th century Britain. This will allow us to compare different built places over time in the next chapter. As above, I will discuss a small number of examples in some detail to represent the wider picture.

To begin with sites associated with the military, the basic mechanics of fort-type plans can be illustrated with a number of sites, beginning with the familiar example of Caernarfon (Fig. 3.17). The plans of Roman forts have always been a central concern of Roman military archaeology, often with respect to the structure of the units using them (e.g., Bennett 1983; Johnson 1983; Wilson 1980). From this point of view, the important thing is the numbers of barracks and the likely numbers of troops they could accommodate, to be set against what we believe we know of the organisation of different kinds of regiments. This, and the other examples that follow, certainly conform to the common, formalised pattern for forts in terms of outline (defensive barrier and ditches, axial gates) and interior arrangement (long barrack/stores buildings, central *principia* flanked by large courtyard

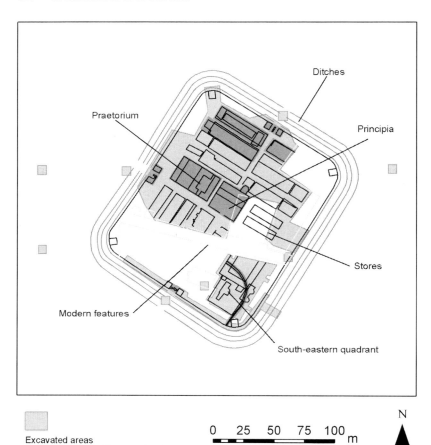

Figure 3.17. Simplified plan of Caernarfon, with key structures and the sites mentioned in the text labelled, and excavated areas added (plan after Casey et al. 1993: 8; Wheeler 1924: f.p. 186).

house [*praetorium*] and *horrea*, etc.). The establishment and maintenance of this regular pattern from place to place may be regarded as an element in the institutional distanciation effected by the bureaucracy of the military, as well as playing a very significant role in structuring the nature of routines within each individual site.

This is not to say, though, that there was no variation between fort sites, and both similarities and differences must be seen as important elements of the relationship between groups of immediately co-present actors and the more distant, even 'imagined', community of the military (cf. James 1999a: 16–18). Caernarfon illustrates this, with the complex sequence of structural changes in the southeastern quarter of the fort (described above) accommodating an unusual administrative function. In the 4th century, there were also modifications to the *principia* and gates and dispersed construction work in the northern half of the fort (the buildings affected are highlighted on the plan [Casey et al. 1993; Wheeler 1924]). The rebuilding of some structures and neglect of others created an overall arrangement with a much more 'localised' appearance in this period. Birdoswald, again a familiar example, presents a similar picture of the tensions between consistency and variation in spatial arrangements at fort sites (Fig. 3.18). Although the key features seem to be present (the *horrea*, however, not being built until the 3rd century), the plans of individual buildings (e.g., those excavated in the 1920s on the eastern side of the fort) and the layout of surveyed structures in the southern half of the fort (which block some roadways) indicate idiosyncratic uses of space—albeit largely undated, given that the latter are only known through geophysical survey (Biggins et al. 1999). The extent of the extramural settlement is also noteworthy, although again dating is a problem; it

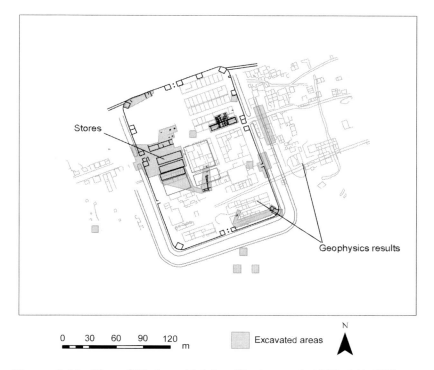

Figure 3.18. Plan of Birdoswald (after Biggins et al. 1999: 161; Wilmott 1997: 10–11).

is possible that its level of occupation may have been reduced later in the Roman period, as at several other *vici* (Bidwell 1997: 76–7). This phenomenon occurs at Housesteads (Fig. 3.19), which has more of its archetypal plan preserved from its original 2nd century phases, and these changes may have enhanced the boundary-marking effect of the walls and the sense of a community turned in on itself.

One other northern site illustrates a slightly different element of late Roman fort planning than has hitherto been observed. South Shields (Fig. 3.20), again a site that we have partly explored already, was altered numerous times in its occupation history in accordance with its role as a supply base as well as a garrison post. In the early 4th century, it appears to have been rebuilt according to a new type of 'cruciform' plan, paralleled elsewhere in the empire, and based around a crossroads with the *principia* removed from its central position in

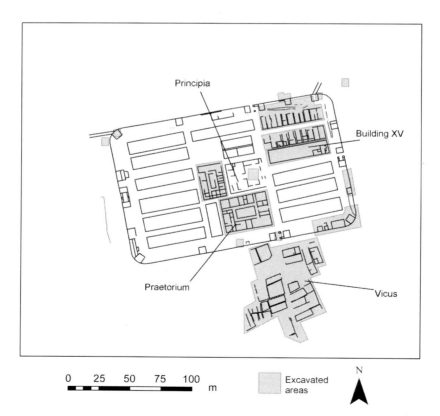

Figure 3.19. Plan of Housesteads (after Birley and Keeney 1935: pl. XXII; Crow 1995: 29).

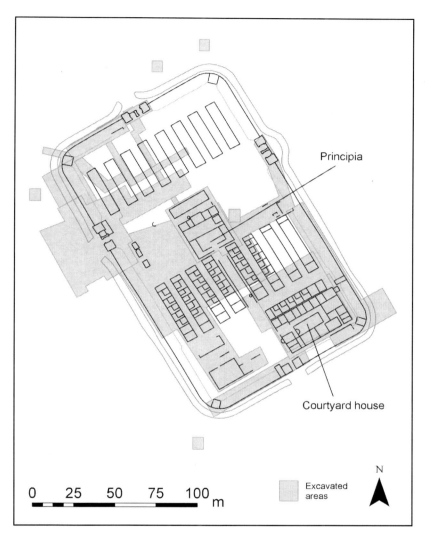

Figure 3.20. Plan of South Shields (after Bidwell and Speak 1994: 34).

relation to the accommodation (Bidwell 1996; Bidwell and Speak 1994: 11–46). This new arrangement is important in terms of regionalisation, with major implications for a distancing of the relationship between soldiers and central authority figures within the unit here, but it is difficult to match at any other site in Britain. It is also only one of several unusual phases in the development of this particular site. The remaining elements of one of these, the supply base portion of the fort behind the *principia*, must not be ignored, particularly as the excavated gateway was apparently in regular use. Nonetheless, this is an important example that—compared with Housesteads or Birdoswald—highlights the potential diversity of fort plans even within one of Britain's military zones.

Examples from the Saxon Shore zone complement this picture, though these all have specific archaeological problems with regard to the interpretation of their internal planning (Fig. 3.21). At Portchester Castle only the bare outlines of a handful of possible structures, and these of different dates, were noted during excavation. These were surrounded by a pockmarked landscape of rubbish pits (Cunliffe 1975). These phenomena relate to the use of building technologies and rubbish disposal methods that were different to those employed on the sites we have considered so far, and while they make the plan of the site more difficult to reconstruct, they indicate quite a different built environment compared to Housesteads, for example. At Richborough, another key Saxon Shore fort constructed in the later 3rd century around the foundations of an earlier monument to Claudius, the only spatial information apart from two small chalk buildings—and a putative *principia*—comes from the distribution of dated pits and scattered 'surfaces' (Bushe-Fox 1926; Cunliffe 1968). Nonetheless, this somewhat negative evidence is important insofar as it indicates that the experience of living in these places may have been

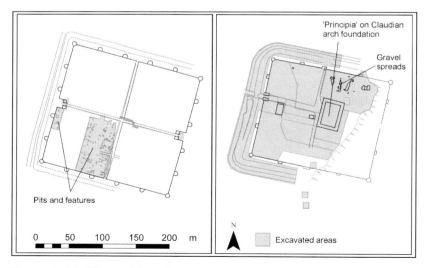

Figure 3.21. Plans of Portchester Castle and Richborough (after Cunliffe 1975: 14; Cunliffe 1968: f.p. 248).

rather different from the stone forts of the west and north (with the possible exception of newer forts in those regions, like Piercebridge [cf. Bidwell 1997: 104]). Although still regular defended enclosures, the arrangements of the streets, open spaces, and buildings and the nature of the defences themselves (being rather larger than those constructed previously elsewhere) were all distinctive.

Turning now to sites of a different order of magnitude, the plans of Caerleon and Chester (Figs. 3.22–3.23) exemplify fortress-sized sites designed to accommodate entire legions, and as such magnify both

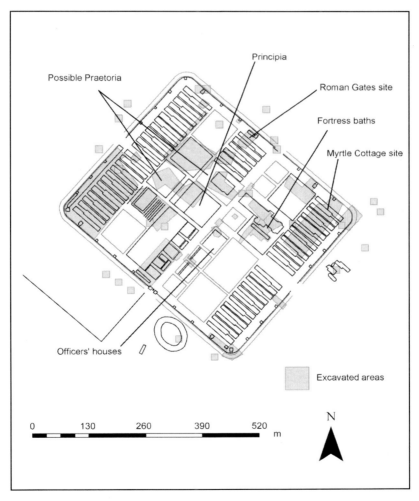

Figure 3.22. Plan of Caerleon (after Boon 1972: 114; Knight 1988: endpiece).

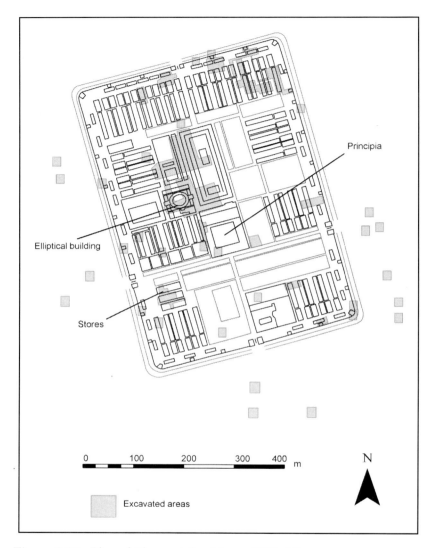

Figure 3.23. Plan of Chester (after Mason 1996: 85).

the consistent and variable features of fort arrangements. Both have the general shape and certain key features (*principia* in the centre, barracks around the edge) that one would expect, but Chester also has some very large structures—of uncertain function—that are not apparent at Caerleon. Nonetheless, the scale of both sites underlines, even more so than in the smaller forts, two key features of the 'military' construction of space: major differentials in power (compare the extent of the barracks with that of the officers' residences, and the *principia*, the administrative and sacred hub of the legion) and, bearing some relation to this, the limited private or individual space as against the dominance of public or corporate space. It is difficult to determine what elements of these plans were in use in the later Roman period (the 'blueprints' used here are a mixture of different, mainly early, phases, and modern extrapolation). While the general arrangement seems not to have been radically altered by the later Roman period, some areas within each site fell out of use, as did some of the axes of movement. Certain buildings were demolished to create open areas, while those still in use were often altered internally. These changes, discussed in more detail in the next chapter, certainly had had an impact on the generic 'camp life' that had been built into the fortresses' design.

Before moving on to consider the spatial arrangements within 4th century towns, it is worth noting that some sites are quite ambiguous in terms of the identity categories to which settlements are typically assigned—military or civilian. Forden Gaer and Leintwardine (Fig. 3.24), both in the eastern central part of Wales, have earthwork defences and were occupied from the later 1st to the 4th centuries (Crew 1980; Stanford 1968). At neither, however, has much internal structural evidence been found to define the nature of the occupation more closely. At Forden Gaer, though, a central building was replaced by a road late in the site's history; at Leintwardine observations in the central area of the enclosure have failed to locate any of the central buildings that one might expect in a fort. These problems highlight the fact that the shape of defensive circuits can be insufficient to determine whether a settlement is a military base or a defended town, and also raise the possibility of the existence of a variety of defended sites that might not fit into the definitions of categories such as 'fort' or 'town', or alternatives like '*burgi*' (Burnham and Wacher 1990: 5–6). Even so, the common element of boundedness is likely to have created some similarities in routines and practices of movement in these sites.

This brings us to towns that are more easily defined as such. In contrast to some of the sites we have looked at so far, the available plan of Caerwent (Fig. 3.25) relates more directly to the 4th century—rather than being a composite—because although the town was established in the later 1st century, the major excavations on the site between 1899 and 1912 were most revealing of the latest structures. Caerwent, which was the *civitas* capital of the Silures, does have some superficial morphological similarities to a fort. These are primarily the defences (not part of the original plan, but constructed in earth in the 2nd century and stone in the early 4th), a central basilican structure (the *forum basilica*),

108 ■ An Archaeology of Identity

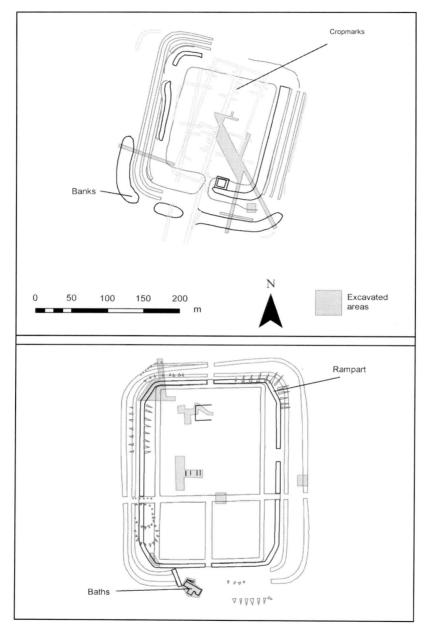

Figure 3.24. Plans of Forden Gaer and Leintwardine (after Crew 1980: 732; Stanford 1968: 259).

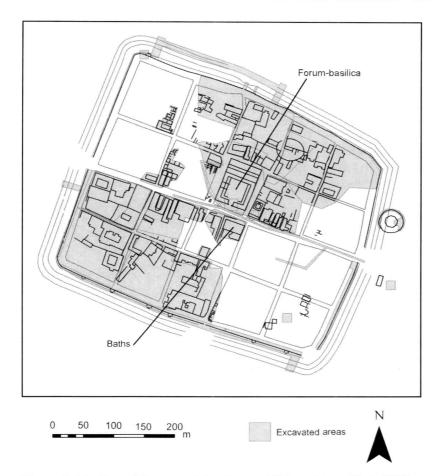

Figure 3.25. Plan of Caerwent (after Brewer 1993: endpiece; Nash-Williams and Grimes 1952: f.p. 248).

and the rectilinear street grid. Apart from a few other public buildings—also mostly central—the rest of the plan contains large and quite dispersed houses. Obviously, these are of rather different designs to the main form of accommodation in a fort (though not to *praetoria* and other officers' houses), and more importantly offer a spectrum of different regionalisations, with more private, noncorporate space. Nonetheless parts of the domestic space could be quite public, if the Italian model of elite social life was followed in this kind of settlement, with male members of the household receiving daily submission from their clients at home, before proceeding to the *forum* and the baths

(Laurence 1994: 122–32). Social arrangements may have been rather different in Britain, however, as we will see in Chapter 5 (cf. Clarke and Robinson 1997). Certainly, in the 4th century, the form of some of the public buildings in Caerwent had changed from their original design, as their internal arrangements—and perhaps their function—was transformed. If some of these changes, described later, can be regarded as similar in kind to those taking place at other sites of superficially different types (such as forts), then it may be that a major trend in the material history of Roman Britain is convergence toward a way of life much reduced in its degree of system integration.

Many of the other towns in Britain are more problematic to discuss in detail. The examples illustrated here (Figs. 3.26–3.29) are Canterbury (*civitas* capital of the Cantiaci), Lincoln (one of the veteran *coloniae*), Cirencester (capital of the Dobunni, and also a 4th century provincial capital), and Wroxeter (capital of the Cornovii). While enough is known about all of them to say that they were irregular defended settlements, containing common public buildings, only at Wroxeter is there anything approaching the kind of detail of other structures that we have for Caerwent (and this from aerial photography—with even less chronological refinement than the Edwardian excavations at the latter site). Although one can point to varying degrees of regularity in street grids, and varying densities of occupation by large houses, little can really be said about the regionalisation of space and movement across these sites.

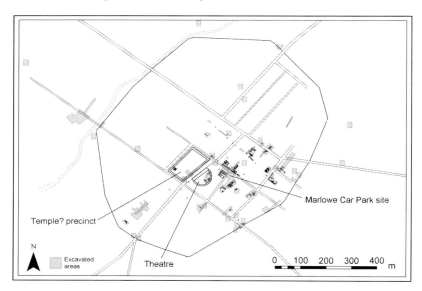

Figure 3.26. Plan of Canterbury (after Bennett 1984: f.p. 50).

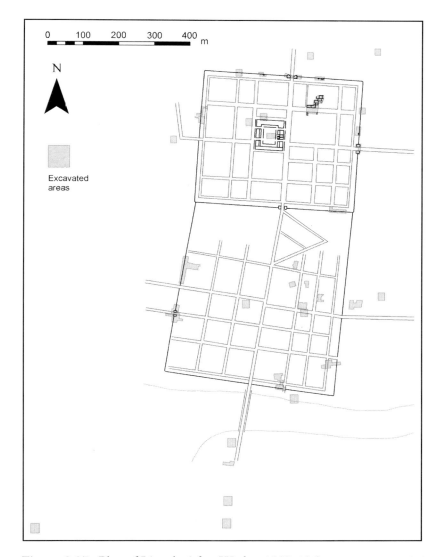

Figure 3.27. Plan of Lincoln (after Wacher 1989: 106).

The only phenomenon that stands out from some of the excavations conducted at these sites is the changing nature of roads. Many were encroached upon over time (e.g., at Canterbury Lane in Canterbury [Frere and Stow 1983: 69–80]), while others seem to have been widened into piazzas (e.g., at the Gaumont Cinema site in Cirencester [Wacher 1965: 101–2]). These suggest important developments in routines of mobility around sites, but the picture is very incomplete. Fortunately,

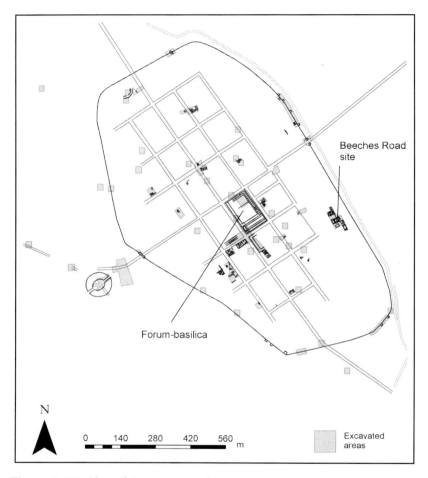

Figure 3.28. Plan of Cirencester (after McWhirr 1986: 15).

rather more insight can be developed from changes in the uses of individual structures, covered in the next chapter.

In this section, some hints about the role of past places in the structuration of social life have begun to emerge. The sites compared have all been towns or forts—or something in between—and both similarities and differences have been highlighted between the morphologies of these sites. Many of these may be regarded as obvious and in little need of interpretation, and many have rarely been anything other than taken for granted. Nonetheless, the argument that will be pursued through the rest of this book is that such similarities and differences are not merely superficial, nor to be explained solely in terms of 'Romanisation', or of the typological history of a particular site that

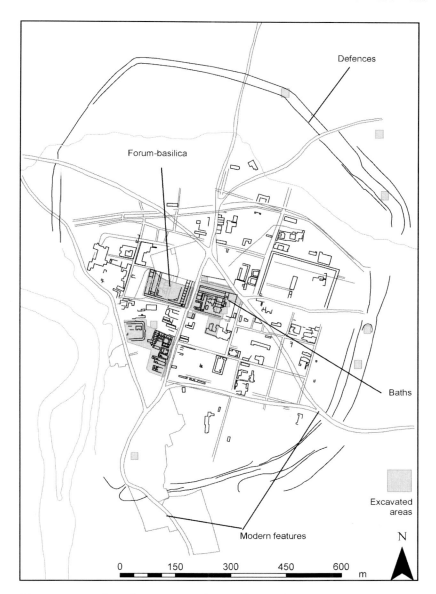

Figure 3.29. Plan of Wroxeter (after Barker et al. 1997: 3).

may, for instance, have developed from a fortress into a *colonia*-class town while keeping its original layout. These places constructed and were constructed by the social activities of the people dwelling in them, and therefore materialised some of the linkages between interactions and institutions of different scales. As social identities are a central element in these relationships, variation between places can be related to the processes of identification in which their inhabitants were engaged.

Indeed, this much is implicitly assumed in the normal identification of forts as 'military' and towns as 'civilian'. Of course, there are distinguishable differences between those sites usually regarded as under either wholly military or civilian authority, and in this section we have seen how some of these can be described in terms of public versus private, or independent versus interdependent spaces, or of the spatial distributions of power. However, the situation is more complex than the traditional picture will allow. First, there are formal similarities between these types of site (boundedness, scale, density) that are distinct from the characteristics of rural sites and may be regarded as key elements of 'Roman' social activity (Laurence 1994: 134–5). Second, there is diversity within each category. The range of distinctive features at the fort sites considered above, from the cruciform plan of South Shields to the ephemeral buildings at Portchester, was much greater in the 4th century than hitherto (with sites like Caerleon and Housesteads preserving much of the 2nd century norm). These must represent changes to the experience of living as a soldier in different places, and as we will see in the next chapter, this process was ongoing through the 4th century. To get closer to what those changes might mean, though, we need to look more closely at the actual buildings in use during this period.

Building plans

Although considerable attention has been directed at the functional significance of building plans in Roman archaeology, in many cases this has relied upon textual sources. While many of the identifications of certain building types with named textual analogues have become firmly established and remain very useful, this has often only come about through considerable modern debate (e.g., the use of the term *principia* for a military headquarters building was still uncertain in the early 20th century [Bosanquet 1904: 226–8]). Even then there is a danger of quashing the potential diversity of labellings in the past. A more artefact-centred approach to function can also be employed (e.g., Allison 2002; Allison et al. 2004; Hingley 1990; Hoffmann 1995), and this will be explored in the next chapter, where important changes in the uses of buildings in the 4th century will also be considered. The focus here will be on more general qualities of the arrangement of spaces and their 'regionalisation' (to use Giddens's term), looking at public and then private structures—with the proviso that this distinction must be qualified in a number of instances, and indeed is one that is quite dynamic during the later Roman period.

Beginning, then, with public buildings, the centrepieces of both fort and town-type settlements were basilican buildings attached to bounded courtyards: the *principia* and *forum basilica*. The formal similarities between these structures, in spite of the frequent individual variations, can be striking (cf. Caernarfon and Caerwent in Figs. 3.17 and 3.25). Indeed these similarities have constituted an important element in arguments for military involvement in town foundation and construction during the later 1st and early 2nd centuries (Millett 1990: 69–74). In terms of their later use, it is difficult to avoid drawing a broad parallel between the similarities of structural form and central position within a settlement, and a common architectural expression of centralised (imperial) authority. However, there are certain specific differences underpinning the use of these buildings by different identity groups. First, the *forum* could be an arena for individual elite display (Laurence 1994: 127–9), whereas the *principia* had much stronger corporate associations to do with a military unit's organisation and traditions. The latter were reinforced by the presence of the shrine of the standards in the central part of the rear range—adding a religious role—and while analogous rooms may have been present in the town *fora*, the conspicuous temples that are found in Gallic examples were moved outside the complex, leaving it as a more overtly commercial and administrative domain (Millett 1990: 72). These are very much differences of regionalisation, which turn seemingly similar locales into more divergent contexts of interaction. As we will see later, however, these are quite dynamic environments in the 4th century.

Another key type of structure common to different kinds of site was baths. One of the characteristic features of many Roman-period settlements in Britain (including villas), bathing facilities must be an important element in any discussion of 'imperial lifestyles'. Though variable across the empire, baths can be associated with certain routines of bodily control and with a variety of other social roles—not least social interaction itself—as venues for meeting and conversation (DeLaine 1999; cf. Todd 2005). Plan forms do vary in Britain, in terms of specific bathing room arrangements (Bidwell 1997: 77–8), but the popularity of the practice in the later Roman period is a more important issue to consider here. At some sites baths were decommissioned during this time. The fortress baths at Caerleon are one such example (Zienkiewicz 1986a, 1986b), and their disuse is one reason

116 ■ An Archaeology of Identity

why the site is believed to have been abandoned by its garrison at the end of the 3rd century. However, it should be noted that temporary closure had occurred on earlier occasions in the site's history, presumably when the garrison was at less than full strength. At Caernarfon the later of the two small bath structures in the southeastern corner was never even finished (Casey et al. 1993). At other sites, however, the baths seem to have remained in use until quite a late stage (e.g., at Caerwent [Nash-Williams 1954]), indicating that, at least in places, the practices associated with bathing as body maintenance, and with bath buildings as foci of interaction, remained important.

While the 4th century was not a prolific period for the commissioning of new public buildings, as noted in Chapter 2, two other types are worth mentioning here. Although new kinds of religious buildings were being built in this period—churches have been tentatively identified at a small number of sites in Britain, including Richborough (Brown 1971)—pagan temples were still being constructed too. At Caerwent, for example, such a building was established next to the *forum* in the late 3rd century, and maintained and repaired through the 4th, in a traditional 'Romano-Celtic' style (Brewer and Guest forthcoming). This created quite a distinct hierarchy of spaces between the interior 'cella' and its surrounding enclosure, which contrasted with the more open planning of the new churches, modelled on the basilican-style of structure. Practices of worship, then, were spatially diverse in this period. The other type of structure that was a distinctive feature of public space in the 4th century is stone defences, with some construction, modification, or refurbishment of walls often dated to this time at both fort and town-type sites (e.g., Chester, York, Lincoln, Cirencester). While there are often dating problems with such features, this may represent the last bastion of official 'public' expenditure (Bidwell 1999; Faulkner 1998: 378–85) and has been interpreted as a re-affirmation of the boundaries between those living in such communities and those living outside (Guest 2002). As important elements in the material landscape of 4th century Britain, these will certainly merit further attention as we build from patterns of practices to identities.

Shifting the focus now to more 'private' or domestic buildings, we can summarise the different types of houses inhabited in towns, farmsteads, and forts. Roman-period domestic architecture in Britain was widely variable, but certain basic forms can be identified across sites of different types. Again, it is important to stress that similar planning of physical space need not imply similar structuring of social space. Nonetheless, in both forts (and their extramural settlements) and towns, residential structures can be divided very crudely into courtyard houses and strip buildings. The former vary enormously in complexity, but typically combined rooms for public business with living/service quarters (sometimes including private baths), while the latter were often workshop and/or retail premises as well as domiciles (Brothers 1996; Laurence 1994: 127–9). Often, the latter could develop into the former, or at least into intermediate types, through the addition of corridors and wings. More coherently planned versions of courtyard houses were also built in forts and fortresses for the more powerful members of those communities. Not found in Britain are the large apartment blocks of the more densely populated Mediterranean towns.

While rural sites are obviously entirely different kinds of built space from the relatively densely populated towns or forts, there are similarities between some rural houses and some of the house types found in towns—particularly those of courtyard plan. This affinity is enhanced, at least in Britain, by the fact that a number of towns are far from densely packed with structures and have the appearance of 'garden cities'. Of course, there is a great range of structures on rural sites, from elaborate villas to many farms of considerable simplicity, with some (especially in the west and north [Hingley 1989: 31–5]) even retaining circular buildings constructed in the Iron Age tradition into the later Roman period. More complex rural structures, though, such as the main building at Rivenhall (an Essex villa), can be paralleled in the sprawling structures at Beeches Road in Cirencester (McWhirr 1986; Rodwell and Rodwell 1985)—or even in fort *praetoria*. Some rural sites in the north and west are defended, too, blurring the boundary between these and small military sites. Interpretation of the internal spaces of villas, in particular, is a matter of some debate; J.T. Smith has suggested that complexes with a number of apparently repeated arrangements of rooms might be occupied by a number of families of equal status, rather than a single wealthy landowner (e.g., Smith 1997). While this theory remains controversial, the formal similarities between house types across different kinds of settlement are potentially significant, with courtyard houses—for instance, perhaps signifying membership of an elite status group with links to the state (cf. Hodgson 1996: 147–9). At the same time, the considerable differences in the surrounding settlement environment would create quite different routines for those living inside such houses.

Although courtyard houses were part of the built environment of fort-type sites, these settlement were of course dominated by a distinctive kind of building: barracks, the particular form of accommodation strongly linked to the military in the Roman world. Although

118 ■ An Archaeology of Identity

clearly a recognisable type of structure that was associated with the imposition of a certain lifestyle distinctive to the military (James 1999a: 16–17), it is important to appreciate the range of variability within the basic format of centurion's quarters and *contubernia* (the individual pairs of barrack rooms; cf. Bidwell 1997: 58–9; Coello 1996: 59; Davison 1996: 162–9). Although some of this variation is undoubtedly related to the particular characteristics of the military units concerned (the most obvious example being the recently discovered cavalry stable barracks at Wallsend, which were built to house both horses and men [Hodgson 1999: 86]), it is equally clear that the size, construction details, and exact number of *contubernia* were subject to some local control. The extent to which this variability was quite a normal part of fort construction is important in the context of one of the major controversies surrounding change in the Roman military: the appearance of 'chalet' barracks in the later empire.

Initially recognised as a distinctive barrack form in excavations at Housesteads (Wilkes 1960: 63–6, 1961: 285–9), and subsequently also at Wallsend (Daniels 1980, 1989), the loose 'type' of a row of detached or semi-detached irregular buildings has also been noted in records of antiquarian work at some other forts (e.g., Birdoswald, Chesters, Greatchesters [Coello 1996: 53–4; Daniels 1980: 173–81]). This plan form, along with a perceived bias in the associated small finds towards 'female' objects and the occurrence of infant burials in some examples, led to the suggestion that these barracks were 'married quarters' for substantially reduced garrisons in frontier forts (Daniels 1980: 189–92; cf. Bosanquet 1904: 235). This idea, however, has been countered on a number of grounds. Even disregarding the problems with gendering small finds, and with locating the origins of the rubbish deposits that contain them, 'female' objects are not actually *more* common in this later structural phase than in earlier ones, but tend to be present quite consistently over time (Allason-Jones 1995: 30, 1999: 45). In terms of plan, recent discoveries at South Shields and reexcavation at Wallsend have suggested that the 'chalet' layout is simply a fairly typical late Roman type, with 3rd century or even earlier origins, suited to a slightly smaller centurial unit. Finally, a posited link between 'civilians' in forts and the abandonment of *vici*, used to support the 'married quarters' hypothesis, has also been questioned on chronological grounds (Bidwell 1991, 1997: 62–7; Hodgson and Bidwell 2004; cf. Coello 1996: 52–6; Hassall 1999: 37; Welsby 1982: 79–90). All of this makes the 'married quarters' idea untenable in its present form.

Nonetheless, Crow (1995: 85–92; 1999: 125–7) is right to point out that there are still considerable variations in 'chalet' plans from site to site, such as between buildings at Housesteads, South Shields, and Wallsend. If one also takes into consideration some of the late modifications to barrack buildings at Caerleon (Evans and Metcalf 1992; Fox 1940), Caernarfon (Wheeler 1924), and York Minster (Phillips and Heywood 1995a; 1995b), as well as the quite different structural traditions hinted at by the 'Saxon Shore' forts of the southern coast (e.g., Burgh Castle, Portchester, Richborough [Figs. 4.10–4.11]), the range of 4th century living arrangements for those inside forts is increased. Although it is possible that the open spaces in the latter forts—and other sites with cleared areas like Chester—were filled with structures of similar plan to those on Hadrian's Wall, but which were not groundfast, nonetheless the degree of localised variation seems to be greater in the 4th century than hitherto, and this must represent a change in the distanciation of military norms. Furthermore, although— on the grounds it has thus far been argued—the 'married quarters' hypothesis is unacceptable, the presence of items such as women's or children's shoes in forts from an early date (Driel-Murray 1995) demands that presuppositions about the day-to-day gendering (or other structuring) of space inside fortified enclosures be reconsidered.

Construction technologies

A final element of the architectural material culture of 4th century Britain that needs to be considered is construction technology. The major element of this that tends to be evident—and which will be the focus here—is the materials used, though occasionally it is possible to speculate about systems of measurement in planning (e.g., Walthew 1981). There are some important characteristics of late Roman structures that can be related in a number of ways to both past and present (archaeological) practices and perceptions. It is certainly the case that late Roman structures noted in excavation have often been labelled as 'rude' or 'rough' by comparison with earlier building phases. Examples come from sites like Wroxeter, South Shields, and Birdoswald (Atkinson 1942: 108; Hooppell 1878: 379–81; Richmond and Birley 1930: 170–1), and in more general terms include designations of 'squatter' occupation at several forts (e.g., Boon 1972: 62–9, 1987: 43; Wheeler 1926: 79–85). It should of course be pointed out that such attitudes maintain an idealised view of the early or 'high' empire that obscures variation between structures, and differing construction 'standards', throughout the Roman period. They also betray an interesting—in the broader context of this chapter—attitude to the particular qualities of materials, with stone being 'civilised', and wood being 'primitive'.

Behind such perceptions lies a very broad interpretation of structural sequences, primarily from forts and towns: many timber buildings of the 1st century were reconstructed in stone at some point in the 2nd, only to be repaired or replaced in timber again in the later 4th or the early 5th centuries. While this has often been couched in Romano-centric terms of colonial 'rise and fall' (e.g., Frere 1987: 296–8; Haverfield 1918b; cf. Grew 2001), to the extent of ignoring the specific circumstances of any changes, such sequences can undeniably be discerned in the material. Examples of late Roman timber constructions, for instance, are numerous and varied: from the small 'stall' structures around the large baths at Canterbury and Caerleon (Blockley et al. 1995a; Zienkiewicz 1986a), to the post- or sill-built free-standing buildings at Portchester, Carlisle, and Chester (Cunliffe 1975; McCarthy 1990; Ward and Strickland 1978) and the important 5th or even 6th century 'hall' structures at Wroxeter and Birdoswald (Barker et al. 1997; Wilmott 1997), as well as the late timber gateway at South Shields (Bidwell and Speak 1994).

If the open areas observed in the plans of several other sites (e.g., Richborough) are also regarded as areas potentially occupied by timber buildings, then clearly there is a phenomenon here to be understood—although the question remains as to whether this is best done at the individual site level, or at a more regional level. There are, however, some further complications. Several examples exist of early timber structures that apparently were not rebuilt in stone at all, such as a gate tower at Caernarfon (Casey 1974), while in many cases even those buildings that have stone walls at ground level employed these as sills for a timber superstructure (e.g., at Lincoln's Holmes Grainwarehouse site [Darling and Jones 1988; cf. Davison 1996: 175–6]). Equally, there are stone structures that were built or rebuilt in the 4th century, ranging from the St. George Street baths in Canterbury to the barracks at Caernarfon (Frere and Stow 1983: 27–40; Wheeler 1924), not to mention various town defences. In some places, though, these constructions involved the use of *spolia*—as at Caernarfon—or drystone techniques rather than mortaring (as at Birdoswald [Richmond and Birley 1930]). Other, more localised, changes in material that can be noted are the use of stone roofing materials instead of tile at some forts in the later Roman period (e.g., at Caerleon and Housesteads [Fox 1940; Wilkes 1960, 1961]); the reuse of wall blocks as flooring material (e.g., at South Shields); and the presence at some forts of poorly dated 'late/ post-Roman' earthwork defences on top of the stone walls (e.g., at Birdoswald and Brecon Gaer [Wheeler 1926]).

What might be the significance of these developments in construction technologies in the 4th century? It is vital, as with the question of 'chalet' barracks, to set supposedly distinctive late Roman practices within the context of the range of previous activities. Although stone architecture is one characteristic often bound up with archaeological definitions of 'Roman-ness' (Haverfield 1923: 36; cf. Reece 1988: 145), indications have been given above that even in forts and towns, there might be differences in the extent to which stone was used, not to mention variation in other structural details like wall-bonding materials and floors. Within this range, the construction of timber halls on stone platforms in 6th century Wroxeter is not necessarily so far removed from the use of sill walls in 2nd century Chester barracks. Furthermore, although the transition to primarily timber architecture has been seen as a defining feature of the post-Roman 'dark ages' (Dark 1994b: 5–6; Edwards and Lane 1988: 2–4), such a view excludes the large numbers of smaller-scale rural settlements that did not use stone throughout the Roman period (Hingley 1989: 23–5, 31) and also ignores the length of time that this transition, insofar as it can be defined at all, actually took, encompassing most of the 4th century as well as the earlier 5th—in other words, three or four generations.

These points allow the distinctive construction technologies of the 4th century to be accounted for as community-level responses to gradually changing circumstances. These might partly involve a reduction in institutional capability, or motivation, to organise the quarrying of stone on a large scale (cf. Reece 1988: 149; Wilmott 1995: 63–7). However, even if or where such a factor was important, any changes must have been mediated through the frames of meaning and understanding of those participating in them—as would happen with any kind of material culture. An obvious possible dimension of these is the perceived permanence of a particular material, and timber buildings might have been quite permanent enough for most people—large stone buildings being more of a state-driven attempt to impress statements of power upon the minds of multiple generations. The one major possible exception to this pattern of 4th century decentralisation is the building of stone town walls, whose significance might simply have been seen in terms of defence or perhaps in the redefinition of boundaries (Guest 2002; cf. Esmonde Cleary 2003; Faulkner 2000; Ottaway 1996). In other respects, however, it is likely that the transformation in practices associated with construction—insofar as it existed at all—differed from region to region, dependent

122 ■ An Archaeology of Identity

not simply on the availability of stone supplies but also upon variable social and institutional dynamics in different areas. These were clearly important *material* changes, though, which (as the next chapters will explore further) were part of a *temporal* flow of activity and as such had *social* significance. Before pursuing these points, one more class of material culture needs to be considered: texts.

Texts as objects

In keeping with my approach to artefacts, I want to elaborate upon some of the ways in which the texts that we can use to write about identities were themselves objects created and used in specific contexts that have particular characteristics in the 4th century. In doing so, I am forced to step outside of the evidence directly coming from Britain—rather as with 'military' funerary assemblages—since most of the written material that is relevant to military and other identities in this period comes from other parts of the empire. In some ways, however, this is more of an opportunity than a problem, as we will see later how different kinds of evidence relating to different levels of a context can be tied into different levels of identification. For now, I will consider the significance of the dearth of insular written artefacts, before making some general points about genres of writing and methods of textual circulation in the Roman period, using specific examples of the most important texts for our purposes in considering the dynamics of identity in 4th century Britain.

While the lack of major historical or other literature surviving from Roman Britain should come as no surprise, given the absence of any long-established literary culture comparable to that of the Mediterranean, it is notable that documentary and epigraphic evidence is also in short supply in the 4th century. This is partly a factor of preservation. The famous examples of documentary material that do survive tend to be found in earlier (therefore, deeper and often waterlogged) stratigraphic deposits, as at Vindolanda. A small quantity of evidence that relates to the 4th century will be referred to below, but the lack of monumental inscriptions is particularly interesting. Very few British sites have produced inscriptions dating to any point beyond the end of the 3rd century. Apart from a handful of building inscriptions (e.g., Tetrarchic ones from Birdoswald and Housesteads) and a few milestones, as well as some lettered mosaics (Bédoyère 1999b: 20–31), there is little sign of public—or indeed private—memory being maintained through monumental writing in this period. This represents a significant change compared to the extensive corpus of public (civic, imperial, military) and private (religious, funerary) epigraphic material from the previous two and one-half centuries of Roman administration. Although inscriptions were frequently reused in various ways within the Roman period, and afterwards (Keppie 1991: 30–6), these factors are unlikely to have wholly created the late Roman epigraphic void.

This brings us to the question of 'epigraphic habit', which is of general interest as a material practice that involved visible constructions of social identity in Roman Britain. A well-established trajectory of research in classical epigraphy (e.g., Dobson and Mann 1973; MacMullen 1982; Mann 1985) has demonstrated that the practice of inscribing (or commissioning the inscription of) words on stone was a particular one, which was certainly not adopted uniformly—either in geographical or social terms—across the Roman Empire. In Britain, many inscriptions are associated with soldiers, either with respect to institutional military activity (building inscriptions, dedications) or more individual proclamations of an origin outside Britain on tombstones (Mann 1985: 206). The latter are often accompanied by largely stereotypical representations of soldiers, showing their equipment and, sometimes, their idealised battlefield role (as with auxiliary cavalrymen depicted riding down barbarians [Ferris 1995]). It is notable that tombstones were not usually erected by British recruits, and this does not seem to be because there were no such recruits, but rather that native groups did not acquire the 'epigraphic habit' (Mann 1985). This, moreover, might be expected, as 'Britons' is largely an outsiders' label (cf. Matthews 1999; Snyder 1998: 72). This might lead us to believe that the lack of 4th century inscriptions resulted from increasing local recruitment, but while it is likely that the latter was occurring, the picture is complicated by a wider decline in epigraphic activity across the empire in the later Roman period (MacMullen 1982). We are thus dealing with wider questions regarding the relationship between practices of writing and social identity in the later Roman Empire.

In Britain, a key part of these must be the extent of Latin literacy in 4th century Britain, but this remains uncertain. Indications in favour of relatively widespread familiarity with the language include curse tablets found at Bath and elsewhere, stamps on ceramics, and quotations and salutations on mosaics (Bédoyère 1999b: 28–9). It has also been argued that the apparent incorporation of a quotation from Virgil on certain coins of Carausius implies an audience receptive to such esoteric references (as might equally be implied by the classical mythology represented on many mosaics [Bédoyère 1999a: 32–6; Smith 1977]).

Carausius's 'image' as a usurper certainly seems to have been created within a Roman idiom of traditional representations of authority and power, although it is uncertain at whom this was directed. Indeed, inscriptions on coins are more generally interesting, as the range of propogandist messages conveyed by imperial types such as the *Gloria Exercitus* ('the glory of the armies') and *Fel Temp Reparatio* ('happy times are restored') issues may well have been targeted directly at the military. Within the military evidence from elsewhere in the empire suggests that orders and ceremonies were conducted in Latin, mixed with expressions from other languages (James 1999a: 16, 21). Nonetheless, in all of these cases, it would be problematic to extrapolate from what are primarily formulaic uses of a language—confined to particular contexts—to greater degrees of fluency, and indeed there is no reason to suppose that indigenous languages were supplanted.

The limited evidence, therefore, suggests that while Latin was probably familiar in some form to many (Millett 1990: 110; cf. Duncan-Jones 1977), at least in towns, forts, and villas, it is very difficult to understand what this meant to the varied social groups living in these and other kinds of settlements. There are, for instance, some indications that clerks or scribes were involved in the production of the Bath curse tablets (Tomlin 1988: 98–101), as with some of the letters of the Abinnaeus Archive from Egypt, which I will draw upon later. Differential knowledge of Latin may therefore have been bound up with a whole range of power dynamics within various social groups, and not necessarily have been perceived simply in terms of opposed 'Roman' and 'native' modes of discourse. All kinds of opportunities, compulsions, and constraints may have influenced the actions of those learning the language. This need to treat the relationship between different forms of written (and spoken) Latin and 'Roman-ness' in a sophisticated way must guide us when we consider the lack of 4th century inscriptions on stone in Britain. No less than the other points made throughout this chapter, this is a distinctive characteristic of the materiality of this period that is likely to have had some significance in terms of people's changing identities.

Obviously, however, such significance can only be interpreted in a somewhat limited way, and for more positive associations of specific practices with specific identities, we will have to turn to texts that do survive from the wider empire. These represent another level of context, above that of everything discussed in this chapter so far. The discourses on identity that these texts contain, especially those focused on military/official categories, take us away from the particularities of life in small communities in Britain and into the ideas that made the

Roman Empire a large-scale institution in itself. At the same time, these discourses should be expected to have some things in common with other forms of material culture, one of the most important being that they were themselves produced in a range of specific contexts. With regard to these contexts, it is worth reviewing the major forms of classical writing, from which individual texts that are useful will be drawn. In addition to the small-scale textualisations such as inscriptions, letters, stamps on ceramics, and curse tablets, there were several genres of larger-scale 'literary' writing—including history, geography, poetry, drama, theology, and technical treatises. Insofar as these categories were defined in more-or-less formal ways by Roman-period authors, they are useful devices for contextualising texts, but there can be considerable overlap between them at quite a fundamental level. They cannot, for example, readily be separated into 'fiction' and 'non-fiction', and this has significant consequences for how they might be understood now.

Thus, while genres such as poetry can often be mined for historical information, it is equally important to consider the poetics of histories and the ways in which such forms of writing constructed a reality as much as represented one. While historical writing in the Roman world was indeed concerned with truth, this was not necessarily a truth inherent *in* particular events, but rather one that the historian might create by imputing a meaning *to* them—as indeed is arguably the case with history today (Atkinson 1990: 1; Comber 1997: 54; Munslow 2000: 89–91; Potter 1999: 5–18). This introduces the notion of a rhetoric of history that cannot be factored out as a distortion, but must be considered as part of the meaning-creating activity—or practice—of the historian. Thus, for example, the work of such earlier Roman writers as Caesar, Tacitus, and Strabo, can be examined not for *what* they say about Britain, but rather *how* they say it—the categories and values of identity that are applied in the act of representing an 'other'. Such ethnographic writing clearly served the Roman political present (Comber 1997: 47), reinforcing the self-definition of Romans at the time when the empire was expanding rapidly, but also allowing room for accommodation between Rome and other peoples (Matthews 1999: 27). Ideals of civilisation and particularly *humanitas* (Woolf 1998: 48–60) were implicit in Roman authors' descriptions of themselves and others, and while the need to classify people may be regarded as a fundamental aspect of social life, these particular formulations have had a profound influence on post-Roman understandings of cultural identity. These were, however, the truths that such authors sought to reveal, just as much as the more obviously political agendas

126 ■ An Archaeology of Identity

in the work of Caesar on himself or Tacitus on Domitian (Comber 1997: 49–54). By the 4th century, an additional form of truth to be considered is the particular religious direction of an author's narrative. Competing Christian and pagan world-views again placed particular facts, like the fall of Rome in AD 410 (Ridley 1982: xiv–xv), in the service of different kinds of reality, for authors and their audiences.

In addition to the possible meanings of 'truthfulness' in classical writing, it is worthwhile to consider some of the practical actions involved in generating and distributing a literary text in this period, and David Potter has provided a useful review of these (1999). The range of sources that could be used by a historian 'inquiring' into truth was diverse, and preferences might vary on an individual basis, or according to the conventions of the time or the subgenre. Later historians, for instance, seem generally to have been less interested in public records and documents and more in personal experience or testimony. Research and composition might be a lengthy process, often involving the use of slaves to read texts aloud or to make notes, and decisions would have to be made throughout about the ordering and interpretation of events and about resolving the inevitable discrepancies in testimonies. Publication and distribution of the 'final' draft was haphazard, and the circulation of different versions of a text was quite likely given both the vagaries of copying and, more importantly, the intervention of grammarians—early professional literary critics who might 'correct' a text to better reflect their idea of what the author ought to have written (i.e., another idea of 'truth'). These factors served to partially detach a text from a single authorial intent (cf. Munslow 1997: 116–7), and it is important to remember how long this process lasted for literary works that became part of the 'manuscript tradition' and thus survived to our own time. Such objects have been part of the material culture of monks and librarians through many centuries beyond the Roman period.

However, for all of these audiences (as for the authors), the texts were material culture that played a vital role in the structuration of social life. In this regard, all forms of texts can be seen fundamentally as media of distanciation—that is, of extending social interactions and negotiations of power across time-space, beyond the limits of individual co-presence (Giddens 1984: 142–4, 181–3; Urry 1991: 163–9). They may thus tend to relate more directly than some other forms of material culture to institutional identities, which also transcend larger portions of time-space (Jenkins 2004: 132–5). Of course, for literary works at least, authorship and circulation were both socially limited— primarily to aristocratic men. Many other social groups would have been reliant upon entirely different frameworks of memory and reality construction than the literate (cf. Fentress and Wickham 1992: 41–51). It is also important to bear in mind that many readings of texts, or indeed recitations of oral narratives, would have occurred in contexts of co-presence with their own social dynamics, entirely distinct from the relationship between the original author and their readers (cf. Thompson 1990: 235–48), rather than in private study. However, such contexts tend to remain archaeologically intangible, and our focus here must remain closer to what the texts do still indicate about their authors' understandings of the social world.

Fortunately, for the exploration of the dynamics of identity in the 4th century, we have examples of texts available from a range of different contexts of production and use. Two written histories are particularly pertinent. Foremost of these is the *Res Gestae* of Ammianus Marcellinus, written in the late 4th century and covering the whole period since the end of Tacitus' history 300 years previously, but only surviving for the years of the mid-4th century. Ammianus' perspective is framed by his former experiences as a high-ranking soldier, as well as by his Greek ethnicity and pagan religious leanings (Barnes 1998: 1–10; Wallace-Hadrill 1986: 13–20). Less is known about the other key writer, Zosimus, whose *Nea Historia* runs to AD 410 and the sack of Rome—as well as, incidentally, the end of Roman Britain. He was apparently a pagan, but writing rather later—in the early 6th century—and worked by compiling information from earlier histories (Ridley 1982). Representing a different genre, the technical treatise, is Vegetius' *Epitoma Rei Militaris*. This manual on the principles of 'military science' seems to have been compiled as a set of constructive criticisms addressed to the military policy of a later Roman emperor, probably Theodosius I. Vegetius himself seems to have been a high-ranking bureaucrat rather than a soldier, a Christian but one with a fondness for traditional Roman literature (Milner 1993: xviii–xxv). All of these texts were constrained in their circulation and use by the factors mentioned above, but all have something to offer on continuity and change in military and other identities in the 4th century.

Three other, more documentary sets of texts are also useful. The 'Abinnaeus Archive' is a collection of correspondence once belonging to a 4th century cavalry officer in the Fayyûm region of Egypt, and containing many letters that shed light on the daily interactions between soldiers and others (Bell et al. 1962). The other two bodies of material are more unique, representing high-level administrative uses of writing that probably had different mechanisms of circulation from more literary works. The Theodosian Code is a major Late Antique collection of laws prepared for Theodosius II between AD 429 and 438 (Pharr 1952), which includes laws—even apparently

128 ■ AN ARCHAEOLOGY OF IDENTITY

obsolete ones—dating back to AD 313. These had usually been issued by emperors to specific officials in specific places, and while they had probably been on public display in those places, how (or even if) they were circulated around the whole empire is by no means certain. Nonetheless, they reflect the attitudes of the highest levels of government to matters of identity and social behaviour. Finally, an even more problematic bureaucratic document is the *Notitia Dignitatum*. This is a list of civilian and military offices across the whole empire, which has been profoundly influential in a number of ways in the construction of historical archaeologies of the later Roman Empire. However, questions surround its dating, location of production, and authorship, while its format may also have made it vulnerable to the accumulation of modifications through mistakes in manuscript copying. The document was most likely maintained from the 390s to the 420s in the office of an imperial secretary, the *primicerius notariorum*, in the western empire (Hassall 1976: 103–4; Welsby 1982: 133–5). Like the law codes, then, this is an artefact that relates to how the central authorities saw the institutions of the empire working in a diocese like Britain.

These texts will all be helpful in the next chapter in constructing narratives, from different perspectives, of how social identities were constructed and transformed in the 4th century. In the context of this chapter, however, it is important to stress once again that despite the additional layers of meaning the writing upon them creates, they are also objects produced and used in specific contexts in the late Roman world, just like the coins or buildings discussed above. On the one hand, this limits easy application of what they say to contexts to which they had no connection, but it also creates opportunities where such connections can be demonstrated. In the following chapters, the place of particular writers and documents in that world will be emphasised, at the same time as the observable patterns in Britain are put into a wider imperial context of themes that run through all of the texts. This approach links the practices of writing in the late Roman period with the other practices involved in living in it, which are evident in all of the material culture from 4th century Britain. In concluding this chapter, it is to the significance of this material culture that we must again turn.

Material practices and identity

This chapter has considered the basic elements of the material conditions of 4th century life in a somewhat provisional and synchronic fashion, but one geared towards thinking about the involvement of these things in a range of contexts of practice. We have seen how different kinds of artefacts are an integral part of practices such as exchanging, appearing, eating, dwelling, building, and writing. Although we have yet to explore the meanings of different ways of conducting such practices, the basic dimensions of similarity and variation within each kind of activity have also been introduced, from the range of available pottery types to the styles of buildings used in forts and towns. According to the tenets of structuration theory set out in Chapter 2, it is precisely through doing such mundane activities as wearing particular items of dress, or dumping rubbish in a certain way, that the relationships between individual people and the social groups and institutions of which they are a part actually become manifest. Since such relationships are the very stuff of identities, the understanding of how different kinds of material evidence can relate to specific practices, sketched out in this chapter, is a vital first step in constructing an archaeology of identity for 4th century Britain. Giddens also emphasises how the context in which an activity is conducted is vital in determining its meaning (e.g., 1984: 71); and that is why, where the data allow, some emphasis has been placed upon locating activities in sites. Locating different ways of performing activities in time will be our concern in the next chapter, but before pursuing these, we need to be very clear about how this contextual fluidity works.

It is not just the case that there are different forms of meaning, as discussed in the introduction to this chapter, or that different types of meaning content might be intended in different situations. It is more that at any particular moment, the potential significance of an act may be either latent—that is, an unintentional aspect of carrying out the activity—or it may be active, made the subject of attention, comparison, or comment. To take a simple example, the habit of living in a 'chalet' barrack might have been a simple matter of routine most of the time for the soldiers inside—an unremarkable part of their world. But if a soldier from another unit, where there were different kinds of barracks, passed through the fort and spoke to some of the garrison, this might suddenly become a topic of conversation—a different way of doing things that signified the identity of both the inhabitants and the visitor. Moreover, through the continued practice of living in any kind of barracks, all of these soldiers were participating in a specific way of life that—again largely unintentionally from their point of view—reproduced the 'military' as a distinct community with a different way of doing things from people living in towns or farms.

All of these issues are accounted for within the framework of structuration theory, which is why it provides such a solid foundation for an archaeology of identity. Essentially, structuration theory stresses not only the central importance of practices in the constitution of social life, but also the ways in which meanings can vary for actors according to the attitude they have toward those practices in specific contexts. This is where the stratified model of consciousness, discussed briefly in Chapter 2, comes in. Traditionally, agency has been defined in relation to choice and intentionality. Certainly, a major aspect of the definition of agency as *active* involvement (used here) is that people are engaged with the world in such a way that they can select their activity from a range of options and could always have 'acted otherwise' (Giddens 1984: 9; cf. Emirbayer and Mische 1998; Macmurray 1957: 84–164; Mead 2002 [1932]). However, this does not mean that only actions that are deliberately selected count as actions, and one of Giddens's major contributions to the understanding of agency has been to point out that people are still acting when they do things entirely routinely, or when the consequences of their actions are not intended. Indeed, the unintended reproduction of social structure is a central element of the theory of structuration, carried forward primarily by routine actions, even though these are still reflexively monitored by the actor (Giddens 1984: 2–16). At the same time, though, the notion of 'discursive consciousness' offers the potential for actors to talk or think critically about situations, and thus enables the deliberate construction or transformation of ways of doing things—and of the identities to which these give shape.

The nature of this distinction between 'practical' and 'discursive' consciousness is vitally important. As with the duality of structure, Giddens is maintaining only a slender division between these concepts. In reality, we are always engaging in a mixture of habitual and discursive action. Even revolutionary scientific ideas, for example, are usually reached by people who are thinking in their habitual language (Baert 1992: 64–5; Crossley 2001: 135–9). Nonetheless, the two frames of action can be considered separately, and need to be if we are to retain the potential for transformative action as well as unthinking repetition (Emirbayer and Mische 1998: 994–1002; Mead 1934: 347–78). As we will see, this has considerable significance in considering how identities work, because it helps us make the vital link between material practices and either implicit or explicit kinds of identification. It is useful, also, to consider an affective or emotional dimension of action, in addition to the habitual and discursive (Archer 2000: 193–305; Bauman 1990: 110–11), lest we forget that people do not just think about what they are doing in a purely cognitive sense, but also have feelings about it.

These conceptual tools will allow us to get a firmer grasp on the significance of the material practices explored in this chapter.

Of course, not all practices are as archaeologically visible as those we have looked at so far, and some of these—like speaking—are extremely important. We can, however, see the kinds of activities that people would have spoken about, even where these leave a material gap, as with the lack of inscriptions in 4th century Britain. Sometimes material invisibility can be a signifying social strategy just as much as visibility (Criado 1995). The materiality of human life, as embodied engagement with a material world, means that the effects of agency are to be found everywhere we look. Sometimes those effects will be unintended; at other times they will be intended. Sometimes they will be the work of a single human, but the actions of that human are never entirely solitary or autonomous because of the internalisation of other people's opinions and values. Sometimes material patterns will result from habitual action; at other times they will have been discursively noticed in the past. In all of these cases, though, we can talk about the people in the past in ways that we understand and in terms of some of the different ways in which they understood their relationships to each other and to the wider world. Thus, we can recover something of their "historically situated agency" (Shalin 2000: 339) and create more sophisticated accounts of the past. To put all of this into practice, and to pursue the meanings of the material patterns that we have begun to examine, it is necessary now to move from a static understanding of 4th century activities to one that reflects the reality of a lived world, by adding the vital dimension of time.

Chapter 4

THE TEMPORAL DIMENSIONS OF 4TH CENTURY LIFE: TRADITIONS AND CHANGE

Studying temporality

In adding an explicitly temporal dimension to the material practices considered so far, it is vital to stress that the separation of subject matter between these two chapters is entirely artificial; all practices are necessarily temporal as much as material—and indeed social. However, establishing the idea of material practices, and the kinds of things it involves in the context of 4th century Britain, constitutes a logical starting point to break into this overlapping complex of ideas for an archaeological study. Time is no less a central concern in archaeology, although it has attracted curiously limited theoretical attention when compared with material culture. This is surprising, as time is of course fundamental to archaeology in more ways than one. As well as constituting one of the basic parameters of archaeological data, in the form of chronology, it defines archaeology in relation to other disciplines: others may study people, but it is only archaeologists who study the material culture of those people in the past without the limits of documentation experienced by historians. This time depth is regarded as a major asset in contributing something to debates in other disciplines (e.g., Binford 1962: 219; Hodder 1991b: 191–2), as it encompasses the greatest possible spectrum of human diversity. In the popular imagination, it is time that adds mystery to archaeologists' work, allowing them to be characterised as 'time detectives' or 'time travellers' (e.g., Fagan 1995). Perhaps because of this central role, however, time is rather taken for granted in both the professional and popular sphere. From a theoretical point of view, it is usually simply treated as almost a dimension of space—a landscape of chronological points within which data must be situated, or a misty chasm that must be crossed in order to engage with the past. Only relatively recently have archaeologists begun to realise that, like other areas of the discipline that have been scrutinised in the last 40 years, temporality requires a bit more critical thought if we are to deal with its complexities.

Much of the debate that has followed from this realisation has been concerned with the relationship between archaeologists' attempts to measure time more efficiently and past people's experiences of the flow of time, which might have been understood in very different ways (see Lucas 2005 for an effective summary). This initially led to an opposition being created between the abstract, 'measured' time of the archaeologist (and the modern West), governed by the clock and a linear progression of years, and the more subjective, 'marked' time of past people or non-Western 'others', governed by significant events and ritual cycles (e.g., Gosden 1994: 2; Shanks and Tilley 1987: 128). However, thanks to insights from anthropology and such antidualist schools of philosophy as phenomenology and pragmatism, it is increasingly being realised that all people experience time in complex ways which combine elements of 'marking' and 'measuring', and which therefore involve different attitudes to past, present, and future (Adam 1990: 44–5, 1994; Gardner 2001b). Understanding these is important because people's views of their own actions, of what is considered possible or impossible, necessary or unnecessary, are very much involved in what they choose to do (Emirbayer and Mische 1998: 973). Moreover, as the archaeological record is fundamentally composed of material patterns of continuity and change, the meanings of these temporal processes to the people who created and experienced them—and indeed whether they were observable at all to them, or only to us—are key issues in more fully understanding those people's lives.

This centrality of time to all human experience has not gone unnoticed by sociologists either, and it is worth noting here that Giddens has been a key player in the recognition of its importance within his discipline (Bryant and Jary 2001: 33). However, in doing so Giddens drew rather uncritically on Claude Lévi-Strauss's structural anthropology and Torsten Hägerstrand's 'time-geography', both of which failed to transcend the typical limits of dualist thinking. For Lévi-Strauss, the distinction between linear or 'irreversible' time and cyclical, 'reversible' time corresponded to a difference between 'hot' and 'cold' societies (Adam 1990: 25–9; Gell 1992: 23–9, 286–93; Giddens 1984: 35–6). The former were more dynamic (i.e., modern), open to change, and aware of their place in the directional flow of history, while the latter were trapped in an eternal present, focusing past and future in a recurrent moment through cyclical rituals. While cautious of some aspects of Lévi-Strauss's work, Giddens (1979: 24–8) adopted the ideas of hot and cold societies (1984: 199) and reversible and irreversible time (1984: 35), using the latter to also describe the difference between daily, routine time scales and a more linear human lifetime. This is problematic; to even refer to activities figuratively as 'reversible' ignores the fact that while undeniably similar, no two routine actions are the same as aspects of their context will have changed (Adam 1990: 26–9; cf. Gregory 1989). This is important because although routine is critical to the continuation of social life in a patterned way, it is equally vital (by virtue of its 'irreversibility') to social change. Indeed, all social life should be conceptualised in terms of a balance between tradition and change or mobility, with even routine actions always being enacted in new contexts, with new potentials.

Giddens has also made use of 'time-geography' in relating time to space (Giddens 1984: 110–19). This school of social geography is a way of mapping people's movements through time-space, in order to show how—through their daily movements—different opportunities for interaction and constraints upon action emerge (Fig. 4.1). This is a useful way of representing graphically the choreography of action, and in a context like Roman Pompeii, it has been used to show how members of the senatorial class moved around the city at certain times in a patterned way, which was integral to the display and practice of their social status (Gell 1992: 190–205; Laurence 1994: 122–32). While helpful, therefore, in adding a temporal dimension to the material contexts of practice, and an improvement on the rather static perspective of society taken by most social theorists (Adam 1990: 13), there are still problems with the representational method used in this approach. This essentially reduces time to another spatial dimension

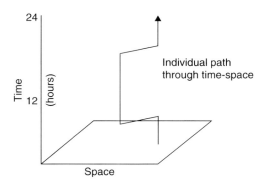

Figure 4.1. An example of the type of 'time-space map' generated by time-geographical studies (cf. Gell 1992: 190–205).

136 ■ An Archaeology of Identity

and treats it as a container *for* action, rather than as something which might be experienced differently *in* action. This is a similar approach to the kind of optimising time budget analysis used in some anthropological and archaeological work on resource acquisition and decision making (Gell 1992: 206–16; Mithen 1990; Smith 1983), with the same flaw: the acceptance of abstract, 'measured' time as the only real form. As such, it is not very helpful in extending Giddens's wider insights into the relationship between agency and structure, as temporality is a part of both and must therefore be treated as a more flexible concept involving different experiences and perceptions, as well as culturally diverse time structures.

It is relatively easy to see how temporality can be part of the definition of structures, with calendars (for example) providing a very obvious kind of 'rule' or 'resource' that actors routinely follow and use, and with organised time being a key part of the structure of many institutions (Roman military calendars, like the *Feriale Duranum*, are excellent examples of this; [James 1999a: 21]). It is equally clear that time must be an element of agency, as 'active involvement' in the world implies an ongoing process. This point is captured well by Mead, stressing a key difference between humans and other species in this regard: "It is because the conscious individual is both an animal and is also able to look before and after that consciousness emerges with the meanings and values with which it informs the world" (Mead 2002 [1932]: 89). This involvement of time in both parts of the duality of structure is certainly in line with Giddens's general approach, but also highlights why the more specific ideas he pursues can be criticised in the manner just outlined. A more open-ended approach, one that seeks to understand the relationship between particular time structures and agents' own 'time-perspectives' (Emirbayer and Mische 1998: 968–70), is required and will be pursued in this chapter.

Since an archaeology of how Roman calendrics impacted upon Romano-British society is not yet possible, this will be done by expanding the description of different material practices in the previous chapter into an analysis of continuity and change, and considering how these phenomena were the products of processes of structuration. The actions of people in small-scale contexts were shaped by structures of wider institutional extent, and these structures had temporal associations of either tradition or fluidity. At the same time, those people's actions were instrumental in creating permanence or shaping transformation in wider structures, and this happened as they made decisions about the uses of artefacts or spaces that were linked to those structures. The medium for this linkage is of course identity, so by establishing the temporal patterns in this chapter, we move a vital step closer to understanding the dynamics of identity in this period. Not only does this kind of approach represent a challenge to traditional accounts of how societies work, where the role of individual actors in shaping social processes has tended to be suppressed by normative or systemic mechanisms (Johnson 1999b: 132–48; Trigger 1989: 148–55, 289–94), but it is essential in a context that occupies an anomalous status in the history of Britain in the 1st millennium, as we saw in Chapter 1.

The 4th century—and even more so the early 5th—is a 'period between periods' where traditional narratives have a problem in explaining a major change. This is largely, I would argue, because of a failure to appreciate that history does not conform to the preferred academic pattern of homogenous, stable periods—which a scholar can specialise in—punctuated by periods of 'transition'. In contrast to many earlier archaeological approaches, the approach adopted here treats change as a built-in feature of social life and stability as an active, rather than a passive, process. The motor of history shifts from 'great men' or hidden structures, systems, and the like to the intentional practices of human agents—or their unintended consequences—in interaction with social structures. If social formations are continually produced and reproduced in daily practice, then there is always the potential for those formations to change, insofar as agents are inherently powerful beings (Giddens 1984: 5–16, 212–3; cf. Cohen 1989: 45–7). This is not quite to say that all history is transitional, which again implies a totalising vision of the past (cf. Bintliff and Hamerow 1995b: 1; Shanks and Tilley 1987: 185). Rather, change occurs at a multiplicity of rates on a multiplicity of levels of social life, producing a multiplicty of narratives. We might therefore try to humanise our terminology and talk about the traditions and mobilities (opportunities for change) that different practices and institutions embody and enable. This perspective opens up a much broader and more meaningful range of ways of understanding 'continuity' and 'change'.

That this is singularly pertinent to the 4th and early 5th centuries in Britain can be reinforced by a brief consideration of the problem of 'collapses'. The status of the end of Roman Britain, both as a historical phenomenon and a subject of academic enquiry, is part of a broader cross-cultural category of 'transition'—the abrupt end of a civilisation. In general terms, explanations for such events have ranged from traditional 'organic' models of decline (ageing) and fall (death) to systemic notions of 'crash' as a sudden departure from 'homeostatic' regulation (Yoffee 1988: 1–9; Renfrew 1979). Much of the foregoing discussion in this chapter, though, demands a rather different approach. At a minimum, this requires sensitivity to changes at different paces 'within' period boundaries, with a view to questioning the

138 ■ AN ARCHAEOLOGY OF IDENTITY

validity of such periods themselves. In turn, a much greater appreciation of the multiple perspectives within any society is called for, not simply those that seem most obvious—typically those of the elite (Scull 1995: 73; Wilmott 1995: 66–7). The choice of whether one describes late Roman Britain as either 'golden age' or 'decline and fall' largely depends upon whether one focuses on elite or nonelite viewpoints; a more complete account must surely consider both.

Equally important is clarity about what we mean by 'collapse'. Partly because of the dominance of elite perspectives upon such things, 'collapse' tends to be discussed in pejorative terms: 'decline', 'fall', 'dark age'. In modern usage, these terms also tend to be contrasted with perceived 'climaxes' or 'highpoints' of a civilisation, particularly within an organic view of culture (Bowersock 1988: 166–7; Tainter 1988: 74–88). While past value judgements should obviously be explored as partial perspectives on social changes, their adoption at face value as 'true' descriptions is equally clearly flawed. Redefining 'collapse' therefore entails consideration of how (socially) widespread any particular changes were, and to what extent they relate to the 'failure' of a political structure as opposed to a 'civilisation' or 'great tradition' (Cowgill 1988: 255–8). Thus, even the fairly neutral definition of collapse offered by Joseph Tainter (1988: 4) as "a rapid, significant loss of an established level of sociopolitical complexity" begs an important question of description: significant for whom? This question opens up previous efforts that have focused on finding an *explanation* for collapse to a more inclusive *interpretation*.

The problems of describing 'what collapses' are closely related to the issue of whom a collapse affects. Any situation interpreted as a 'fall', often followed by a 'dark age' (characterised by changes in settlement patterns, literacy, etc. [Renfrew 1979: 482–5]), is simply, in the first instance, a change in an established level of archaeological visibility. Given that the most visible kinds of material—stone architecture, ceramics, texts, and so forth—need not constitute the totality of material culture used at any particular time, we must allow for some lifestyles being less immediately obvious than others, as well as exploring the relationship between archaeological visibility and active social strategies (Criado 1995; Tainter 1988: 197–9). *Describing* collapses therefore requires consideration of multiple, partial perspectives situated within a general practice-based approach to the meaningful use of material culture, as outlined in Chapter 3. It follows that attempts to *explain* collapses will be inadequate if they do not accommodate the diversity of social life. This is certainly a flaw in many of the typical explanations of collapse such as environmental change, cultural 'inflexibility', invasion, class conflict, and the cost/benefit value of social complexity (Tainter 1988: 39–90, 91–127). Such causal phenomena do not account for discernible changes in material culture as themselves meaningful.

Moving beyond the limitations of explanation, and tackling also the problems of description, requires an attempt at interpretation and understanding. Cause-and-effect linkages are insufficient as accounts of the ways in which different people in the past constructed and reproduced varying social formations (Hodder 1999: 69–70; Munslow 2000: 37–43). A fuller reading of collapse—as with the rise or initiation of cultural episodes—needs to explore the range of meanings that might be invested in those symbols that disappear or persist, the extent to which changes in material culture represent changes in routines of action, and the ways in which these transformations in meaningful practices are bound up with transformations in social identities. These are all constant features of social life, but vary in tempo. Situations described in the language of 'collapse' (by contemporaries or those looking back) may well represent dislocations in power relations, redefinitions of institutionalised identities, and shifts in some modes of interaction—but these phenomena will affect different people in different ways, seeming more or less rapid, intelligible, or desirable. Symbols associated with a particular ideology might be actively rejected, or a change in modes of interaction might simply be worked through in ways that involve gradual modifications to a suite of material practices (cf. Reece 1989: 235–6). All of these issues need to be explored at a range of scales rather than simply as generalisations. In this way, 'collapse' serves as an example of how trying to capture the nuances of all social processes forces us to focus on the balance between fixity and fluidity—or tradition and mobility—that is a critical feature of the temporal character of social life, and our main concern in this chapter.

Biographies of assemblages

Coins and small finds

We can begin by returning to the higher-resolution forms of data considered in Chapter 3. As already noted there, coins are a kind of material culture whose main value for the archaeologist is typically chronological, and this allows long-term patterns in the use, loss, and discard of this kind of object to be reconstructed. These will also help us in constructing a broader picture of continuity and change in different regions and on specific sites. In this way, the 'biographies' of the individual coins, which might involve all sorts of specific meanings and values that are difficult for us to reconstruct, become integrated into biographies of assemblages and thus of places. It is from these more aggregate sets of material stories, underpinned by their connection to practices, that we can interpret the social significance of continuity and change. Use of the term 'biography' to refer to shared stories of assemblages or places is only intended loosely; it has become more widespread as a way of talking about the different phases of use that an object might go through, and even rather carelessly to anthropomorphise artefacts (Knappett 2002: 98; Meskell 2004: 55–8; Spector 1991). Here the term is used more as a metaphor for the collective story that a group of artefacts or structures can tell (cf. Evans 2001: 26–7). Nonetheless, the ways in which specific coins and other finds were used in specific activities and contexts (discussed in Chapter 3) will be vital guides in interpreting the broader temporal patterns here in socially significant ways, even if some of the meanings attached to individual objects have been lost.

For coins, we have a useful baseline for comparing different assemblages over time in the British Mean of coin supply to Britain mentioned already (Fig. 3.8). Indeed further work in this vein has established patterns of supply to particular groups of sites (e.g., Lockyear 2000; Reece 1993b, 1995; Ryan 1988), and some of these will be examined further below. This in itself suggests that aggregate scales of artefact analysis are relevant to the shared, meaningful practices of particular communities of past actors, at the same time as being sensitive to variation between them. In this section, I will compare assemblages from a range of sites and regions to see how continuities and changes in coin use created patterns of similarity and difference between them. A sound methodological basis for such comparison is provided by Richard Reece (1995), whose 21-period system for the division of Roman coinage in Britain has already been introduced. These methods are fairly simple. Having converted the list of coin finds from any site into a 21-period format (they are conventionally listed by emperor), the initial analytical step is to turn the actual numbers of coins into a figure of 'coins per thousand' (period total ÷ overall total × 1000). This serves the same purpose as a percentage, in permitting comparisons between lists of different sizes, but produces larger numbers that are more convenient for graphic output. These numbers can be directly plotted on a line graph without further manipulation, but the result is not very useful for comparative purposes. If, for example, the coins/1000 numbers for Caerleon are displayed (Fig. 4.2), several peaks and troughs are immediately obvious, but to be able to comment on the significance of these variations over time, they need to be related to the overall pattern of coin loss in Britain.

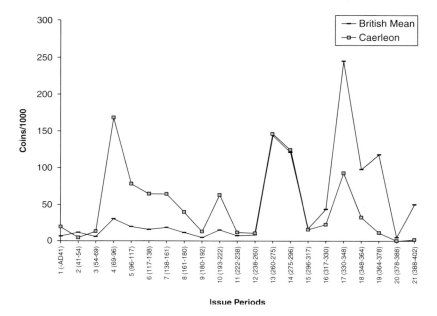

Figure 4.2. Caerleon coins/1000 and the British Mean (data from Gardner 1997: 83–9; Mean from Reece 1995: 183).

It was for this purpose that Reece derived the British Mean from the coin lists published in his compilation of coin data, *140 Sites* (also shown on Fig. 4.2 [Reece 1991, 1993b]). The general background that this provides allows some assessment of whether changes in a site's coin graph represent something happening at *that site*, or something common throughout Britain. If individual site curves are constructed, therefore, from coins/1000 minus the British Mean for each period (also expressed in coins/1000), they can be compared in terms of their degrees of difference from the Mean. If this is done for a number of sites, however, the graphic representation quickly becomes confusing as 'average' values all cluster along the *x*-axis (representing the Mean [see Fig. 4.3]). One way around this is to introduce a cumulative calculation that spreads the curves according to the differential pace at which coins are lost over the 21 periods of time. This allows a visual comparison of coin loss at different sites through time.

To implement this stage, the coins/1000 for each period are added cumulatively, both in the British Mean list and for the site list(s). Each cumulative period total on the Mean list is then subtracted from the site totals. This method permits ready graphic comparison (Fig. 4.4) and is the basis for much of this section, although only selective examples will

142 ■ An Archaeology of Identity

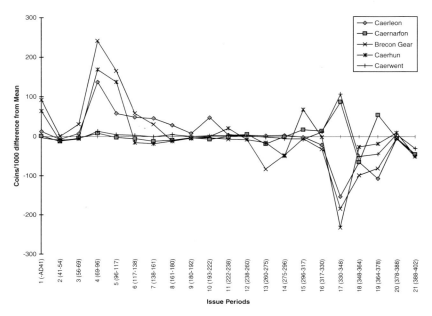

Figure 4.3. Western sites coins/1000 minus the British Mean, noncumulative (data from Gardner 2001a: 833–8).

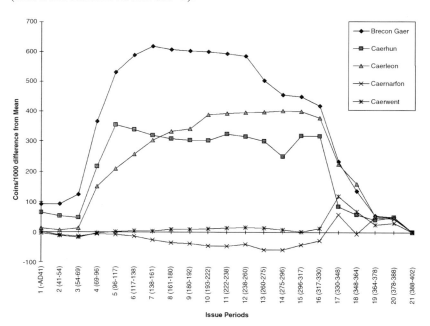

Figure 4.4. Western sites coins/1000 minus the British Mean, cumulative (data from Gardner 2001a: 833–8).

be illustrated. In reading these graphs, we must remember two points: first, the actual number of coins from different sites is widely variable, but this is masked by the method; and second, the positions of points on the graph has relative rather than absolute significance, and it is actually the lines connecting them that are more important. Because the lines follow cumulative movement against the Mean, they move up when the numbers are above average, straight when average, and down when below average. While early differences may cause two site curves to be widely separated, if both start to become parallel (perhaps in the 3rd century), then this indicates that they are now similarly average. Equally, even if a site curve is always above the x-axis, it is not always above average—only when the line is moving up. Hopefully these points will become clearer once we have looked at a few examples.

To begin with, we can compare coin loss patterns by region (see Fig. 2.4 for the locations and types of sites mentioned here and in subsequent sections). A selection of sites from modern Wales is shown in Figure 4.5, illustrating the main trends in this area. The sites fall into three major groups: (1) those that have a strongly above-average surge around Period 4—the Flavian period in the later 1st century AD when many were actually established—after which they have average coin loss until the late 3rd or early 4th century; (2) those that are below average until significantly adopting coin use in the later 3rd century; and (3) those sites that follow the Mean much more closely. All of the first group are fort- or fortress-type settlements, with Caernarfon exceptional amongst such sites in appearing in the third group; the second group is composed of farms and villas. In the 4th century periods, there is considerable variation at least until the middle of the century, but all sites are average or below towards the end. Assuming that coin loss corresponds in some way with coin use, these trends suggest that usage was quite polarised in western Britain in the 1st and 2nd centuries, only spreading into rural areas away from forts in the 3rd century, while the 4th century was a time of flux.

The northern area of Britain might be expected to follow a similar pattern, but it is not quite that simple (Fig. 4.6). There is a general regional division between the northeast and the northwest, with the latter demonstrating more strongly above-average coin loss in the earlier part of the Roman period, and the northeast appearing more average throughout. This means that coin supply to the northwest was more episodic, with a significant conquest-period presence becoming more variable over time. Importantly, though, in both regions the 'military' and 'civilian' sites hang together—unlike in Wales—relating to a more rapid adoption of coin-use by at least some of the local population, as

144 ■ An Archaeology of Identity

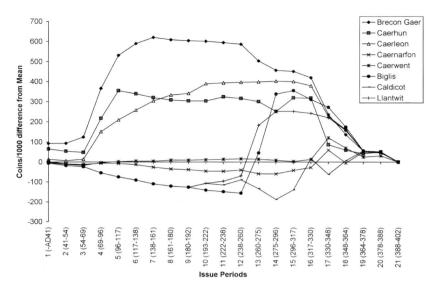

Figure 4.5. Coin deposition at selected sites in Wales (data from Boon 1988a, 1988b; Gardner 2001a: 833–8, 841–2).

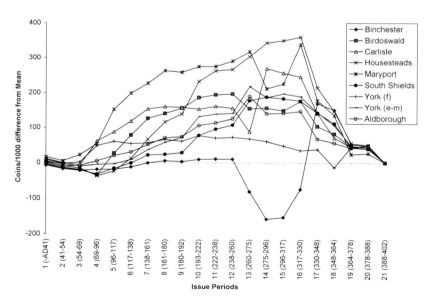

Figure 4.6. Coin deposition at selected sites in northern England (data from Gardner 2001a: 854–64; Reece 1991: 22).

well as the longer occupation history of northern forts compared to western ones. The other areas of Roman Britain show considerable variation among coin loss patterns (Fig. 4.7). Much of this variation relates to individual site histories: the later 3rd century foundation of 'Saxon Shore forts' like Burgh Castle for instance, accounts for their late Roman flourish on the graph. However, two things are broadly apparent. One is that the southwest of Britain was generally late in adopting coinage; the other is that many sites in central and southeastern Britain display average coin loss in the 1st and 2nd centuries—meaning that they were not such centres of coin use as the western forts in this period, though were still part of the monetary system, but became considerably more diverse in the 3rd and 4th centuries. This latter period was the time when coin use really seems to have increased at many sites, albeit not at one consistent moment. Among other things, this highlights why discussion of the impact of Roman colonialism on Britain should not be confined to the conquest period, but treated as a process with different phases of impact.

While comparing sites by region highlights how different parts of Britain adopted or changed coin-using practices at different points in time, it is useful to look at these patterns from another angle to get a fuller perspective on the factors that might account for them; one way of doing this is to focus on site types. Examples of site curves for (smaller) forts and (larger) fortresses are shown in Figure 4.8. These reinforce the distinctions between sites in the west, north, and southeast, which are primarily based upon their occupation histories: many forts in Wales seem to have been at least partially abandoned after the 2nd century, while those in the north were more consistently inhabited and those in the southeast were founded later in the 3rd century. Superficially, and rather obviously given that military pay was a major reason for the existence of Roman coinage in the first place (Reece 1977), this pattern might suggest that coin use remained a consistently identifiable part of military practice. On the other hand, we have already seen that the contexts of deposition have a particular character in the 4th century, which must be taken into account in interpreting the significance of this apparent stability (see below). Furthermore, the changing structure of the wider context of coin-use must also be considered. While high coin use may have been a distinctive and noticeable characteristic of military practice in a late 1st century western fort, this was not the case in 4th century eastern Britain, where many other types of site were also occupied by coin-using people. It is through this kind of attention to the dynamic context of particular practices that we can take more account of the conditions affecting situated

146 ■ An Archaeology of Identity

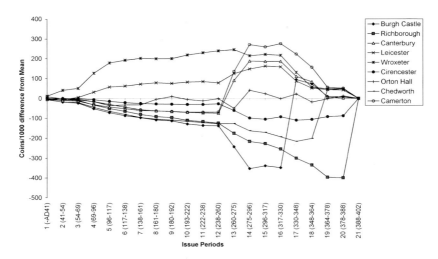

Figure 4.7. Coin deposition at selected sites in central and southern England (data from Esmonde Cleary 1996; Gardner 2001a: 869, 871–5, 877–8, 880–2, 886–90; Reece 1991: 23, 25).

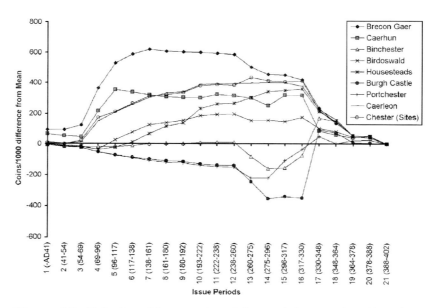

Figure 4.8. Coin deposition at selected fort and fortress sites (data from Gardner 2001a: 833–5, 849–55, 857–8, 869, 876–7).

THE TEMPORAL DIMENSIONS OF 4TH CENTURY LIFE ■ **147**

actors at different times, rather than homogenising people across the whole of the Roman period into simple categories of identification.

Indeed, the nature of this wider context becomes clearer if we look at other site types. The group of major towns that were *civitas* capitals is variable (Fig. 4.9). Some of these (e.g., Wroxeter) started as legionary bases, which accounts for the early peaks, but there may also be regional factors at work; at some of these sites (e.g., Silchester), people seem to have been using coins in numbers from an early point in their history, while others (Canterbury, Cirencester) lagged behind until the 3rd century or later. This suggests that official administrative status did not have a direct bearing on coin-using activity. Other towns and small settlements of lower (if any) official status, shown in Figure 4.10, also show a good deal of variation in their early patterns but are quite consistent in the later Roman period, with later 3rd century peaks and then below-average curves in the mid- to late 4th century. Moving away from towns, many of the curves for farms and villas are quite similar, though villas usually have greater absolute numbers of coins (Fig. 4.11). Interestingly, these show an even later period of high coin loss, coinciding to some extent with the decline in towns but also indicating a focus on the rural southwest as a coin-using area in this period (cf. Reece 1993b: 867–8). Clearly, 'exchanging' or other practices within which coins were used were not uniform in later Roman Britain. A final graph (Fig. 4.12) of large temple sites underlines this in comparison with other site types: these western pagan temples clearly flourished late in terms of coin loss, hinting at a religious dimension to coin use that may even represent an alternative type of practice involving coins (Peter Guest pers. comm.). At the least, these show that the changing patterns of coin use over time relate to a combination of unique events in site histories, regional variations, and functional/typological factors—both in terms of different site types and different types of coin-using practice.

When we tie these longer-term—and more extensive—patterns to the insights into coin use and deposition practices discussed in Chapter 3, an interesting picture begins to emerge. These indicated that coins of all periods were common finds in later Roman refuse deposits, and that this was linked to the increase in the availability of small denominations in this period. One major implication of this change, which can now be seen in a fuller chronological perspective, can be expressed in terms of the temporality of action discussed above. The patterns observed suggest widespread changes in the use of coins— and hint at changes in practices of rubbish disposal—in daily life over the later part of the Roman period. The increasing routinisation of coin

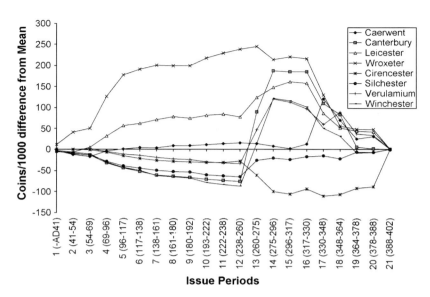

Figure 4.9. Coin deposition at selected *civitas* capitals (data from Gardner 2001a: 838, 871–5, 880–2, 886–90; Reece 1991: 19–22).

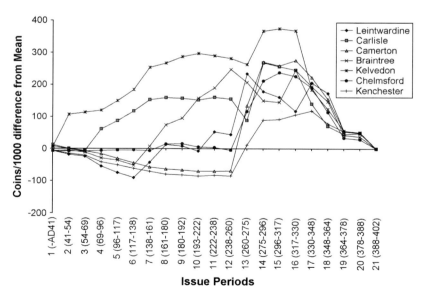

Figure 4.10. Coin deposition at selected other towns and settlements (data from Gardner 2001a: 855–6; Reece 1991: 23–4; Stanford 1968: 294–5).

The Temporal Dimensions of 4th Century Life ■ 149

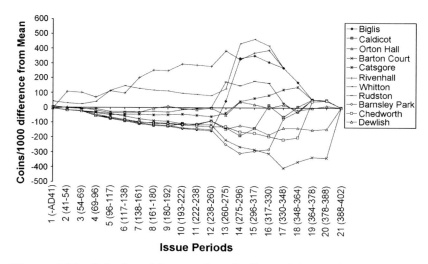

Figure 4.11. Coin deposition at selected villas and farms (data from Boon 1988(a) and b; Esmonde Cleary 1996; King 1986; Reece 1991: 23–6; 1993c).

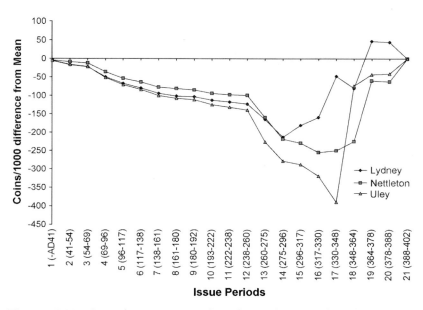

Figure 4.12. Coin deposition at selected temple sites (data from Reece 1991: 28).

150 ■ An Archaeology of Identity

use across most types of site indicated by the data illustrated here, in practices that had at least something to do with 'exchange', had significance in terms of perceived relationships between individuals or individual communities and the empire. The state clearly imposed considerable symbolic capital onto coins, with propagandist reverse types such as the *Fel Temp Reparatio* issues ('the restoration of happy times' [Casey 1984: 20]), and changes in the range of contexts of use and discard of such coins must entail different perceptions of them as cultural objects with specific associations (cf. Butcher 2001: 22). In other words, the value of such messages may have diminished with that of the coins. Furthermore, the apparent increase in the rate of turnover of coin issues in the later 3rd and 4th centuries represents some change in the temporal relationship of individuals to the empire. This might be seen as a partial breakdown in the eternal image of the empire when compared to individual lifespans, previously represented by old coins remaining valuable decades after their production.

These themes will be pursued further in Chapter 5, but the fact that coins were part of specific practices does serve to indicate that the larger-scale, aggregate patterns presented above are likely to be meaningful in terms of continuity, change, and identity. These seem to indicate that a mixture of factors governed the formation of a coin assemblage over time: regionality, site type, periods of occupation, and nature of coin use. To take one of the clearer patterns as an example, some forts/fortresses stand out (along with certain sites near to them) as being distinctive in the early Roman period, with an 'unusual' pattern of coin use compared to other sites—though this disappeared later on. This 'functional' pattern is accompanied by a 'historical' one, relating to the apparently early abandonment of many of the western fort sites; those like Caernarfon, with a more continuous occupation history, have quite different profiles, as do those established later in other areas. The dispositions of these sites, and their relationships with neighbouring ones, adds a 'regional' dimension—differences between the west, north, and southeast. Finally, variation in the level of coin use, particularly in the 4th century, can be detected by comparing sites (such as Housesteads, Caernarfon, and York) that have different coinage patterns but comparable stratigraphic sequences. Other notable phenomena revealed in these aggregate lists include some grouping of rural sites and divergent town profiles (cf. Reece 1993b: 864), as well as a marked westward shift in later coin deposition in southern Britain (cf. Reece 1995: 197). All of these amplify the impression from the analysis of the 4th century contexts of coin finds that coin use and discard were quite variable practices across the temporal and spatial span of Roman Britain. As such, they offered considerable potential for the dynamic negotiation of different identities.

To turn to the other major category of material culture where higher-resolution data are available, the patterns observed for small finds in the previous chapter can be given a fuller chronological context too. Aspects of the depositional chronology of certain types of objects were considered to some extent in the previous chapter, but here this can be given fuller attention by breaking down the functional categories of artefacts found at selected sites according to their stratigraphic phasing. To show how this method of comparison can work with a familiar example, the first site illustrated is Caernarfon. The weighting of the assemblage towards the later Roman period noted in the analysis of the kinds of contexts in which finds occurred is confirmed here (Fig. 4.13). Importantly, these later deposits included some typologically early objects, such as a 2nd century brooch in Phase 10A (Cat. No. 6 [Allason-Jones 1993: 166]). The question of whether this is residuality or prolonged use remains a difficult one to resolve, as contemporary objects were also found in contexts of this period. The 'Roman Gates' excavation in Caerleon (Evans and Metcalf 1992 [Fig. 4.14]) provides a different perspective, where the assemblage is spread across a broader range of periods. This is partly because there was a good deal of construction activity in the 2nd century. What is notable here is that the relative proportions of material—some 'military', some personalia, many 'fittings'—remained quite consistent throughout the site's history, perhaps indicating consistent patterns of use of different kinds of objects, and thus the continued importance of certain kinds of activities.

Some further light on this, as well as on the relationship between use and deposition, is shed by the data from the Blackfriars Street site in Carlisle, a major military town on the northern frontier (McCarthy 1990 [Fig. 4.15]). This has a mixture of tightly stratified groups (e.g., Period 3), and some sizeable ones that must be residual (Periods 15 and 18). Here, though, it is possible to match increases in artefact numbers within the Roman period with major construction and abandonment episodes. In Period 3, for instance, structures fronting a road were rebuilt, while in Period 8, there was a hiatus in occupation before new structures were again erected. This means that the deposition of material for building make-up, and the dumping of rubbish in open areas, were probably the main sources of artefacts; the objects themselves may thus represent a fairly random sample of things in use and circulation at these points— including some that were dropped or discarded long ago, some that had remained in use for some time, and some that were quite new.

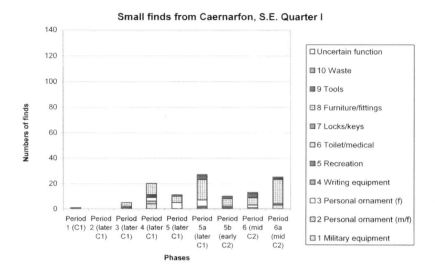

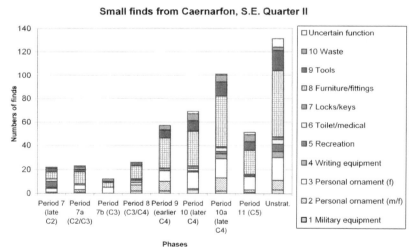

Figure 4.13. Small finds patterns through time: Caernarfon (data from Allason-Jones 1993; Allen 1993: 226–8; Coulston 1993: 214).

The potential mixing of objects in this way, already observed at other sites, is a significant obstacle to interpretation of the presence of particular identity groups at any particular period. However, a new element here is the consistency of patterns of functional distribution over time, and this offers hope that different cycles and circumstances of deposition do not unduly compromise the overall picture of the range of activities happening on the site.

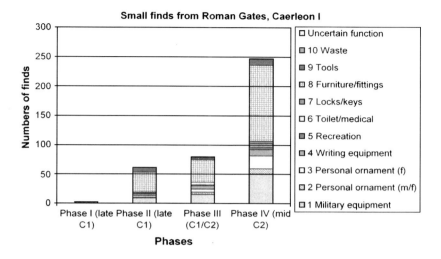

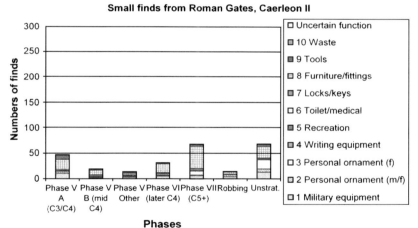

Figure 4.14. Small finds patterns through time: Caerleon (data from Webster et al. 1992).

This picture is confirmed by another familiar site, of a different kind to the examples just cited: Orton Hall Farm (Fig. 4.16). The profile of small finds deposition over time shows both consistency in the dominant functional categories represented, and a relationship with the more intensive phases of site construction and activity—such as Period 3—as well as some bias towards the latest phases. However, it is important to note that this bias is not sufficient to compromise the integrity of the earlier phases, and does not carry quite the same implication of increased 4th century deposition as seems to have been

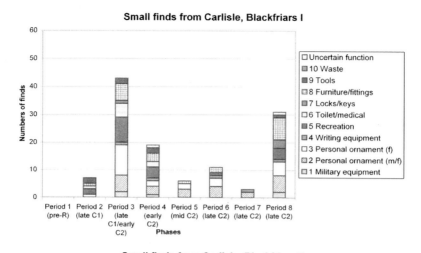

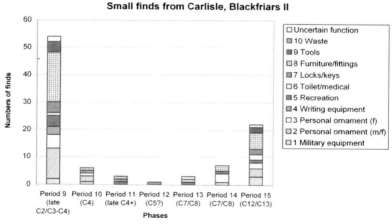

Figure 4.15. Small finds patterns through time: Carlisle (data from Caruana 1990: 105–62).

common for coins. This much can be confirmed by a breakdown of the coins found on the site by phase (Fig. 4.17). This shows the same degree of likelihood that early coins would end up in later contexts as was noted previously at other sites. The contrast with the small finds pattern here means that the increased turnover of coins in the 4th century, as already discussed, is likely to be a real phenomenon and not simply a product of residuality or other post-depositional transformations. While small finds certainly occur in late or unstratified contexts, and will have included old artefacts, there are signs—at least from this site—that they were being deposited more evenly throughout

THE TEMPORAL DIMENSIONS OF 4TH CENTURY LIFE ■ 155

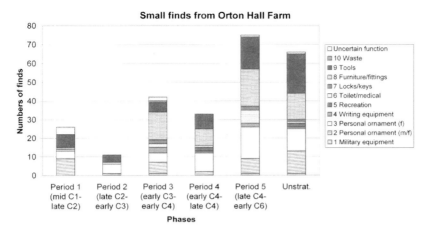

Figure 4.16. Small finds patterns through time: Orton Hall Farm (data from Mackreth 1996: 92–102).

Issue Periods	1 mC1-lC2	2 lC2-mC3	3 mC3-eC4	4 eC4-lC4	5 lC4-eC6	U/S	No prov.
1							
2						1	
3							
4					1		
5							
6			1				
7						1	
8			1			1	
9						1	
10							
11							
12						1	
13					2	1	2
14			2		2	6	1
15							
16							1
17			1	1	5	5	2
18					1	1	1
19					3	3	1
20						1	
21					1	1	
?			1		1	9	

Note: 1 coin in ?/U-S is missing from list – may be period 14.

Figure 4.17. Table of coin deposition through time at Orton Hall Farm (data from Esmonde Cleary 1996).

156 ■ An Archaeology of Identity

the profile, and in consistent functional assemblages. This supports the notion that the practices within which they were engaged were much more stable than those of coin use.

Overall, then, taking this broader temporal perspective on small finds deposition shows that although for several sites the later Roman period produced the largest deposits, they do not necessarily differ in composition from previous phases. The occurrence of finds in contexts much later than their date of manufacture is of course a persistent phenomenon, which can be accounted for either in terms of redeposition of refuse or of prolonged use of the artefacts themselves. At some sites, it is certainly possible to suggest that refuse dumping within an excavated area is likely to derive from occupation elsewhere, and may include quite old material—as at Blackfriars Street in Carlisle. At others, it is equally possible to suggest that old objects were still being used, as we saw is probably the case in mid-4th century Birdoswald (analysed in detail in Chapter 3). Taking object typologies into account is also important, and generally speaking these change at a much slower rate than coins. Many types, in fact, are difficult to date with precision—hence the lack of detailed analysis of this aspect of the data here—and a cycle of change of around a century in duration, covering the introduction, use, and obscelence of particular styles has been suggested by Hilary Cool (2000). The even greater longevity of some broad object styles, such as penannular brooches, that might span the whole Roman period (Barker et al. 1997: 211) can be taken to support the notion that artefacts of considerable antiquity might remain in use for a long time.

It has also become clear that the consistent overall pattern of functional categories from different types of sites is robust over time (cf. Cooper 2000: 82–5). Although exceptions to this can often be related to particular depositional environments, it would seem that a similar range of objects—at a very coarse-grained level—were in use on sites of different 'types' throughout the Roman period. While this means that 'appearing' and certain other practices were important in communities of all types, it also means that there are no easy distinctions between specific identity groups at this level. Even though 'military' objects, for example, might be more common within fort sites, they do occur on rural settlements (during all periods) and in towns. At the latter, and indeed in forts, it is often the case that many of these objects cannot be dated with precision, and therefore a given general percentage of 'military' objects need not reflect conditions in any particular period—such as the 4th century, when some have suggested towns had more of a military population (e.g., Faulkner 2000: 167–8).

Beyond such general statements, it becomes a question of whether finds of very specific types within other categories (e.g., crossbow brooches) are of significance in marking out particular identity groups. This is indeed likely to be the case within a basically homogenous suite of material culture.

We have already noted how some such subcategories of objects have been given 'official' or other statuses, particularly based upon studies of continental burial evidence (Swift 2000: 45–52, 99–117), although we also saw some of the pitfalls of these identifications with the example of Oudenburg. From a more temporal perspective, the association between specific find types and identities also has to be questioned. The presence or absence of certain artefacts on a particular site does not necessarily allow the occupation at that site to be characterised straightforwardly as 'official', 'military', 'civilian', or anything else. Crossbow brooches, for instance, certainly occur on town as well as fort sites (e.g., Wroxeter [Barker et al. 1997: 209]). Such objects can relate to the activities of certain individuals who moved through a settlement, or stayed there only for a short time, and not necessarily to the whole community living there on a more permanent basis. This reminds us of the problems with making easy associations between artefacts and communities, and defines some of the limits of what can be inferred from assemblages. Nonetheless, we have so far observed some differences in the temporal dynamics of assemblages of coins and small finds, and begun to link these to the practices that were discussed in the previous chapter. This process can be continued with the finds relating to eating.

Pottery and animal bone

The patterns of pottery supply in the 4th century that we looked at in Chapter 3 can readily be given a temporal perspective by comparing developments within this period with earlier phases of activity. Unfortunately, the examples used previously do not have sufficient differentiation within the 4th century to give us much leverage on changes over time, so different examples will be used here—though again representative of forts, farms, and towns.

Although the published groups from Birdoswald exclude the major imported Samian ware, the changes between different phases are indicative of the range of local and nonlocal fabrics used at different times (Fig. 4.18). Here, local wares were important to begin with, then were gradually superseded by pottery from further afield in the 3rd and early 4th centuries, especially BB1 from Dorset. This was a

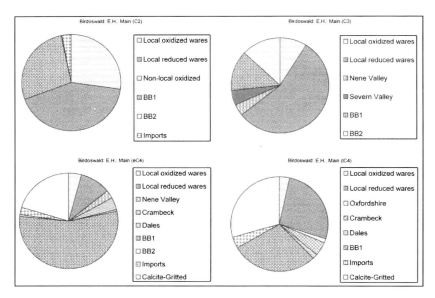

Figure 4.18. Pottery supply through time: Birdoswald (coarseware percentages by weight, C2 = 2nd century etc.; data from Wilmott 1997: 234).

very widespread ware right up the western side of Britain. In the later 4th century, though, the emphasis was more localised again, with northern regional fabrics (particularly calcite-gritted wares) being more important. This pattern is representative of many other military sites, such as South Shields and Caerleon (Bidwell and Speak 1994; Greep 1986), but also—on a smaller scale—of farms. The small site of Llandough, a putative 'villa' in southern Wales (Owen-John 1988 [Fig. 4.19]), clearly experienced a decrease in the diversity of available wares in the 4th century (BB1 being a relatively local ware here). At Cirencester (Fig. 4.20), also in western Britain but a major town, the diversity of wares is certainly greater than at Llandough, but the patterns of change are similar: the rise of certain big, widespread industries, followed by a contraction to more localised supply in the 4th century, including versions of shell-tempered fabrics from the South Midlands similar to the calcite-gritted wares of the north.

While these examples represent only a very small sample of the pottery information available for British sites, they offer some interesting information when put together with other material and examined in terms of processes of transformation. It is clear that in spite of the differences observed earlier between forts and towns on the one hand, and farms on the other, locally produced ceramics were generally

THE TEMPORAL DIMENSIONS OF 4TH CENTURY LIFE ■ 159

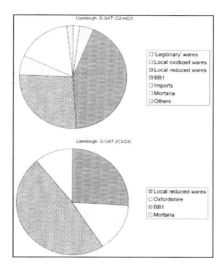

Figure 4.19. Pottery supply through time: Llandough (coarseware vessel percentages; data from Hartley 1988: 171; Webster, P.V. 1988).

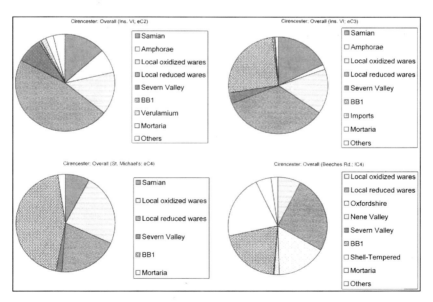

Figure 4.20. Pottery supply through time: Cirencester (Estimated Vessel Equivalent percentages; data from Cooper 1998).

the mainstay of pottery supply through time. While this might have an 'economic' explanation in terms of transport costs or exchange networks, I think it also has important implications for foci of identification—which were primarily local or, at most, regional—and this applies to communities inhabiting sites of all kinds. At the same time, these communities were part of a more general and perhaps abstract community of practice across Roman Britain, where forms in different fabrics were often similar (BB1 and Samian forms were widely copied, for instance), or certain trends were followed across a number of production centres (there are several different calcite-gritted/ shell-tempered wares in the later 4th century, making products in the same forms [Tyers 1996: 74–8]). Forts and towns also have something in common beyond this pattern: the greater diversity of wares available in the mid-Roman period. While again unsurprising from a 'commercial' point of view (these are bigger population centres), this potentially makes these ostensibly different 'military' and 'civilian' sites quite similar with respect to the lifestyles of the people inhabiting them. However, even more telling is that on sites of all types, the predominant trend over time—particularly within the 4th century in particular—is toward the more local and regional fabrics, where even the successful South Midlands shell-tempered ware did not match the earlier distribution of BB1. This implies a dynamic tension between the local and the more global patterns in the ceramic industry.

This pattern can be amplified somewhat if we look to animal bone as a source of evidence for what was consumed in these vessels, although chronological variation within the 4th century is difficult to pin down from the currently available data. The three sites illustrated earlier are merely put into a longer-term perspective here, therefore, with the addition of one other example that shows how a more anomalous depositional context can be evident in such assemblages (Fig. 4.21). This is Caerleon, where at the fortress baths, there is clearly evidence for the provision of chicken as a snack food for construction workers engaged in building the complex (O'Connor 1986: 225–9). This apparently continued as a practice for the baths' users in the 2nd century, but the dumping of cattle butchery refuse became a factor from the 3rd century, and pig was an important component of the 4th century deposits with a slight decline in cattle. This is interesting, bearing in mind what was said about the importance of pig as a possible military preference earlier; cattle has also been given this association, although less distinctively so by the 4th century (Stallibrass 2000: 71). What this means about the occupation of later Roman Caerleon is a matter to consider later. The increasing importance of cattle over time at

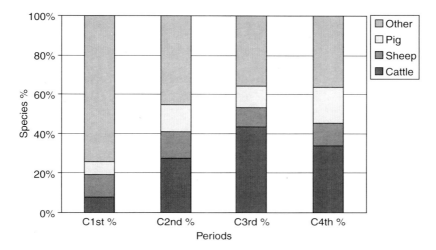

Figure 4.21. Animal bone patterns through time: Caerleon (M.N.I. data from O'Connor 1986).

another fort site is demonstrated at Caernarfon (Fig. 4.22), although again pig was important.

An example of a town site is provided by Lincoln (Fig. 4.23), where the 4th century again had a higher degree of cattle dominance than earlier periods, when sheep were more important. Almost more significant than the proportions here is the fact that the 4th century assemblage indicated large-scale organised butchery, taken by one of the specialists working on this material as indicative of both a significant late Roman population and a considerable degree of organisation (Dobney 2001: 44). These are important points to which we will return below, as changes to the use of spaces at a range of other sites also involve large-scale butchery. Finally, and turning again to the farmstead of Orton Hall Farm, this was also clearly reliant on cattle more than any other species (Fig. 4.24), but again its importance fluctuated somewhat.

Overall, these examples show that different types of sites were part of a broadly similar pattern of meat consumption in the Roman period. While the increasing preference for cattle is often associated with growing 'Romanisation', this clearly did not proceed at an even pace; nonetheless, it provides an important background pattern that might have formed a salient degree of common practice between different communities, especially in the 4th century. It is important to note, though, that within this pattern there are some variations, and each site illustrated here has an individual trend. One cannot read too much into these variations, given the potential for problems with the

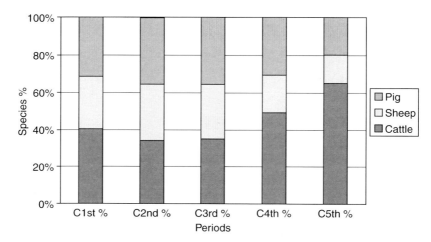

Figure 4.22. Animal bone patterns through time: Caernarfon (M.N.I. data from Casey et al. 1993: 76–8; Noddle 1993).

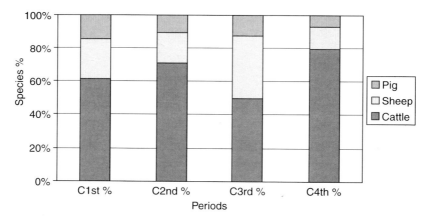

Figure 4.23. Animal bone patterns through time: Lincoln (fragment count data from Dobney et al. 1995: 20–61, 132–3).

comparability of quantified bone data, but like the stability of the pig preference at at least some military sites over time (cf. King 1999b: 169–73, 183), these small changes may have been meaningful. They do at least serve to indicate that, as recent work on very important aspects of the data such as the structure of herds and butchery methods is also beginning to indicate (Stallibrass 2000), local circumstances of supply played some role in the precise combinations of meat consumed at individual sites.

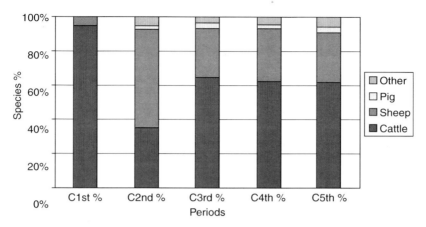

Figure 4.24. Animal bone patterns through time: Orton Hall Farm (bone number data from King 1996).

To summarise these patterns in relation to eating habits is difficult without much further work on both ceramic and faunal assemblages, not to mention botanical remains and other kinds of serving equipment such as glassware. Fortunately, this is a growing area of research (e.g., Cool 2004a; Evans 2001; Hawkes 2002; Stallibrass 2000). From what we have looked at here and in Chapter 3, a couple of key points can be made, however. The comparisons of pottery supply place the emphasis on localised supply to sites of all types, albeit with forts and towns more likely to have greater numbers of extra-regional imports. This pattern is visible throughout the Roman period, though with some shifting dynamics over time. In the 4th century, especially later on, there were several strong regional sources of pottery supply, with the widely popular wares of earlier periods (like Samian or BB1) disappearing or contracting somewhat in their distribution, even if their forms remained influential across Britain. New centres for the production of calcite- or shell-gritted fabrics emerged, but these—along with the existing regional industries (e.g., Oxfordshire)—were always an addition to the even more locally produced wares that appear on all sites, particularly in reduced fabrics (cf. Tyers 1996: 75–8). There are also some ethnically distinctive fabrics within this localised pattern, such as the short-lived 'Frisian' ware at Housesteads (Jobey 1979; Tyers 1996: 76–7). Thus, the consumption of ceramics had different local, regional, and supra-regional dimensions, which interacted in different ways over time.

The same picture emerges from the evidence of faunal assemblages. Again, small-scale variation between sites is visible, relating to

164 ■ AN ARCHAEOLOGY OF IDENTITY

some localised diversity in practices throughout the Roman period. Beyond this, cattle are clearly the majority species on most sites—although more variation might be expected on rural sites in the more marginal parts of Roman Britain, such as the north (Stallibrass 1995: 134). While a cattle-dominated diet has been associated with the arrival of the Roman military in Britain (King 1999b: 178–83), the sheep-dominated nature of the late Iron Age diet may have been overemphasised by earlier researchers (Grant 1989: 136–7). Moreover, the proportion of cattle on individual sites fluctuates, in some cases declining slightly in the 4th century. While such broad patterns cross-cut site types, a preference for pig as the secondary species to cattle does seem to be a phenomenon largely restricted to fort-type settlements and persists through time. It is increasingly being recognised by archaeozoologists that the animals consumed in Roman Britain were primarily being supplied from the immediate hinterland of sites, rather than transported over long distances (Grant 1989: 137–40; Stallibrass 2000: 71), and they were commonly slaughtered at the point of consumption. This is one factor behind the small, local variations in site consumption patterns. Like the pottery patterns, this factor indicates a tension between global and local 'norms', that may have been increasing in the 4th century. Locally variable practices—linked to fundamentally local supply mechanisms—existed within broader (regional and 'British') patterns of similarity. These shifted over time, mixing diverse late Iron Age traditions with those from other parts of the empire (especially the other northwestern provinces), but most importantly allowing for a diverse range of scales of social identification. The implications of these will be our concern in the next chapter.

Artefacts, time, and biography in Roman Britain

In the foregoing sections, a considerable range of material culture has been surveyed, including artefacts rarely considered in histories of Roman Britain. A number of patterns—at a variety of scales—have emerged in the evidence of coinage, ceramics, faunal remains, and small finds, and these will be more fully explored and integrated in Chapter 5. Here I will attempt to summarise briefly the major points that have emerged and suggest how they might relate to the temporal dimension of structuration.

The relatively high resolution of the coin data examined above enabled a range of regional, historical, typological, and archaeological patterns to be identified. The possibility of variation in the use of coins was detected in different regions and periods. In addition, a balance between local and regional factors in the supply and use of ceramics was identified, as well as a background commonality of practice across the British provinces, based on common forms influenced particularly by the very widespread industries of earlier times (such as Samian and BB1). A similar balance or tension was found in animal bone patternings, along with a more specific trend relating to the persistent degree of pork consumption at a number of fort sites. A consistent relationship between proportions of functional small finds categories at a number of sites was also established. All of these types of artefacts can be linked to specific practices (from eating to exchanging) and the analyses of coins and small finds in Chapter 3 demonstrated how—even though such artefacts are mainly found in contexts related to rubbish disposal—there are still grounds for believing that context-level artefact distributions *can* indicate something of the nature of activities in particular areas of sites, and therefore of the changing pattern of activities in such areas. This is the case even as the artefacts themselves are sufficiently diverse to make the characterisation of whole site communities in terms of simple identities (like 'military' or 'civilian') rather more difficult than is usually thought.

Through all of these material studies, the temporal characteristics of artefacts have frequently been significant—the dates of manufacture or deposition of objects, and, related somehow to these, the time when they were in use. The problem remains of how to relate these dates and times to the practices of human agents, and how to understand the temporalities of these practices themselves, which are likely to have been of central importance in the construction of different kinds of identity. This takes us back to the relationship between measured and experienced time discussed above, and how these ideas need to be unified within the frame of human action. The measurement of time used in the analysis of artefacts in this chapter is undoubtedly 'our' time, rather than that of the people living in the communities of Roman Britain, but it does bear some relationship to that experience in the sense that we are able to discern when things changed quickly or slowly, and how long traditions of practice persisted. We are also able to gain some insights into the measured time of these people: the coinage, for instance, does not bear the dates of emperors in the abstract 'years AD' formula that we use, but relates the passage of time to more embedded social phenomena—e.g., the titles of the emperor, his achievements, and other significant events of the past (sometimes quite distant, such as the founding of Rome) or future. More material that relates to this theme will be discussed below, when we consider textual narratives

166 ■ An Archaeology of Identity

of continuity and change, but here we have already seen some of the potentially divergent temporalities of material practices—as in the increasing tempo of coin discard in the 4th century, at a time when many other small objects were being used in quite traditional ways, or the gradual cycles of change in pottery supplies.

While mundane when discussed in material terms, the fixity or fluidity of these kinds of patterns relates fundamentally to the negotiation of identities. Indeed, it is through this relationship that artefacts and places can be said to have narrative biographies similar to those of people, as discussed above (cf. Hodder 1993b: 268–70). It is very difficult to extract individual object biographies from the great number of artefactual 'life-stories' that accompany the aggregates of material culture that have been our main concern here. This is not, though, too serious an obstacle to the exploration of the part these artefacts play in the lives of past human actors. On the contrary, I would argue that although I have only begun in this chapter to draw out some of their meanings, the variety of similarities and differences between patterns of different scales encountered above suggests that artefactual biographies *can* be aggregated in terms of human biographies, precisely because they are part of human *social* agency. The relationship between things and people is formed through the regularities of practices at a particular place, which fits with the notion that shared meanings—such as those relating to social identities— derive from repeated practices. At the same time, there is sufficient variation to allow for the ways in which these meanings can be changed and contested. In this fashion, the aggregations quickly transform the objects of analysis from biographies of things into biographies of places, and then into biographies of people acting in relation to each other in those places. The first of these transformations will be our concern in the next section.

Biographies of places

Spaces in use

Having discussed the material parameters of built space in the previous chapter, it is now time to consider the changing ways in which those spaces were used throughout the 4th century. Assigning functional interpretations to spaces—even in the very general terms of public/official and private/domestic used so far—is always difficult, and as with artefacts 'function', must be interpreted broadly. Here, therefore, I will look at dimensions such as the negotiation of social status, which are as much a part of the ongoing practices of 'dwelling' in a particular place as any more technically defined purpose like sleeping or food preparation. In paying attention to how these practices changed over time, I will not only consider changes and continuities within the late Roman period, but also highlight how these compare with the phases preceding it. After considering how some spaces were used, I will turn in the next section to look at stratigraphic features commonly described as pertaining to 'disuse'. It will become clear, however, that this is an inappropriate term for an activity—refuse disposal—that was an important, if changing, part of the life of all Roman-period settlements. Actual abandonment, and how this is best described and understood, will also be considered at this point as a phenomenon that occurs throughout the history of Roman Britain, and not just at the period's 'end'.

In the last chapter, the broad distinction between between public and private uses of space was deployed without much critical attention. However, this division requires some further examination, as it is a major axis of change in the 4th century. There are some kinds of buildings that seem to cross the boundary between these categories by their very nature. Some of these are a factor of archaeological imprecision in the understanding of material culture, as is the case with many rectilinear rural settlements in northern England (Collingwood 1931; Greene 1978), which have long been controversial: are they fortlets or farms? As the finds evidence is inconclusive in most cases, it is difficult for us to answer this question. Other kinds of structure are ambiguous because of past overlaps in status, as in the case of official houses like *praetoria* (or indeed barracks) or buildings interpreted as *mansiones* (inns, such as in the extramural area at Chester [Mason 1980]). In the latter case, the interpretation is usually based on a combination of form (courtyard building) and scale (size taken to imply official involvement). These are buildings and spaces with a use that either combined official and private functions in the past, or in which the finds and formal qualities cannot be used to differentiate their status in the present. In the 4th century, it seems that this ambiguity becomes more commonplace across formerly clear-cut 'public' and 'private' spaces, as several examples can be used to demonstrate.

If we take the category of administrative buildings first, the *fora* of towns and the *principia* of forts, there are many interesting patterns over time. Of course individual structures at different sites will always have their own idiosyncracies across the whole of the Roman period. At several, though, there are more dramatic transformations in the late Roman period. In some places, this amounts to what has been described as decommissioning—in the *principia* at Caerleon, for

168 ■ An Archaeology of Identity

instance (apparently demolished at the end of the 3rd century [Boon 1970])—or at least a reduction in the range of original functions, as in the *basilica* at Caerwent (with a progressive process of demolition and industrial use through the mid-4th century [Brewer and Guest forthcoming]). Other alterations are less substantial but equally important: the in-filling of the *aedes* (shrine) cellar and of the heating system in the *principia* annexe at Caernarfon; subdivisions of the *principia* structure at Housesteads; and new, fairly temporary structures in the *fora* at Leicester and Wroxeter (Atkinson 1942; Bosanquet 1904; Hebditch and Mellor 1973; Wheeler 1924). At York and South Shields, and indeed at Cirencester, the alterations to some of the partitioning and access arrangements in the central building have been interpreted as increasing the exclusiveness of authority, with more restricted admission to still grandiose official buildings (Bidwell and Speak 1994; Holbrook and Timby 1998a: 113–121; Phillips and Heywood 1995a; cf. Bidwell 1996: 7). At many of the other examples noted here, though, it is possible that public space is being subdivided and appropriated for other, unofficial and private purposes—or perhaps authority adapted to local conditions—representing significant changes in regionalisation.

Horrea at Birdoswald and South Shields also underwent changes, though the modifications to the former (already referred to in Chapter 3) are perhaps more significant than the conversion of some of the latter to barracks, since other store buildings remained in use at South Shields. At Birdoswald, alterations in the nature of supply and/or storage arrangements must be inferred from the excavated sequence, indicating both the decommissioning of the *horrea* as stores and the conversion of one of them to domestic uses (Wilmott 1997: 220). Building XV at Housesteads may be a similar case, with a bath suite inserted in around AD 300 (Leach and Wilkes 1962). The addition of baths here is notable, and while we have already seen that this kind of structure was still popular at some sites in the 4th century, there are examples of abandonment too. Caerleon has already been mentioned in this regard, and after the baths were disused, small structures were built in the surrounding portico (Zienkiewicz 1986a, 1986b). Very similar changes have been noted at Binchester, after a phase when the private officers' baths were apparently opened up to a wider public in the early 4th century; Canterbury in mid-century; and Wroxeter in the late 4th/early 5th centuries (Barker et al. 1997; Blockley et al. 1995a; Ferris and Jones 1991; Frere and Stow 1983: 27–40). Clearly, this kind of change was a phenomenon specific to some sites and not others, meaning that the range of amenities available in individual settlements was increasingly disparate.

Other types of public or official building also underwent changes, though in some cases their exact significance is unclear. Several good examples come from Chester. The amphitheatre here has little sign of post-3rd century use (also the case at Caerleon), and as with those places where baths were abandoned, this is notable given the quite specific practices of corporate entertainment and perhaps training associated with this kind of structure (Newstead and Droop 1932). A group of buildings near the *principia* have more complex sequences. The unique 'elliptical building' (see Fig. 3.23 [Newstead and Droop 1939; Petch 1978: 17–22]) is actually an element of continuity in the site's structural history. Planned but not completed in the late 1st century, it was finally finished in the early 3rd and used into the late 4th, along with an adjacent bath block (Mason 1996). However, the building immediately to its north—and the very large structure north of the *principia*—were both subdivided in the 4th century, with hearths being set up, while the *horrea* in the southwestern part of the fort seem to have been demolished in the later 3rd century (Petch 1978: 17–22; Petch and Thomson 1959; Strickland 1982). The late Roman uses of these buildings must have been quite different from those of earlier periods. Examples of other large enclosures, with various functions, which underwent fairly major changes in the 4th century can be found at sites like Canterbury (including floors and hearths on top of a probable temple plaza), Wroxeter, and Cirencester (Bennett 1978: 275–7; Bushe-Fox 1916; Holbrook 1998). Again, therefore, structural adaptation is a widespread phenomenon across some—but not all—forts, fortresses, and towns.

Turning now to patterns of change in domestic architecture, we begin with those that also had some 'official' status, as referred to above. Small-scale alterations, rebuildings, and other structure-specific developments are of course to be expected in houses throughout their lives. The immediate concern in comparison with public buildings, however, is to see whether there are any *patterns* of change in the later Roman period. Looking at *praetoria* in forts, it is notable that detailed excavated sequences are not common. At Housesteads, however, occupation in the 4th century was recorded in a reduced and heavily modified part of the courtyard house complex, and the under-floor heating system was filled in (Charlesworth 1975). The same developments have also been found at Binchester and South Shields—even though the latter structure was newly built at the beginning of

170 ■ An Archaeology of Identity

the 4th century, with strong Mediterranean affinities (Ferris and Jones 1991; Hodgson 1996). Unfortunately, little detailed information is available on the large courtyard building known at Piercebridge, nor of possibly similar buildings such as one at Caister-on-Sea (Darling and Gurney 1993). Nonetheless, the few sequences there are point to physical changes to this particular kind of locale, by the late 4th century, which are likely to have undermined previous distinctions in the regionalisation of space between those living in the *praetorium* and the rest of the fort's population. This might be even more the case in those forts with similarly subdivided domestic spaces—the 'chalet' barracks.

With town houses, it is more difficult to generalise, and again there are surprising limitations to the number of coherently excavated and/or recorded examples. The largely 4th century plan of Caerwent is certainly dominated by courtyard buildings, at least some having developed from multiple strip buildings. Detailed information on the various phases, however, is lacking. At Carlisle, the best-known structures at Blackfriars Street and Castle Street remained essentially strip plan throughout their history—though not all were occupied in the 4th century (McCarthy 1990, 1991). A great range of structural histories are represented in the houses of towns like Canterbury, Cirencester, Leicester, Lincoln, and Wroxeter. As a couple of examples, at the Marlowe Car Park sites in Canterbury (Blockley et al. 1995a), some of the houses in the area excavated were disused from early in the 4th century—their sites accumulating 'dark earth'—while others were being modified and rebuilt, one with new private baths. Although few houses have actually been excavated at Wroxeter, one of those recorded by Bushe-Fox (1913) and that dug by Kenyon (1980) were both occupied through the 4th century with minor alterations. The histories of these buildings are likely to represent the localised concerns of their (private) owners, as well as developments in the wider settlement. The evidence described above that *praetoria* have similarly individual patterns of change in the 4th century is potentially important.

Indeed, there is overlap in a different direction visible at some 4th century locations—between town houses and farms. This is not just evident in the sense of formal similarities between some large town houses and villas, which had been evident in earlier periods, but more in the functional sense of the potential for farming activity in town buildings. This has been raised with respect to structures like those at the Beeches Road site in Cirencester, described in the excavation report as an 'urban farm', partly on the basis of finds evidence as well as a 'barn'-like structure accompanying the main houses (McWhirr

1986: 77–8). It is also relevant to the problem of interpreting the build-ups of 'dark earth' over some disused urban structures (see below). As with all of the above changes, though, an essential problem is whether these kinds of ambiguity were recognisable or important to different social groups living in or around such structures. The extent to which the regionalisation of space is only partly a factor of its built component is important to stress here; it also depends upon what people *do* in a space. Even though changes in official buildings seem to create formally similar environments to some houses, their influence on social practices must be considered. We can, however, get further with this in many of the cases discussed here, where the stratigraphic and artefactual information permits meaningful interpretation of real ambiguities—compared to cases like the rectilinear settlements of the north mentioned above, where the ambiguity is simply uninterpretable from current evidence.

To summarise some of the main characteristics of spaces that seem to change in the 4th century, across the different types so far discussed, a key feature that perhaps indicates the appropriation of official space for more private—or even domestic—use is subdivision into smaller, more independent units. This happens in Binchester's baths, for example, and the Housesteads *praetorium* (Charlesworth 1975; Ferris and Jones 1980, 1991). In many of these cases (Binchester again being one), there are also signs, often from dumps of waste material (see below), that 'industrial' practices such as metalworking or livestock slaughter have replaced other functions. It is true that this kind of change could occur in earlier phases of the Roman period (happening at Chester in the 2nd century, for example, in the vicinity of the *principia* and *praetorium* [Matthews 1995]). Moreover, even in the 4th century, there are places where changes in plan form are associated with a change in nature (a seclusion) of official status, rather than its diminution—as in the *principia* at York and the *forum basilica* at Cirencester (Holbrook and Timby 1998a: 113–21; Phillips and Heywood 1995a; Wacher 1964: 9–14); it is also the case that 'industrial' activity may still be officially—even militarily—organised (cf. Faulkner 2000: 126–30). Nonetheless, the regionalisation of what had been planned as homogenous kinds of 'official' built space clearly diversified over time, at a local level, and this certainly happened more commonly from the end of the 3rd century than previously.

Other specific structural changes have also been referred to, including the in-filling of hypocaust systems, both in some baths and in other kinds of building where they were used for heating. To those examples mentioned above, we could add some of the barracks at

172 ■ AN ARCHAEOLOGY OF IDENTITY

South Shields (Bidwell and Speak 1994); the St. George's Street Baths in Canterbury (Frere and Stow 1983); and houses at Saltergate in Lincoln (Colyer and Jones 1979: 84–8). In all of these cases, the hypocausts had only been inserted earlier in the 4th century. It is not suggested here that the reasons for these changes need be the same across this wide spectrum of different places. Nonetheless, this phenomenon does seem to be another important element in the constellation of structural changes taking place across Roman Britain in the 4th century. From these kinds of alterations to the plan or structure of particular buildings, some understanding of changing circumstances of co-presence and regionalisation can be reached, either in terms of the privatisation of some spaces or the abandonment of particular practices of heating others. Other spaces, however, remained official or in use for practices like bathing, so there is no consistent pattern—more one of increasing localised variation in what spaces were in use, and for what purposes. One other repetitive practice has been mentioned in connection with some of the changes discussed in this section, and this needs to be considered in more depth as potentially adding considerably to understanding how uses of space changed. This is the disposal of rubbish.

Disposal, disuse, and dwelling

Before evaluating the evidence for changing refuse disposal practices in Roman Britain, it is necessary to address briefly the concept of 'rubbish' itself. Although a theme of some interest to processually oriented archaeologists, in the context of site formation processes and ethnoarchaeology (e.g., Rathje 1992), recent approaches to the meaningful use of material culture have tended to neglect the meaning of waste (exceptions include Lindenlauf 2004; Moore 1986). What 'rubbish theory' there is fits into ideas about tackling the issue of value (Thompson 1979; cf. Kopytoff 1986). This work is indeed important, though its emphasis is primarily on objects as rubbish rather than on the cultural life of middens and other deposits of mixed materials. The former is relevant to our understanding of some of the practices involving the coins and small finds discussed in Chapter 3, particularly when considering whether some change in value categories can be associated with the apparently increased deposition of material in the late Roman period. It is equally essential, however, to understand the significance attached to the dumping of quantities of pottery- and/or bone-rich earth in different places in the 4th century. Certainly, ideas about cultural standards of cleanliness have structured interpretation of some sites in the late Roman period (e.g., Caerleon and Portchester [Boon 1972: 67–9; Cunliffe 1975: 423–8]). Any re-evaluation of the ways in which archaeological deposits relate to changing living practices at these or other sites must, therefore, turn a critical eye to the problem of whether such standards existed at all.

As will be shown, the evidence actually suggests that the spatial organisation of waste disposal was fairly loose at most sites across Britain throughout the Roman period. This does not mean, though, that rubbish disposal was not highly structured conceptually. As Thompson has argued (1979: 1–4), social groups may have very strict discursive standards of cleanliness—observed in many contexts of routine practice—while seemingly ignoring unconcealed and prolific dumping of certain kinds of waste. Thus, a 'squalid' occupation of a building may not seem so to those living in it. Before looking at this theme in more depth, it is worth noting the kinds of things that count as rubbish in this context, and the methods that were used for their disposal. The normal assumption is that everything found as material culture on Roman-period sites—all the categories of artefacts discussed so far—ended their lives as generalised 'rubbish'. While this may be largely true, it obscures some of the variation in artefact biographies referred to above, particularly the potential for objects to spend some time as 'antiques'. It also implies that objects dumped in a heap or buried in a pit—two of the major methods of disposal—had lost all significance, even though there is a range of evidence for the persistence of ritual disposal in Roman Britain (e.g., Poulton and Scott 1993), and rubbish-bearing deposits were frequently used in construction activities. Such practices imply a distinctive cultural attitude to waste that is worth exploring.

To survey this sphere of practice in the earlier parts of Romano-British history, there is a wide range of evidence to suggest that many sites had their 'squalid' areas. Both pits and dumps were used at sites of different types, and while extramural areas were used for the deposition of rubbish at times when enclosed settlements were fully occupied, any 'vacant lots' within such sites were certainly used whenever available. Rubbish dumps outside the walls of forts and towns are underrepresented archaeologically because excavation has usually concentrated on the interior arrangements, but they are known at sites like 2nd century Caerleon (Knight 1964), 2nd century Brecon Gaer (Jones 1993), and 3rd century Cirencester (McWhirr et al. 1982). Of course, it is rarely possible to determine whether all of this material was generated inside the walled area or if it derived from extramural habitations. Conversely, the refuse deposits very commonly

174 ■ An Archaeology of Identity

used in the construction of features like floor make-up in the buildings inside the walls may well have been imported from outside. While this complicates the spatial analysis of finds, there are examples where dumped material is very likely to have come from the immediate vicinity—as with the so-called 'alley deposit' of 2nd century pottery beneath a barrack window at Birdoswald (Richmond and Birley 1930), the workshop waste at certain sites in Chester (2nd century and later [Matthews 1995; Strickland 1982]), and domestic waste in various parts of Caerleon (in the 2nd and 3rd centuries [Nash-Williams 1929; Zienkiewicz 1993]). These rubbish deposits, which were sometimes quite extensive, had simply been put (or accumulated) in the nearest convenient space that was not in immediate use as a thoroughfare or activity area.

The disposal of rubbish, at least in built-up areas (rural settlements had rather more diffuse patterns of deposition), can thus be characterised as relatively unrestricted. While areas in regular occupation may have been kept clean, and some organised extramural dumping probably took place at some sites, rubbish was otherwise deposited in many locations and might also have been reused in construction. More organisation is apparent in the disposal of latrine waste, involving specialised structures at least at some sites (Housesteads has the best-known example [Simpson 1976: 133–43, 150–2]), while negative evidence for the recycling of materials like glass and metal also implies some collection or formalised disposal procedure. This particular set of practices, common to many sites, allows the change to a supposedly 'squalid' way of life in the later Roman period to be recontextualised. It is also important to bear in mind that a refuse deposit in a room may relate to 'construction' (used as floor make-up), to 'occupation' (material accumulating on floors that people live on), or to 'disuse' (rubbish dumps in otherwise abandoned rooms or structures). It is likely that confusion of these different types of context has occurred in the past, leading to some misinterpretation of the extent and nature of the occupancy of particular spaces. This point will be returned to below, but suffice it to say here that people in different settlements through the Roman period frequently lived in close proximity to their rubbish.

In this light we can see that while important shifts in the spatial location of refuse disposal in the 4th century did undoubtedly occur, they were rarely inconsistent with earlier practices either in forts or towns, which might be regarded as traditional aspects of 'dwelling'. What is important is the kinds of location that were taken over for disposal, rather than the activity of disposal itself, and this ties in with the theme of the appropriation of 'public' space referred to above. Examples of this include the dumping of refuse in the *frigidarium piscina* of the Caerleon fortress baths through most of the 4th century (Zienkiewicz 1986a); accumulations of rubbish in streets adjacent to the Caerwent *forum* and York *principia* (Brewer and Guest forthcoming; Phillips and Heywood 1995a); waste disposal in the central baths at Binchester after ca. AD 350 (Ferris and Jones 1980, 1991); prolonged later 4th century dumping in the northern *horreum* at Birdoswald (Wilmott 1997); and similar changes in the Marlowe Car Park baths in Canterbury and a large courtyard structure in Cirencester (Blockley et al. 1995a; Holbrook and Timby 1998b; Timby et al. 1998). Examples of ostensibly more private spaces being turned over to rubbish disposal functions—while the use of adjacent rooms went unchanged—include the centurion's quarters of Barrack VI at Myrtle Cottage, Caerleon, and parts of the courtyard house at South Shields, in the later 4th century (Fox 1940; Hodgson 1994a, 1994b).

Generalised dumping in areas of open ground was also an increasingly important feature of the landscape of a number of sites during the 4th century. As we saw in Chapter 3, after the demolition of the courtyard house and disuse of an earlier bath block, the southeastern part of the fort at Caernarfon was primarily a rubbish disposal area (involving pits and dumps), although ephemeral evidence of some other activities (structural and 'industrial') was also recorded (Casey et al. 1993). At a very different kind of site not considered so far, the small, later 4th century coastal station at Filey in North Yorkshire (Ottaway 1997; cf. Dobney 2001: 44), the yard surrounding the central watchtower was filled with dumped material, occasionally sealed with clay (a feature noted elsewhere as a way of sealing noisome rubbish—e.g., at Portchester [Cunliffe 1975]). Evidence of rubbish accumulating in the areas immediately outside town or fort walls (in the ditches or the space between these and the walls) comes from several sites, including Birdoswald, South Shields, and Lincoln (Colyer et al. 1999). Similar practices are also widely known on the earth ramparts inside stone defences, as at Portchester. It can be difficult to decide whether the latter was primarily a disposal activity or part of rampart construction/modification, though both factors may have been important. Quantities of refuse also seem to have been used as landfill on the Lincoln waterfront (Dobney et al. 1995). Significant though these large-scale 4th century rubbish disposal activities may be, at least in terms of understanding the density and spatial practices of the resident community, to interpret them as signs of increased 'squalor' in this period would be to ignore earlier precedents. It has already been

176 ■ An Archaeology of Identity

noted, for instance, that vacant plots in Chester were dumpsites before the 4th century, and rubbish was certainly incorporated into both fort and town ramparts in the 2nd or 3rd centuries at several sites (e.g., York and Leicester [Buckley and Lucas 1987; Miller 1928]).

Nonetheless, and as suggested above, even if the essential practices associated with rubbish disposal did not change a great deal in the 4th century, the spaces chosen did—and significantly so. The increasing 'privatisation' of space has been discussed already, and this is certainly part of the story. Another aspect of the problem is whether the spatial dynamics of refuse disposal offer any means of understanding the density and location of settlement in various kinds of site. This is a key aspect of site function (or identity) in many discussions of towns (e.g., Reece 1980) and forts (e.g., Daniels 1980): if a town has low occupancy, it is really a village; if a fort has low occupancy, then it may only be home to 'squatters'. Several sites have sufficient coverage of excavation to allow us to look at areas of settlement in relation to refuse disposal in the later Roman period, to pursue this question further. These are illustrated in Figures 4.25–4.30, using a range of different categories of evidence, translated in most cases into a graded artefact-density distribution. Caerleon is a good place to begin, and it can be compared quite directly with Chester (Figs. 4.25–4.26).

These plans illustrate very clearly the problem of distinguishing areas used for rubbish disposal from areas used for other activities. For instance, the fortress baths at Caerleon have produced considerable quantities of finds, but these are mostly from large dumps and beg the question of where the people generating this rubbish were living. The answer might be in those areas where deposition is slight (e.g., some of the barracks in the western corner), although closer proximity might be suggested by some of the examples referred to above, as well as by the structural evidence from Caerleon itself. This is focused on the eastern part of the site and along the main lateral street, the *via principalis* (cf. Gardner 1997: 30, 1999). Changes in the use of the baths are surely significant; however, not only do these fit with similar developments at a range of other sites, but they are also precedented at Caerleon. The baths were apparently in disrepair in the later 2nd century and were closed through much of the 3rd, perhaps because garrison reductions made the heating of such a large structure unnecessary (Zienkiewicz 1986a: 37–50). The 4th century changes, then, need not be taken in themselves as indications of military abandonment at the end of the 3rd century (*contra* Boon 1987: 43). Most of these comments also apply to Chester, where a similar historical sequence has generally been proposed (McPeake 1978;

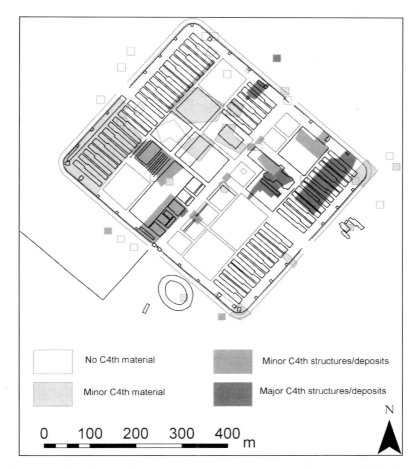

Figure 4.25. Plan of Caerleon: activity density (plan after Boon 1972: 114; Knight 1988: endpiece; data from Gardner 2001a).

cf. Strickland 1994). Here it is the north central areas of the site that seem most heavily used, even if the amounts of material deposited (or at least reported) tend to be less than for Caerleon.

We can compare these legionary fortresses with a couple of auxiliary fort sites. Housesteads (Fig. 4.27) presents a more consistent pattern of activity, with the distribution of finds suggesting rubbish deposition both inside living quarters and up against the northern defences (from the 2nd century). Unfortunately, deficiencies in the detail of the available data affect some of the excavations here, and these are a problem in a small site. Nonetheless, it seems that life was continuing in the fort, with some important changes in the planning

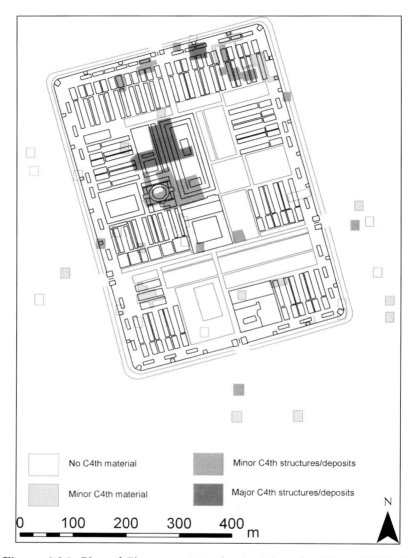

Figure 4.26. Plan of Chester: activity density (plan after Mason 1996: 85; data from Gardner 2001a).

of space but little change in the practices of rubbish disposal. A more complex example is Portchester Castle (Fig. 4.28). Disposal methods at this site included both pit digging and rampart-back dumping, and although the former has been associated more with a 'civilian' phase in the settlement's occupation (Cunliffe 1975: 427–8; Reece 1997: 6–7),

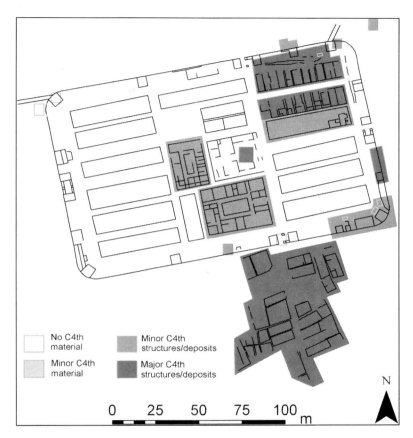

Figure 4.27. Plan of Housesteads: activity density (plan after Birley and Keeney 1935: pl. XXII; Crow 1995: 29; data from Gardner 2001a).

it is unlikely that such a simple link can be made (see above). It is true that the use of pits in this part of Portchester is relatively limited chronologically, to the period AD 325–45 (although coin dates are lacking for many pits), and it may follow that there was a greater density of occupation at this time—or different arrangements of structures—necessitating the burial of rubbish away from activity areas. The subsequent period, to AD 364, was interpreted by the excavator as more 'ordered', partly on the basis of a relative dearth of coins (Cunliffe 1975: 425), although this pattern compares with coin deposition at other forts in the region. Indeed, dumping continued, seemingly spreading to cover a road surface. This does suggest a major shift of spatial practices, significantly affecting aspects of mobility and regionalisation within the enclosure. Overall, though, it seems that

180 ■ An Archaeology of Identity

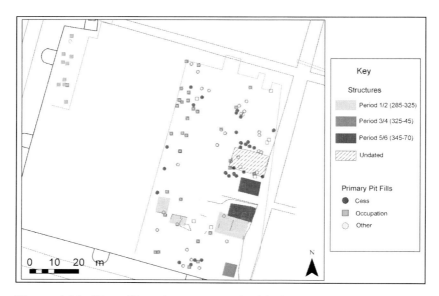

Figure 4.28. Plan of Portchester: pits and rubbish (plan after Cunliffe 1975: 14; data from Cunliffe 1975).

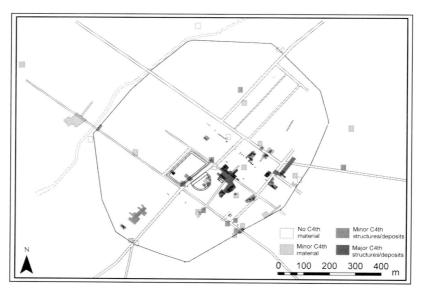

Figure 4.29. Plan of Canterbury: activity density (plan after Bennett 1984: f.p. 50; data from Gardner 2001a).

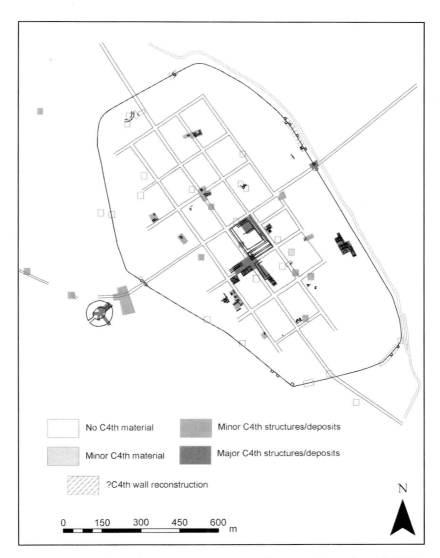

Figure 4.30. Plan of Cirencester: activity density (plan after McWhirr 1986: 15; data from Gardner 2001a).

the changing spatial patterns of rubbish disposal in the fort cannot reliably be associated with either 'military' or 'civilian' identity groups; rather, fluctuating local priorities in the organisation of space generated comparable changes in sites of all kinds. Changes in the character of occupation might be indicated if certain key buildings were transformed in function, but even this was a widespread phenomenon that need not be associated with the withdrawal of official or military presence. We must remember that these institutions were themselves susceptible to change.

Postponing further discussion of this issue to Chapter 5, it remains here to look at a couple of town sites (Canterbury and Cirencester) and compare the patterns of activity in these two examples with a reasonable coverage of excavated material. Quite a varied picture comes from the former (Fig. 4.29). The town has a good spread of excavated sites and low-intensity deposition is common among these throughout the 4th century. Greater numbers of finds that are more likely to relate to rubbish dumping occur in a few places, often linked with structural activity. These include the Marlowe Car Park baths area, which was large enough to suggest that ongoing building and occupation was consonant with rubbish dumping in very close proximity (and the build-up of so-called 'dark earth'). The overall picture is of a mixed landscape of inhabited structures and open plots used for rubbish dumping—rather like 4th century Caerleon. Detailed finds information is lacking from many of the excavations in Cirencester, but what is available underlies the synthesis presented in Figure 4.30. This indicates a more consistent spread of occupation across the town than in Canterbury, with rubbish dumping likely to be occurring in close proximity to areas of accommodation (e.g., at Beeches Road [McWhirr 1986]), as well as in what had been public buildings (Holbrook and Timby 1998b; Timby et al. 1998). Although this contrast between Canterbury and Cirencester is somewhat artificial, based as it is upon poorly distributed evidence, it does raise an important issue regarding the abandonment of sites in Roman Britain.

The problem of distinguishing 'occupation debris' from 'refuse dumps' has already been aired. Another way of looking at this is to ask if sites with little or no 4th century material (or indeed material of any specific period) are unoccupied, or merely clean. Obviously, deposits of refuse indicate the presence of some people, and disposal activity is a form of use. The impression from the majority of sites considered here is that this kind of use was rarely far removed from places of habitation, and available space was readily exploited. This is true throughout the Roman period, although 'availability' is something that certainly seems to have increased in the 4th century, partly as some former public buildings changed in function. Stratigraphic factors must also be taken into account, as mentioned in Chapter 3: reduced levels of large-scale construction in the 4th century will have left rubbish deposits undisturbed, in contrast to earlier phases.

It is important to note this progressive abandonment of some built-up sites (cf. Reece 1980), as the changes in material culture in the early 5th century can make this seem rather an abrupt period of 'collapse'. Another widely discussed aspect of this phenomenon is the 'dark earth' found in the late Roman stratigraphy at many town-type sites, some of which have been mentioned above. Uncertainty remains as to the composition—which is somewhat variable from site to site—and origin of this kind of deposit. Potential explanations for it range from imported garden soil to the accumulated decay of successive timber buildings (Blockley et al. 1995a: 260–6; Courty et al. 1989: 261–8; Ottaway 1992: 111–2). The importance of relatively ephemeral structures at several later Roman sites has already been noted, but the organic content of many dark earths also suggests that the growth of vegetation on areas of waste ground used for rubbish disposal is a major part of the story (perhaps following from timber/daub structural phases). The increased incidence of this in the later 4th century is probably related to the lack of a centralised infrastructure to clear such vegetation, already indicated by the changes to public buildings, and even if some of these deposits are garden soils, they are likely to have been private concerns (Perring 1991: 78–81). Interestingly, dark earths are rarely found on fort sites, even where rubbish disposal activities spread to more parts of the intramural area, and even though some central functions appear to change; this suggests that these changes did not mean the abandonment of all maintenance activities at such sites. There are also, of course, local exceptions to the transformation in the manifestations of authority in towns, such as the late sequence of possibly 'official' buildings in the baths area at Wroxeter (Barker et al. 1997). This is to be expected amidst the fragmentation that we are beginning to see in the later Roman period in Britain.

Traditions and transformation in spaces

A wide range of sites, representing some of the best archaeological data available from Roman Britain, have been considered in this section to look at changing patterns in the planning and habitation of built space. As with the more portable forms of material culture discussed, these data are inconsistent and problematic, and it is particularly difficult to consider detailed interpretation of the functionality of different spaces. Nonetheless, a number of important observations have been made, and these can be developed further here and tied into some of the other patterns noted above. As might be expected, elements of continuity and change can be detected in the relationships

184 ■ An Archaeology of Identity

between different kinds of sites, as expressed in the organisation of space. While the changes are certainly important and indicative of transformations in a variety of social practices in the 4th century, the continuities are equally notable. Indeed, the latter suggest that some of the persistent notions of later Roman 'squalor' (e.g., Faulkner 2000: 123–6) are insensitive not only to variant cultural perspectives on rubbish, but also to much earlier evidence of the activities taken to be symptomatic of 'decline'.

While significant developments in site planning are difficult to pick out from a long-term background of individual idiosyncracy (on the one hand) and from incomplete evidence (on the other), changes in the layouts of individual structures offer major opportunities for understanding the dynamics of identity in Roman Britain. At the same time, an impression of increased variation in site arrangements can be discerned in the larger-scale evidence, cutting across established categories like 'town' and 'fort', with their respective 'civilian' and 'military' associations. While the rigidity of such associations can certainly be questioned on some levels throughout the Roman period, the grounds for doing so are increased in the 4th century—particularly in the latter part of that century, as comparable changes in established routines of practice affect both groups of sites. The main trend evident in these changes is an orientation towards more localised priorities in the construction and use of space. While such local variation was obviously not absent in the 1st or 2nd centuries, its increase must relate to changes in the distanciation of state institutions.

Thus, a fort like South Shields, located on the eastern coast and apparently the base of a newly arrived unit at the beginning of the 4th century, seems fully integrated into the current norms of military practice elsewhere in the empire for much of the period. Meanwhile, the communities living in the inland northern forts—like Housesteads and Birdoswald—and those of the west seem to have had more freedom to keep doing things their own way (cf. Reece 1997: 8–10). The southeastern forts were different again. This impression of variability is reinforced when transformations to individual structures are considered. These were increasingly common in the 4th century and generally constituted radical alterations to the regionalisation of key spaces like *principia*, *horrea*, and *praetoria*, which can at the very least be considered in terms of 'public' and 'private'. The latter dimension seems to have become more important than the former, with the appropriation of what were previously corporate spaces for other uses. Where these spaces had been critical to specific, socially significant uses of co-presence and interaction (as in bathing or collective meetings/rituals in *basilicae*), then it must be concluded that aspects of the structuration of social life were also undergoing change. This is likely, in turn, to have had an impact on the construction of social identities.

A key part of the evidence for such modifications in function—which are difficult to describe in more specific terms—is the location of rubbish disposal. Importantly, there is evidence from a number of sites that the supposedly 'squalid' conditions of 4th century settlements were actually fairly typical throughout the Roman period. Rubbish was disposed of or used in close proximity to other activities, and it is therefore likely that it was regarded in quite different ways than modern Western sensibilities would appreciate. One implication of this is that 'cleanliness' and 'order'—or the lack thereof—cannot be taken as reliable indications of identities such as Roman/native, civilised/uncivilised, or military/civilian. Another implication requires some reconsideration of the artefactual material from these sites. The importance of 4th century refuse dumps as artefact-bearing deposits now appears to relate to gradually reducing intensity of occupation. If earlier intramural refuse deposits existed, as we know they did in some contexts, many may have been disturbed or reused in new construction activity. Those of the 4th century were not reused and were not disturbed because the appropriate kinds of construction activity were no longer occurring. Another important feature of the 4th century evidence—that new areas were being taken over for rubbish dumping in place of previous functions—can be understood as an aspect of the same phenomenon of the gradual abandonment of built-up sites.

Nonetheless, this rubbish was being generated and dumped by people living in these sites. If it did incorporate old material, these people must also have been doing something to disturb this material (if it was not still in use), as well as discarding their own. Moreover, for some of the reasons discussed above, the increased frequency of disposal of things like coins is unlikely to be purely a factor of this stratigraphic imbalance. While it is clear that the inhabitants of forts and towns had changing priorities in the use of spaces—particularly public ones—in the 4th century, this does not indicate complete abandonment of these sites or, indeed, the total transformation of the ways of life or institutional connections of the residents. The disposal of rubbish in newly available spaces is important by virtue of the nature of some of those spaces, but not in terms of attitudes towards refuse in built-up areas. Furthermore, comparison of different kinds of material culture and the contexts in which these were found indicate mismatches in deposition which do not tally with a simple account of the 4th century deposits as the final resting places of all earlier rubbish

186 ■ An Archaeology of Identity

(e.g., at Causeway Lane, Leicester [Connor and Buckley 1999]). Some of the other potential reasons for variation in disposal patterns thus carry weight, coexistent with the undeniable changes in the use of intramural space in the 4th century.

That these changes are common to forts and towns is also of some importance. The architecture of different kinds of settlement is, and always has been, one of the key aspects of the archaeological distinction between broad identity groups, such as 'military' and 'civilian' in this case. This is rightly so, as the distinctive environments of the town—with its arrangement of elite houses and arenas of elite display (*forum*, baths, theatre [cf. Laurence 1994: 122–32])—and the fort—with its strongly regionalised spaces geared towards disciplined corporate life (cf. James 1999a)—were vital to the structuration of the communities inhabiting them in the later 1st, 2nd, and part of the 3rd centuries. In the 4th century, several elements of these distinctive spaces remained, such as the forts' barracks. However, just as we have already seen from the finds evidence that there are grounds for questioning the exclusivity of both environments, and for rethinking these categories in terms of mobilities between them, so we have also seen in this chapter that common changes can be traced in both types of settlement in the 4th century. These erode the distinctions between town and fort, and blur them into a more generalised category that also remains distinct from rural sites only in the relatively intense level of deposition. It is precisely because the earlier built environments were important to the structuration of social groups that changes in those environments can be interpreted as representing changes in identities, as we will see in Chapter 5. At the same time, there is continued evidence of ties to larger communities such as general rubbish disposal practices, the inhabitation of barracks, and various kinds of 'official' use persisting in some specific structures. It is to these larger communities that we turn in the final part of this chapter.

Writing Roman history

In examining continuity and change in the wider empire, three of the more narrative texts introduced in Chapter 3 will be most useful—the documentary sources being more synchronic in their specification of practices and behaviour associated with particular identities, and thus more appropriately dealt with in the next chapter. The discussion of the archaeological evidence in the foregoing sections has highlighted some of the ways in which changes in material practices in this period are invariably coloured by a sense of impending collapse, and this is only partly because of the prejudices of modern scholars when confronted with new types of construction or of rubbish disposal location. Several 4th century (or slightly later) authors also constructed narratives of decline, and considering some of these in detail will point out how they might have been associated with particular identity groups, giving us one way to flesh out all of the material that we have considered so far in terms of such groups in Chapter 5. We can begin with the most central source for all 4th century imperial histories: Ammianus Marcellinus.

Ammianus' *Res Gestae* has formed the backbone of almost all modern accounts of this period from at least the time of Edward Gibbon in the 18th century. Indeed, Gibbon much admired Ammianus and helped to establish the view that he was an essentially reliable historian—even the 'last great historian' of the ancient world (Barnes 1998: 1–10; Wallace-Hadrill 1986: 13–20). However, recent deconstruction of Ammianus' writing (Barnes 1998) has revealed the many layers of meaning embedded in the text as transmitted, and some of the ways in which these were engaged in the construction of a particular reality. We have already noted certain aspects of the writer's life and personality (Barnes 1998: 1–2, 54–128, 187–95): he identified himself as a Greek; he was from an upper-class background and served as a high-ranking soldier; he was a pagan (and possibly apostate) in an increasingly Christian empire; and he was male, with very conventional (i.e., patriarchal) views on gender roles. He also had an ambivalent attitude to Rome itself, having been expelled from the city during a famine in the 380s as a 'foreigner', yet retaining a fundamental respect for the classical tradition represented by the city (cf. Wallace-Hadrill 1986: 16–17, 33–5). Stylistically, he used excursuses and other literary conventions in a variety of ways to arrange his 'facts' in a narrative focused on military and state affairs, and on the personalities of emperors. He has often been compared to Tacitus, but while he made some effort to emulate his illustrious predecessor, he clearly had his own agendas.

These agendas are important in any attempt to understand the kind of social reality that Ammianus was constructing for himself and for his audience. Whereas Ammianus' perspective has often been treated as a prism through which to view late Roman life, here the prism itself is of interest. It—or rather he—does convey something of the changing social life in that world, but mainly insofar as Ammianus-as-author was a part of that world. His own nexus of identities and the ways he perceived those of others must relate to other social groupings and categorisations current at the time. So, with respect to continuity and change, several comments can be made. Ammianus' paganism is an important element of his political and social conservatism and his insistence on traditional Roman values as the answer to the troubles of the day, particularly the influxes of barbarians into the eastern empire in the later 4th century (Wallace-Hadrill 1986: 34–5). While he rarely makes pointed remarks against Christians (though see, e.g., XXII.5 [cf. Barnes 1998: 79–94]), his pagan loyalties are clear from his glorification of the apostate emperor Julian, and from more subtle references to the changes that were taking place in the empire.

Thus, the surviving books begin with an account of the vices that are besetting Rome, corrupting the moral fibre of the city (XIV.6). The extravagance and ostentation of the contemporary aristocracy of the city is contrasted with the austerity of its ancestors who founded the empire, and who lived like common soldiers (XIV.6.7). At the end of his history, this point is reinforced with reference to the way that the Goths—who were initially admitted to the empire as settlers and allies—were treated by Roman officers and administrators, leading to a revolt that culminated in the major Roman defeat at Adrianople in 378. In contrast to some other tribes, particularly the Huns, Ammianus portrays these Goths as relative innocents driven to destruction by corrupt Romans (XXXI.4). This theme of moral decay also runs through Ammianus' more general treatment of the military. While there are times when he paints a positive picture of the soldiers—particularly when they are fighting to defend the empire, in battle scenes that are themselves formulaic examples of Roman literary convention (e.g., XVI.12)—it is more usual for him to refer to their brutality and fickleness (e.g., XVIII.8, XX.4, XX.11, XXII.4, XXVI.2). Of course, Ammianus describes himself as a former soldier (XXXI.16), but it is clear from other references (e.g., his unfamiliarity with travelling on foot [XIX.8]) that he had been an officer of high rank, while most of his complaints are directed against idle and decadent soldiers of lower status.

These perspectives on the changes occurring in the empire are thus related to Ammianus' religion and to his understanding of morality, as well as to his relatively high status and to some of his own personal experiences—such as his expulsion from Rome. Indeed, these factors were probably important in his decision to write the *Res Gestae* at all, and to write it in the particular way that he did, with its focus both on Julian and on the importance of earlier Roman history (Wallace-Hadrill 1986: 20–22). These features combined to cement the identity of pagan Rome as an eternal touchstone for moral strength, and to account for the contemporary crisis in terms of the abandonment of this strength. This is, therefore, one highly conservative perspective on change in the Roman Empire. Another, with similar but much more explicit prejudices, comes from Zosimus. He wrote his *Nea Historia* rather later than Ammianus, in the 6th century, when the western empire had ceased to exist. His major theme was the fall of Rome, and Zosimus blames this quite overtly upon Christians and barbarians. How much of this is his own opinion, and how much is inherited from the three or more writers upon whom much of his work was based, is uncertain (Ridley 1982). Nonetheless, it again highlights some of the clear axes of different identities in the period, and how these were interpreted as accounting for continuity and change.

As with Ammianus, military affairs are a key focus for these issues, but Zosimus' account is slightly different. Soldiers are consistently denigrated, except in the stock battle accounts (e.g., I.7, I.9, I.33, II.13, II.33–4, III.21, IV.23), and there are certainly similarities here with some of the things that Ammianus wrote about. Indeed, this negative perception of lower-class soldiers seems to have been a feature of male aristocratic attitudes to the military since the early imperial period, when the link between a 'civilian' status (citizenship), military service, and a particular form of noble masculinity began to be undermined by increasingly wide recruitment (Alston 1998). Having lost its monopoly on martial violence to the lower classes of Roman and (noncitizen) provincial society, the elite began to despise the soldiers. Although citizenship had become a much more widely held right by the 4th century, and all 'Roman' soldiers were again citizens (and could on occasion be 'manly' [Zosimus IV.23]), the citizen/noncitizen distinction within the military was supplanted by that of Roman/barbarian. This provided the opportunity for some elite writers—such as Zosimus—to dismiss soldiers as barbaric when they sought reasons for reverses in the fortunes of the empire. Indeed, this is where Ammianus and Zosimus differ somewhat. The former certainly could be prejudiced against barbarians such as the Huns (XXXI.2–4), but as we have seen above, he was more interested in internal processes of change. For Zosimus, the blame lay more clearly with the incomers (e.g., IV.59), who were defined as members of distinctive ethnic groups based upon such qualities as 'customs' or laws as well as language and religion (V.20). From such accounts, we can start to pick up on some of the ways that particular traditions were defined as key parts of Roman culture by *some* Romans, although—as we will see with other categories of identity in Chapter 5—this is only a partial perspective. The fact that traditional paganism was central to this culture, as Zosimus saw it (e.g., II.7), makes this partiality very clear—most of the 4th century Roman emperors, after all, were Christian.

190 ■ An Archaeology of Identity

All of this is more important for our purposes than the fact that Zosimus is also the historian who provides the main reference to the 'rescript of Honorius', telling the British cities to look after their own defences (VI.10). While there is some debate about whether this refers to Britain at all, or a region in Italy with a similar name (e.g., Bartholomew 1982; Thompson 1977, 1983), all of the material evidence discussed so far seems to indicate compellingly that there were changes in the first decade of the 5th century, and indeed well before this point. Interpreting the meaning of these changes to people experiencing them is a more challenging endeavour, but we are beginning to get a good picture of how elite Romans might have seen some of them from their restricted viewpoint. The final writer to consider for the moment is Vegetius, who confirms these impressions. Like Ammianus' *Res Gestae*, Vegetius' *Epitoma Rei Militaris* was influential long after its composition, in this case being popular in the medieval period as a handbook for the conduct of warfare. This is therefore a good example of how all texts are capable of different readings, with a political tract being used as a technical manual in a different context.

In criticising contemporary—i.e., late 4th century—military practice, Vegetius drew on material from other sources and praised former Roman techniques. Like Ammianus, then, he was a conservative commentator who believed in the importance of Roman traditions; however, he was also a Christian (Milner 1993: xviii–xxv). This emphasises the point that the complexities of identity politics in the period should not be obscured by the rhetoric of writers like Zosimus. Vegetius echoes Zosimus, though, in his diagnosis of the problems—and solutions—facing Rome in the 4th century. This is closely tied to issues of recruitment (e.g., Book I). At heart, the *Epitoma* is a plea to stop hiring 'barbarians' and return to the 'old Roman' standards and values (even though these seem somewhat poorly understood, at least in technical terms [Milner 1993: xvii–xviii]). Overall, then, the literary construction of 'Roman tradition' is an important trend in some of the key writings of this period. Given the context of this writing, produced by high-status individuals, it is suggestive of a fundamentally conservative state ideology, and comparison with some of the laws passed in the 4th century will bear this out in the next chapter. However, it is also important to note that this creation of social and ethnic ideal types also comes with hints at variation or change, such as the fact that 'Roman values' could be appropriated by pagans or Christians. This tension between stability and tradition, and fluidity or mobility, is the key theme in this chapter, cutting across many forms of material culture—including written texts.

Tradition, transformation, and structuration

The views that we have just considered are interesting and lie behind many of our current understandings of Late Antiquity across the empire. While they represent the opinions and understandings of people who were well placed to know about the events taking place in this period, they are also highly partial. Not only do they relate much more to the Mediterranean—and the eastern part of the Mediterranean at that—than to northern provinces like Britain, but their authors' views were clearly structured by attitudes to class, gender, religion, ethnicity, and morality, which are unlikely to have been shared by every other person in the empire. In order to understand this period, and how the people living in it understood it themselves, we need to recover a broader range of possible perspectives on how changing practices related to changing identities. Before developing this fully in the next chapter, it is worthwhile making more explicit some of the temporal dimensions of the practices that we have observed at a range of sites over the course of the last two chapters, as a counterpoint to the explicit discourses of tradition and transformation produced by men like Ammianus, Zosimus, and Vegetius.

In Chapter 3, we saw how the material culture of later Roman Britain could be—and indeed should be—interpreted in terms of the activities of which it was a part. It must be stressed here that there is a great deal of potential for future analysis of this kind, as is already being pursued by a small number of researchers (e.g., Allison 2002; Dobres 2000), dependent though it is upon high-resolution material evidence. Here, we can examine a number of specific actions—such as appearing and exchanging—and aspects of dwelling: building, making, using, maintaining, and dumping. These can be connected in alternative ways to the simple, linear path of manufacture, use, and deposition proposed by Schiffer (1972), reflecting the overlapping engagement of different kinds of material culture within social practices. Returning to some key sites, we can explore both the variable and the routine in such practices. At Caernarfon, for example, the southeastern corner of the fort—which has been studied in detail in earlier chapters—preserves evidence of many kinds of actions. This area was given over, for a period of approximately 80–100 years, to a range of activities of individually short duration. Compared to the rest of the enclosure, this area was open, and earlier buildings—barracks, a courtyard house, baths—were long disused. This remained so for three generations of the fort's inhabitants, during which time people continued to use the area for the disposal of rubbish (either by dumping or the digging of pits) and for the manufacture of artefacts. Despite the lack of architectural order, then, this became a place of routine practices and associations with only occasional disturbances, such as the construction of a long, timber-lined drain across the area.

The artefacts that were deposited here each had individual biographies, and no doubt these had involved many other places than that in which they ended up. Even lacking detailed excavation of the rest of the fort and its environs, we can begin to understand some of the dynamic practices within which these objects were engaged, through their temporality and their functionality. The most immediate practice contexts are the actions surrounding their deposition. Coins and other small artefacts frequently occur in the same kinds of matrix—pit fills, dumps, and drain fills. As such, they seem to be mixed rubbish derived from elsewhere, and this fits with the general use of this area. Where the objects are intrinsically dateable, many seem to have been old when dumped, although it is vital to note that an archaeologist's measured age for an artefact might not correspond with a past individual's experienced age for it. This might depend, for instance, on when an individual encountered it and whether she or he was aware of any characteristics of age that it bore—such as the name of an emperor in the case of coins. Bearing this in mind, it has already been noted that there seems to be an increased 'turnover' of coins in the 4th century, and thus in all likelihood a change in the temporal relations between people and at least one category of things. This is much less obvious in other 'small find' object categories, given our coarser understanding of the temporality of style changes, but there do seem to be fairly slow cycles of transformation (Cool 2000). The number of antiques (if these were not simply redeposited) and general continuities in the repertoire of small goods would indicate conservatism, but there are several styles of objects (e.g., bracelets) that can be dated broadly to the 4th century, and sometimes its second half—indicating that this slow pace of change was continuing. What this evidence gives us, then, is a set of overlapping temporalities: the continuity in the general use of space contrasted with the short-lived activities taking place in it; the increased turnover of coinage compared with the slower change of personal objects; and the constant engagement with objects and materials from the past in a site that had been inhabited for two and one-half centuries, happening as new features were created.

Moving to a different local context, the west gate area at Birdoswald has evidence for a similar tension between routine and change, and between unity and division within the activities of the community. As with Caernarfon, dumping is the major practice to which the excavated 4th century contexts directly relate, but in addition there are elements of the site that were involved in 'moving' (the structural sequence of the gateway) and 'maintaining' (the sequence in the southern *horreum*, Building 197). With regard to the dumping, the pattern is very similar to Caernarfon, both in terms of the relative location—within the walls of the fort, in an area no longer used for its initial constructed purpose (Building 198)—and in terms of the significant features of temporality and functional materiality associated with the artefacts. In view of the major modification to the use of Building 198, the maintenance of the gate and roads is significant, as is that of Building 197. The former attests to the continuation of established routines of moving, which apparently persisted into the 5th or 6th century when the portal was reinforced in timber. However, the latter actually indicates changes in routine in the mid-4th century, as the building was maintained only after the in-filling of the subfloor cavities (originally provided to ventilate stores) and its new use involved the provision of domestic hearths. This was also a period when the nature of pottery supply was changing at the site, creating further differences between this site and others in different regions. Nonetheless, the suite of small finds deposited in the dumps in the northern *horreum* was entirely typical, and again we therefore have overlapping processes of continuity and change in the different practices performed by the same people.

Routines of movement are also key parts of the sequences at South Shields and York Minster. Elements of continuity at South Shields are represented in the ongoing maintenance of the southwestern gate, even as there were several changes in the ditch layout to the front of this. Comparisons of the artefactual material also indicate signs of ordered, routine practices in this most architecturally disciplined of 4th century forts, with spatial segregation of dumping—in the area outside the gate rather than the *principia*—and a corresponding concentration of coins and personal objects in these extramural deposits. This only changed late in the occupation, with a dump containing personal objects behind the *principia* and major changes in the nature of dwelling at the courtyard house site (Hodgson 1994b). Dwelling, moving, and ordering are—in addition to dumping—also the main practices represented at York Minster. Once again, while the temporal and functional features of the artefacts reinforce the points made with regard to Caernarfon, we can see the same distinction between the *principia* and places of dwelling, movement, and dumping in terms of the number of finds and the proportion of personalia, highlighting the different social/depositional environment of the *principia*. There are stronger indications here than at the other sites so far considered that these artefact distributions are stratigraphically post-Roman, but they do fit with the general 4th century patterns elsewhere, suggesting that the objects have not been disturbed too much. Routines of movement were, however, certainly being changed in the 4th century—both inside buildings and around them—as internal partitions were rearranged and some alleys disused.

Change is a dominant feature of the 4th century picture at another pair of sites, the *praetorium* at Binchester (Ferris and Jones 1980, 1991) and the Marlowe Car Park baths in Canterbury (Blockley et al. 1995a, 1995b). Although artefact distributions of the kind incorporated in the discussion so far cannot readily be constructed for these sites, the structural sequences referred to above furnish indications of transformations in very specific routines associated with bathing. Through the 4th century, the large structure partially excavated in the centre of Binchester acquired baths, was partitioned into smaller units, and then was converted into a smithy and slaughterhouse with dumping in the bathing area. This cluster of changes in the practices conducted in a particular place—dwelling of different kinds, bathing, butchering, making, dumping—is indicative of the considerable dynamism in this particular community at this time. Much the same can be said of the baths at Marlowe, which saw a much longer-established tradition of bathing disrupted in the mid-4th century when rubbish dumping, manufacture, exchange (the erection of 'market' stalls), and other activities moved in. Some blockage of preexisting routes around the baths also occurred. Despite the intensity of the changes at both of these sites, particularly with regard to the disappearance of the aspects of bathing associated with the body, it is worth noting that the new configurations of regionalisation were, like bathing, highly interactive. These new practices would themselves become routine over time intervals to be measured in years.

Two more sites can be examined with regard to the practices of dwelling. Portchester and Housesteads both have sequences of structures that indicate the gradual but continuous pace of change in the 4th century (Cunliffe 1975; Daniels 1980; Wilkes 1960, 1961). This process of structured transformation is very much at the heart of structuration (Giddens 1979: 64; cf. Adam 1990: 25–9). At Housesteads, the 'chalet' barracks in the northeastern part of the fort certainly do embody elements of continuity, even if this is simply by virtue of their position in relation to existing axes of movement in the fort and to the walls. However, they also represent an extension of the earlier parameters of variation within barrack buildings—making for changes in practices such as construction and maintenance—as well as to movement in the structures themselves. Portchester can be made to yield a similar story. Although the arrangement of space within the walls is quite different from Housesteads, it sees elements of continuity (orientation and situation of structures; dumping practices on the banks) and change (in the appropriation of certain areas for pit digging and in the use of routeways) through its life. Finally, one form of practice not included in the discussion so far—but embodying the same kinds of tension—is the act of burial described at Oudenburg. Here, as seen in Chapter 3, established and institutionalised norms could be modified and a community simultaneously united and divided by different aspects of the process of burying. As I shall discuss in the next chapter, these tendencies—which cut across a great range of different practices—can be understood as the building blocks of social identification.

Chapter 5

THE SOCIAL DIMENSIONS OF 4TH CENTURY LIFE: INTERACTIONS AND IDENTITIES

Studying sociality

In moving from the dynamic material practices that we have been examining in the last two chapters to their significance for people at the time, we come finally to their interpretation in terms of identity. Like materiality and temporality, this is a fundamental dimension of connection between agency and structure, since the way that people relate to themselves, each other, and more abstract social formations is very much through concepts of identity (Jenkins 2004: 1–7). Families, ethnic or religious groups, wealth classes, genders, and age grades are fundamental framing devices for how people live, and they are all based upon—and shaped by—the ways in which people behave: how they dress, how they eat, and how they build and use spaces. Similarities and differences in these activities are the building blocks of social life, and as such they are both controlled by institutions and enacted by individuals. They are therefore likely to be a major factor behind the patterning in archaeological material. Developing an approach to identity that appreciates this pivotal role in processes of structuration is an important additive, albeit a sympathetic one, to Giddens's own work. This theoretical agenda will be pursued throughout this chapter, using particularly the work of Richard Jenkins (1996; 2004) in conjunction with a much more synthetic approach to the different kinds of evidence considered in the previous chapters, now that their connection to practices has been firmly established. By way of introduction, though, we need to consider previous archaeological approaches to identity, focusing on the dimension that has perhaps been of longest-standing interest: ethnicity.

As with material culture itself, interpretations of identity groups in 20th century archaeology have moved from essentialism to pluralism.

198 ■ An Archaeology of Identity

Partly reflecting broader shifts in archaeological thinking that have introduced pluralist modes of interpretation, this also relates to the debate in anthropology over primordial and instrumental definitions of ethnicity. The former, which took ethnicity to be an essential and natural part of human life, has strong ties to the biologically and linguistically homogenous 'cultures' or 'peoples' of traditional approaches to prehistory, and indeed history (Hall, J.M. 1997: 17–8; Jones 1997: 65–83, 1999: 219–22). The shift to an instrumental view of cultural identity in anthropology, and indeed sociology, owes much to the work of Fredrik Barth (1969), who was influenced by the great interactionist scholar Erving Goffman, also one of Giddens's inspirations (e.g., Giddens 1984: 36–7; cf. Jenkins 2004: 22, 186; Chapter 2 above). In this view, ethnicity is essentially a flexible tool for social power that has a contingent—rather than a natural—reality.

Initially, this perspective had limited impact in archaeology, thanks to the disinterest shown toward identity by early New Archaeologists (Jones 1997: 26–7). However, instrumentalist ideas became increasingly important in the 1980s, linked to the growing appreciation of the sheer complexity of archaeological and ethnoarchaeological patterning that was a major spur towards post-processualism (Hodder 1982b; Shennan 1989). In the 1990s, this has been developed further, partly in conjunction with the increased interest in agency and practice (e.g., Hall, J.M. 1997; James 1999b; Jones 1997; Stark 1998). The centrality of ethnicity and other dimensions of identity to archaeology today also owes much to the realisation that, as well as being important in the past, these issues are the major ones at stake in contemporary political disputes involving archaeological heritage. The problems that we face in dealing with these are really testimony to the complexity of identity, which—like agency—makes it hard to define (Jones 1997: 56–65). To take ethnicity as a paradigmatic example, it "is a term that only makes sense in a context of relativities, of processes of identification, and that nevertheless aspires to concrete and positive status both as an attribute and as an analytical concept" (Tonkin et al. 1996: 23). The most useful recent definitions deployed in archaeology are those of Siân Jones (1997: xiii, 84–7) and Stephen Shennan (1989: 14), who treat ethnicity as a self-conscious, ascribed social category distinguished by notions of shared origin, descent, and 'culture'. This category is typically structured in opposition to ethnic 'others' based on abstract stereotypes. While these stereotypes might be made to seem very natural and 'real' to people (the process of 'reification'), they are still abstractions, and the range of behaviour on which they are based is invariably much more fluid and complex in actual experience. Individuals are typically able to change their affiliations, and more importantly to 'have' multiple ethnicities (or none at all), expressing different group identities in different contexts of interaction (cf. James 1999b: 70–7). An individual in Britain in the Roman period, for example, is thus likely to have had a number of nested affiliations that might be termed 'ethnic' at varying sociospatial scales, up to and including 'Roman'.

But how are these 'ethnicities' worked out in practice? A key feature emphasised by Barth (1969) is the boundary. Whereas the essentialist view of cultures tended to focus on what lay within coterminous boundaries of ethnicity, language, and so forth, with the boundaries themselves largely ignored—very much a normative approach—Barth drew attention to the overlapping of boundaries in more complex ways (cf. Shennan 1989: 11–14). He stressed that the boundaries themselves need to be treated as foci of active maintenance and interaction. Comparison between one group and another is the key element in the construction of ethnicities, but this does not mean that there will be a simple process of differentiation between the two groups. Rather, different types and levels of identity, and different kinds of practice (involving material culture or other media such as gesture and language), may cross-cut in various ways. In some circumstances, markers chosen for certain ethnic boundaries will draw upon those used in the negotiation of gender or age divisions (Hodder 1982b: 85, 185–9; Jones 1997: 114–29). Furthermore, the marking of a boundary, which may be manifest in some aspects of material culture but not others, certainly does not make it impermeable to ideas, objects, or people. Above all, the definition and maintenance of boundaries of all kinds is a *performative* process (Goffman 1959; cf. James 1999b: 72–6; Jenkins 2004: 106): it depends upon people *doing things* in particular ways.

In other words, identities are a key element in structuration, forming part of 'structure' as social groups but also penetrating the ways in which agents see themselves and choose actions. Viewing identities from a structurationist perspective also helps to account for how their characteristics change through time—as actors select different identities to perform, or try to change the rules of belonging to a certain group—as well as the impact of power relations, which will play a major role in structuring daily practices and determining whether constructed stereotypes of identity succeed or fail. This gives us the idea that identity is very much a two-way process, as individuals absorb and accommodate to categories imposed upon them by others, but equally reproduce and potentially transform those categories through their own actions. Richard Jenkins describes this process as the 'internal-external dialectic of identification', and uses it to connect the broad social boundaries shaping collective identities in terms

200 ■ An Archaeology of Identity

of 'insiders' and 'outsiders' to the way individuals typically consider both their own impulses and the views of others when undertaking a course of action (a view of selfhood established by Mead [Jenkins 2004: 17–26]). This conception helps bring structure into action, and action into structure.

The construction of boundaries through stereotypes of similarity and difference also raises an issue with the relationship between material and textual discourses, addressed already at various points in this book. Both Siân Jones (1999) and Jonathan Hall (1997: 142) have argued that the kinds of ethnic identity formulated in written culture are more abstract and stereotyped than those of material culture, and that we therefore cannot expect to find the same kinds of identities being represented in these different media. It is certainly the case that the 'nominal' aspects of past identities—the specific titles or labels (analytically distinguishable from the 'virtual', lived, or experienced aspects [Jenkins 2004: 22])—are difficult to define without writing. It is also clear, from recent studies of the authors of the Roman and early medieval periods, that textual constructions of ethnicity reify simplified forms of more complex identities. This work has produced significant insights on two levels. First, focusing on what the texts are written *about*, the validity of the fluid, situational model of ethnicity has been demonstrated by the range of ethnic 'markers' referred to in various sources—including 'customs' and laws as well as origins—and the way that different ethnic entities seem to appear in different kinds of context (Geary 1983: 18–21; Pohl 1997: 11–21). Second, with regard to what the texts were written *for*, links can be made between a tendency of writers working in 'the classical tradition' in Europe to talk about stable, homogenous ethnic groups and political agendas of state formation or imperial expansion (Geary 1983: 21–5; Lucy 1998: 18–9; Matthews 1999; Pohl 1997: 16; Woolf 1998: 48–76). Interestingly, these discourses would seem to have strong resonance with the political interests of those writing histories for emergent European nation-states in the 18th to 20th centuries (cf. Hingley 2000; Lucy 1998: 20).

However, as we will see below, stereotyping and the simplification of complex identities in contexts of interaction can be regarded as a very common feature of the construction of social identities of all kinds (Jenkins 2004: 124–31). This process can draw upon the 'fixing' or objectifying properties of material culture as much as on those of written (or, indeed, spoken) language to make these simple identities seem 'real'. While the emphasis placed by Jones (1999: 228–9) and Hall (J.M. 1997: 136) on the transience and multiplicity of material culture meanings is not entirely misplaced, and helps to free it from normative text-determined classifications, it is also problematic. It falsely distances writing itself from practice: the abstract concepts of spoken language are materialised, being inscribed on an object, and this is an active cultural practice that creates social categories (cf. Jenkins 1997: 62–3). In addition, one cannot ignore the very solidity of material things that allows them to be used, at least some of the time, to reify meanings beyond the limits of spoken language (Tilley 1999: 263–70). Material culture meanings certainly can be multiple and fluid, but part of their power derives from their suggestion of permanence as *routinised* in practice. It is precisely for this reason that ethnic groups can seem so real to those living in them. This process also creates critical opportunities for the archaeological interpretation of material culture.

All of the comments made so far in relation to ethnicity are pertinent to other dimensions of identity. Indeed, the 'multidimensional' ethnicity model is part of a more generally pluralistic approach to human social identities, which can be explored in relation to individuals and to groups (Jenkins 2004; cf. Wiessner 1989). Another key aspect of identity, for instance, is occupational role. In some situations, as in the case of the Roman military, this may overlap in various ways with certain ethnic—or at least cultural—identities (i.e., 'Roman'); it is also likely to be closely related to social status, itself an important kind of identification (Jenkins 1997: 59–60). Occupation is an aspect of identity that is firmly based upon routines and habitual activities, as Giddens discusses with reference to Goffman's concept of 'framing': "the ordering of activities and meanings whereby ontological security is sustained in the enactment of daily routines" (1984: 87). Within the context of Roman military activity, discipline—particularly in relation to the body—was a major aspect of the latter, and there were also 'occupational' subdivisions such as skill specialisms, ranks, and units (James 1999a: 15–21). These are characteristic of a fairly concrete type of institution, the 'organisation' (Jenkins 2004: 22–3). Later in this chapter, the military will be treated as this kind of identity group within Romano-British society , rather than—as some scholars have suggested it should be—within the framework of a more unusual and highly enclosed type of institution, the 'total institution' described by Goffman in the context of lunatic asylums (Goffman 1961; Pollard 1996; Shaw 1983; cf. Alston 1999; Giddens 1984: 154–8; Haynes 1999a: 8–9; Pollard 2000: 251–2). The connections between military units and other communities in Roman Britain, which strengthened over time, make such a model untenable.

Other dimensions of identity—including gender, age, kinship, and religion—will also be relevant in different ways. We might characterise some of these various identities (self, gender, sometimes ethnicity) as primary and important in early socialisation, and others as secondary (often, as in the case of occupation, achieved rather than ascribed [Jenkins 2004: 62–6; Musolf 2003: 245–74]). Nonetheless, all can be treated as sets of culturally constructed categories requiring maintenance and negotiation on the part of actors, at the same time as having associated structural features and obligations. These are effected in the interactions that make up daily life (Giddens 1984: 83–9) and thus provide much of the substance of the duality of structure. The literature on these topics is substantial, and I will merely note here some of the themes that will be explored in more depth below.

Gender is a social category capable of diverse constructions, as distinct from biological sex—itself not necessarily a clear-cut 'given' (Conkey and Spector 1984: 15–6). In a later section, we will confront some of the problems of the association of certain kinds of artefacts with women and men, and pursue some of the ways in which soldiers' identities were bound up with masculinity (cf. Allason-Jones 1995; Alston 1998; James 1999a: 16–9; Treherne 1995). Age classes are another key aspect of identity, which have already been given some attention in the context of Roman culture as a whole (Harlow and Laurence 2001; cf. Hodder 1982b: 72–85). As we will see, there is evidence of important differences between ancient and modern understandings of infancy. Kinship was also important in societies such as that of Roman Britain, and some of the later Roman changes in material culture in sites such as forts can be related to the increasing prominence of local identities based on this kind of social bond (cf. Allason-Jones 1999; Hassall 1999). Finally, religion was a pervasive aspect of life in the context at hand, and one—both in the early Roman period with the arrival of new gods, and in the 4th century with the rise of Christianity—highly susceptible to the formation of self-conscious identity groups.

Amidst this bewildering range of relevant social identities, all of which might be important in different contexts, it is useful to return to the concepts of discursive and practical consciousness to again link the study of identity to structuration theory. Certain aspects of identity may require active signalling, to others and/or to oneself (Grahame 2000; Wiessner 1989: 56–7); these are equally likely to be amenable to explicit discussion on some level. However, social identities must also be routinised in practice (i.e., become part of practical consciousness) if they are to form a significant element of an individual's own sense of self-identity. It is fundamentally through such routinisation that identities serve to structure human interaction, at the same time as they are themselves reproduced (Giddens 1984: 4–28, 60, 83–90). The relationships between people that are structured in this way are inevitably relationships of differential power, leading to the formation of hierarchies. Equally, though, they can lead to the formation of communities—collectivities that do things together in a more or less organised fashion (Jenkins 2004: 160–75; Wenger 1998). While we can differentiate between collective groups in a range of ways—institutions, organisations, or communities (see below)—this point gives us the opportunity to address an important question raised in Chapter 2, which has become part of the 'agency debate' in archaeology (e.g., Dobres 2000: 133): to what extent do groups have agency?

Though in a sense merely abstractions from the flow of interaction between people, institutions are certainly 'real' in their effects and consequences for actors, and in this way are also 'real' in the practices of actors. This is indeed how they come to appear to 'have' agency. However, while this must be accounted for in interpreting actors' own motivations and understandings of their world, it is the *people* whom we are studying, and lest we confuse rather than inter-relate agency and structure, "We should beware . . . of investing collectivities with the kind of substance or agency with which embodiment allows us to endow individuals" (Jenkins 2004: 81; cf. Giddens 1984: 220–1; Handley and Schadla-Hall 2004; and *contra* some of my own earlier thoughts on this, esp. Gardner 2004b: 43). This very reification has inhibited many students of the Roman military, for instance, rendering them incapable of understanding the people within that institution, and especially the ways in which those people reproduced military traditions yet also transformed them over the centuries of their existence. Thus, how people lived and shaped identities, but were also constrained by them to act in certain ways, will be our main foci here. The consequences for broader-scale 'institutional' narratives will be addressed in the final chapter, but it is at the smaller scale, where concrete social interactions occur, that the more nuanced narratives that have been missing from much Roman archaeology are to be found. We have already begun to examine these, and now we can start to look for connections between patterns of practice and identities.

From practices to identities

The building blocks of identities

Linking practices to the production and reproduction of social identities entails a consideration of some of the qualities of presence and absence associated with different activities—that is, how the people who are co-present in a particular interaction might be part of larger but more abstract communities (cf. Giddens 1984: 142–3). This, in turn, requires us to understand how artefacts materialise the connections between individuals and groups, but also to appreciate that these connections are dynamic and flexible. In this way, materiality, temporality, and sociality are fully intertwined as the fabric connecting the two parts of the duality of structure. Having already highlighted the importance of materiality and temporality in previous chapters, however, it is sociality that needs to be stressed here.

In any situation, in addition to physical constraints on 'what is possible'—which are always partly socially constructed—there are a range of enablements and constraints generated by the internal-external dialectic of identification: what is expected/believed of oneself, by oneself or by others, according to identity categorisations. These will be reproduced or transformed in the interaction between actors in specific time-space contexts. This is therefore a process of identity *negotiation*, with a variety of factors—particularly power relations—affecting the degree to which particular identities are fixed or fluid. Nonetheless, in all but the most extreme cases, the duality of structure holds good. Structure, which as rule and resource can be conceived as institutionalised identities, is both enabling and constraining. Even the most rigid and naturalised social categorisations can be resisted, subverted, or undermined (Jenkins 2004: 149). This is because the actual complexity of social life means that any individual may be categorised in a number of ways. Such complexity is manifest in the archaeology of later Roman Britain.

To return, then, to the material practices to which this archaeology relates, it is possible to develop some of the specific examples discussed in previous chapters in terms of presence-availability and distanciation and generate some interpretive principles for their relationship to identity construction. These examples, and others that have been considered at a broader scale of empirical resolution, can be grouped according to some of the inter-related practice themes identified so far: exchanging, appearing, dwelling (which encompasses moving, building, maintaining, inhabiting, and depositing), working, and eating. Through the similar or different ways in which such practices were performed, embodied individuals negotiated different aspects of identity. While this process relies heavily upon interaction and therefore co-presence, the internal-external dialectic of identification also allows for the impact of absences—that is, distant or imaginary presences (cf. Giddens 1984: 37; Urry 1991: 170–1).

Practices can have discursive identificatory significance, even when one is physically alone, if the imagined presence of particular absent others is an active influence (perhaps evoked through material culture). Even if not discursively formulated at a particular moment, however, identity is an immanent feature of all routine practices. Indeed, a general point worth emphasising is that although the notion of an internal-external *dialectic* implies a relationship with discourse and therefore discursive or reflective consciousness, this dialectic is usually sufficiently routinised to be an element of habitual action (cf. Jenkins 2004: 25), and thus of even the most mundane activities. It also underpins their emotional or affective content.

The practices that have been listed above illustrate this point well. Those associated with exchange demonstrate in particular the intersection between routinisation/presence and distanciation/absence (Gregory 1989: 205); the same can be said with regard to writing. Although the time-space contexts of exchange involving coinage are lacking from most sites in a literal sense (with some exceptions—for example, the 'market stalls' at Canterbury around the Marlowe Car Park baths), at a slightly larger scale, we can perceive both stable and fluid aspects of coin-using practices. Insofar as coins can be assumed to be associated with exchange, they are characterised by both presences and absences. As objects, they occur very commonly on almost all sites and can thus be seen as an element in routines relating to acquisition and use in contexts of interaction. At the same time, the extent to which these routines were similar from place to place depends upon the coins as expressions of distanciation—materialised as symbols of the state's political and economic power *over* interactions. In this respect, coins are embedded in processes of institutionalisation. Nonetheless, the micro- and macroscale material patterns in Britain point to shifts in the balance between presence and absence across time-space. Chronologically and regionally distinct groupings of coin loss curves, in tandem with the increased discard of coins from many sites, imply that as coins became more *present* in some locations from the late 3rd century, they also became less *absent*—less tied to the institutions (and thus identities) of the Roman state. This is in turn suggestive of the shifting range of specific kinds of action that 'exchanging' as a general practice might encompass, and what other mechanisms or kinds of objects it might involve.

Similar themes run through practices of appearing, where an even greater range of actions and potential identifications must be considered. On all of the sites subject to microscale analysis in Chapter 3, 'personal objects' were as numerically significant as coins in the categories of portable material culture encountered. Many of these objects can quite readily be associated with appearing in a particular way, and thus very much with the internal-external dialectic of identification. The common dominance of such objects in small finds assemblages across the full spectrum of Romano-British sites suggests the fundamental importance of appearing in defining and creating identities across an extremely wide range of time-space contexts. These artefacts were also part of practice contexts such as bathing, moving, and dwelling, each of which might involve people interacting with a range of others (co-present or distant/imagined) of varying degrees of familiarity. On the one hand, the importance of personal objects at a spectrum of sites of different scales—from isolated farms or communities on Hadrian's Wall to large towns in the southeast—suggests that such objects could be engaged in very localised identificatory practices (relating, for example, to age or gender within a family), albeit within larger communities of practice across Britain that probably structured some of the norms of display. On the other hand, some objects—such as crossbow brooches—were probably part of more distanciated institutional identities related to the state. Even so, their association with embodiment, as worn objects rather than detached symbols, suggests exactly the tension between fixity and fluidity that is so important in understanding social life. These were things that could be worn in different ways and move between contexts in which their meaning might change. They were symbols of an abstract state, but they were not detached from real people.

Practices associated with dwelling are even more complex, and even more likely to entail significant intersection between specific locales of co-presence and structures of distanciation. The built environment of a site obviously looms large in defining contexts of social interaction. It is important, though, not simply to view it as a container for action, but rather as an integral part of it—a *place*, not just a space (Gregory 1989: 204–8). This can be seen not only in the ways in which fort sites were institutionally, as well as architecturally, built (James 1999a: 16), but also in the manner in which they were transformed in different ways, in different places, through the 4th century. These changes—clearly visible at sites like Birdoswald, South Shields, and Binchester—were effected in building, maintaining, moving around, and inhabiting structures. They must represent significant changes in the nature of dwelling in these places and of identities, because these were transformations of an established and institutionalised set of practices. Equally, people dwelling in other kinds of site drew upon certain traditions, often modifying them over the course of the later Roman period. While vernacular building traditions may only loosely be described as institutions in themselves, they are as likely to relate to institutionalised identities—such as kinship relations and hierarchical status—as those in forts are to relate to the more organisationally concrete institutions of the military. Changes in townscapes, particularly, must then be seen as being of equal importance to understanding the transformation of practices of dwelling across Britain as those in forts. Part of their significance comes from the likely correspondence between places of dwelling and places of work (cf. Gregory 1989: 201), providing an area of overlap between these kinds of practice. All of these kinds of sites, however, were still linked by networks of roads, which must have facilitated the continued distanciation of some elements of institutional structures into the late 4th century and beyond.

'Working' obviously encompasses a broad range of practices and may be closely linked with appearing and dwelling. Working may involve a high degree of routinisation, and in an organisational setting, these routines may be linked to structures of distanciation—as in the bureaucratic procedures of the state. Writing was undoubtedly a practice related to the latter, and it is certainly assigned a key role in distanciation by Giddens (1984: 200–1; cf. Gregory 1989: 204–13). Like exchange, though, it could have diverse meanings in a variety of circumstances of localised co-presence (cf. Thompson 1990: 235–8). In such situations, particular working practices serve as axes of similarity and difference between individuals and groups at a local scale— as indeed do practices of dwelling. In these respects, the 'work styles' of people in towns and forts must stand in some contrast to rural patterns of activity, particularly in the north with its dearth of intermediate sites—although we have seen some evidence for overlap in the possibility of 'urban farms'. While the work style of many state servants was structured as a feature of institutional distanciation, the most distinctive working practice associated with military identity— violence—is scarcely represented in the material data. This will be discussed at more length in the next section, but although weapons are found at various sites, these do not occur in contexts specifically associated with large-scale warfare, being more readily linked to policing and defence duties (and thus partly also with practices of appearing). Tools of other kinds are frequent finds on a wide range of sites, indicating that specific practices associated with manufacturing, butchering, and so on (for which other evidence includes deposits of bone, etc.) might occur in similar ways in a variety of time-space contexts.

Finally, we might consider practices associated with eating and the interplays between fixity and fluidity that can be seen in the patterning of pottery and animal bone. The resolution of the material in this regard is less amenable to interpretation of microscale variation in eating practices, important as these are likely to be. The immediate social contexts of the procurement, preparation, cooking, and eating of food might be expected to vary between some of the different kinds of dwelling encountered in Roman Britain—such as a barrack room and a farm—but it is not clear what consequences changes in these dwellings would have had for eating practices. Nonetheless, the meso- and macroscale picture is relatively clear. This indicates fairly global norms of practice in terms of pottery forms and animals consumed, against which a more localised network of supplies (suggested by regionalised ceramic industries and on-site butchery) allowed for variation, which seems to have increased later in the 4th century. These patterns cross-cut sites of different types (with the exception of an important and stable correlation between higher numbers of pig bones and fort sites). They are commensurate with the critical tension between the creation of homogenising identities from the similar elements of routine practices, and the potential for fragmentation of these identities that is inherent in the small variations in conduct among places and persons.

Social change is primarily the theme of a later section, but it is clearly an implicit element in all that has been said so far. The understanding of detailed material patterns in terms of practices emphasises the importance of both stability and transformation, and of similarity and difference. This approach is the key to an integrated understanding of material and textual meanings as outlined in Chapters 2–3. Essentially, material culture participates in—and indeed constitutes— the same kinds of discourses of simplification and reification as written texts. Equally, though, while created consistencies are socially real and consequential (Jenkins 2004: 119), they are still *created*, drawn from a much more diverse and complex range of practices at different scales under conditions peculiar to particular contexts. We have seen some of the potential for this not only in the patterns of activity just discussed, but also in the descriptions of continuity and change in the Roman Empire written by people like Ammianus Marcellinus. To construct an archaeology of specific identities, then, we need to take account of both the common practices that allow for wider communities to be constructed by such writers—and more importantly by the people living in them—and also the variations that relate to overlapping identities with a different focus (such as gender) or that allow for different scales of identity in a more spatial sense. I will now try to demonstrate how this can work with one of the most visible categories in the context we have been discussing.

Locating distinctive practices: defining military identity

The starting point for interpreting the nature of military identities in the 4th century must be the isolation of particular kinds of practice that might be associated with these types of identities. While this isolation is an analytical step in the first instance, it also reflects certain features of social life just discussed—particularly the reification of abstract, stable stereotypes, selectively drawn from the complexities of daily interactions. Initially, I will focus upon the most overtly institutionalised practices evident in the material and textual patterns outlined so far, taking such institutionalisation to be implicitly relevant to the definition of what is 'military'. In this regard, some general comments on institutions and organisations will be helpful. For Giddens, institutions are "the more enduring features of social life" (1984: 24), which may be classified in various orders: political, legal, and economic. However, these analytical tools are rather crude, and we require further resolution to filter out some of the other likely institutionalised features of life in later Roman Britain and focus on the distinctive characteristics of 'the military' and other associated levels of identification.

It is thus necessary to bring in Richard Jenkins's useful distinction between institutions and organisations (2004: 142–4). Whereas the former label might be applied to a wide range of practices that are 'stretched' across time-space, organisations have a specific internal-external dialectic, involving relationships of similarity and difference both at the organisational boundary (members being distinguished from nonmembers by recruitment procedures and participation in the shared goals of the organisation), and within it (subdivisions of power and role 'inside' the organisation). Although organisations and organisational identities—like institutions in general—entail a degree of abstraction from the complexities of day-to-day living, being defined by only selected aspects of behaviour, they are obviously still dependent upon interaction for their reproduction. What they do is generate predictable and routine activities, and harness them for particular goals, at the same time as reifying these specific routines as natural and 'normal' for the group (Giddens 1984: 179–80; Jenkins 2004: 145–59). In this section, I will focus on those practices that have most bearing upon the creation of an organised identity across the Roman military, leaving until a later section the detailed consideration of the broader range of complexities (consisting largely in any individual's participation in an *intersecting range* of institutions) and their significance in the social life of people across Roman Britain.

210 ■ An Archaeology of Identity

Even before reaching this point, though, we will not be able to ignore the importance of divisions within an organisation, which alert us to the potential significance of nested tiers of identifications (e.g., rank, unit), and that may have their own sets of organisational goals. While closely associated with a wider 'military' identity, these should not be collapsed into it.

Remaining at a broad level for now, however, one of the most obviously institutionalised practices that ought to be involved with military identification is writing. Certainly, it is from writing *about* 'military' identity groups that many of our pre-understandings concerning the existence and nature of such identities come. The specific nominal labels denoting 'military' or associated identities (such as unit titles) that occur in a range of sources—and particularly the *Notitia Dignitatum*—will be discussed further below. Here, our focus is more upon the practices from which identities emerged, and in the context of writing it is necessary to consider the range of textual technologies used in the military bureaucracy. This is somewhat problematic with respect to later Roman Britain, mainly because of the dearth of directly related evidence. Moreover, some of the most important examples of record keeping in this period are associated with 'state' organisation (as is the case with the *Notitia*), rather than specifically 'military' organisation. This institutional blurring is actually rather significant and will be pursued at a later point.

However, examples from other, often earlier contexts—such as the Vindolanda tablets and the 3rd century papyri found at Dura-Europos in Syria—do indicate particular forms of writing associated with military organisations, in the form of unit strength reports, festival calendars, and so forth (Bowman 1994: 34–9; James 1999a: 16–21). In the 4th century, however, these are rare even in the Abinnaeus Archive (although matters such as recruitment and leave do appear indirectly), which is much more a collection of correspondence. It must largely be assumed, therefore, that some such specifically institutionalised practices continued in this period (perhaps, for instance, to keep the compiler of the *Notitia* informed [Hassall 1976: 103–4]) and that these did serve to make military units organisationally distinct in the extent and form of literacy. Indications from some of the earlier sources, however, suggest that military paperwork was both quite variable from area to area and (perhaps obviously) was more concerned with 'internal' identity categories like rank, rather than an outsider's discourse of 'the military' (Bowman 1994: 34–5); where the latter does appear it tends to be with reference to 'soldiers'—i.e., individuals, not an institution. Writing, then, can be seen as engaged in both the external (somewhat distinctive bureaucratic practices) and internal (variable ways of administering subgroupings; different degrees of use according to rank) moments of the dialectic of identification at the organisational level. It may have been either explicitly 'military' or not, depending on the particular context of co-presence in which it appeared (and therefore also on the dialectic of identification at the interactional level). It was also dynamic over longer intervals of time, as the decline of inscriptions relating to soldiers (and indeed, therefore, of representations [Coulston 1990]) in the 4th century, noted in Chapter 3, indicates.

Similar issues of scale and perspective can also be highlighted by drawing particular institutionalised practices of dwelling from the sites discussed in previous chapters, and attempting to link these in to 'military' identities. The association between fort architecture and the Roman military is obviously well established and rightly so, even if part of the inspiration for this book is the problem of 'civilian' occupation of fort sites. While the simple dichotomy this implies will be undermined throughout this chapter, it is still valid to ask on what level, and in what particular ways, life in a fort might be labelled 'military'. In this fashion, we can distinguish (in the same way as Reece has done for towns [1988: 126]) 'fort life' from 'life in forts'—the one being a specific way of life intimately linked to the fort environment, the other simply living of a more generic kind that happens to be occurring in a fort-shaped space. While it is easy to oversimplify past lives by careless use of labels such as 'military', this does not mean that similar strategies of stereotyping played no part in those lives. With respect to potentially military aspects of dwelling, an understanding of these must come from those aspects of space associated with organisation—though, as we will see, even here there is room for other identifications than simply 'military'.

The ideal model of a fort is certainly appropriate to the military as an institution. Ignoring the variation between sites for the time being, forts do have certain important common features: a regular boundary marked by a large barrier; a network of straight axes of movement; a central focus of sanctified authority; and a markedly differentiated hierarchy of dwelling spaces (standard barrack rooms, end barrack rooms, courtyard houses). These features imply a disciplining of space (Giddens 1984: 145–58; James 1999a: 16), but they can also be related to the external and internal divisions that characterise organisations. The external community is defined not only by the wall, but by the singularity of the internal arrangement of space (which is, for instance, different from towns). Members are both united and divided by architectural expressions of power, corporate homogeneity, and status distinction. If we add writing—which facilitates the extension of discipline in time as well as space—and a notional common goal of domination, fort architecture can clearly be related to an organisational discourse; the latter, by virtue of its spread across the empire, can in turn be associated with a large-scale, abstract identity like 'militariness'—which is simultaneously made real through a range of practices conducted in specific places. This, however, is counter-balanced by the complexity of the people actually moving through these places.

Even in a 4th century fort like South Shields that conforms fairly closely to the ideal type, questions need to be asked about the extent to which this arrangement of space actually did discipline the lives of those inhabiting it, as well as about the other axes of identification that might be more prominent than 'militariness' at interactional scales. While some of the corporate dimensions of the fort as dwelling place would seem to relate to a larger-scale identity (similarities in architecture from place to place; spaces used for activities associated with imperial cult or law), others are more localised. The 'unit' itself is an obvious focus here, one that is most immediately manifest in the fort as a whole and movement around it in the course of a day's activities. Further internal subdivisions of rank or status are also very immediate in the distinctions among barracks, *praetorium*, and *principia*. In these senses, to members of the organisation, the 'military' as a pan-imperial identity (James 1999a) is only the top tier of an extensive hierarchy of identities bound up with dwelling in this place.

While this broad 'militariness' may also be important in interactions with nonmembers, the boundary is blurred because of the other people moving in or around the fort, who add a range of competing institutions (e.g., of gender distinction) as well as an alternative definition of 'military'—in the sense of a 'fort-based community' rather than an overarching organisation consisting only of soldiers (James 1999a: 23). These alternatives are obviously not incompatible, and each might be appropriate under different circumstances. The presence of people who were not members in the organisational sense is indicated in the finds evidence and, given the likely strength of the connections— marriage, kinship, friendship, enslavement, clientship—between these and soldiers (notwithstanding other, more transient visitors), the organisational homogeneity of the fort is disrupted. Thus, while fort architecture is strongly associated with specific aspects of dwelling as part of the organisation of Roman military units, the relationship between these (and 'the military' as a broader identity group) and other members of a fort community—also 'military'—at an interactional scale is complex. Each label only applies from a certain point of view.

Some reference has already been made to the importance of a particular suite of institutionalised practices to 'military' identities: those classed as 'working,' which—in this case—primarily means organised violence (along with associated activities like training). Although Giddens has distinguished 'military power' from 'policing power' (Cohen 1989: 177), some of the texts in the Abinnaeus Archive suggest that Roman soldiers could serve either function, at least in mid-4th century Egypt, and indeed that both were implicated in the particular constitution of any 'military' identity (Bell et al. 1962: 1–15; cf. Bagnall 1993: 173). As already noted, the material culture of violence is actually quite poorly represented in the direct sense in the archaeological evidence from Roman Britain. Weapons are relatively rare finds, and when they do occur are not confined to fort sites (e.g., there are spearheads at Barton Court Farm [Miles 1986]); the same is also true of fortifications. Either these indicate that soldiers moved around outside of the organised space of forts, or that other categories of people had access to 'the means of violence' (Cohen 1989: 177). Probably both occurred; the latter has certainly been suggested as an explanation for the diversity of defended sites in northern Gaul in this period, which include hilltop 'refugia' (Brulet 1990: 309–13). The ambiguity of many of the latter highlights the important point that 'military' identity, as discussed so far (and see below), tends to be strongly associated with the state and state-organised violence, and this allows some distinction between this identity group and other potential sources of control over violent action.

Indeed, regardless of whether soldiers had exclusive rights in the use of force in provincial society, they are profoundly associated with violence in textual constructions of 'militariness', and this finds close parallels in material practices of 'appearing' (see below). In the writings of late Roman historians, but also in some of the more documentary sources, soldiers are generally characterised as fundamentally aggressive. There are of course exceptions, and it is important to note that this aggression can be valued positively (as in the service afforded to the state by brave soldiers in battle [e.g., Ammianus, XVI.12]) as well as negatively (as in the harassment of villagers or tendencies towards mutiny and indiscipline [e.g. Abinnaeus Archive, Text 28; Ammianus, XX.4]). However, in these sources, we also find that this particular 'military' characteristic is not free from complications, as it is closely bound up with gender, status, and—increasingly in the 4th century—ethnic identifications. Soldiers were portrayed as violent not simply because they were soldiers, but also because they were men, often of low status, and associated by the Mediterranean elite with the trend towards 'barbarisation' in frontier provinces. Mention has already been made of the significance of changing aristocratic conceptions of masculinity, evident in the portrayal of common soldiers in literature (Alston 1998); this merely took on new nuances in the 4th century. None of this is intended to deny the centrality of violence to military identity or to the congealing of subunit groups in the traumatic conditions of fighting, but merely to point out that in both literary discourses about soldiers and in the material discourses of soldiers about themselves, 'military' might have been a simplifying identity—but it was not simple.

This combination of an 'occupational' identity—which can be constructed on different levels—with others relating to masculinity, status, and ethnicity (as well as state service) can also be seen in practices of 'appearing' that might be linked to 'militariness'. There are serious limitations, though, to the material available directly to us, as many elements of whatever 'uniform' soldiers might have had in 4th century Britain do not survive archaeologically—garments like the tunics, trousers, boots, and cloaks believed (on the basis of representational and archaeological evidence from other parts of the empire) to constitute an important medium for the construction of military identity in the 3rd century (James 1999a: 18–21). The only material in the northwestern empire that allows us to trace the continuation or transformation of this important aspect of 'appearing' into the 4th century is metalwork: particularly the crossbow brooches and belt fittings discussed in Chapters 3–4. These items, along with weapons and armour (probably carried/worn in a smaller range of contexts), potentially constructed a distinctive form of embodiment for a soldier, based on sounds and smells as well as visual appearance (James 1999a: 21). This would find support in some textual constructions of soldierly appearance (e.g., Vegetius, II.12).

However, as with some of the other practices discussed above that might be distinctively 'military', this label should not be applied too loosely in the present, even if it might have been an oversimplification in the past. As with any other aspect of organisational identity, appearance relates to cross-cutting institutions as well as to those that are linked to the organisation on different levels: the state, a particular unit or rank, masculinity, personal wealth or status, regional identities, and religious affiliations were all potentially involved in constituting the meaning of dress elements, which—some of the time—were engaged in the definition of military identity. Many of these other institutions will be dealt with in a later section; here, I am only concerned with those that cluster around 'militariness'. Some of the objects referred to earlier in connection with this identity, particularly belt fittings and crossbow brooches, need to be considered here, but their distribution within Britain is problematically wide (making it difficult to associate them definitively with mobile soldiers *or* nonsoldiers), while the burial evidence from Oudenburg does not really support the notion of a rigidly defined uniform (cf. Philpott 1991: 140, 188–9; Swift 2000: 43). This is perhaps to be expected given the potential diversity of the individual biographies of each individual object.

There is little doubt, from other evidence, that similar items could be employed in the construction of generalised 'official' status (as in Ammianus, XXII.10; cf. Zosimus, VI.19.2); at smaller scales, it is conceivable that minor variations in form could have significance in terms of rank (Reece 1999a: 154–61; Swift 2000: 36–52; cf. Ammianus, XIX.11), though regional identities might also have been signified by these. Textile elements, too, might have had rather wider currency than the soldiers (James 1999a: 19), although a mixture of commonplace and specific items may well have been worn (Theodosian Code, XIV.10). In each case, we return to the importance of context as pinning down meanings. Thus, for example, the crossbow brooches found at Caernarfon—even if worn by soldiers—might have primarily signified rank or status to both wearer and audience within this community (along with more individual biographical features), only coming to mean 'military' if the soldier travelled to Caerwent (where more brooches were found). On the route between these places, though, passing through areas less familiar with state representatives, such objects might primarily mean 'Roman' or 'official'—again, both to wearer and audience (linked through the internal-external dialectic) within the context of each specific interaction. The complexity of the organisation of the late Roman state thus means that even with 'official' markers, both external and internal boundaries could have a range of connotations, and a specifically 'military' identity is but one of these.

'Exchanging' is one kind of practice that, as argued previously, cannot readily be pinned down to any possible dimensions or expressions of military identity in the 4th century, although this needs some qualification. While it is certainly the case that the increase in the incidence of coin use in Britain (uneven—regionally and socially—as this was) diluted the distinctiveness of its association with fort communities in the 1st and 2nd centuries, there might still have been particular features of coinage associated with 'militariness'. These are largely invisible at the level of assemblages as they concern individual issues or denominations, and the messages struck onto them. There has been some interest in whether the pay of state servants remained the leading factor in pulling coins into a diocese like Britain, even after the apparent shift to supply 'in kind', as such individuals still seem to have received money in the form of donatives—which might be distinctive issues (Casey 1988; Reece 1977). If this was the case, though, we are dealing both with a blurred 'military'/'state' identity, and with something that would probably vary from unit to unit. Slightly less problematic, however, are certain legends on some 4th century coins, such as *Gloria Exercitus*—'the glory of the armies' accompanied by depictions of armed figures. Although such coins passed through the hands of many different people (this example being one of the more common 4th century types in Britain), such images would have been a strong element in the construction of a pan-regional military identity, stereotyping soldiers in the eyes of members and nonmembers of this celebrated organisation.

The final practice context for which there are some signs of distinctiveness that can be linked to 'military' or associated identities is eating. While both pottery and animal bone generally relate to other dimensions and scales of identification (as we will see below), one feature of the bone assemblages from a number of fort sites—the high incidence of pig—stands out. This is important because of the established background, from earlier periods, of pork as a more commonly Italian food preference retained by some elements in the Roman military, albeit usually legions (King 1999a: 139). Along with architecture, this distinguishes the inhabitants of forts in a way that may be closely linked to certain traditions. Whether these traditions were discursively constituted as such, or simply reproduced in practical consciousness as the 'way things are done' (cf. Giddens 1984: 200–1), is arguable, but both circumstances are possible—and indeed likely, given that it seems that this was not a completely uniform phenomenon common to all forts, but rather a feature of particular practices in certain places.

At some of these places, we may be dealing with specific, routinised traditions of long-established communities (e.g., at Caerleon or York), while at others there may have been more self-conscious differentiation (as at the more recently established community at Portchester). In either case, and dependent upon the balance between routinisation of these practices and their discursive formulation in particular interactions, the emphasis on communities of place (perhaps closely tied to a particular unit) begins to fracture the idea of a common 'military' identity. Indeed, this again highlights an issue raised previously in this section: that in attempting to understand the use of 'military' as a specific identity label in the past, we must be alert to the scale(s) at which it had significance. Stereotyping and reifying though it may have been, other (equally institutionalised) labels may have been more important at the scale of interactions within a fort community, even if in our terms these would all be treated as 'military'. This problematic relationship between labels and experience will, in the next section, take us closer to the distinctive character of life in later Roman Britain.

The social world in late Roman Britain

Understanding military identities: the nominal and the virtual

Having located some of the major areas of practice with which 'military' and related identities might have been associated (both practically and discursively), as well as some intersecting institutions, we need to explore how these fit together in terms of the nominal and virtual aspects of 'military' identification. This distinction permits an even more refined understanding of the recursive relationship between the institutional and interactional scales of social life in the construction of identities in later Roman Britain. In particular, it allows us to fully exploit the variation in the available evidence with regard to both the different labels and names associated with 'military' organisations, and the localised experience of living in these organisations. The latter are well represented in a range of subtle ways when the practices discussed above are examined in more detail. The nominal-virtual relationship is thus critical in dealing with both fixity and fluidity; as Jenkins writes, "[I]t allows us to think about the fact that abstractly collective institutionalised identifications . . . are occupied by embodied individuals, yet are also independent of them" (2004: 142). This independence, however, cannot, be absolute, and it will be argued in a later section that the transformation that we describe as the 'decline and fall of the Roman Empire' was indeed *effected* by the actions of embodied individuals reshaping institutions over time, albeit largely unintentionally; as a consequence, there were multiple viewpoints about the significance and extent of this change.

Already, in the preceding section, some of the potential complexity of the nominal aspects of 'the military' has emerged. 'Military' itself, while tending to be employed as an all-encompassing label in present usage, had specific uses and contextual connotations in Roman-period discourses, even if it was also—and at the same time—as stereotyping and simplifying as any other social categorisation. The picture is further complicated by the frequent intersection of identity boundaries of different types (i.e., internal and external) in routine interactions. Other labels that can be linked to 'military', but that are not the same thing and relate to different levels of social identification within this institution, include those for armies, soldiers, grades of units (e.g., *comitatenses, limitanei*), unit titles, ranks, organisational subunits, place of posting, and possibly social/officers' clubs. While these are all likely to have been of greater importance in microscale interactions involving people familiar with soldiers, 'military' identity—as a primarily macroscale identity—might still be drawn upon in stereotyping an individual in other contexts of interaction, though quite possibly involving a close congruence with a more generalised state identity. Thus, even ignoring other, potentially highly significant institutionalised identities such as gender, the complexity of the relationships among state, 'military' (as a generalised institution), and submilitary organisational identities constitutes a wide range of potential boundaries (and material meanings) to be drawn upon in any particular context.

Disentangling these requires a closer look at 'military' as part of the nominal dimension of identification, and attention to some of the documentary and literary evidence for labelling practices. Ammianus often draws a distinction between military and civilian authority within state affairs (e.g., XX.5, XXI.16), just as he often distinguishes between soldiers (*milites* or *armati*) and other citizens (e.g., XIX.8, XXI.10). His discourse is thus one of distinctiveness and division along nominal lines, in both high politics and daily life. The former is also reflected in the highest level of categorisation in the *Notitia Dignitatum*: the overall title ('*Notitia Dignitatum omnium, tam civilium quam militarium*'). These 'civil' and 'military' offices are indeed partly nominally distinct—with *vicarii* in control of administration and *duces* and *comites* in charge of units of soldiers—but the latter title, and others like *magister*, also applies to court officials. Units are distinguished by their titles (e.g., *numerus barcariorum Tigrisiensium* [*Occ.* XL.22]) and places of posting (for the *limitanei* frontier troops, not the mobile *comitatenses*—an important element of sub-'military' differentiation). Other internal organisational boundaries are dealt with below, but it is important to note here that the impression of rigid military/civil separation in state affairs is belied by the use of a term for soldiers (*milites*) for other state servants than those under arms, in laws of the Theodosian Code (Pharr 1952: 155, fn. 23). It is also evident from the Abinnaeus Archive that there could be considerable jurisdictional confusion in matters such as tax collection between nominally 'civil' and 'military' authorities (e.g., Text 13).

The organisational structure behind any notion of 'military' identity furnishes a highly fractured series of unit and rank classifications. While the detail of the *Notitia Dignitatum*'s account of the hierarchy of state offices cannot be matched elsewhere, the general principles of naming organisational statuses are found in other sources, including Ammianus (e.g., XVIII.9) and the Abinnaeus Archive (e.g., Texts 1–3). Mention has already been made of the division between mobile *comitatenses* and static *limitanei*, and the location of the latter in a fixed posting creates quite a specific identity focus lacking for the former (in Text 1 of the Abinnaeus Archive, for example, the unit is often referred to by its posting rather than its title). Other larger-scale groupings of units might take the form of 'army/armies' (*exercitus* [Vegetius III.1]), perhaps under the command of one of the *magistri militum* or an individual *comes* or *dux*. Individual units, however (as we will see below), seem a much more important focus of identification. Their titles were quite variable, involving different combinations of unit type (e.g., *numerus, equites*), 'ethnic' name or place of origin, the name of an individual or an imperial title, or some other honorary or functional description. Below this nominal scale, there were a series of smaller official or semi-official group categories—*centuria, contubernium*, and perhaps *collegium*—and individual statuses or ranks— from the commander of the unit, such as a *tribunus* or *praefectus*, to a soldier (e.g., Theodosian Code, VII, *passim*; cf. Pegler 2000; Southern and Dixon 1996: 55–64). Although all of these are associated fairly directly with the *armatae militiae* (the armed service [Pharr 1952: 155, fn. 23]), they constitute an elaborate network of similarity and differ- ence, as well as a series of potential links to the wider social world— e.g., to similar rank structures in the administration, to places, or to ethnicities created or legitimised by the Roman establishment).

To summarise, the 'military'—the institutionalised profession of soldiers—was clearly constructed as a specific community (James 1999a), and we should not doubt that this could be 'really' conse- quential in terms of interactions, as indicated in the discussion of par- ticular practices above, and by sources such as the Theodosian Code. The laws contained in this document closely regulated soldiers' behav- iour, from clothing to supply. However, such laws—some of which had to be repeated several times, indicating that they may not have been effective—are themselves part of the process of identity creation. 'Military' identity, like all identities, was a construction—a nominal abstraction—which, aside from other cross-cutting identity categories (to be examined in the next section), simplified a more complex set of relationships between soldiers and other state representatives on the one hand, and within the category of soldiers on the other. In both cases, boundaries were almost certainly contested (e.g., in jurisdic- tional disputes), as these classifications entailed differential power or status. The point is that while 'the military' was a real identity that can perhaps be situated analytically as a large-scale or macrolevel social institution, it sits at the centre of a whole cluster of organisational identities that are at least as likely to have been negotiated in material or textual discourses of similarity and difference. All of these identities might be immanent in any particular context, even if not discursively formulated at that point, and all of course were also abstractions serving to regulate interactions—but subject to considerable virtual variation. This variation can be seen quite clearly in the material patterns from 4th century Britain.

To illustrate the discussion of the relationship between the virtual and the nominal dimensions of identification, I will focus on a couple of sites only: South Shields and Housesteads. South Shields, in its reconstructed form of the early 4th century, bears many indications of the institutionalised practices that can be related to 'military' identity. These features—including the hierarchy of accommodation, the formality of the layout, the finds of crossbow brooches, and the maintenance of a *principia* structure that was kept clear of generalised rubbish—can all be seen as part of a distinctive lifestyle. However, there are also many smaller-scale signs of variation and change that can be understood in terms of the virtual consequences of other nominal aspects of identity. The discursive formulation of any of the aforementioned characteristics as 'military' would depend on the context of discourse—perhaps if comparison were being made with people from surrounding settlements, towns further south, or another unit, although even here this would only be likely if the interaction was proceeding from a point of total unfamiliarity. In many other circumstances, the virtual aspects of life in this place would be engaged in the construction of other kinds of identification.

Those pertaining to rank and hierarchy within the unit organisation are fairly obvious. Both in terms of dwelling and very likely appearing, differences between ranks were marked; more subtle are distinctions between groups who were nominally of the same rank. The individual rooms of particular barracks had their own unique biographies, and as places of dwelling themselves, these biographies were created by the actions of the small groups inhabiting them. For example, each pair of rooms had its own localised sequence of fireplaces or of partitioning arrangements (Bidwell and Speak 1994: 43–4). These divisions formed the internal organisational structures of another nominal entity—the unit. In this case, the *Notitia* has been used to assert the identity of this as the *numerus barcariorum Tigrisiensium* ('unit of Tigris bargemen' [e.g., Bidwell and Speak 1994: 42]), part of the northern *limites* command of the *Dux Britanniarum* (*Occ.* XL). While scepticism towards the *Notitia* is always healthy, because of the problems surrounding its composition, here the nominal and virtual aspects of identification can be brought together well. A newer unit apparently brought into South Shields from the east of the empire would appropriately account for some of the more strongly institutionalised elements of the site (see above and Chapter 4), linking to other elements of the empire-wide military identity group (and other groups particular to the central/eastern empire—as in the case of the 'Mediterranean' officer's house [Fig. 5.1]) rather than local traditions. This permits a contrast with some of the other sites on Hadrian's Wall apparently occupied by more long-established—and perhaps lower status—units, such as Housesteads.

Although much of the detailed patterning is less well understood at Housesteads, it seems that there is more variation from the institutionalised ideal found at South Shields in the early 4th century. This is the case not simply for the different levels of nominal identity (e.g., ranks) mentioned in connection with the latter, although the virtual experience of these might well be different here (Jenkins 2004: 142), but also in terms of the nominal/virtual relationship at the particular

Figure 5.1. Photograph of the interior of the reconstructed 4th century officer's house at South Shields.

level of unit/place identities. In the *Notitia*, Housesteads is occupied by the *cohors prima Tungrorum*, which seems from other evidence to have been in post from the early 2nd century (Crow 1995: 56–63; *Notitia Occ.* XL.40). This is an older type of unit, part of the *legio/cohors/ala* system of the early empire that was supplemented by units with titles like '*numerus*' in the later period. Some scholars have rejected the length of continuous occupation that the *Notitia* suggests, disbelieving that a unit could persist in garrison for so long, particularly as various 'frontier disasters' have been postulated for later Roman Britain (e.g., Frere 1987: 17–26). However, the evidence for these is flimsy (cf. Hodgson 1991: 84–7), and more importantly the site's 4th century material culture would be appropriate to this kind of nominal identification—i.e., a long occupation by an 'old-fashioned' type of unit (cf. Bidwell 1997: 104).

Thus, while 'military' institutionalised features of life are certainly evident, and there are still signs of organised change (such as the wholesale rebuilding of barracks as 'chalets'), the form of these barracks and their subsequent development (Crow 1995: 85, 2004: 103; Wilkes 1960, 1961), as well as significant modifications to the *principia* (Bosanquet 1904: 208–25), could be accounted for in terms of a more deeply embedded attachment to the localised routines of small-group life and to a particular sense of 'place' as constructed through these (Fig. 5.2). Interestingly, the apparent arrival of another unit in the 3rd century (the *cuneus Frisiorum*), which may be synonymous with the *numerus Hnaudufridi* and which is attested epigraphically

Figure 5.2. Photograph of one of the 'chalet' barrack rooms at Housesteads.

(Crow 1995: 59–60), seems to have little impact on these routines apart from the appearance of a relatively short-lived, but distinctive, 'Frisian' ware—perhaps because they were housed outside the fort (Crow 2004: 79–81; Jobey 1979). Even if this ceramic link is valid (and there are problems with dating based on similar wares from other sites), the new ware need not have persisted for more than a generation, and does not correlate with the other, later signs of change. Overall, then, this seems to be quite an insular community in the 4th century, with traditions mixing institutional and developing local features, and change responding to local priorities as much as to outside influences (cf. Crow 1995: 91). In these circumstances, unit/place and other small-scale foci are likely to have been at least as important in routine identifications as 'the military'. It is worth noting that such insularity also seems to develop over the course of the 4th century at South Shields, particularly with a different pattern of occupation in the courtyard house. While the institutional similarities between these units can be partly understood in 'military' terms, the common development of place-oriented differences relates to equally strong localised identities.

Similar points of comparison can be drawn out with all kinds of sites, highlighting variations that are relevant to different nominal statuses (as is partly the case with South Shields and Housesteads) and different virtual experiences of similar nominal identities (as with the differences between Housesteads and the barracks/stores sequences at Birdoswald, also home to a long-established unit [Richmond and Birley 1930; Wilmott 1997: 14, 195–202]). These comparisons emphasise the importance of localised scales of identification, both in nominal and virtual aspects, and this leads us to an important point with regard to one of the archaeological problems outlined in Chapter 1: the identification of different assemblages as 'military' or 'civilian'. From what has been said so far in this chapter, it should be clear that 'military' assemblages cannot be straightforwardly identified in 4th century Britain because soldiers were not confined to forts, because nonsoldiers lived in forts, and above all because the 'military' as a meaningful identity label in the past may have been latent in many of the interactions taking place at forts or elsewhere—but was much less important in many of these than smaller-scale identifications with different foci, which created different material patterns.

While the possession of a certain degree of social power might be regarded as a distinctive feature of being a soldier in many situations (and many of the letters in the Abinnaeus Archive relate to such power [e.g., Text 28]), this was still relative to rank, unit status, and other relations with the local community. At least in the Egyptian context of the Archive, these were extensive, encompassing patronage, property dealings, and family connections (e.g., Texts 3, 21, 35, 58, 60, 62, 80–82). A soldier's status also owed something to the social background and gender of the individual (cf. Ammianus, XIX.8, XX.4; see below). Furthermore, even some of the most institutionalised practices that one can associate with 'militariness', such as particular aspects of dwelling, were not only virtually variable in forts but could be subject to major dislocation if soldiers were based in towns (e.g., Theodosian Code, VII.8–9). The problems this caused in discipline were a common motif for Late Antique writers (e.g., Zosimus, II.34), and while this is partly a product of the discourse of 'the soldiers' constructed by the literary class, it may well also reflect one genuine situation in which 'military' identity became discursively contested—away from any specific architectural environment—encouraging soldiers to 'act the part' to maintain some of their distinctiveness.

In this section, through an examination of similarities and differences at various scales of practice and in nominal and virtual aspects of identification, I have tried to demonstrate that while military identity was socially real in late Roman Britain, it was itself an abstraction of a complex cluster of associated identities, which—importantly—are likely to have been more commonly drawn upon in the kinds of small-scale interactions to which much of the material patterning at individual sites relates. Military identity was expressed in specific contexts, such as in the discourses of writers who were addressing themselves to those who did not live with soldiers, or in material discourses at points of contact with others (as when on the move through town or countryside, although the artefacts engaged in these would 'mean' different things in other circumstances). Unfortunately, some of these discourses—such as those expressed through material like garments or through particularly aggressive behaviour—are not archaeologically visible. Nonetheless, it is possible to assess the relationships between those elements of military and related identities that can be located in practices, and a host of other, overlapping identifications that would have been of considerable importance in small-scale interactions. It is to these that we now turn.

The military and the Roman state

In the preceding section, one of the most important areas of institutional blurring located in several practice contexts was that between military identity and others associated with the Roman state, and this is worth pursuing further. Partly this is because it is a key element in understanding the nature of power structures in late Roman-period Britain and is therefore important in charting social change. Furthermore, this particular overlap also leads us into a broader spectrum of what might be (somewhat inappropriately) termed 'civilian' identities, which actually cross-cut 'military' identities in a range of ways. As with the different sublevels of the latter, it is likely that, with regard to 'state' identities, the engagement of material culture in identification can only be seen in terms of 'either/or' oppositions if these are seen as dynamic. It should not be a question of identifying which artefacts universally 'meant' military instead of official, or vice-versa, but rather of locating practice contexts when one or other such meaning was more prominent, given that both might be available. This requires the comparison of a more diverse spectrum of sites than the forts that dominated the previous section, and in particular the examination of certain aspects of towns.

Before proceeding with this discussion, it is worth noting that the complexity of the relationship between 'military' and 'civil' service in the late Roman Empire (which is indeed not peculiar to this period of Roman history) has long been recognised (e.g., Tomlin 1976), and is indeed an element in the casting of the 4th century empire as an authoritarian state. Even so, a slightly contradictory picture is often presented whereby military and civil authority were rigidly separated by Diocletian (e.g., Frere 1987: 331–2), while at the same time the late Roman state was highly militaristic, to such an extent that it has been compared with modern states like Nazi Germany (e.g., Faulkner 2000: 98, 110). Both viewpoints are based on an over-reliance on certain written sources—in the latter case, bodies of codified law like the Theodosian Code—as well as a failure to engage with multi-vocality (see below). The problems of assuming that such laws (which were, it must be remembered, only *codified* in the early 5th century) represent social life across the empire have already been touched upon above (and see Cameron 1993a: 26–7, 45–6, 111–2). Notwithstanding this, analogies with modern totalitarian states are clearly problematic, both in terms of the different modern constructions of nationhood and of the vastly superior technologies of surveillance and control available to modern states. One aspect of states like Nazi Germany does, however, resonate with some of the situations referred to in, for instance, the Abinnaeus Archive: jurisdictional conflict between different branches of the state service.

This can be used to account for some of the confusion in the ways such identities were constructed in different written discourses.

226 ■ An Archaeology of Identity

Even in the nominal dimension of identification, there is considerable overlap. Mention has already been made of some of the problems surrounding labels like *militiae*, used in distinction to 'civilian' or 'citizens' in some contexts (e.g., by Ammianus, who also uses *armatae* for soldiers [XX.5.7, XIX.8.4, XXII.2.4]) but applied to all servants of the emperor(s) in others (e.g., the Theodosian Code, VII.1.5, necessitating the specific labelling of soldiers as 'armed'). In the *Notitia*, in spite of the distinction made in the overall title, several of the ranks and offices occur commonly in both the superficially 'civilian' and 'military' branches of the service (e.g., *comites*, *magistri*, and more junior *officium* ranks). Again, though, this seems to run somewhat contrary to some of Ammianus' remarks on the importance of separation between 'military' and 'civil' administration (e.g., XXI.16; XXVII.9). This situation should not be surprising, and the contexts of these various sources must be taken into account. Ammianus' assertions of some of the distinctive aspects of military identity—bearing in mind that he had been a (high-status) soldier himself—may precisely indicate increased boundary blurring or contestation, while the compilers of the Theodosian Code were creating a more centralising vision for the emperor over a century after the promulgation of some of the laws they were gathering. During this time, the virtual connotations of nominal labels may well have changed significantly. The *Notitia* might also be expected to present a more homogenising picture than some other sources.

The blurred and contested boundary between 'military' and 'official' identities can be pursued through the virtual consequences of these nominal labels, and these are clearly apparent in some of the conflicts over tax collection and other duties in the Abinnaeus Archive (e.g., Texts 13, 14); similar problems might have occurred with judicial authority. Locating such 'official' practices in material contexts from Britain entails focusing once again on institutionalised or organised phenomena, but this is problematic. These specific kinds of 'working' need not have quite the same 'lifestyle' implications as membership in an armed unit. Nonetheless, one possible avenue to pursue is the similarity between *forum* and *principia* structures. While no doubt functionally distinct in detail (although both generally were used for administration and judgement), there are some parallel changes in these kinds of structure in the 4th century. One of the most interesting comparisons is between the changes to the *principia* at York (Phillips and Heywood 1995a, 1995b) and those to the *forum* at Cirencester (Holbrook and Timby 1998a: 113–21; Wacher 1964: 9–14), both involving similar modifications to—and restrictions of— access in the *basilica* in ways suggestive of continued administrative use.

Of course, at other sites (e.g., Caerwent and Wroxeter, or Caerleon and Housesteads [see Chapter 4]), such structures seem to have undergone more radical changes, involving partial demolition or reuse for light industrial or other activities and thus perhaps a diminution of some public functions. So here we have a re-emphasis on the importance of localised trajectories, with some sites, perhaps maintaining stronger ties to the central state, having more—or just different—'official' practices than others. The church was also developing more elaborate administrative structures in this period, and these may be another part of this picture. It has been suggested, for example, that the timber-framed buildings constructed over the demolished baths *basilica* at Wroxeter were associated with an ecclesiastical official (Barker et al. 1997: 237–8). As with 'military' identity, then, 'official' identity could be multifaceted.

There are other 'organised' practices evident in towns that might relate to 'official' identities, though these again constitute similarities with forts and differences from farmsteads and villages, potentially marking out both of the former as 'official' communities. Taking a broader perspective to structural sequences through dwelling practices, while the institutionalisation of space in town sites clearly differed from those in a fort, with the fluidity of arrangements of houses and streets evident at sites like Canterbury's Marlowe Car Park (Blockley et al. 1995a), there were important similarities. These included the relative density of settlement—with corresponding implications in terms of rubbish disposal—and also, in many cases, the enclosure of space within walls. Eating practices can also be seen as institutionalised in somewhat similar ways. Large-scale slaughtering of animals at a late date is indicated at towns like Lincoln (Dobney et al. 1995) and Cirencester (Holbrook and Timby 1998b; Timby et al. 1998), while ceramic supply is as diverse as it is for forts, and more so than for farms. There are also signs of the active maintenance of roads and open spaces in several towns (e.g., Cirencester [Holbrook and Salvatore 1998: 23–5]). Exchanging and appearing are more complicated, as the former seems to be subject to more regional variation, while the indications from small finds assemblages are that the latter involved common elements across fort, town, and farmstead sites—even for 'official' metalwork, which does occur on farms and villas (e.g., Orton Hall Farm [Mackreth 1996]).

Of course, one explanation for some of these 'organised' practices might be the presence of soldiers in towns—and indeed on farms with certain metalwork finds (cf. Fulford and Timby 2000; Salway 1993: 274–5). This brings us to the heart of the 'military'/'official' problem.

It is simply not possible to distinguish between these identity groups on the basis of current evidence for material practices. While aspects of a 'military' lifestyle can be identified in highly structured locales, this does not mean that soldiers did not move around. Even if the crossbow brooch and belt combination was exclusively worn by official personnel (and there is certainly doubt about this [Philpott 1991: 189, 229]), there is no way to distinguish those who also carried weapons and belonged to named units. It is possible that evidence for large-scale slaughtering of animals in towns indicates the presence of concentrations of state servants, but again these need not be what we would consider soldiers. Perhaps, however, this is not such a negative point. The similarities (some elements of costume and nominal titles) and differences (routines of dwelling) between different kinds of state servants can be seen as organisational boundaries that might find discursive expression in different situations, and these can be envisaged as varying throughout Britain.

Some of the similarities between forts and towns have already been noted, and it is likely that both might have been viewed as 'official' by those living in other kinds of settlement (regardless of whether towns were themselves by this stage nothing more than 'administrative villages' [Reece 1980]). However, 'officials' probably also moved through or lived in small towns/villages, villas, or farms (hence perhaps some of the metalwork finds). The exact connotations of particular identities would have been dependent also on the regional context, creating significant virtual, experienced differences between nominally related identifications. The communities in the forts of Hadrian's Wall and other parts of the north and west were the main representatives of 'official' status in those areas, and in those interactions where that kind of identity was at stake, it must have been effectively synonomous with 'soldier'. In central and southern Britain, with a greater spectrum of settlement types and variable kinds of official lifestyles, the distinctions between soldiers and other state servants may have been more pronounced and/or contested—especially when these were brought to the fore in circumstances of co-presence, as when soldiers moved through or stayed in a town. For the 'officials' to be found in small towns or villas, the range of local interactions that would involve construction of this kind of identity (as opposed to patron or master, perhaps) can only be guessed at.

Notwithstanding these important variations, the main conclusion from this section must simply be that 'military' and 'official' identities overlapped sufficiently to act as potential sources of social tension (or, indeed, solidarity), as well as to complicate the interpretation of much material culture. This tension might well be reflected in some of the discourses of military and civil authority in the textual sources, through which the greater distinctiveness of the 'military' community might have been constructed in reaction to an increasingly less distinctive range of practices. Another implication of this overlap is that the label 'civilian' becomes highly problematic when applied to material assemblages—even more so than 'military'. We have seen in this section that, in contexts where it might have been discursively formulated with reference to certain branches of the state service, these overlapped in a range of ways with 'military' service. Where it related more to the lives of those who were not 'official' in any sense, it—like military status also—overlapped with a whole range of other identities, and these are the subject of the next section.

Intersecting institutions: gender, religion, and local identities

The range of identity categories to be considered here is considerable. All of these can be regarded as to some extent 'institutionalised'—that is, constructed abstractions from the complex and dynamic flow of everyday life, serving to make it more predictable and routine.

Gender identities were certainly an important part of the social world of late Roman Britain and intersected in various ways with other categories. The writing of gender identities in late Roman textual sources presents a construction of such identities from a very particular point of view. In various specific examples, the aristocratic males of late Roman society delineated quite strong distinctions between men and women. Ammianus not only makes several comments about the ideal of masculinity, with reference to soldiers (see below), but also refers to women in a derogatory fashion (e.g., XXII.4, XX.4, XXVII.7, XXXI.2). Zosimus makes similar remarks (e.g., I.39.2, III.3.5, IV.23.2; cf. also Theodosian Code IX.24.1). These frequently characterise women as unstable or emotionally chaotic, and this presents an interesting realm of intersection between practices and identities; this kind of behaviour is similar, in the eyes of elite authors, to the disruptive violence of soldiers—as opposed to the more ordered kind the latter group are also sanctioned to deliver. For the high-status males involved in writing histories and laws, female identity is thus comparable to aspects of low-status male identity and (as we shall see) to barbarian identity, and this commonality is defined in terms of particular practices. While we can thus situate the perspective of such authors, locating other kinds of practice that might represent different views of gender—not least those of women—is problematic with the material data directly available in 4th century Britain.

230 ■ An Archaeology of Identity

Even with practices of appearing, which are very likely to have involved gender identities in some way, there are obstacles to identifying practice contexts in which particular artefacts were actually worn, as such material occurs primarily in contexts of rubbish disposal. The pitfalls of gendering artefacts inhibit interpretation even at quite crude levels of analysis. Some of these problems have already been addressed in Chapter 3. Even in burial contexts, many graves in 4th century Britain were unfurnished, such as in Cirencester's Bath Gate cemetery (McWhirr et al. 1982). In other cases where there are more finds, such as at Oudeburg, the burials have often been 'sexed' on the basis of assumptions about the grave goods rather than physical anthropology (though the latter can also be problematic). While there are cases where independent sexing has occurred, and where there are correlations with particular artefact types (Philpott 1991: 233) such as bracelets and hairpins, these still relate to the construction of gendered (and/or other) categories in a practice that is geared towards 'fixing' a person's identity, and this may well create differences with everyday life. Similar potential difficulties obviously apply to the use of depictive material as straightforward representation (e.g., Reece 1999a: 159–60), although of course we are lacking this kind of material in the specific context of 4th century Britain. Other possibly significant evidence, like the sizes of shoes, can still be gendered in different ways: as Carol van Driel-Murray admits, her evidence for women and children in forts could also be interpreted as an indication of young male concubines (1995: 19). These problems are serious and in themselves indicate that gender identities are rarely immobile or uncontested.

Nonetheless, norms represented in contexts like burial are unlikely to bear no relation to daily life, particularly where artefacts are commonly found in settlement contexts as well. The association of bracelets or hairstyles requiring pins with women, for instance, is significant in the view of the widespread occurrence of such items on almost all of the sites mentioned so far. Changes in these artefacts over time will be indicative of changes in the construction of gender identities and thus gendered experience. Therefore, as Hilary Cool has noted, the declining incidence of hairpins towards the end of the 4th century indicates a shift in women's hair dressing that may reflect the imposition—or acceptance—of less elaborate styles due to the spread of Christian moral conventions. These were perhaps replaced as gendered symbols by shale bracelets and necklaces, more common in this period (Cool 2000: 54–5). The subtleties of meaning content—and therefore expressions of power relationships—within these general patterns are likely to have been variable, and may now be largely incomprehensible. However, the centrality of such items and other 'personalia' to the consistency of 'small finds' assemblages across all kinds of sites is an indication of the importance of the construction of gendered identities in daily life (cf. Jenkins 2004: 49–61; Musolf 2003: 245–74). While subject to the contingencies of particular interactions, which might transform gender symbols into age or status symbols, these finds clearly relate to the practices associated with 'appearing'. Gender identities are also likely to have had implications in terms of 'working' and 'dwelling', and while the gendering of particular spaces is very difficult to penetrate (cf. Allison et al. 2004), the finds evidence plotted out in detail in Chapter 3 supports Driel-Murray's (1995) suggestion that forts were by no means male-only environments.

More can be said about the relationship between masculine gendered identity and military identity. This is true at least for the more positive ideal types constructed in the written sources, with the bravery of the soldiers being a quality also of 'manliness'. This kind of equation might also be found in other practices and practice contexts. Some of the aggressive actions of soldiers referred to in the Abinnaeus Archive, and also qualities of the costume of soldiers (and/or other officials), may have been engaged in the construction of 'manly' as much as 'military' identity. How men in other professions constructed their masculinity is difficult to say on the basis of the material at hand, although domestic power relations perhaps constituted one sphere for this. It is clear, though, from some other aspects of the written material that there were different kinds of manliness, and also that not all soldiers were 'men' in the same sense. The trends discussed by Richard Alston (1998) for earlier periods can be discerned in the way that Ammianus simultaneously idealises and despises the uncouth manliness of the common soldiers (e.g., XIV.10, cf. XVI.12). The difference between the masculinity of different social classes, perhaps another element in the officer/men distinction made so architecturally real in fort planning, along perhaps with age statuses (Laurence 2000), adds another cluster of identificatory practices with which material culture from forts (particularly small finds and garments) must have been engaged.

While charting the relationships between nominal and virtual aspects of ritual and religious differentiations is in some ways more problematic than with gender, there are actually rather more clear indications from the material considered in Chapters 3–4 of the broad kinds of activity that may have cross-cut the identifications discussed so far in this section. These come primarily from the practice contexts of human burial and other kinds of structured deposition, the dedication of stone monuments, and the construction of sacred spaces. The main issues at stake, in terms of identity, are related to how the transition from organised 'pagan' cults to state-sponsored Christianity affected the daily practices of different groups, given that religious activity infused much of life (cf. Millett 1995: 36). The change might have sharpened some boundaries, such as those of gender, and eroded others. For example, Mithraism—a hierarchical pseudo-Persian cult—was strongly associated with 'military' identity in the 2nd and 3rd centuries, so its decline probably had an impact on that category. Some comment has already been made on the problems of burial archaeology in 4th century Britain, particularly in relation to forts. For the burial grounds that we can compare, such as those at the fortress/*colonia* at York (e.g., Wenham 1968) or outside the walls of Cirencester (McWhirr et al. 1982), there is a good deal of variation within the superficially homogeneous pattern of a shift from cremation to inhumation in the late Roman period. This suggests that the practice of inhumation was used in a range of localised identity construction practices (cf. Philpott and Reece 1993). Clear religious affiliations are difficult to pick out of these, Newarke Street in Leicester (Cooper, L. 1996) being a relatively rare example of a small but homogeneous cemetery that is believed to be Christian.

Other specific practices are more notable. One is the small number of cremations discovered near the fort of Birdoswald in the 1950s (Wilmott 1993). Although only seven burials were recorded, the persistence of the practice of cremation into the 4th century is important against the inhumation-dominated background. Lacking a clear regional context for burial practices, this is difficult to interpret and the indeterminacy of inhumations as either pagan or Christian is inhibitive, but perhaps this example relates to the preservation of locally specific traditions (cf. Cool 2004b for a 3rd century example of particular burial practice at Brougham). Another feature of several fort sites in the 4th century—and indeed much earlier in some cases—is the presence of intramural infant burials (e.g., South Shields, Portchester, York [Bidwell and Speak 1994; Cunliffe 1975; Hall, R.A. 1997]). Although found in some cemeteries (e.g., Trentholme Drive in York [Wenham 1968]), the practice of interring infants in areas of otherwise 'domestic' occupation is something that also cuts across site types (examples include Barton Court Farm, Butchery Lane in Canterbury, and the Wroxeter baths *basilica* [Barker et al. 1997; Miles 1986; Williams and Frere 1949]). On the other hand, this practice is not known at all sites and may reflect community-specific traditions or individual religious preferences, but where it does occur, it is perhaps indicative of a differentiation in 'personhood' between very young children and others. Also in connection with burial, it is worth noting the apparent disappearance in the 4th century of the practice of erecting stone funerary monuments. While this phenomenon applies to other kinds of religious dedication too, it also affects imperial and civic inscriptions (see Chapter 3). As such, it probably relates to a broader cultural change and, while possibly having a religious dimension, cannot be pinned down to this in particular.

Other kinds of ritually structured deposition are also worth considering. One example comes from South Shields (Snape 1994). Here, a collection of 'head'-associated objects (cattle skulls, fragments of stone/ceramic faces and heads) were deposited in one of the silted fort ditch terminals. This is certainly interesting but is very unlikely to be unique. The place of structured deposition in Roman-period contexts has been discussed relatively little, although the fort at Newstead, north of Hadrian's Wall, has been the focus of some attention (e.g., Clarke and Jones 1996; cf. Poulton and Scott 1993). The interpretation of the digging and filling of many of the 2nd century pits here, which have a range of contents including human remains, as in some sense 'ritual' has profound implications if extended to other sites and periods. Although the detailed analysis of pit contents and construction elsewhere is beyond the scope of this book, indications of a more 'religious' attitude to rubbish disposal (especially in pits or wells), and also to building, can be found at some sites. These include the possible burial of infants as foundation deposits (e.g., at York [Hall, R.A. 1997]); finds of human bone amongst other 'rubbish' (e.g., at Chester [Newstead and Droop 1932]); and the occurrence of infant bones in several of the 'cess pits' at Portchester (Cunliffe 1975), suggesting an important alternative interpretation to Cunliffe's more prosaic understanding of these (cf. Chapter 4). Such practices need not be associated with particular organised 'cults', pagan or Christian; the important point is that they cross-cut different kinds of sites and confirm that religious attitudes constitute an identity category that overlaps and intersects with others.

Certain built spaces should also be associated with ritual activities on 4th century sites, though again there are problems in interpreting the nature of those activities. The temple of Mithras at Caernarfon is one example (Boon 1960), believed to have been abandoned in the 3rd century and destroyed in the mid-4th century by zealous Christians. If this event did happen, it is apparently not part of a widespread phenomenon, as indications from other sites are of differing local decisions on religious matters. For example, the cleanliness of the *principia* at

234 ■ An Archaeology of Identity

South Shields—compared to other structures—through most of the 4th century might not simply be related to the 'nondomestic' nature of the building's use, but also to the importance of the rituals conducted in it for the identity of the unit. Something similar might have happened at York. This contrasts with the changes in the *principia* at Housesteads, where rubbish and workshop activity seem to be features of the 4th century phases (Bosanquet 1904). Again, though, we must be wary of disassociating metalworking from ritual, and it is worth noting that both South Shields and Housesteads—along with a handful of other sites like Richborough—have possible evidence for early churches (Brown 1971; Rogers 2005).

Other kinds of temple structure paint a similarly diverse picture. Even as the *forum basilica* at Caerwent was undergoing significant changes, a recently built temple was being maintained next door apparently into the later 4th century (Brewer and Guest forthcoming). In contrast, a temple explored by Bushe-Fox (1914) at Wroxeter was apparently abandoned at the beginning of the 4th century, while the putative temple complex in central Canterbury also appears to have been demolished and overlain with floors and hearths in the 4th century (see, e.g., Bennett and Nebiker 1989). Baths, as spaces that could be associated with temples and were certainly the site for various rituals of 'appearing', seem subject to the same vagaries of different locations, with some prospering and others declining in use. Generally, while much of the detail of ritual activity is undoubtedly lost and some sacred aspects of spaces cannot be recognised, the indications are that religious activities in the 4th century were sufficiently fluid to encompass a range of activities in different places. There was of course considerable diversity even in Christian belief and practice at this time (cf. Petts 2003: 160–1). Indeed, the suggestion that there was not a single, homogenous doctrine of conduct that can be associated either with particular groups or with the whole population can also be detected in texts from other parts of the empire. Religious themes were downplayed—at least explicitly—by Ammianus, while religious identities barely appear in the Abinnaeus Archive (Bell et al. 1962: 30–3). There is also evidence for the celebration of diverse festivals even in the more rapidly Christianised east (Salzman 1990).

The 'local' focus of the significance attached to different practices is equally clear when we consider ethnic identities, even if those that figure in many of the written sources are considerably more global. One of the fundamental axes of differentiation for many writers of the later 4th century was between 'Roman' and 'barbarian'. Roman identity, as constructed in such writing, was itself very complex, intersecting with various cultural characteristics (e.g., 'traditional values' of virtue and law [Ammianus, XXI.13; Zosimus, II.5–7]), religion (either classical pagan or Christian, depending on the writer [e.g., Ammianus, XVII.4; Vegetius, II.5]), citizenship, and sometimes the military (Vegetius, I.28). 'Barbarian' identities, particularly from the later 4th century, were constructed largely in opposition to this (e.g., Ammianus, XVI.12, XXXI.2; Zosimus, IV.30–35). Some of the later laws of the Theodosian Code contain interesting proscriptions regarding 'barbarians' (e.g., against provincials marrying them [III.14.1]; against the wearing of trousers or long hair in Rome [XIV.10.2–4]), and these are clearly features of ethnic stereotyping and discrimination—typically indicative of contact and confusion rather than distance (Jenkins 2004: 127–31). It must be doubted that the distinction between 'Romans' and 'barbarians' was as clear cut as these written discourses attempted to make it, particularly in frontier regions like Britain.

This begs the question of whether such identities were constructed in some of the other practice contexts that we have looked at, and this actually seems unlikely. Although it has been argued that the military identity group developed an explicitly barbarian aspect (Halsall forthcoming), this is not really supported by the material from Britain. The latter rather suggests a provincial (or, technically, diocesan) focus that might be regarded as 'Roman' by people in the free north and 'barbarian' by people in Rome—and that was part of a broader distinction between frontier and Mediterranean provinces (cf. James 1999a: 21–3). However, such identities would be much less likely to arise in daily interaction than smaller-scale identities, and apart perhaps from some 'ethnic' titles and small elements of material culture, there is little evidence for such a discursive 'barbaric' formulation. Only occasional finds of boar-tusk dress ornaments have been associated with attempts to appear 'barbaric' (e.g., at Caernarfon [Boon 1975]), and belt fittings can certainly no longer be taken as indicators of this kind of identity. Once linked to incoming Germanic troops, these items are now—as we have seen—primarily associated with late Roman officialdom (Millett 1990: 216; cf. Hawkes and Dunning 1961). As will be argued below, the emphasis of the patterns from Britain (as manifest in the full range of practices, especially dwelling, eating, and appearing) is firmly upon more localised variations within a provincial norm, with as many internal frontiers as external ones.

The idea of a provincial norm draws our attention to another tier of ethnicity, the 'peoples' of which classical authors were fond of writing. These include 'tribal' units within provincial areas and broader groupings either inside or outside the empire—such as Britons and Gauls, or Saxons and Franks (e.g., Ammianus, XIX.5–6, XXVIII.3, XXX.7). These nominal identities not only appear in literary writing, but are also a feature of unit and other titles in the *Notitia Dignitatum* (e.g., the *cohors prima Tungrorum*, listed as the unit at Housesteads [*Occ.* XL.40]); more generalised titles with ethnic connotations include words like *laeti* and *gentiles* (e.g., in *Occ.* XLII.31–70). Clearly, such ethnic unit titles cannot be treated as faithful designations of the origins of all members, although as nominal identities, they may well have played a part in particular unit loyalties—and, perhaps, elements of costume or fighting style (Halsall forthcoming), although the archaeological support for this is limited. More relevant here, though, is a consideration of whether soldiers and others might have shared ethnic identities such as that of 'Gauls' or 'Britons'.

While the thrust of the material patterns discussed in Chapters 3–4 would certainly allow for commonalities that might form the basis for such identifications (whether in practices of eating or appearing, for instance), there are many variations. As a result, these broader identities are only likely to have been discursively formulated in contexts of comparison with significant difference. These would be most likely to occur outside of Britain (and the discourse of 'Britons' in Late Antique writers is primarily an outsiders' one), but the lack of settlement evidence from northern Gaul is an obstacle to defining the potential extent of such 'difference' here. The reverse need not be true: encounters with 'outsiders' in Britain are—given the strength of localised identities—likely to have been conducted in fairly localised terms and need not have led to the construction of a self-conscious 'Britishness', although this might have depended upon an individual's familiarity with literature (cf. Matthews 1999). For similar reasons, the internal boundary between town/fort and country in a number of material aspects cannot be simply described in terms of 'Roman'/'Briton' (cf. Guest 2002). Overall, there are no clear indications for the construction of a British identity in material practices, primarily because the circumstances in which this might have happened are unrepresented. An analogous situation is the way in which the Abinnaeus Archive contains almost no reference to these kinds of ethnic identities, as these were only latent in daily interactions.

It is, then, primarily more localised identities constructed through the routine practices that dominate the material patterns. These include 'spatial' identities from the level of households to communities and regions, and related spheres of identification such as kinship. As with all identities, relations of similarity and difference are key to understanding these associations. Several examples of dwelling practices can be related to very small-scale spatial identities: the individual 'chalet' units at Housesteads (Wilkes 1960, 1961), the structural sequence of an individual complex like Barton Court Farm (Miles 1986), or the different trajectories of individual houses in Canterbury (e.g., at the Marlowe Car Park site [Blockley et al. 1995a, 1995b]). At a more site-specific or community level, there are practices associated with dwelling that encompass more than a single structure, such as 'organised' butchery (e.g., Lincoln [Dobney et al. 1995: 10–11]), rubbish disposal (e.g., Caernarfon [Casey et al. 1993]), and the maintenance of internal thoroughfares (e.g., Caerleon [Zienkiewicz 1988]). Particular traditions, for instance of eating, have also been referred to above, as well as the importance of changes to many structures that reflect local rather than global priorities. These site-specific virtual identities will have been intimately bound up with nominal dimensions such as a unit or place name. In turn, these could be nested within more regional identities. Small settlements in northern Britain, for instance, characterised by having only small amounts of 'Roman' material culture (e.g., Huckhoe [Jobey 1959]), might be similar to others nearby but quite different to the Wall communities, which might in themselves have constituted a regionally distinctive identity group.

Indeed, there is considerable general potential for regional scales of identification, based partly on 'dwelling' but also evident in practices like exchanging and eating (cf. Perring 2002: 130–1). Many of the coin patterns noted in Chapter 4 vary on a regional basis, with changes through time affecting ostensibly similar kinds of site (like forts) depending on where they are (e.g., the west or the northeast). Equally, while pottery forms in the 4th century do tend toward homogeneity (and this carries across the Channel too), a noticeable trend through the later part of the century is the tendency for particular industries to supply particular areas (notwithstanding the traditional reliance on local wares). There were also some regionally distinctive forms (Tyers 1996: 77). While such regional patterns may have corresponded to 'tribal' identities, and indeed it is possible that these were a more likely focus than 'Britons' for ethnogenesis inspired by classical/administrative ethnography, once again we must consider the circumstances under which such regional patterns might have been discursively 'noticed'. These are most likely to have involved individual mobility, which is unfortunately precisely the kind of action that is difficult to track in material contexts. It is also important to note that these regional patterns are not homogenous, bounded distributions, but trends within which there is considerable site-specific variation. This does not mean that regional 'ethnic' identities were not constructed through items like pottery, but does underline the importance of interactional contact between people who did things differently and their discursive formulation.

Finally, there are a number of other institutionalised identity categories that might have had considerable importance, but which are difficult to track in specific material contexts—even burial—given the potential complexity of the relationships between them (cf. Philpott 1991: 228–33). Social statuses relating to wealth and ranking based upon kinship or other forms of social standing are likely to have been constructed through certain aspects of burying and appearing, as well as dwelling and eating. The difference between the courtyard house and the barracks at South Shields could be interpreted purely in terms of organisational rank, but wider social class was probably also important here. Identities broadly relating to 'class'—including *honestiores* and *humiliores* (high and low status), patron and client, and also free/freed/slave—are a feature of diverse written sources, ranging from the Theodosian Code (e.g., VI, XIII, XIV) to the Abinnaeus Archive (e.g., Text 64). Detecting such specific nominal elements of identification, and their virtual correlates, in the material at hand, however, is problematic. Differentiation between individual artefacts, between burials in a cemetery, or between houses in a town is certainly evident in many cases, but particular associations in particular practice contexts are elusive, and one-to-one correlations between— for instance—villa size and wealth are unsustainable given the potential for regionally or socially distinct 'regimes of wealth' hinted at by some of the coinage patterns (e.g., Dinorben [Hingley 1989: 34–5]).

The same difficulties apply to two other important dimensions of status: occupation and age. Even without the emphasis on the legal status of different professions in the Theodosian Code (e.g., XIV.7), the common identification of persons by trade in the Abinnaeus Archive (e.g., Text 42), and Vegetius' comments on the suitability of different professions for soldiering (I.7), there is ample evidence for craft specialisation in British contexts. From the smithing and butchering common to many formerly 'public' sites in the 4th century, to the production of pottery and other goods, making and working practices could provide important grounds for identity construction. From this perspective, the occupation of 'soldier' is little different from others. However, whether all professions were as institutionalised as the legal documents suggest—and as state/military-related identities could be—is another matter. Nonetheless, occupational identities could overlap: evidence of a range of industrial practices in forts, for instance, implies that soldiers could be smiths or belong to other 'trades'. Generally, though, the social organisation of labour in Roman-period Britain is poorly understood, and there is much potential for further research along the lines of Peacock's (1982) attempt to develop models for pottery production.

There are even problems with age, another status that appears in some of the texts (e.g., Ammianus, XV.12), and which is *a priori* likely to be important in some fashion. While the infant burial practices referred to earlier indicate one age-based practice, very much tied into perceptions of the link between age and personal identity, there is very little evidence relating to puberty or any of the other potential life-course events of individuals in 4th century Britain (cf. Laurence 2000). A couple of possible exceptions from burial contexts include the deposition of certain artefacts more commonly with young women than men, and the relatively high incidence of decapitation among older women; in neither case, though, is the rite uniform (Philpott 1991: 77–88, 232–3; Swift 2000: 72–4). Indeed, this might be expected from the emphasis on local practices discussed above with reference to religion. The overall dearth of evidence is unfortunate, as one could certainly envisage age intersecting in significant ways with masculinity in the identity of the soldier, furnishing alternative dimensions of similarity and difference to the professional one in a range of interactions.

A topography of 4th century identities

In this chapter, we have explored how dynamic material practices can be connected to a model of identity that emphasizes the importance of multiple categories in any individual's life, and on the way each of these may come to the fore in different situations. The range of potentially important categories in late Roman Britain has been discussed, along with the possibilities for—and problems inhibiting—their archaeological recovery. Sometimes the latter are serious, but the fundamental point is that the similarities and differences that structure patterns of archaeological material bear some relationship to people's ways of doing things in the past, and that these are the building blocks of identity.

To summarise this discussion, before examining continuity and change in late Roman Britain in Chapter 6, the key dimensions of identity can be mapped (Fig. 5.3). This diagram indicates a number of things. It stresses that identity—as a necessary part of social relationships—is one of the qualities of human life that connects agency and structure. Individuals are shaped by identities as structural categories, but they also internalise those categories to define themselves. Equally,

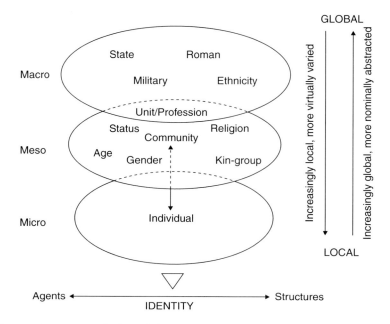

Figure 5.3. A stratified model of identification in later Roman Britain (cf. Gardner 2004b: 42).

structures are shaped by the actions of people, but those people are living largely according to the rules of behaviour that their identities afford them. This centrality of sociality to the process of structuration has begun to be developed beyond Giddens's own formulations by others (esp. Jenkins 1996, 2004), but we have also seen how this overlaps with two other critical dimensions—materiality and temporality—that also bridge the gap between structure and agency.

As far as Figure 5.3 goes, this means that all of the categories listed in the main part of the diagram have both 'individual' and 'institutional' qualities—even that of 'the individual', which always has some socially constructed attributes (through naming conventions, ideas of personhood, and so on). All are available to be put into practice in specific contexts of interaction between different people, according to the circumstances of that interaction. These will dictate what identities are noticed, imposed, or chosen, as interpretations of the meaning of specific actions—whether these are ways of eating food, wearing dress items, or using space. The vertical dimension of the diagram indicates the scale of community that a particular identity takes as its point of reference. At the smallest scale in the Roman world, we have the discrete individual, which may well have been perceived somewhat differently from the modern individual (cf. Fowler 2004) but certainly existed as an important category. Next come medium-scale identities such as a particular place or a grouping, which—while universal in some senses (as with gender)—were probably constructed in more regionally variable ways across the Roman world. At the top level come macroscale identities, where the category specifically refers to a 'global' community such as the profession of the soldiers across the empire, a major ethnic entity, or the empire itself.

The larger-scale identities are more abstract (as nominal statuses) from the daily flow of life, based on a small selection of qualities such as the occasional observation of 'Roman' law or the possession of citizenship. These may mean very different things in different local contexts, but at the abstract level of the empire, they are a unifying identity—at least in theory. They will also have some bearing on practice, through which they come to be tangible for the people living within their orbit, as in the availability of Roman coins to facilitate payment of taxes; how those coins are actually used in exchange may again vary. The lower scale of identities are intrinsically more varied in practice, but are also linked by common threads. While being an individual is by definition an individual experience unlike that of anybody else, there are nonetheless *ways* of being an individual that are common to particular societies. Again, then, the importance of identity is that being based on the simple principle of similarity and difference, it allows for highly fluid associations of people with a wide range of different communities, from themselves to a whole empire. This accounts for just some of the potential variability of meanings attached to material culture in the late Roman period—or indeed any period—and this is why pinning down material meanings is so difficult. Nonetheless, from patterns in the distribution of material culture in space and time, we can think about which kinds of identities were most commonly constructed by people in particular contexts.

There is indeed a broad range of these in the Roman Empire, with the degree of mobility afforded to people—particularly in organisations like the military—potentially bringing them into contact with a great variety of others to whom they might be defined as 'Roman', as 'military', or as 'British', 'Gaulish', or 'Greek'. However, many of the material patterns discussed in this book relate to smaller-scale ways of life and to more narrow traditions of particular places. This is undeniably a partial product of the nature of archaeology. We cannot dig up a soldier travelling from the Tigris to the Tyne, with all of the encounters along the way that made him feel different or seem different to others—sometimes a Roman, sometimes a semi-barbarian, sometimes a man,

242 ■ An Archaeology of Identity

sometimes a pagan, sometimes just a soldier. We can only dig up the places. Nonetheless, the patterns of local adaptation we have seen at a wide range of 4th century sites indicate an already fragmented world becoming even more so. This will produce equally fragmented stories, which defy grand narratives, of what happened in Late Antiquity. In the final chapter, we will see how the archaeology of identity therefore becomes, of necessity, an archaeology of multiple perspectives.

Chapter 6

CONCLUSION: ROMAN BRITAIN IN THE 4TH CENTURY

The dynamics of identification in late Roman Britain

Contextualising the 4th century: structuration and change

The empirical and theoretical problems that were outlined in the first two chapters of this book have been explored in the last three chapters through studies of the overlapping material, temporal, and social dimensions of life in late Roman Britain. Now we can integrate these themes more fully to consider some of the different available narratives of social change in the 4th and early 5th centuries.

As with each stage of the discussion to this point, structuration theory provides useful concepts with which to work in analysing these processes. One of these, a major plank of structuration theory as a whole, has already been highlighted: Giddens's focus on the unintended consequences of routine action, which complements people's ability to make deliberate decisions to change a way of doing things (Giddens 1979: 210–22). He has also, however, considered larger-scale, more dramatic shifts, which relate to significant disruptions of ontological security—fundamental changes to someone's way of life—that may be imposed upon them. These are referred to as 'critical situations' at the individual level, and 'critical thresholds' where such situations are widely experienced across society (e.g., Giddens 1979: 228, 1984: 61, 246). As we saw in Chapter 2, there have been criticisms of Giddens's emphasis on routine as minimising the potential for such changes, but these concepts go some way to show that this need not be the case, even if his treatment of 'traditional societies' is flawed (e.g., 1984: 199). Indeed, the core concepts of structuration theory have already been useful in understanding the temporal dynamics of practice; now they will be equally helpful in constructing a multiscalar and multi-tempo approach to social change in 4th and 5th century Britain.

244 ■ An Archaeology of Identity

We can begin to work through this by examining the relationships between practices and identities from a long-term perspective, and attempting to position many of the networks of identity discussed in the previous chapter within a fuller context. This demonstrates that many significant elements of 4th century practices are prefigured in various ways, although caution should be exercised here to avoid teleological argument. The balance between routine and transformation can be detected in a basic aspect of the practice of dwelling—its 'whereness'—if we consider the degree of settlement mobility over time. There were episodes of 'hiatus' or 'abandonment' throughout the period at many farmsteads in Roman Britain, although in most cases, these can be interpreted in terms of shifts in the settlement focus away from the excavated areas. So, for example, at Orton Hall Farm, Barton Court Farm, and Caldicot (Mackreth 1996; Miles 1986; Vyner and Allen 1988), there were small changes in the location of the settlement, spread over generational time. In these and other cases, different rooms or elements within larger structures also fluctuated in and out of use. Similar situations can also obviously be found in forts, fortresses, and different kinds of towns (e.g., Canterbury, Caerleon, Carlisle [Blockley et al. 1995 a, 1995b; Evans and Metcalf 1992; McCarthy 1990, 1991]), though the pace can be a little more rapid, at least in certain phases. While the motives for such shifts might be widely varied, the important point is that the background to the 4th century developments in settlement occupation and abandonment is far from unchanging. Sometimes changes were quite extreme, as with the abandonment of many western forts in the 2nd century, but in other places, there were gradual cycles of transformation paced at generational intervals or greater.

If we focus on more specific aspects of dwelling over prolonged periods, it is equally clear that many general patterns of action became established well before the 4th century. One that has already been addressed is rubbish disposal. More or less organised practices of depositing refuse are evident from an early stage in the development of quite nucleated settlements like forts or towns. These included both extra- and intramural dumps, the latter often in otherwise unused open spaces (e.g., Caerhun, Lincoln, York, Cirencester, Chester [Baillie Reynolds 1938; Gilmour 1981; Hall, R.A. 1997; Holbrook and Timby 1998b; Strickland 1982; Timby et al. 1998]). All of these individual incidences of deposition probably had specific circumstantial motivations, and perhaps variable religious connotations, but they serve to make the large late deposits like those at Beeches Road, Cirencester (McWhirr 1986), the Lincoln waterfront (Dobney et al. 1995), or the courtyard of the Filey coastal signal station (Ottoway 1997) seem less unusual and more traditional. This does not mean that there were not changes in the significance of the locations of such activity in the 4th century, but it does highlight continuities in a highly routinised practice across a wide range of sites. People's contact with this 'rubbish' must have been a familiar and regular experience and a key part of the materiality of Roman Britain.

There were also some long-term similarities in the *ways* in which certain things changed. Modification of buildings was not an innovative practice, at least on a general level. For example, the turrets on the walls of Caerleon were generally disused as defensive structures in the early 2nd century and replaced by rampart buildings or cookhouses (e.g., at the eastern corner [Hawkes 1930]), while the northern gate at South Shields was already blocked and used as a metalworking area in the 2nd century (Dore and Gillam 1979). Similar changes to turrets and gates occurred at Birdoswald in the 2nd and 3rd centuries. While these seem to relate to localised priorities, as referred to in previous sections, it is important to distinguish between the different organisational implications of various functional changes—i.e., how significantly such changes affected the routines involved in the reproduction of the organisation. Turning turrets into cookhouses, or narrowing gateways, occurs on a fairly widespread basis and thus reflects local concerns common to the kinds of organisation living in a fort. Other major functional changes, like the replacement of barracks with a courtyard house at Caernarfon in the 2nd century (Casey et al. 1993), are more unique, but still involve the establishment of a new regime that seems to have connections to wider institutional structures.

It will be argued below that some kinds of change occurring in 4th century sites are different to these relatively minor modifications, being dictated much more overwhelmingly by the needs of a specific community in a specific place. Nevertheless, it is still important to note the degree of variation between individual sites in all periods. It is clearly not the case that every fort, for instance, was identical in form until some point in the late 3rd century. Although barracks were fairly consistently laid out, there was still variation in the number of rooms, dimensions, and so forth, and more substantial changes (i.e., the appearance of 'chalet' barracks) do occur in the late 2nd or 3rd century (e.g., at Wallsend [Hodgson 1999]). Variation between individual structures might also have been significant, as between the layouts of adjacent officers' quarters in the York Minster barracks, in the early 2nd century. Similarly, in towns, *forum* structures might vary in a range of ways from one site to the next (e.g., between Leicester with

246 ■ An Archaeology of Identity

unusual side ranges, and Cirencester with its cross-colonnade [Hebditch and Mellor 1973; Holbrook and Timby 1998a: 113–21]). This highlights the fact that social practices always entail a balance of similarity and difference, or stability and change, and that it is never easy to create simple cultural or temporal categories with an absolutely standardised identity.

Some fairly long-term continuities can be identified in a range of other practices, particularly appearing and eating. The analysis of small finds groups in Chapter 4 demonstrated that similar kinds of objects—notably personalia associated with dress and appearance—generally dominated most assemblages, at least from the 2nd century. Although there were obvious changes in the particular styles of artefacts used (for example, the rise to prominence of crossbow brooches and twisted wire bracelets in the 4th century [cf. Cool 2000]), as well as presumably some of their associations (such as gender or official roles), the overall emphasis of small finds groups across a range of sites followed similar trends. Equally, with material associated with eating, patterns that can be discerned as changing from one perspective are quite stable from another. Thus, the range of pottery available at particular sites did vary over time, but there was always a core element of local supply; at the same time, many forms changed in detail within a broad continuity of repertoire (e.g., BB1), or deliberately copied old-fashioned imported forms (e.g., Oxfordshire-ware Samian copies). Faunal representation also fluctuated in detail, but the dominance of cattle across different site categories had become an established feature in the 2nd century.

The other general categories of practice defined earlier are more problematic. Coin use does appear to change quite significantly over time, and in conjunction with regional and site-typical factors, illustrates an important point that might also apply to ceramics, but that is not visible from the data at hand. The 'military' sites of the 1st and 2nd centuries were distinctive in their coin loss patterns, but by the 3rd and 4th centuries, this distinctiveness disappeared and regional patterns became more dominant. 'Working' and 'writing' (in insular terms) cannot be tracked in the material from British sites at the general level of current interest, and it is not helpful to go too deeply into the similarities (language, format, stereotyping ethnography) and differences (style of language, political agendas) between Tacitus and Ammianus, for example. An understanding of long-term change must rather rely on the main points set out above with regard to dwelling and certain other practices. Superficially, these imply that the number of overlaps and blurrings in provincial culture that make 'military' assemblages hard to define in the 4th century are applicable to some earlier patterns, too. The precise timing may vary, but even in the 2nd century, some of the important changes were beginning.

However, to avoid treating this as an inevitably 'unfolding' process that happened of its own accord, divorced of human agency (cf. Giddens 1984: 228–33), it is important to dig a little deeper into these changes. The demise of exclusive patterns of coin loss, ceramic supply, or small finds (at different rates) after the 1st century indicates that soldiers were increasingly just one element in provincial society. However, this was never a homogenous culture, nor was this pattern of development inexorable and unidirectional. It is one thing to say that from an early point in the occupation, women were an important part of fort communities, and that gender identities were therefore an important focus for articulation in appearance-related material culture. This does not mean, though, that the meaning of these identities was thereafter a given constant. On the contrary, they—and all other identities—were continually changing by virtue of being continually constructed. In this process, the balance between tradition—for Giddens, the ultimate form of routinised practice (1984: 200)—and mobility or fluidity (Urry 2000a: 30–2) was dynamic over time and variable between people in different places or social groups. This seems to be the implication of the tension between continuity and change outlined throughout this section, and of the ways this cuts across different communities. These might have different traditions (e.g., 'local' or 'military'), and different degrees of mobility (e.g., through access to writing or transport technologies), and these intertwined in a particular range of permutations in the 4th century—to which we now turn in detail.

Structured transformation within the 4th century

In reviewing the tempos and trajectories of change over the course of the 4th century, it is again appropriate to make use of the broad categories of practice that I have drawn out of the material culture patterns outlined in Chapters 3–4. By exploring the balance between reproduction and transformation across different dimensions of social life in Britain (different sites, regions, social identity categories), an understanding of how these processes relate to those of preceding and later periods can be achieved. As with the longer time-perspective of the previous section, a considerable range of insights can be gleaned from looking at changes in patterns of dwelling. While these certainly occurred in the 4th century, both their pace and their nature were highly variable. Some seem to have been major adjustments to routine, while others were in themselves routines of modification. Frequently, these circumstances have been confused by archaeologists. For example, the barrack rebuilding sequence excavated at Birdoswald in the late 1920s (Richmond and Birley 1930) was interpreted—as was fashionable at the time—in terms of specific, short-lived events of widespread impact, such as the visits of Constantius or Count Theodosius to Britain in the 4th century. Later excavators at Birdoswald, however (e.g., Wilmott 1997), have taken the view that such changes were rather more gradual and mundane.

Such differences of approach relate in part to certain problems with the archaeological measurement of change, primarily chronological resolution. If even the results of a fairly small-scale, localised action like the digging of a pit can only be dated to a span of several years, there is little hope of deciding how 'routine' such an action was (did it impact upon individuals' lives on a daily, weekly, or monthly basis?), and the temptation to link material changes to more specific historical dates can be strong. Nonetheless, we can make some judgements on tempos of change, and more importantly on how seriously they altered existing institutional routines—even if the 'critical situations' where these are effectively destroyed are likely to have been rare (Giddens uses the example of concentration camp prisoners to illustrate the extent to which 'normal life' can be broken down in such situations [1984: 60–4]; see below). For example, even though the changes within South Shields at the beginning of the 4th century were quite extensive, they can be interpreted as creating a newly organised level of routine. Many subsequent developments at this place represent continual modifications to this routine but were probably not viewed by the inhabitants as drastic changes.

One ingredient in the likely impact of particular changes is the history of a site. In spite of the phenomenon of settlement shift noted above, many sites (such as South Shields) possessed fundamental threads of continuity that might appear to those dwelling in them as material culture encountered during building or the digging of pits. Again, this must have been a key characteristic of the materiality of life in Roman towns and forts, generating connections with the past. This might also apply on a larger scale to forts that were more definitively abandoned. Some of the forts in the west—such as Brecon Gaer or Caerhun—were essentially given up in the 2nd century, yet sporadic later material suggests that these sites were not simply forgotten and indeed must have provided an element of relatively unchanging continuity in the landscapes of this region. The forts on Hadrian's Wall, although certainly changing internally, might equally be defined in their relationship to old structures—including the Wall itself and its largely abandoned turret buildings. Some sites founded later, however, do show how quickly patterns of routine specific to a particular place might become established—as with refuse disposal practices at Portchester (Cunliffe 1975), where the pit-digging episode is one (actually quite prolonged) feature against a background continuity of dumping against the back of the fort wall.

Taking some of these points into account, several changes noted at various sites in the 4th century can be seen as routine modifications (rather than major disjunctures) with superficially limited organisational impact. This does not mean, however, that such changes were inconsequential. The reproduction of any institution (i.e., any identity) produces unintended consequences of action that can constitute some of the unacknowledged conditions of action for subsequent episodes (Giddens 1984: 5). The incorporation of these into new routines transforms the institutions involved. Examples of this kind of transformation include the changes to the living spaces in the 'chalet' barracks at Housesteads (Wilkes 1960, 1961), the courtyard house at South Shields (Bidwell and Speak 1994), and the houses of Carlisle (McCarthy 1990), as well as the use of an open area of Caernarfon—after the cessation of building activity—for rubbish disposal and manufacturing (Casey et al. 1993). Such developments were increasingly common in the second half of the 4th century, and it seems likely that this is the period when cumulative small-scale transformations—made as a result of mundane local decisions—really began to undermine the distanciation of state structures in some parts of Britain.

More significant changes can be brought into this picture too, although these still tend to occur against a backdrop of persistent routines. At Caerleon, for instance, the apparent demolition of the *principia* (Boon 1970) and disuse of the baths (Zienkiewicz 1986a), represent quite major changes, but in other parts of the fortress, routines of street maintenance—or of periodic occupation of barracks—continued (e.g., Fox 1940; Zienkiewicz 1988). While the baths were adapted to new uses (principally refuse disposal), the 4th century activity in the *principia* is not well understood and should not constitute decisive evidence for the withdrawal of every last soldier. Similarly, the structural sequence at nearby Caerwent, which includes a *forum* converted to metalworking use by the mid-4th century but continued use of the adjacent *basilica* rooms, temple, and baths (Brewer and Guest forthcoming; Nash-Williams 1954), represents a mixture of the persistence of certain traditions and the transformation of others. Thus, at sites like these, there were clearly changes in routines, particularly some of those associated with organisational structures of the Roman state. At the same time, there were also many continuities—as well as examples of very organised practices—that can be interpreted in terms of modified or decentralised state structures working more fully within the local dynamics of specific communities (whether through individual aristocrats or armed units).

Different tempos of change can be constructed for other practices on the basis of various patterns in the material culture, although in many cases the most direct practice context for these is rubbish disposal and, therefore, part of dwelling. Some of the changing temporal features of coinage have already been discussed in Chapter 4. At a broad level, the later 3rd century seems to be something of a watershed for coin use at many British sites. Although there was variation at other points in time, particularly between those sites occupied by a coin using community from the mid-1st century and those not (i.e., between soldier-dominated communities and others), many sites in the 2nd and early 3rd centuries display a 'flat', average curve of coin loss, or one that is slightly below average (see Chapter 4). From the 260s, however, a much more volatile and fractured picture emerges, with fewer distinctions between different kinds of site and more regional patterns. Clearly, some of these features relate to site occupation histories (e.g., sites not established until the 3rd century), but there seems to be little doubt that coin use became more widespread, but also more spatially and temporally variable, in the later 3rd and 4th centuries. This may owe something to uneven coin supply (and certainly there are more episodes of coin copying to meet shortfalls in this period than previously), but if so, this must still have been mediated in meaningful ways.

Indeed, this is confirmed by the contextual information for coin loss presented in Chapter 3, from which it is clear that depositional practices relating to coins had a specific character in the 4th century. Although part of this is due to stratigraphic over-representation of some 4th century deposits, other indications (for instance, from comparisons between dates of minting and dates of context formation) suggest that there were real increases in the tempo of the use and loss of coins at various kinds of site. At the same time, comparison between dated pottery groups and coins can highlight sites at which coin-use can only have formed a small part of exchanging practices. Thus, for instance, the quantities of 4th century pottery found at the fortress baths site in Caerleon are not matched by coin finds in the same way as the relatively more prolific coinage from the southeastern quarter of Caernarfon. Moreover, some sites have no coinage at all but at least some pottery (e.g., Apperley Dene [Hildyard 1952]). All of this serves to indicate that the 4th century was a more fluid period in routines of exchanging coins (and perhaps other ways of using them) than previously, and that this runs contrary to the imagery of many 4th century issues. These have much more consistently formalised imperial portraits than earlier coins (also found in other sculptured media), as well as special motifs that stressed the enormous length of 'Roman' tradition. One example of the latter is the phoenix depicted on some *Fel Temp Reparatio* coins, indicating that Rome would rise again if legends that it would not last longer than 1200 years—AD 348 was the city's 1100th anniversary—came true (Reece and James 1986: 32).

The apparent increase in the fluidity associated with a material category bearing strong nominal and virtual identifying links to the Roman state is important when contrasted with the evidence for practices like eating and appearing. These show rather less intensive patterns of change, and perhaps more of a tradition-based emphasis in the construction of local or gender identities. Although not discussed in detail in Chapter 4, typological change in ceramics in the 4th century was limited, with certain established forms remaining dominant (Tyers 1996: 74–5). The evidence for pottery supply shows gradual changes, occurring primarily in the later 4th century, although tight chronological control over these is relatively poor (in part because of the typological stability of 4th century wares). Changes in patterns of species representation in animal bone assemblages are also difficult to map with any resolution, but the continuity of the cattle-dominated pattern at many sites into the 5th century is indicative of the lack of substantial change in the 4th.

'Appearing' is a little more tangible, as several of the groups of small finds represented by stratigraphic period in Chapter 4 have multiple 4th century phases. However, some of these groups are very small, and of course the problems of potential residuality and stratigraphic over-representation (also encountered with coins) are once again significant. Nonetheless, the 4th century groups at Caernarfon, for instance, are fairly consistent, while the same can be said of the groups from the Carlisle and Orton Hall Farm. The fluctuations in size of different groups within sites like these are an important dimension of variation, but are difficult to relate to changes in the use of objects and more likely to reflect deposit size. There is a tendency toward increased deposition in the late and post-Roman layers in places, but there are also sites with sizeable early groups, producing a somewhat different picture to that noted for coins (e.g., also Causeway Lane in Leicester [Connor and Buckley 1999]). Even if there is some increasing discard, it is important to note that—where they can be dated at all—artefact styles seem to change relatively slowly. Later 4th century crossbow brooches, for example, have their origins in mid-3rd century P-shaped brooches, and although there are thus definite changes in the 'personal object' repertoire (and probably in some of their associations), these are sufficiently gradual to imply that there was a good degree of stability in routines of appearing, across the full spectrum of sites, through much of the 4th century.

While changes in insular writing in the 4th century are simply inaccessible, it has been possible to look at some of the narratives of change in the writings of authors outside of Britain. Transformations in various aspects of Roman life do figure in the works of Ammianus, Zosimus, and Vegetius, though it is perhaps notable that Zosimus—who makes much of the military crisis (for him, related to 'barbarisation' [e.g., IV.30.1])—was writing with a hindsighted perspective on the early 5th century, from the viewpoint of the early 6th. Ammianus, whose extant writings run to a point identified by many as the beginning of this crisis, seems to give rather less emphasis to these supposed developments in the military (though cf. XXXI.4), placing more of the blame for the problems on changes in the moral fibre of the Roman citizenry (e.g., XXVIII.4). Clearly, this is as much a factor of Ammianus' particular perspective as anything Zosimus wrote is of his, and it is interesting to note the threads of traditionalism and conservatism that run through Ammianus' narrative (e.g., XXXI.5; moral decay was itself a well-worn literary theme), and indeed inform its very construction (Barnes 1998: 193–5). Vegetius also places a great deal of emphasis on the importance of Roman traditions (e.g., I.28). Although neither of these viewpoints necessarily tells us much about how the Roman world was changing in the 4th century, they do give us some examples of how particular individuals reacted to the changes they saw by clinging to—or creating—a traditional past.

All of these material and textual perspectives on change in the 4th century demonstrate that there were more and less rapid transformations in this period—as indeed in any period. The tempo and character of change varied between different spheres of life, different communities or regions, and different identity groups. Many transformations were gradual, reflecting a slow and entirely routinised drift of traditions. It is important to recognise that tradition not only is far from immutable, but that there are different kinds of tradition, and this is very clear from the data. The relative stability of certain practices of 'appearing' across a range of sites, for instance, suggests that traditional ways of constructing gender identities probably remained quite widespread even if the specific artefacts or identities themselves subtly altered, perhaps in response to new religious beliefs. Other, place-specific developments in different kinds of site can be related to community traditions, regardless of whether these cross-cut other categorisations such as unit identities. Alongside these transmutations of tradition run more rapid or more drastic changes, and these seem to particularly afflict institutions with ties to the late Roman state, whether coinage or certain kinds of dwelling. Although these do not indicate an immediate cessation of organised life, and indeed can be seen in terms of a decentralisation of state power, the effects of these changes in the later 4th century might have taken various structural contradictions to crisis point in the early 5th. This period therefore requires even more detailed consideration.

The early 5th century: a 'critical threshold'?

The problems of the archaeology of the first half of the 5th century in Britain have already been discussed, and can briefly be summarised. Materially, there is an apparently sudden disappearance of the most visible features (coins, pottery, stone architecture), while the relatively slender written sources speak (at something of a temporal or spatial remove) of usurpations and military and administrative problems leading to the severing of ties with the empire. Since it is now widely accepted that the Saxon '*adventus*', which is in itself highly problematic, was not directly related to the end of Roman Britain (e.g., Reece 1989), attention has focused on finding an internally generated reason for the evident changes, such as tax revolts (e.g., Faulkner 2000: 174–8). While isolated events involving powerful political actors— during the first decade of the 5th century—may certainly have had a genuine impact affecting the highest levels of the imperial structure in Britain, they need to be placed in the context of longer-term patterns to account for their particular effects, without making them seem predetermined. These effects were rather different to earlier episodes of usurpation or currency crisis (like the later 3rd century or the mid-4th), but are still likely to have involved varying degrees of influence from different social groups within and outside the British provinces. As such, they would have been perceived rather diversely by such groups, giving rise to different accounts of 'prosperity' or 'decline'.

As in previous sections, consideration of changes in different practices at the beginning of the 5th century can be a useful approach to this problem. The most obvious change that affects a wide range of sites is simply abandonment. In part, this phenomenon is defined archaeologically by changes in portable material culture (see below),

254 ■ An Archaeology of Identity

but it is also a stratigraphic phenomenon that can only represent a significant break with tradition in a range of places. However, this change was neither rapid nor uniform. Indeed, of few sites in Britain can it be said that occupation simply stopped one day in AD 410. Settlement shift of one kind or another was a feature of many sites throughout the Roman period, and many abandonments occurred during the 4th century. Often these were still within otherwise occupied settlements, and sites no longer serving as actual places of residence might still be used for entirely routine practices like rubbish disposal (e.g., Blackfriars Street in Carlisle [McCarthy 1990]). In addition, there are oft-cited examples of sites that were apparently not abandoned at any point in the period under consideration (especially Birdoswald and Wroxeter [Wilmott 1997; Barker et al. 1997]). The status of such sites is debated; some doubt the veracity of the claims made on unsurprisingly tenuous evidence, while others contend that more examples might be found with more sensitive excavation techniques (cf. Burnham 1999).

The problem is one of archaeological visibility. If the sequences at sites like Birdoswald and Wroxeter are to be believed, timber was preferred to stone as a building material in the early 5th century, though of course it had never actually gone out of use for such purposes. If unavailability of newly quarried stone is held to account for its declining use, this might be related to changes in organisational power (cf. Reece 1988: 149). However, there does seem to have been sufficient cohesion at local levels—for instance in various forts of the Wall—to reuse stone and then build major structures in timber (e.g., at Birdoswald and South Shields [Wilmott 1997; Bidwell and Speak 1994]) and to use earth to reinforce defences where necessary (e.g., Birdoswald again and Housesteads [Crow 1988]). These represent precisely the kinds of localised responses to priorities seen increasingly in dwelling practices in the 4th century, which suggest that unit-level organisations might still be quite strong, even if their traditions were now unique combinations of local and institutionalised elements. The similarities between such communities might well have formed the basis for some larger-scale identities up to a regional level. The persistence of localised institutional traditions may also be held to account for the kinds of architectural changes seen in the vicinity of the baths *basilica* at Wroxeter (Barker et al. 1997) or the *forum basilica* at Cirencester (Timby et al. 1998).

Changing visibility also underlies the difficulties in understanding transformations in other practices, though as with dwelling, this would have been meaningful in the past. Those practices of eating involving pottery vessels, and of exchanging involving coinage, would clearly have been affected by the cessation of production of the former and of importation of the latter. Again, though, tempos of change were varied rather than uniformly catastrophic. We have already seen how use of coinage become more erratic in the 4th century, and discard of coins increased, perhaps making their final disappearance less remarkable (cf. Butcher 2001: 24). Change in pottery supply is rather more inexplicable, unless it is accepted that many sites away from forts and towns had only ever received sporadic and small quantities of vessels (as seems the case at Apperley Dene and Huckhoe, for example [Hildyard 1952; Jobey 1959; cf. Going 1992]). In both coins and pottery, then, ubiquity of form in the 4th century may have been less 'noticeable' than regionally and socially specific patterns of variation, which contributed to a fracturing of social relations that became increasingly local in focus. These changes were gradual, and even the likely duration of the final cessation of pottery production—spread over a period of years—means that they operated through routinised mechanisms. This is supported by the way that the latest datable materials still tend to appear in refuse deposits, which indicates that some routines of dwelling were continuing even as others were changing.

Gradual as many of these transformations were, they did make a real difference to various lifestyles in Britain, but we need to consider which identities were most affected and other kinds of evidence. Dating the 'end' of use of the finds that I have associated with appearing as a practice is problematic (cf. Cool 2000). Although in terms of dated deposits, it is obviously difficult to extend their use beyond that of coins or pottery, there are reasons for believing that appearing did remain a significant practice and one upon which persistent identities depended. That pottery, in particular, was not produced at local levels after the collapse of the major industries may be indicative of genuine economic incapacity (cf. Cooper, N.J. 1996), perhaps associated with a breakdown of inter-regional contacts and with a corresponding decline in the necessity to define and express regional identities. An identity category such as gender, however, might be expected to persist in importance, and in spite of the possibility of increased late small find discard, it is notable that the limited range of artefact types that can be given a 5th century date includes metalwork and beads (e.g., penannular brooches from South Shields [Croom et al. 1994]). The precise repertoire of styles may well have changed (and of course we have no idea how garment fashions might also have developed), and the kinds of gender identities negotiated through them need not have remained constant. Nonetheless, the persistence of this fundamental axis of differentiation should come as no surprise, and it is entirely possible that 'personal items' occurring in 'sub-Roman' or unstratified contexts were still in use for a long time after AD 410.

But what about 'official' and 'military' identities? So far, I have presented a picture of gradual change with an emphasis on the transformation of routine rather than an abrupt dislocation, and on the unintended consequences of these small modifications as a key mechanism behind larger-scale developments. In large part, this is because—from a broad perspective—the observed changes take place over a generation or more, and while any individual may certainly have experienced a period of dislocation (even a 'critical situation'), this need not have been any more serious than those experienced at other small-scale moments of disruption to routine (e.g., when a house was abandoned in the 2nd century). It remains persistently held, however (e.g., Bédoyère 1999a: 164), that if there was a 'crisis' or 'collapse' in the early 5th century, it must have affected the aristocratic or official classes—those connected to the state (which, according to writers like Zosimus, 'abandoned' Britain) and to towns, villas, and forts (the most visible of 'deserted' sites). This seems to be an oversimplification, that does not take into account the gradual decentralisation of state power in Britain that we have charted through the 4th century, nor the wide range of perspectives with which such processes might have been viewed within the identity groups concerned.

This decentralisation is evident in the variety of virtual experiences, across a range of practices and practice contexts, of what were nominally similar identities (see above). It is, as also stated above, belied by the tenor of the law codes of the early 5th century, at least if these are taken at face value. However, the context of these codes is important. They were compilations of decrees, issued to specific people by specific emperors in response to specific situations. As such, they are actually indicative of the fairly ad hoc fashion in which the imperial system worked. We have already seen how different communities in Britain had varying kinds of organisation, which may have been more or less linked to the ideologies of the central state. Clearly, some of these organised forms of life persisted beyond the claim of Roman emperors to the territory of Britain. This means that the series of changes in late 4th and early 5th century Britain cannot be neatly separated into those affecting the elite, as opposed to those affecting others. What is likely is that constructions of broader communities like 'military' or 'official' were now themselves rather more localised (e.g., confined to a specific group of communities on the Wall), and thus perhaps not requiring the same kinds of expressive material discourse as previously. Throughout this process of change in the late 4th and

5th centuries, the tension between tradition and mobility persisted, although manifest in different kinds of tradition and different kinds of mobility to the earlier 4th century. Crucially, while these changes were structured by traditions, they happened because of the actions of people across Britain, who were shaping—at least as much as being shaped by—the 'end' of Roman Britain. These people did this not through widespread rebellion or disaffection, but by taking small decisions about how to live in particular communities, unintentionally transforming society into something that, by the mid-5th century, looked rather different from the mid-4th. The institutionalised transformation of the military, then, is part of a story not of 'collapse' (cf. Wilmott 1995) but rather of structuration, a product of the agency of people living in small communities across Britain.

This process, of necessity, will have been perceived variably by people in different places and with different associations. The broad trajectory of changes may have increasingly favoured localised 'communities of practice' (groups with common patterns of action [Wenger 1998]) rather than more global ones, but as we have seen, this is because the specific changes in each place were often very particular. Each community, then, will have had a different sense of what changed and what stayed the same. In some places, inequities in power relations will have remained strong—perhaps at Birdoswald, for instance. The transformation of materiality in this place may have thus been of relatively low significance in the day-to-day lives of either rulers or ruled. In other places, though, a more genuine social transformation probably did accompany the more visible cessation of pottery production, for example, or the abandonment of some urban structures. Nonetheless, people had left their houses in towns before; the only difference this time was in terms of scale. Those administrators who still lived in towns into the 5th century may have regretted this accelerated change, but some may have remained and adapted to the new way of life; others had withdrawn some time before. No place or category of people was unaffected by the processes of transformation during the 4th century, because all were involved in creating them, but as these were the largely unintentional products of decisions taken with diverse motives, they would also be regarded with diverse feelings. Those who most noticed Britain's departure from the empire's official structure might have been those who felt that it was already a semi-barbarous frontier diocese of limited value—that is, the literate elite of the central empire. To what extent the multifaceted picture in Britain connects with that of the wider empire is the next issue to consider.

258 ■ AN ARCHAEOLOGY OF IDENTITY

Late Roman Britain and the late Roman Empire

Given the complexity of social factors involved in accounting for the range of regional and local material patterns in late Roman Britain, it would be surprising if there was any single story to be told about transformation across the whole Roman Empire in this period. If we look just across the Channel to northern Gaul, this is immediately confirmed as a number of novel features arise that show a particular constellation of processes at work. These are partly a product of the kinds of evidence available: we have already noted the greater preponderance of cemetery data relative to settlement data in this part of Gaul. Nonetheless, distinct similarities to, and differences from the British situation can be observed. The former include the presence of frontier communities like Oudenburg, mentioned in Chapter 3, which appears to be much like the forts on the opposite side of the Channel. Pottery also seems to follow the same kinds of regional trends in the later 4th century that we have seen in Britain (Brulet 1990: 61–78). More differences can be found, though, in some other types of site common in northern Gaul—such as towns with small fortified enclosures (e.g., Alet [Brulet 1991: 155–7; Langouët 1977]) and fortified hilltop 'refuges' (e.g., Furfooz [Brulet 1978, 1990: 153–86]). Both of these phenomena indicate a different pattern for the organisation of military or other security arrangements than that found in Britain, presumably related to the greater threat of invasion from across the Rhine (King 1990: 172–88). While our main literary sources for these invasions were probably engaged in some of the same deliberate constructions and exaggeration of these problems that we noted earlier (Heather 1997: 78–9; Wood 1992), another distinctive characteristic of the archaeology of northern Gaul is that episodes of cultural contact seem to be quite widely represented in cemetery evidence.

This comes from sites like Frénouville, a rural burial ground with approximately 650 graves dating from the 3rd to the 7th centuries (Pilet 1980a, 1980b, 1980c). Interestingly, while there were changes in the burial rite here, including a general shift in grave orientation in the 5th century and the introduction of burials with weapons in the early 6th, these supposed signs of Frankish influence were not accompanied by significant immigration: the physical anthropology suggested a consistent population over time. While such analyses can be questioned (cf. Reece 1982: 354, 1999b: 795–6), this is clearly a different kind of phenomenon to any we have encountered in Britain. Even the 'intrusive' burials at Lankhills, an urban cemetery, are much smaller in number than the apparent change at Frénouville (Swift

2000: 69–77). The picture at Frénouville can also be matched at several other sites, including the nearby burial ground at St. Martin de Fontenay (Pilet 1994: 102–3) and that at Furfooz, closer to the Rhine. These represent episodes of cultural contact within a 'Late Antique' context that do not visibly occur in Britain, because of the problems surrounding material culture use between the beginning of the 5th century and the arrival of Anglo-Saxon artefacts—and people—later in that century. Thus, they are not strictly comparable to what we have seen in 4th century Britain. This, though, is precisely the point: these regions of the empire, as close as they are physically, experienced quite different social changes at different times. The transition from empire to what came after was everywhere a locally negotiated phenomenon.

This regionalism can be found within imperial institutions themselves too. The different pattern of military-associated sites in northern Gaul (compared to Britain) has already been noted, and in other parts of the empire, there are also signs of different practices well within the 'Roman period'. A major feature of the material culture of late Roman Britain is the indeterminacy of the distribution of different kinds of artefacts with regard to 'military' or 'civilian' identities. This is partly thanks to modern misinterpretation of the nature of these identities and requires us to look at the archaeology of practices, rather than simply things, in order to distinguish distinctive ways of acting that relate to specific groups. Such an approach has been adopted in this book. However, the question that remains to be addressed is what all of this means in relation to the integration of soldiers with other sectors of society. There is indeed major variation in the pattern of this integration across the empire, as some recent studies have indicated. Nigel Pollard (1996, 2000), working on soldiers living in urban contexts in Syria, has argued that the institutional boundaries around the army in this region remained quite strong despite—or perhaps because of—a good deal of interaction with, and physical proximity to, other people. In Egypt, by contrast, Richard Alston (1995, 1999) has suggested considerable social integration, as indeed the Abinnaeus Archive that we have looked at in some detail appears to confirm. These differences may relate to regional variation in recruitment and garrisoning arrangements, with more dispersed and locally recruited soldiers in Egypt than in Syria, as well as to differences in the kinds of contexts of interaction highlighted in the evidence from each area (Pollard 2000: 166–7). They underline, though, the conclusions of this book: that superficially global and simple identities will always be constructed in diverse ways in diverse contexts.

260 ■ An Archaeology of Identity

To return to Britain, then, this question of interaction must be answered with a view to time, place, and kinds of identity. We have seen how a multitude of identities were bound up with soldiers' lives, and that many of these would have been more important than simply 'being a soldier' in any specific interaction. In the early 4th century, as in previous periods, there were distinctive practices that united military communities along the Wall, for example, and seem to have separated them from the majority of the rural population in this region. There were also contacts with soldiers from outside of Britain—for instance, through new units and perhaps recruits. Nonetheless, even at this time, there is a good deal of evidence that nonsoldiers were part of these 'military' communities (James 1999a: 23), living in and around those forts. These communities were probably themselves a significant source of new recruits, hereditary recruitment being expected by the Roman authorities (Theodosian Code VII.22), although recruitment and veteran settlement remain difficult issues to penetrate given the lack of epigraphic evidence in this period (see Chapter 3). These communities, in turn, differed from those in the south—where a wider degree of interaction might be expected—and probably from those remaining in the west of Britain. I have argued that the means to negotiate these regional 'military' identities persisted in the later 4th century, but with declining attachment to any broader military community, and with the balance shifting to local communities with their important nonsoldier element. Those units that were not withdrawn from Britain, but remained to be transformed into new kinds of social grouping (like that at Birdoswald), may no longer have been 'military' in the official sense. They did, though, probably retain many of their internal structures and external relationships of power.

Interaction between soldiers and others, like every other kind of identity relationship in this period, was thus dynamic and variable. In detail, it will have shifted rapidly from context to context as soldiers interacted with each other at one moment, with family at another, or with strangers from a farming community at yet another. On the broader level, looking at the institutional structures of 'military' identity over time, change was slow but continuous, as the cumulative effects of small-scale actions and decisions weighed against the influence of the larger-scale imperial community, increasing the variation within that community until it became meaningless. This variation is the key to understanding Late Antiquity. The dominant grand narratives for this period have emphasised either change brought on from without (mainly in the form of barbarian invasions) or, alternatively, weakness within— from Ammianus' moral decay to the modern emphasis on a widening gap between contributions made and benefits received by taxpayers and beneficent aristocrats. By contrast, I would suggest that there was no one factor explaining the end of the Roman west, or the shifting place of the military within that society. Rather, there was a great diversity of responses to the continual tension between continuity and change, and between local and global communities of practice (cf. Hingley 2005; Wenger 1998). In different regions and different settlements, these created different stories, but in every case it was through the everyday actions of people going about their lives— conducting themselves in accordance both with their own desires and with others' expectations of them—that anything happened at all. What this means for our future studies of the Roman Empire is the subject of the final sections of this book.

The archaeology of complex identities

To put them in general terms, the conclusions of this book are that the social world of the late Roman Empire is too complex to be satisfactorily represented by either a simplistic use of category labels or by simple stories of 'decline and fall'—or indeed of 'transition' or 'transformation'. All of these things—stereotypical labels, sudden changes, slow changes, continuities—were parts of that world, but to different degrees in different places. The grand narrative approach thus describes some of what was going on, but to add to that, we need to explore local and everyday perspectives on this period. That is what I have tried to do in this book, adapting this approach both to the people who lived in a community like Birdoswald and to the authors of a document like the Theodosian Code, whose response to the changes happening across the empire was to attempt to reimpose legal order upon it. The latter example reminds us that there were 'globalising' discourses in the Roman Empire, even in the 5th century, but these still need to be anchored to their contexts of production—and then to the great diversity of contexts in which they were received. The implications of this complexity apply to all parts of Roman history, however, and are equally important in replacing the narrative of 'Romanisation' in the earlier phases of Roman occupation. Foremost amongst these implications is that investigations of identity in archaeology must exploit the insights into the interpretation of material culture that have been generated within post-processual archaeology.

A key question that lay behind the research upon which this book is based is how one might define 'military assemblages' in later Roman sites in Britain. The complex nature of the material patterns we have looked at would seem to defy any attempt to do this. Part of the problem here is a basic issue of circularity of argument. If one is attempting to classify an assemblage of artefacts—or even a single object—as representing a simple, monolithic identity group like 'the military', where does one begin? Certain fixed markers of 'militariness' have to be assumed for other types of artefact to be associated with them. Perhaps the most obvious such marker is a site type, the fort, within which 'military' material culture might be most pristine. However, as we have seen, the occupation of forts is by no means this simple in any period. Moreover, in the late Roman period, it is precisely the ambiguous nature of the occupation of forts and fortresses (like Caerleon) that have begged the question of what constitutes a 'military' assemblage. An alternative way to provide some kind of military benchmark would be to test the material patterns against something like the *Notitia Dignitatum*, a supposedly independent record of military dispositions. While comparison between this document and occupation patterns at forts is interesting, it cannot safely be assumed that the correlations between units in the *Notitia* and on the ground are exact; nor, indeed, is this document really an independent source in the sense required by a 'testing' methodology (cf. Kosso 1995). It is itself a product of specific discourses about official identities and therefore only one way of defining what we mean by 'military' when trying to talk about assemblages.

This situation has not, however, ended in a logical impasse. Indications of the importance of military identities come not only from the full range of textual material, but also from certain aspects of the material culture patterns that relate to strongly institutionalised practices; in a fortified site on Hadrian's Wall, this institution is pretty likely to be 'military' on some nominal (and virtual) levels. Such an argument is still in some respects a text-determined one, but insofar as the texts are *dependently* related to at least some of the material, being produced through some of the same institutionalised practices as those activities that we might label 'military', they are germane to the definition of this label. It is, however, certainly not the case that all aspects of material patterning on any particular site relate to such identities in the same way—hence the empirical problems with defining *a* 'military' assemblage, or any other based on monolithic identity groupings. In essence, the overall picture is sufficiently complex to require the involvement of a much more varied and dynamic range of identity categories.

This conclusion is important because it effectively invalidates the whole question of defining a 'military assemblage', at least in the terms in which it has conventionally been stated. The understandings of the nature of material culture and its relationships to social identity that have been developed through this book render simplistic labellings of assemblages and artefacts as 'military'—or anything else—highly suspect. Variation within the military community (cf. Reece 1997) and other state organisations alone would be sufficient to render any goal of finding a unique and homogenous material 'signature' impossible, even without the cross-cutting identity groupings which will blur the boundaries further. While both military and civilian categories were certainly elements in various complexes of identity in the late Roman world, both explicitly (discursively) and implicitly (practically), it is simply inappropriate to attempt to characterise any assemblage of artefacts in such dichotomous terms, if we are attempting to penetrate the lived experiences of the people we are studying. Where recent attempts to find 'material signatures' of different categories have had more success than with this particular opposition (e.g., Evans 2001; cf. Allason-Jones 2001), these still need to be understood in terms of the boundaries that were created between people at the time, and how the labels that we use for convenience relate to recognisable categories in the past.

In other words, such terms were used—and they must therefore still be used—but only within a rather different understanding of the social world of which they were a part. As we saw in Chapter 5, the involvement of material culture in the virtual experience of superficially fixed nominal identity labels is extremely important, but this process is fundamentally dependent upon context and should not distract us from the polysemy of material culture or the multi-dimensionality of social identity. To label an assemblage as 'military' in the present might capture something of similar processes of simplification in the past, but it does nothing to further a fuller understanding of how this and other identifying strategies were made to work by past people. Therefore, 'military' as a label is both less useful and more useful than has hitherto been appreciated. Designating an assemblage as 'military' both underplays the likely complexity of the social dynamics in which this material culture was deployed, and dilutes the utility of various connotations of 'military' that are important in understanding such dynamics. Some of the key problems in the archaeology of late Roman Britain, as discussed in Chapters 1–2, thus need to be radically reconceived. The most appropriate framework for understanding military and other kinds of identity will be one that can handle the dynamic tension—the duality—between fluid/complex and static/abstract identities. In this book, I have tried to ground such a framework in the duality of structure in Giddens's structuration theory. This is because the core of this body of theory is not just a sophisticated account of the complications of social life, but also of how all of these are worked out in *practice*—and I would argue that it is upon this concept (i.e., the meaning of artefact patterning in terms of similarities and differences in activity) that the archaeology of identity should be based. I hope to have demonstrated the value of such an approach in this book, but it requires detailed, comprehensive, and above all comparable data to be published from excavations in the future.

An empire for the 21st century?

In putting this approach into practice, I have tried to develop three themes that have been left underdeveloped within the structurationist framework. These are the dimensions of materiality, temporality, and sociality, which provide the crucial links between agents and structures. Actors are corporeal, temporal, and social beings, interacting with a physical, temporal, and social world. Each of these concepts can be used to define and understand the nature of agents, but also of structures, and they overlap in many ways. Although I have broken them down to build the argument of this book, the connections between the themes considered in different chapters should be clear, as should the overall point that detailed attention to all of these qualities of human life is necessary to an archaeology of practices. Identity is, therefore, only one aspect of the significance of practice, and one could write about the archaeology of different themes based upon the same framework—such as power, subsistence technologies, or representation. Nonetheless, identity is a key issue not just in Roman archaeology (in part because of its culture-historical legacy), but also in archaeology's engagement with a wider public. The approach that we take to dealing with identity is thus not just important for our own purposes, but for the knowledge that we present to the world around us.

This begs two related questions. One is to what extent these kinds of concerns make the approach discussed in this book 'fashionable', but at variance with the nature of the context we have been considering—rather the sentiment expressed by Sheppard Frere in the quotation cited at the beginning of Chapter 2. It is true that the modern/postmodern world might have a different balance between different kinds of materiality, temporality, and sociality, compared to later Roman Britain. However, this does not undermine the applicability of these concepts to understanding the latter, given that these are fundamental aspects of human life. On the contrary, the evidence we have surveyed is incomprehensible without considering these concepts, or the process of structuration in which they were embedded. The second question is what the perspective offered in this book means for the ways in which identity politics are understood in the present. In this regard, I think that—as in the consideration of identity itself—a balance between similarity and difference, between present pasts and past presents, is absolutely vital, rather than the perpetual swinging of the theoretical pendulum from positivism to relativism and back again. Through such a balanced approach, I have tried to rewrite the story of later Roman Britain as an interacting mixture of social processes and local decisions, producing a fractured and complex narrative. This resists simplification and I make no apology for this.

Social life is complicated, and while we try to break it down and analyse it, this is only so that we can achieve a more comprehensive understanding of an inherently multifaceted and diverse reality. If the first years of the 21st century are anything to go by, it will be increasingly important to counter resurgent 'black-and-white' moralities and mendacious political simplifications of the world with a balanced tolerance of diversity and an appreciation of nuance and complexity. The kinds of stories archaeologists write are a small part of this process, but they are not insignificant and they frequently offer justification and legitimacy for present actions. This is a responsibility that archaeologists—as people living in the present, not the past— cannot afford to shirk.

BIBLIOGRAPHY

Adam, B. 1990. *Time and Social Theory*. Cambridge: Polity Press.

Adam, B. 1994. Perceptions of time. In T. Ingold (ed.) *Companion Encyclopedia of Anthropology: humanity, culture and social life*, 503–526. London: Routledge.

Allason-Jones, L. 1993. Small Finds. In P.J. Casey, J.L. Davies, and J. Evans (eds.) *Excavations at* Segontium *(Caernarfon) Roman Fort, 1975–1979*, 165–210. London: C.B.A. Research Report 90.

Allason-Jones, L. 1995. 'Sexing' small finds. In P. Rush (ed.) *Theoretical Roman Archaeology: second conference proceedings*, 22–32. Aldershot: Avebury (Worldwide Archaeology Series 14).

Allason-Jones, L. 1999. Women and the Roman army in Britain. In A. Goldsworthy and I. Haynes (eds.) *The Roman Army as a Community*, 41–51. Papers of a conference held at Birkbeck College, University of London, 11–12 January 1997. Portsmouth, RI: Journal of Roman Archaeology, Supplementary Series 34.

Allason-Jones, L. 2001. Material culture and identity. In S. James and M. Millett (eds.) *Britons and Romans: advancing an archaeological agenda*, 19–25. York: Council for British Archaeology (Research Report 125).

Allason-Jones, L. and Miket, R. 1984. *The Catalogue of Small Finds from South Shields Roman Fort*. Newcastle: Society of Antiquaries of Newcastle upon Tyne (Monograph Series 2).

Allen, D.A. 1993. Roman glass. In P.J. Casey, J.L. Davies, and J. Evans (eds.) *Excavations at* Segontium *(Caernarfon) Roman Fort, 1975–1979*, 219–228. London: C.B.A. Research Report 90.

Allison, P.M. 1997. Why do excavation reports have finds' catalogues? In C.G. Cumberpatch and P.W. Blinkhorn (eds.) *Not So Much a Pot, More a Way of Life: current approaches to artefact analysis in archaeology*, 77–84. Oxford: Oxbow Books (Oxbow Monograph 83).

Allison, P.M. 2002. *Pompeian Households: an analysis of the material culture*. Los Angeles: Cotsen Institute of Archaeology.

Allison, P.M., Fairbairn, A.S., Ellis, S.J.R., and Blackall, C.W. 2004. Extracting the social relevance of artefact distribution in Roman military forts. *Internet Archaeology*, 17, http://intarch.ac.uk/journal/issue17/allison_toc/html.

Alston, R. 1995. *Soldier and Society in Roman Egypt: a social history*. London: Routledge.

Alston, R. 1998. Arms and the man: soldiers, masculinity and power in Republican and Imperial Rome. In L. Foxhall and J. Salmon (eds.) *When Men Were Men: masculinity, power and identity in classical antiquity*, 205–223. London: Routledge.

Alston, R. 1999. The ties that bind: soldiers and societies. In A. Goldsworthy and I. Haynes (eds.) *The Roman Army as a Community*, 175–195. Papers of a conference held at Birkbeck College, University of London, 11–12 January

1997. Portsmouth, RI: Journal of Roman Archaeology, Supplementary Series 34.

Ammianus Marcellinus. *The Later Roman Empire (A.D. 354–378) (Res Gestae)*. 1986. Translated by W. Hamilton; Introduction by A. Wallace-Hadrill. Harmondsworth: Penguin Books (Penguin Classics).

Ammianus Marcellinus. 1935ff. Translated by J.C. Rolfe. London: Heinemann (Loeb).

Andrén, A. 1998. *Between Artifacts and Texts: historical archaeology in global perspective*. Translated by A. Crozier. New York, NY: Plenum Press.

Appadurai, A. (ed.) 1986. *The Social Life of Things*. Cambridge: Cambridge University Press.

Archer, M.S. 1995. *Realist Social Theory: the morphogenetic approach*. Cambridge: Cambridge University Press.

Archer, M.S. 1996. *Culture and Agency: the place of culture in social theory*. Cambridge: Cambridge University Press (2nd edition).

Archer, M.S. 2000. *Being Human: the problem of agency*. Cambridge: Cambridge University Press.

Arnold, C.J. 1984. *Roman Britain to Saxon England*. Beckenham: Croom Helm.

Arnold, C.J. 1997. *An Archaeology of the Early Anglo-Saxon Kingdoms*. London: Routledge (2nd edition).

Atkinson, D. 1942. *Report on Excavations at Wroxeter (the Roman City of Viroconium) in the County of Salop 1923–1927*. Oxford: Oxford University Press/Birmingham and Midland Institute with Birmingham Archaeological Society.

Atkinson, P. 1990. *The Ethnographic Imagination: textual constructions of reality*. London: Routledge.

Attfield, J. 2000. *Wild Things: the material culture of everyday life*. Oxford: Berg.

Baert, P. 1992. *Time, Self and Social Being*. Aldershot: Avebury.

Bagnall, R.S. 1993. *Egypt in Late Antiquity*. Princeton, NJ: Princeton University Press.

Bailey, D., Barford, P.M., Bayley, J., Bird, J., Dickinson, B., Freestone, I., Green, M.J., Hartley, B., Joy, J., Macpherson-Grant, N., Mainman, A.J., Pollard, R., Redknap, M., Rigby, V., Simpson, S., Stow, S., Taylor, M., Thompson, I., Timby, J., Vince, A., and Wilson, M. 1995. The pottery. In K. Blockley, M. Blockley, P. Blockley, S.S. Frere, and S. Stow, *Excavations in the Marlowe Car Park and Surrounding Areas, II: the finds*, 583–920. Canterbury: Canterbury Archaeological Trust (The Archaeology of Canterbury, V).

Baillie Reynolds, P.K. 1938. *Excavations on the Site of the Roman Fort of Kanovium at Caerhun, Caernarvonshire*. (Collected reports on the excavations of the years 1926–9 and on the pottery and other objects found, largely reprinted from Archaeologia Cambrensis). Cardiff: Kanovium Excavation Committee.

Baker, P.A. 2003. A brief comment on the TRAC session dedicated to interdisciplinary approaches to the study of Roman women. In G. Carr, E. Swift, and J. Weekes (eds.) *TRAC 2002: proceedings of the twelfth annual Theoretical Roman Archaeology Conference, Canterbury 2002*, 140–146. Oxford: Oxbow Books.

Balbaligo, Y. 2006. Egyptology beyond philology: agency, identity and the individual in ancient Egyptian texts. In R.J. Dann (ed.) *Current Research in Egyptology 2004*, 1–19. Oxford: Oxbow Books.

Baldwin, R. 1985. Intrusive burial groups in the late Roman cemetery at Lankhills, Winchester—a reassessment of the evidence. *Oxford Journal of Archaeology*, 4.1, 93–104.

Bapty, I. and Yates, T. (eds.) 1990. *Archaeology after Structuralism*. London: Routledge.

Barker, G. 1991. Two Italys, one valley: an Annaliste perspective. In J. Bintliff (ed.) *The* Annales *School and Archaeology*, 34–56. Leicester: Leicester University Press.

Barker, P., White, R., Pretty, K., Bird, H., and Corbishley, M. 1997. *The Baths Basilica Wroxeter: excavations 1966–90*. London: English Heritage (Archaeological Report 8).

Barnes, B. 2000. *Understanding Agency: social theory and responsible action*. London: Sage Publications.

Barnes, T.D. 1998. *Ammianus Marcellinus and the Representation of Historical Reality*. Ithaca, NY: Cornell University Press.

Barrett, J.C. 1997. Romanization: a critical comment. In D.J. Mattingly (ed.) *Dialogues in Roman Imperialism*, 51–64. Portsmouth, RI: Journal of Roman Archaeology, Supplementary Series 23 (International Roman Archaeology Conference Series).

Barrett, J.C. and Fewster, K.J. 2000. Intimacy and structural transformation: Giddens and archaeology (with a comment by L. MacFadyen). In C. Holtorf, and H. Karlsson (eds.) *Philosophy and Archaeological Practice: perspectives for the 21st century*, 25–38. Göteborg: Bricoleur Press.

Barth, F. 1969. Introduction. In F. Barth (ed.) *Ethnic Groups and Boundaries: the social organisation of culture difference*, 9–38. London: Allen and Unwin.

Bartholomew, P. 1982. Fifth-century facts. *Britannia*, 13, 261–270.

Bauman, Z. 1990. *Thinking Sociologically*. Oxford: Blackwell.

Bédoyère, G. de la. 1999a. *The Golden Age of Roman Britain*. Stroud: Tempus Publishing.

Bédoyère, G. de la. 1999b. *Companion to Roman Britain*. Stroud: Tempus Publishing.

Bell, H.J., Martin, V., Turner, E.G., and Berchem, D. van (eds.) 1962. *The Abinnaeus Archive: papers of a Roman officer in the reign of Constantius II*. Oxford: Clarendon Press.

Bell, J. 1992. On capturing agency in theories about prehistory. In J.-C. Gardin and C.S. Peebles (eds.) *Representations in Archaeology*, 30–55. Bloomington: Indiana University Press.

Bennett, J. 1983. Fort sizes as a guide to garrison type: a preliminary study of selected forts in the European provinces. In *Studien zu den Militärgrenzen Roms III*, 707–716. Vorträge der 13 Internationalen Limeskongresses, Aalen. Stuttgart: Konrad Theiss Verlag/Landesdenkmalamt Baden-Württemberg.

270 ◾ An Archaeology of Identity

Bennett, P. 1978. 77–79 Castle Street, Canterbury, Stage II. In Interim report on excavations in 1978 by the Canterbury Archaeological Trust, 275–7. *Archaeologia Cantiana*, 94, 270–278.

Bennett, P. 1984. The topography of Roman Canterbury: a brief re-assessment. *Archaeologia Cantiana*, 100, 47–56.

Bennett, P. and Nebiker, D. 1989. No. 76 Castle Street. In Interim report on work carried out in 1989 by the Canterbury Archaeological Trust, 283–286. *Archaeologia Cantiana*, 107, 281–375.

Benton, T. 2001. A stratified ontology of selfhood. Review of *Being Human: the problem of agency* by Margaret S. Archer (2000). *Journal of Critical Realism*, 4.2, 36–38.

Berggren, K. 2000. The knowledge-*able* agent? On the paradoxes of power (with a comment by B. Chan and T. Georgousopoulou). In C. Holtorf and H. Karlsson (eds.) *Philosophy and Archaeological Practice: perspectives for the 21st century*, 39–51. Göteborg: Bricoleur Press.

Berkhofer, R.F. 1995. *Beyond the Great Story: history as text and discourse*. Cambridge, MA: Belknap Press/Harvard University Press.

Bidwell, P.T. 1991. Later Roman barracks in Britain. In V.A. Maxfield and M.J. Dobson (eds.) *Roman Frontier Studies 1989*, 9–15. Proceedings of the 15th International Congress of Roman Frontier Studies. Exeter: University of Exeter Press.

Bidwell, P.T. 1996. Some aspects of the development of later Roman fort plans. *The Arbeia Journal*, 5, 1–18.

Bidwell, P. 1997. *Roman Forts in Britain*. London: Batsford/English Heritage.

Bidwell, P. 1999. Review of *Excavations and Observations on the Defences and Adjacent Sites, 1971–90* by P. Ottaway (1996). *Britannia*, 30, 414–415.

Bidwell, P. and Speak, S. 1994. *Excavations at South Shields Roman Fort: volume 1*. Newcastle: Tyne and Wear Museums/Society of Antiquaries of Newcastle upon Tyne (Monograph Series 4).

Biggins, J.A., Robinson, J., and Taylor, D.J.A. 1999. Geophysical survey [at Birdoswald]. In P. Bidwell (ed.) *Hadrian's Wall 1989–1999*, 157–160. Handbook of the 12th Pilgrimage of Hadrian's Wall, 14–21 August 1999. Carlisle: Cumberland and Westmorland Antiquarian and Archaeological Society/Society of Antiquaries of Newcastle upon Tyne.

Binford, L.R. 1962. Archaeology as anthropology. *American Antiquity*, 28.2, 217–225.

Binford, L.R. 1981. *Bones: ancient men and modern myths*. New York: Academic Press.

Binford, L.R. 2001. *Constructing Frames of Reference: an analytical method for archaeological theory building using hunter-gatherer and environmental data sets*. Berkeley: University of California Press.

Bintliff, J. and Hamerow, H. (eds.) 1995a. *Europe Between Late Antiquity and the Middle Ages*. Oxford: Tempus Reparatum/B.A.R. International Series 617.

Bintliff, J. and Hamerow, H. 1995b. Europe between late Antiquity and the Middle Ages: recent archaeological and historical research in western and southern Europe. In J. Bintliff and H. Hamerow (eds.) *Europe Between Late*

Antiquity and the Middle Ages, 1–7. Oxford: Tempus Reparatum/B.A.R. International Series 617.

Birley, E. and Keeney, G.S. 1935. Fourth report on excavations at Housesteads. *Archaeologia Aeliana*, Series 4, 12, 204–259.

Bishop, M.C. 1989. O Fortuna: a sideways look at the archaeological record and Roman military equipment. In Driel-Murray, C. van (ed.) *Roman Military Equipment: the sources of evidence*, 1–12. Proceedings of the Fifth Roman Military Equipment Conference. Oxford: B.A.R. International Series 476.

Bishop, M.C. 2002. *Lorica Segmentata, Vol. I: a handbook of articulated Roman plate armour*. Duns: Armatura Press/JRMES Monograph No. 1.

Bishop, M.C. and Coulston, J.C.N. 1993. *Roman Military Equipment*. London: Batsford.

Blagg, T.F.C. and King, A.C. (eds.) 1984. *Military and Civilian in Roman Britain: cultural relationships in a frontier province*. Oxford: B.A.R. British Series 136.

Blockley, K., Blockley, M., Blockley, P., Frere, S., and Stow, S. 1995a. *Excavations in the Marlowe Car Park and Surrounding Areas, I: the excavated sites*. Canterbury: Canterbury Archaeological Trust (The Archaeology of Canterbury, V).

Blockley, K., Blockley, M., Blockley, P., Frere, S., and Stow, S. 1995b. *Excavations in the Marlowe Car Park and Surrounding Areas, II: the finds*. Canterbury: Canterbury Archaeological Trust (The Archaeology of Canterbury, V).

Boon, G.C. 1960. A temple of Mithras at Caernarvon—Segontium. *Archaeologia Cambrensis*, 109, 136–172.

Boon, G.C. 1970. Excavations on the site of the *Basilica Principiorum* at Caerleon, 1968–69. *Archaeologia Cambrensis*, 119, 10–63.

Boon, G.C. 1972. *Isca: the Roman legionary fortress at Caerleon, Mon*. Cardiff: National Museum of Wales.

Boon, G.C. 1975. Segontium fifty years on: I. *Archaeologia Cambrensis*, 124, 52–67.

Boon, G.C. 1987. *The Legionary Fortress of Caerleon—Isca*. Cardiff: National Museum of Wales.

Boon, G.C. 1988a. The coins. In J. Parkhouse, Excavations at Biglis, South Glamorgan, 51–52. In D.M. Robinson (ed.) *Biglis, Caldicot and Llandough: three Late Iron Age and Romano-British sites in south-east Wales, excavations 1977–79*, 1–64. Oxford: B.A.R. British Series 188.

Boon, G.C. 1988b. The coins. In B.E. Vyner and D.W.H. Allen, A Romano-British settlement at Caldicot, Gwent, 91. In D.M. Robinson (ed.) *Biglis, Caldicot and Llandough: three Late Iron Age and Romano-British sites in south-east Wales, excavations 1977–79*, 65–122. Oxford: B.A.R. British Series 188.

Bosanquet, R.C. 1904. Excavations on the line of the Roman wall in Northumberland: 1. The Roman camp at Housesteads. *Archaeologia Aeliana*, Series 2, 25, 193–300.

Bowersock, G.W. 1988. The dissolution of the Roman empire. In N. Yoffee and G.L. Cowgill (eds.) *The Collapse of Ancient States and Civilizations*, 165–175. Tucson: University of Arizona Press.

Bowman, A.K. 1994. *Life and Letters on the Roman Frontier: Vindolanda and its people*. London: British Museum Press.

Brandt, R. and Slofstra, J. (eds.) 1983. *Roman and Native in the Low Countries: spheres of interaction*. Oxford: B.A.R. International Series 184.

Brewer, R. 1988. Ironwork. In J. Parkhouse, Excavations at Biglis, South Glamorgan, 56–57. In D.M. Robinson (ed.) *Biglis, Caldicot and Llandough: three Late Iron Age and Romano-British sites in south-east Wales, excavations 1977–79*, 1–64. Oxford: B.A.R. British Series 188.

Brewer, R. 1993. *Caerwent Roman Town*. Cardiff: Cadw.

Brewer, R. and Guest, P. Forthcoming. *Caerwent Forum-Basilica*. London: Society for the Promotion of Roman Studies.

Brickstock, R.J. 1994. The coins. In P. Bidwell and S. Speak, *Excavations at South Shields Roman Fort: volume 1*, 163–176. Newcastle: Tyne and Wear Museums/Society of Antiquaries of Newcastle upon Tyne (Monograph Series 4).

Brothers, A.J. 1996. Urban housing. In I.M. Barton (ed.) *Roman Domestic Buildings*, 33–63. Exeter: University of Exeter Press.

Brown, P.D.C. 1971. The church at Richborough. *Britannia*, 2, 225–231.

Brulet, R. 1978. *La Fortification de Hauterecenne à Furfooz*. Louvain-la-Neuve: Institut Supérieur d'Archéologie et d'Histoire de l'Art (Publications d'Histoire de l'Art et d'Archéologie de l'Université Catholique de Louvain XIII).

Brulet, R. 1990. *La Gaule Septentrionale au Bas-Empire: occupation du sol et défense du territoire dans l'arrière-pays du Limes aux IVᵉ et Vᵉ siècles*. Trier: Selbstverlag des Rheinischen Landesmuseums Trier (Trierer Zietschrift 11).

Brulet, R. 1991. Le *Litus Saxonicum* continental. In V.A. Maxfield and M.J. Dobson (eds.) *Roman Frontier Studies 1989*, 155–169. Proceedings of the 15th International Congress of Roman Frontier Studies. Exeter: University of Exeter Press.

Bryant, C.G.A. and Jary, D. 2001. Anthony Giddens: a global social theorist. In C.G.A. Bryant and D. Jary (eds.) *The Contemporary Giddens: social theory in a globalizing age*, 3–39. Houndmills: Palgrave.

Buchli, V.A. 1995. Interpreting material culture: the trouble with text. In I. Hodder, M. Shanks, A. Alexandri, V. Buchli, J. Carman, J. Last, and G. Lucas (eds.) *Interpreting Archaeology: finding meaning in the past*, 181–193. London: Routledge.

Buchli, V. and Lucas, G. (eds.) 2001. *Archaeologies of the Contemporary Past*. London: Routledge.

Buckley, R. and Lucas, J. 1987. *Leicester Town Defences (Excavations 1958–1974)*. Leicester: Leicestershire Museums, Art Galleries and Records Service (Leicestershire Museums Publication No. 85).

Burnham, B.C. 1999. Review of *Wroxeter: life and death of a Roman city* by R. White and P. Barker (1998), and *The Baths Basilica, Wroxeter: excavations 1966–90* by P. Barker et al. (1997). *Britannia*, 30, 422–424.

Burnham, B.C. and Wacher, J. 1990. *The 'Small Towns' of Roman Britain*. London: Batsford.

Bury, J.B. 1923. *History of the Later Roman Empire: volume I.* London: Macmillan and Co.

Bushe-Fox, J.P. 1913. *Excavations on the Site of the Roman Town at Wroxeter, Shropshire, in 1912.* London: Society of Antiquaries (Reports of the Research Committee of the Society of Antiquaries of London, I).

Bushe-Fox, J.P. 1914. *Second Report on the Excavations on the Site of the Roman Town at Wroxeter, Shropshire, 1913.* London: Society of Antiquaries (Reports of the Research Committee of the Society of Antiquaries of London, II).

Bushe-Fox, J.P. 1916. *Third Report on the Excavations on the Site of the Roman Town at Wroxeter, Shropshire, 1914.* London: Society of Antiquaries (Reports of the Research Committee of the Society of Antiquaries of London, IV).

Bushe-Fox, J.P. 1926. *First Report on the Excavation of the Roman Fort at Richborough, Kent.* London: Society of Antiquaries (Reports of the Research Committee of the Society of Antiquaries of London, VI).

Butcher, K. (with contributions by D. Perring, P. Reynolds, and P.W. Rogers) 2001. Small change in ancient Beirut. The coin finds from BEY 006 and BEY 045: Persian, Hellenistic, Roman and Byzantine periods. *Berytus*, 45 (Archaeology of the Beirut Souks, Volume 1).

Cameron, A. 1993a. *The Later Roman Empire.* London: Fontana Press.

Cameron, A. 1993b. *The Mediterranean World in Late Antiquity, AD 395–600.* London: Routledge.

Caruana, I.D. 1990. The small finds. In M.R. McCarthy, *A Roman, Anglian and Medieval Site at Blackfriars Street*, 85–196. Kendal: Cumberland and Westmorland Antiquarian and Archaeological Society/Carlisle Archaeological Unit (C.W.A.A.S. Research Series 4).

Casey, P.J. 1974. Excavations outside the north-east gate of Segontium, 1971. *Archaeologia Cambrensis*, 123, 54–77.

Casey, P.J. 1984. *Roman Coinage in Britain.* Aylesbury: Shire Publications (Shire Archaeology Series, 2nd edition).

Casey, J. 1988. Postscript to 'The interpretation of Romano-British site finds'. In J. Casey and R. Reece (eds.) *Coins and the Archaeologist*, 55. London: Seaby (2nd edition).

Casey, P.J. 1992. The end of garrisons on Hadrian's Wall: an historico-environmental model. *Institute of Archaeology Bulletin*, 29, 69–80.

Casey, P.J. 1993. Coins. In P.J. Casey, J.L. Davies, and J. Evans (eds.) *Excavations at* Segontium *(Caernarfon) Roman Fort, 1975–1979*, 122–164. London: C.B.A. Research Report 90.

Casey, P.J. 1995. Roman coins. In D. Phillips and B. Heywood, *Excavations at York Minster, Volume I: Roman to Norman: the Roman legionary fortress at York and its exploitation in the early Middle Ages A.D. 71–1070. Part 2: the finds*, 394–413. Swindon: Royal Commission on the Historical Monuments of England (edited by M.O.H. Carver).

Casey, P.J., Davies, J.L., and Evans, J. (eds.) 1993. *Excavations at* Segontium *(Caernarfon) Roman Fort, 1975–1979.* London: C.B.A. Research Report 90.

274 ■ AN ARCHAEOLOGY OF IDENTITY

Charlesworth, D. 1975. The commandant's house, Housesteads. *Archaeologia Aeliana*, Series 5, 3, 17–42.

Clarke, S. and Jones, R. 1996. The Newstead Pits. In C. van Driel-Murray (ed.) *Journal of Roman Military Equipment Studies*, 5 (for 1994), 109–124.

Clarke, S. and Robinson, D.J. 1997. 'Roman' urban form and culture difference. In K. Meadows, C. Lemke, and J. Heron (eds.) *TRAC 96: proceedings of the sixth annual Theoretical Roman Archaeology Conference, Sheffield 1996*, 162–172. Oxford: Oxbow Books.

Coello, T. 1996. *Unit Sizes in the Late Roman Army*. Oxford: Tempus Reparatum/B.A.R. International Series 645.

Cohen, A.P. 1994. *Self Consciousness: an alternative anthropology of identity*. London: Routledge.

Cohen, I.J. 1989. *Structuration Theory: Anthony Giddens and the constitution of social life*. Houndmills: Macmillan.

Collingwood, R.G. 1931. A Roman fortlet on Barrock Fell, near Low Hesket. *Transactions of the Cumberland and Westmorland Archaeological and Antiquarian Society*, Series 2, 31, 111–118.

Collingwood, R.G. 1993 [1946]. *The Idea of History*. Oxford: Oxford University Press (revised edition, edited by J. van der Dussen, incorporating lectures 1926–8).

Colyer, C., Gilmour, B.J.J., and Jones, M.J. 1999. *The Defences of the Lower City: excavations at the Park and West Parade 1970–2 and a discussion of other sites excavated up to 1994*. York: C.B.A. Research Report 114, edited by M.J. Jones (The Archaeology of Lincoln, VII–2).

Colyer, C. and Jones, M.J. (eds.) 1979. Excavations at Lincoln. Second interim report: excavations in the lower town 1972–8. *The Antiquaries Journal*, 59, 50–91.

Comber, M. 1997. Re-reading the Roman historians. In M. Bentley (ed.) *Companion to Historiography*, 43–56. London: Routledge.

Conkey, M.W. and Spector, J.D. 1984. Archaeology and the study of gender. *Advances in Archaeological Method and Theory*, 7, 1–38 (ed. M.B. Schiffer; New York: Academic Press).

Connolly, P. 1998. *Greece and Rome at War*. London: Greenhill Books.

Connor, A. and Buckley, R. 1999. *Roman and Medieval Occupation in Causeway Lane, Leicester: excavations 1980 and 1991*. Leicester: University of Leicester Archaeological Services/Leicester City Museum Service (Leicester Archaeology Monographs 5).

Cool, H.E.M. 2000. The parts left over: material culture into the 5th century. In T. Wilmott and P. Wilson (eds.) *The Late Roman Transition in the North: papers from the Roman Archaeology Conference, Durham 1999*, 47–65. Oxford: Archaeopress/B.A.R. British Series 299.

Cool, H.E.M. 2004a. Some notes on spoons and mortaria. In B. Croxford, H. Eckardt, J. Meade, and J. Weekes (eds.) *TRAC 2003: proceedings of the thirteenth annual Theoretical Roman Archaeology Conference, Leicester 2003*, 28–35. Oxford: Oxbow Books.

Cool, H.E.M. (ed.) 2004b. *The Roman Cemetery at Brougham, Cumbria: excavations 1966–67*. London: Society for the Promotion of Roman Studies.

Cool, H.E.M., Lloyd-Morgan, G., and Hooley, A.D. 1995. *Finds from the Fortress*. York: Council for British Archaeology/York Archaeological Trust (The Archaeology of York: The Small Finds, 17/10).

Cooper, L. 1996. A Roman cemetery in Newarke Street, Leicester. *Transactions of the Leicestershire Archaeological and Historical Society*, 70, 1–90.

Cooper, N.J. 1996. Searching for the blank generation: consumer choice in Roman and post-Roman Britain. In J. Webster and N. Cooper (eds.) *Roman Imperialism: post-colonial perspectives*, 85–98. Leicester: University of Leicester, School of Archaeological Studies (Leicester Archaeology Monographs 3).

Cooper, N. 1998. The supply of pottery to Roman Cirencester. In N. Holbrook (ed.) *Cirencester: the Roman town defences, public buildings and shops*, 324–352. Cirencester: Cotswold Archaeological Trust (Cirencester Excavations V).

Cooper, N. 2000. Rubbish counts: quantifying portable material culture in Roman Britain. In S. Pearce (ed.) *Researching Material Culture*, 75–86. Leicester: University of Leicester, School of Archaeological Studies (Material Culture Study Group, Occasional Paper No. 1).

Cotterill, J. 1993. Saxon raiding and the role of the late Roman coastal forts of Britain. *Britannia*, 24, 227–240.

Coulston, J.C.N. 1990. Later Roman armour, 3rd–6th centuries AD. *Journal of Roman Military Equipment Studies*, 1, 139–60.

Coulston, J.C.N. 1993. Worked stone. In P.J. Casey, J.L. Davies, and J. Evans (eds.) *Excavations at* Segontium *(Caernarfon) Roman Fort, 1975–1979*, 214–218. London: C.B.A. Research Report 90.

Courty, M.A., Goldberg, P., and Macphail, R. 1989. *Soils and Micromorphology in Archaeology*. Cambridge: Cambridge University Press.

Cowgill, G.L. 1988. Onward and upward with collapse. In N. Yoffee and G.L. Cowgill (eds.) *The Collapse of Ancient States and Civilizations*, 244–276. Tucson: University of Arizona Press.

Crew, P. 1980. Forden Gaer, Montgomery. *Bulletin of the Board of Celtic Studies*, 28 (May 1980), 730–742.

Criado, F. 1995. The visibility of the archaeological record and the interpretation of social reality. In I. Hodder, M. Shanks, A. Alexandri, V. Buchli, J. Carman, J. Last, and G. Lucas (eds.) *Interpreting Archaeology: finding meaning in the past*, 194–204. London: Routledge.

Croom, A.T., Allason-Jones, L., Griffiths, W.B., Hooley, A., McLean, S., and Snape, M.E. 1994. Small finds. In P. Bidwell and S. Speak, *Excavations at South Shields Roman Fort: volume 1*, 177–205. Newcastle: Tyne and Wear Museums/Society of Antiquaries of Newcastle upon Tyne (Monograph Series 4).

Crossley, N. 2001. *The Social Body: habit, identity and desire*. London: Sage Publications.

Crow, J.G. 1988. An excavation of the north curtain wall at Housesteads 1984. *Archaeologia Aeliana*, Series 5, 16, 61–124.

Crow, J. 1995. *The English Heritage Book of Housesteads*. London: Batsford/ English Heritage.

Crow, J. 1999. Housesteads—*Vercovicium*. In P. Bidwell (ed.) *Hadrian's Wall 1989–1999*, 123–127. Handbook of the 12th Pilgrimage of Hadrian's Wall, 14–21 August 1999. Carlisle: Cumberland and Westmorland Antiquarian and Archaeological Society/Society of Antiquaries of Newcastle upon Tyne.

Crow, J. 2004. *Housesteads: a fort and garrison on Hadrian's Wall*. Stroud: Tempus Publishing.

Crummy, N. and Eckardt, H. 2003. Regional identities and technologies of the self: nail-cleaners in Roman Britain. *The Archaeological Journal*, 160, 44–69.

Cunliffe, B.W. (ed.) 1968. *Fifth Report on the Excavations of the Roman Fort at Richborough, Kent*. London: Society of Antiquaries/Oxford: Oxford University Press (Reports of the Research Committee of the Society of Antiquaries of London, XXIII).

Cunliffe, B. 1975. *Excavations at Portchester Castle, Volume I: Roman*. London: Society of Antiquaries (Reports of the Research Committee of the Society of Antiquaries of London, XXXII).

Daniels, C. 1980. Excavations at Wallsend and the fourth-century barracks on Hadrian's Wall. In W.S. Hanson and L.J.F. Keppie (eds.) *Roman Frontier Studies 1979, Part I*, 173–193. Papers presented to the 12th International Congress of Roman Frontier Studies. Oxford: B.A.R. International Series 71(i).

Daniels, C.M. 1989. Wallsend—*Segedunum*. In C.M. Daniels (ed.) *The Eleventh Pilgrimage of Hadrian's Wall*, 77–83. Newcastle upon Tyne: Society of Antiquaries of Newcastle upon Tyne/Cumberland and Westmorland Antiquarian and Archaeological Society.

Dant, T. 1999. *Material Culture in the Social World*. Buckingham: Open University Press.

Dant, T. 2005. *Materiality and Society*. Maidenhead: Open University Press.

Dark, K.R. 1992. A sub-Roman re-defence of Hadrian's Wall? *Britannia*, 23, 111–120.

Dark, K.R. 1994a. *Civitas to Kingdom*. Leicester: Leicester University Press.

Dark, K.R. 1994b. *Discovery by Design*. Oxford: B.A.R. British Series 237.

Darling, M.J. (with D. Gurney) 1993. Caister-on-Sea: excavations by Charles Green 1951–1955. *East Anglian Archaeology*, 60 (Gressenhall: Field Archaeology Division, Norfolk Museums Service).

Darling, M.J. and Jones, M.J. 1988. Early settlement at Lincoln. *Britannia*, 19, 1–57.

Davies, J.A. 1997. Coins. In T. Wilmott, *Birdoswald: excavations of a Roman fort on Hadrian's Wall and its successor settlements: 1987–92*, 321–326. London: English Heritage (Archaeological Report 14).

Davison, D.P. 1996. Military housing. In I.M. Barton (ed.) *Roman Domestic Buildings*, 153–181. Exeter: University of Exeter Press.

DeLaine, J. 1999. Introduction: bathing and society. In J. DeLaine and D.E. Johnston (eds.) *Roman Baths and Bathing, Part I: bathing and society*, 7–16. Portsmouth, RI: Journal of Roman Archaeology, Supplementary Series 37.

Derrida, J. 1988. *Limited, Inc.* Translated by S. Weber. Evanston, IL: Northwestern University Press.

Dewey, J. 2002 [1922]. *Human Nature and Conduct.* Amherst, NY: Prometheus Books.

Dietler, M. and Herbich, I. 1998. *Habitus*, techniques, style: an integrated approach to the social understanding of material culture and boundaries. In M.T. Stark (ed.) *The Archaeology of Social Boundaries*, 232–263. Washington, DC: Smithsonian Institution Press.

Dixon, K.R. and Southern, P. 1992. *The Roman Cavalry: from the first to the third century AD.* London: Batsford.

Dobney, K. 2001. A place at the table: the role of vertebrate zooarchaeology within a Roman research agenda. In S. James and M. Millett (eds.) *Britons and Romans: advancing an archaeological agenda*, 36–45. York: Council for British Archaeology (Research Report 125).

Dobney, K.M., Jaques, S.D., and Irving, B.G. 1995. *Of Butchers and Breeds: report on verterbrate remains from various sites in the City of Lincoln.* Lincoln: City of Lincoln Archaeology Unit (Lincoln Archaeological Studies 5).

Dobres, M.-A. 2000. *Technology and Social Agency.* Oxford: Blackwell.

Dobres, M.-A. and Robb, J.E. 2000. Agency in archaeology: paradigm or platitude? In M.-A. Dobres and J.E. Robb (eds.) *Agency in Archaeology*, 3–17. London: Routledge.

Dobson, B. and Mann, J.C. 1973. The Roman army in Britain and Britons in the Roman army. *Britannia*, 4, 191–205.

Dore, J.N. and Gillam, J.P. 1979. *The Roman Fort at South Shields: excavations 1875–1975.* Newcastle: Society of Antiquaries of Newcastle upon Tyne (Monograph Series 1).

Driel-Murray, C. van. 1995. Gender in question. In P. Rush (ed.) *Theoretical Roman Archaeology: second conference proceedings*, 3–21. Aldershot: Avebury (Worldwide Archaeology Series 14).

Duncan-Jones, R.P. 1977. Age-rounding, illiteracy and social differentiation in the Roman empire. *Chiron*, 7, 333–353.

Dymond, D.P. 1974. *Archaeology and History: a plea for reconciliation.* London: Thames and Hudson.

Dyson, S. 1989. The relevance for Romanists of recent approaches to archaeology in Greece. *Journal of Roman Archaeology*, 2, 143–146.

Edwards, N., and Lane, A. 1988. *Early Medieval Settlements in Wales AD 400–1100.* Cardiff: University College/Bangor: University College of North Wales.

Elliott, A. 2001. *Concepts of the self.* Cambridge: Polity Press.

Elton, G.R. 1991. *Return to Essentials: some reflections on the present state of historical study.* Cambridge: Cambridge University Press.

Elton, H. 1996a. *Warfare in Roman Europe, AD 350–425.* Oxford: Clarendon Press.

Elton, H. 1996b. *Frontiers of the Roman Empire*. London: Batsford.

Emirbayer, M. and Mische, A. 1998. What is agency? *American Journal of Sociology*, 103.4, 962–1023.

Esmonde Cleary, A.S. 1989. *The Ending of Roman Britain*. London: Batsford.

Esmonde Cleary, S. 1993. Approaches to the differences between late Romano-British and early Anglo-Saxon archaeology. *Anglo-Saxon Studies in Archaeology and History*, 6, 57–63 (ed. W. Filmer-Sankey; Oxford: Oxford University Committee for Archaeology).

Esmonde Cleary, S. 1996. The coins. In D.F. Mackreth, Orton Hall Farm: a Roman and early Anglo-Saxon farmstead, 92–93. *East Anglian Archaeology*, 76 (Manchester: Nene Valley Archaeological Trust).

Esmonde Cleary, S. 2003. Civil defences in the West under the high empire. In P. Wilson (ed.) *The Archaeology of Roman Towns*, 72–85. Oxford: Oxbow Books.

Evans, D.R., and Metcalf, V.M. 1992. *Roman Gates Caerleon*. Oxford: Oxbow Books.

Evans, J. 1990. From the end of Roman Britain to the 'Celtic West'. *Oxford Journal of Archaeology*, 9.1, 91–103.

Evans, J. 1995. Roman finds assemblages, towards an integrated approach? In: P. Rush (ed.) *Theoretical Roman Archaeology: second conference proceedings*, 33–58. Aldershot: Avebury (Worldwide Archaeology Series 14).

Evans, J. 2001. Material approaches to the identification of different Romano-British site types. In S. James and M. Millett (eds.) *Britons and Romans: advancing an archaeological agenda*, 26–35. York: Council for British Archaeology (Research Report 125).

Fagan, B. 1995. *Time Detectives. Archaeology: revealing the mysteries*. London: Simon & Schuster.

Faulkner, N. 1998. Urban stratigraphy and Roman history. In N. Holbrook (ed.) *Cirencester: The Roman Town Defences, Public Buildings and Shops*, 371–388. Cirencester: Cotswold Archaeological Trust (Cirencester Excavations V).

Faulkner, N. 2000. *The Decline and Fall of Roman Britain*. Stroud: Tempus Publishing.

Fentress, J. and Wickham, C. 1992. *Social Memory*. Oxford: Blackwell.

Ferrill, A. 1986. *The Fall of the Roman Empire: the military explanation*. London: Thames and Hudson.

Ferris, I. 1995. Insignificant others: images of barbarians on military art from Roman Britain. In S. Cottam, D. Dungworth, S. Scott, and J. Taylor (eds.) *TRAC 94: proceedings of the fourth annual Theoretical Roman Archaeology Conference, Durham 1994*, 24–31. Oxford: Oxbow Books.

Ferris, I.M. and Jones, R.F.J. 1980. Excavations at Binchester, 1976–9. In W.S. Hanson and L.J.F. Keppie (eds.) *Roman Frontier Studies 1979, Part I*, 233–254. Papers presented to the 12th International Congress of Roman Frontier Studies. Oxford: B.A.R. International Series 71(i).

Ferris, I.M. and Jones, R.F.J. 1991. Binchester—a northern fort and vicus. In R.F.J. Jones (ed.) *Britain in the Roman Period: recent trends*, 103–109. Sheffield: University of Sheffield (J.R. Collis Publications).

Fincham, G.R. 2002. *Landscapes of Imperialism: Roman and native interaction in the East Anglian Fenland*. Oxford: Archaeopress/B.A.R. British Series 338.

Fowler, C. 2004. *The Archaeology of Personhood: an anthropological approach*. London: Routledge.

Fox, A. 1940. The legionary fortress at Caerleon, Monmouthshire: excavations in Myrtle Cottage Orchard, 1939. *Archaeologia Cambrensis*, 95, 101–152 (reprinted Cardiff: National Museum of Wales c.1941).

Frank, T. 1970. Race mixture in the Roman empire. In M. Chambers (ed.) *The Fall of Rome: can it be explained?* 47–54. New York: Holt, Rinehart and Winston (2nd edition).

Freeman, P.W.M. 1993. 'Romanisation' and Roman material culture. Review of *The Romanization of Britain* by M. Millett (1990). *Journal of Roman Archaeology*, 6, 438–445.

Freeman, P. 1996. British imperialism and the Roman empire. In J. Webster and N. Cooper (eds.) *Roman Imperialism: post-colonial perspectives*, 19–34. Leicester: University of Leicester, School of Archaeological Studies (Leicester Archaeology Monographs 3).

Frere, S. 1987. *Britannia: a history of Roman Britain*. London: Pimlico (3rd edition).

Frere, S. 1988. Roman Britain since Haverfield and Richmond. *History and Archaeology Review*, 3, 31–36.

Frere, S.S. and Stow, S. 1983. *Excavations in the St. George's Street and Burgate Street Areas*. Maidstone: Kent Archaeological Society/Canterbury Archaeological Trust (The Archaeology of Canterbury, VII).

Fromm, E. 1998 [1966]. *Marx's Concept of Man*. New York, NY: Continuum.

Fulford, M.G. and Timby, J. 2000. *Late Iron Age and Roman Silchester: excavations on the site of the* forum-basilica, *1977, 1980–86*. London: Society for the Promotion of Roman Studies.

Gardner, A.N. 1997. *The Nature and Extent of Fourth Century Occupation in the Roman Fortress of Caerleon*. MA Dissertation, University of London.

Gardner, A.N. 2001a. *'Military' and 'Civilian' in Late Roman Britain: an archaeology of social identity* (3 volumes). PhD thesis, University of London.

Gardner, A. 2001b. The times of archaeology and archaeologies of time. *Papers from the Institute of Archaeology*, 12, 35–47.

Gardner, A. 2002. Social identity and the duality of structure in late Roman-period Britain. *Journal of Social Archaeology*, 2.3, 323–351.

Gardner, A. 2003a. Debating the health of Roman archaeology. Review of 'Whither Roman Archaeology?', a day conference held at the University of London, 16 November 2002. *Journal of Roman Archaeology*, 16, 435–441.

Gardner, A. 2003b. Seeking a material turn: the artefactuality of the Roman empire. In G. Carr, E. Swift, and J. Weekes (eds.) *TRAC 2002: proceedings of the twelfth annual Theoretical Roman Archaeology Conference, Canterbury 2002*, 1–13. Oxford: Oxbow Books.

Gardner, A. 2004a. Introduction: social agency, power, and being human. In A. Gardner (ed.) *Agency Uncovered: archaeological perspectives on social agency, power, and being human*, 1–15. London: UCL Press.

Gardner, A. 2004b. Agency and community in 4th century Britain: developing the structurationist project. In A. Gardner (ed.) *Agency Uncovered: archaeological perspectives on social agency, power, and being human*, 33–49. London: UCL Press.

Gardner, A. Forthcoming. Agency. In H.D.G. Maschner and R.A. Bentley (eds.) *Handbook of Theory in Archaeology*. Walnut Creek, CA: AltaMira Press.

Geary, P.J. 1983. Ethnic identity as a situational construct in the early Middle Ages. *Mitteilungen der Anthropologischen Gesellschaft in Wien*, 113, 15–26.

Gell, A. 1992. *The Anthropology of Time: cultural constructions of temporal maps and images*. Oxford: Berg.

Gero, J.M. 2000. Troubled travels in agency and feminism. In M.-A. Dobres and J.E. Robb (eds.) *Agency in Archaeology*, 34–39. London: Routledge.

Gerrard, C. 2003. *Medieval Archaeology: understanding traditions and contemporary approaches*. London: Routledge.

Gibbon, E. 1994 [1776–1788]. *The History of the Decline and Fall of the Roman Empire*. Edited by D. Womersley (3 volumes). London: Allen Lane (Penguin Press).

Giddens, A. 1979. *Central Problems in Social Theory: action, structure and contradiction in social analysis*. Houndmills: Macmillan.

Giddens, A. 1984. *The Constitution of Society: outline of the theory of structuration*. Cambridge: Polity Press.

Giddens, A. 1993. *New Rules of Sociological Method*. Cambridge: Polity Press (2nd edition).

Gilfillan, S.C. 1970. Roman culture and dysgenic lead poisoning. In M. Chambers (ed.) *The Fall of Rome: can it be explained?*, 55–59. New York: Holt, Rinehart and Winston (2nd edition).

Gilmour, B. 1981. St. Mark's. In M.J. Jones (ed.) Excavations at Lincoln. Third interim report: sites outside the walled city 1972–1977, 92–101. *The Antiquaries Journal*, 61, 83–114.

Godsal, P.T. 1909. The conquest of Britain by the Angles; in the light of military science. *Journal of the Architectural, Archaeological and Historic Society for the County and City of Chester and North Wales (Chester Archaeology)*, 16, 70–96.

Going, C.J. 1992. Economic 'long waves' in the Roman period? A reconnaissance of the Romano-British ceramic evidence. *Oxford Journal of Archaeology*, 11.1, 93–117.

Goldsworthy, A.K. 1996. *The Roman Army at War, 100 B.C.–A.D. 200*. Oxford: Clarendon Press.

Goffman, E. 1959. *The Presentation of Self in Everyday Life*. Harmondsworth: Penguin.

Goffman, E. 1961. *Asylums: essays on the social situation of mental patients and other inmates*. Harmondsworth: Penguin.

Gosden, C. 1994. *Social Being and Time*. Oxford: Blackwell.

Gosden, C. 2004. *Archaeology and Colonialism: cultural contact from 5000 BC to the present*. Cambridge: Cambridge University Press.

Gosden, C. and Marshall, Y. 1999. The cultural biography of objects. *World Archaeology*, 31.2, 169–178.

Grahame, M. 2000. *Reading Space: social interaction and identity in the houses of Roman Pompeii*. Oxford: Archaeopress/B.A.R. Supplementary Series 886.

Grant, M. 1960. *The World of Rome*. London: Weidenfeld and Nicolson.

Grant, M. 1968. *The Climax of Rome: the final achievements of the ancient world AD 161–337*. London: Weidenfeld and Nicolson.

Grant, A. 1989. Animals in Roman Britain. In M. Todd (ed.) *Research on Roman Britain: 1960–89*, 135–146. London: Society for the Promotion of Roman Studies (Britannia Monograph 11).

Graves-Brown, P.M. (ed.) 2000. *Matter, Materiality and Modern Culture*. London: Routledge.

Greene, K. 1978. Apperley Dene 'Roman fortlet': a re-examination, 1974–5. *Archaeologia Aeliana*, Series 5, 6, 29–59.

Greep, S.J. 1986. Coarse pottery. In J.D. Zienkiewicz, *The Legionary Fortress Baths at Caerleon, II: the finds*, 50–96. Cardiff: National Museum of Wales/Cadw.

Greep, S.J. 1988. Worked bone. In J. Parkhouse, Excavations at Biglis, South Glamorgan, 58. In D.M. Robinson (ed.) *Biglis, Caldicot and Llandough: three Late Iron Age and Romano-British sites in south-east Wales, excavations 1977–79*, 1–64. Oxford: B.A.R. British Series 188.

Gregory, D. 1989. Presences and absences: time-space relations and structuration theory. In D. Held and J.B. Thompson (eds.) *Social Theory of Modern Societies: Anthony Giddens and his critics*, 185–214. Cambridge: Cambridge University Press.

Grew, F. 2001. Representing Londinium: the influence of colonial and post-colonial discourses. In G. Davies, A. Gardner, and K. Lockyear (eds.) *TRAC 2000: proceedings of the tenth annual Theoretical Roman Archaeology Conference, London 2000*, 12–24. Oxford: Oxbow Books.

Groenman-van Waateringe, W., Beek, B.L. van, Willems, W.J.H., and Wynia, S.L. (eds.) 1997. *Roman Frontier Studies 1995*. Proceedings of the 16th International Congress of Roman Frontier Studies. Oxford: Oxbow Books (Oxbow Monograph 91).

Guest, P. 1999. The interpretation of Roman coins—practice and theory. In A. Leslie (ed.) *Theoretical Roman Archaeology and Architecture (the Third Conference Proceedings)*, 200–212. Glasgow: Cruithne Press.

Guest, P. 2002. Manning the defences: the development of Romano-British urban boundaries. In M. Aldhouse-Green and P. Webster (eds.) *Artefacts and Archaeology: aspects of the Celtic and Roman world*, 76–89. Cardiff: University of Wales Press.

Hall, J.M. 1997. *Ethnic Identity in Greek Antiquity*. Cambridge: Cambridge University Press.

Hall, R.A. 1997. *Excavations in the* Praetentura: *9 Blake Street*. York: Council for British Archaeology/York Archaeological Trust (The Archaeology of York: The Legionary Fortress, 3/4).

Halsall, G. Forthcoming. *Barbarian Migrations and the Roman West.* Cambridge: Cambridge University Press.

Hamilton, S. 1999. Lost in translation? A comment on the excavation report. *Papers from the Institute of Archaeology*, 10, 1–8.

Handley, F.J.L. and Schadla-Hall, T. 2004. Identifying and defining agency in a political context. In A. Gardner (ed.) *Agency Uncovered: archaeological perspectives on social agency, power, and being human*, 135–150. London: UCL Press.

Harlow, M. and Laurence, R. 2001. *Growing Up and Growing Old in Ancient Rome: a life course approach.* London: Routledge.

Hartley, K.F. 1988. Mortaria. In H.S. Owen-John, Llandough—the rescue excavation of a multi-period site near Cardiff, South Glamorgan, 171. In D.M. Robinson (ed.) *Biglis, Caldicot and Llandough*, 123–178. Oxford: B.A.R. British Series 188.

Hassall, M.W.C. 1976. Britain in the Notitia. In R. Goodburn and P. Bartholomew (eds.) *Aspects of the* Notitia Dignitatum, 103–117. Papers presented to the conference in Oxford, 13–15 December 1974. Oxford: B.A.R. Supplementary Series 15.

Hassall, M. 1999. Homes for heroes: married quarters for soldiers and veterans. In A. Goldsworthy and I. Haynes (eds.) *The Roman Army as a Community*, 35–40. Papers of a conference held at Birkbeck College, University of London, January 11–12, 1997. Portsmouth, RI: Journal of Roman Archaeology, Supplementary Series 34.

Hassall, M. 2000. Pre-Hadrianic legionary dispositions in Britain. In R.J. Brewer (ed.) *Roman Fortresses and Their Legions*, 51–65. London: Society of Antiquaries/Cardiff: National Museums and Galleries of Wales.

Haverfield, F. 1918a. Roman Cirencester. *Archaeologia*, 69 (1917/18), 161–200.

Haverfield, F.J. 1918b. Roman Leicester. *The Archaeological Journal*, 75, 1–46.

Haverfield, F. 1923. *The Romanization of Roman Britain.* Oxford: Clarendon Press (4th edition, revised by G. MacDonald).

Hawkes, C.F.C. 1930. Report on the excavations carried out in the eastern corner in 1929. *Archaeologia Cambrensis*, 85, 141–196 (reprinted Cardiff: National Museum of Wales ca.1941).

Hawkes, S.C., and Dunning, G.C. 1961. Soldiers and settlers in Britain, fourth to fifth century. *Medieval Archaeology*, 5, 1–70.

Hawkes, G. 1999. Beyond Romanization: the creolization of food. A framework for the study of faunal remains from Roman sites. *Papers from the Institute of Archaeology*, 10, 89–95.

Hawkes, G. 2002. Wolves' nipples and otters' noses? Rural foodways in Roman Britain. In M. Carruthers, C. van Driel-Murray, A. Gardner, J. Lucas, L. Revell, and E. Swift (eds.) *TRAC 2001: proceedings of the eleventh annual Theoretical Roman Archaeology Conference, Glasgow 2001*, 45–50. Oxford: Oxbow Books.

Haynes, I. 1999a. Introduction: the Roman army as a community. In A. Goldsworthy and I. Haynes (eds.) *The Roman Army as a Community*, 7–14. Papers of a conference held at Birkbeck College, University of London,

11–12 January 1997. Portsmouth, RI: Journal of Roman Archaeology, Supplementary Series 34.

Haynes, I. 1999b Military service and cultural identity in the *auxilia*. In A. Goldsworthy and I. Haynes (eds.) *The Roman Army as a Community*, 165–174. Papers of a conference held at Birkbeck College, University of London, 11–12 January 1997. Portsmouth, RI: Journal of Roman Archaeology, Supplementary Series 34.

Heather, P. 1997. Late antiquity and the early Medieval West. In M. Bentley (ed.) *Companion to Historiography*, 69–87. London: Routledge.

Hebditch, M. and Mellor, J. 1973. The forum and basilica of Roman Leicester. *Britannia*, 4, 1–83.

Heidegger, M. 1962 [1927]. *Being and Time*. Oxford: Blackwell (7th edition, translated by J. Macquarrie and E. Robinson).

Higham, N. 1992. *Rome, Britain and the Anglo-Saxons*. London: Seaby.

Hildyard, E.J.W. 1952. A Roman site on Dere Street. *Archaeologia Aeliana*, Series 4, 30, 223–238.

Hill, J.D. 2001. Romanisation, gender and class: recent approaches to identity in Britain and their possible consequences. In S. James and M. Millett (eds.) *Britons and Romans: advancing an archaeological agenda*, 12–18. York: Council for British Archaeology (Research Report 125).

Hines, J. 1996. Britain after Rome: between multiculturalism and monoculturalism. In P. Graves-Brown, S. Jones, and C. Gamble (eds.) *Cultural Identity and Archaeology*, 256–270. London: Routledge (TAG).

Hingley, R. 1989. *Rural Settlement in Roman Britain*. London: Seaby.

Hingley, R. 1990. Domestic organization and gender relations in Iron Age and Romano-British households. In R. Samson (ed.) *The Social Archaeology of Houses*, 125–147. Edinburgh: University of Edinburgh Press.

Hingley, R. 1996. The 'legacy' of Rome: the rise, decline and fall of the theory of Romanization. In J. Webster and N. Cooper (eds.) *Roman Imperialism: post-colonial perspectives*, 35–48. Leicester: University of Leicester, School of Archaeological Studies (Leicester Archaeology Monographs 3).

Hingley, R. 1999. The imperial context of Romano-British studies and proposals for a new understanding of social change. In P.P.A. Funari, M. Hall, and S. Jones (eds.) *Historical Archaeology: back from the edge*, 137–150. London: Routledge (One World Archaeology Series 31).

Hingley, R. 2000. *Roman Officers and English Gentlemen: the imperial origins of Roman archaeology*. London: Routledge.

Hingley, R. (ed.) 2001. *Images of Rome: perceptions of ancient Rome in Europe and the United States in the modern age*. Portsmouth, RI: Journal of Roman Archaeology, Supplementary Series 44 (International Roman Archaeology Conference Series).

Hingley, R. 2005. *Globalizing Roman Culture: unity, diversity and empire*. London: Routledge.

Hodder, I. 1974. The distribution of Savernake Ware. *Wiltshire Archaeological and Natural History Magazine*, 69.2, 67–81.

284 ■ An Archaeology of Identity

Hodder, I. 1982a. Theoretical archaeology: a reactionary view. In I. Hodder (ed.) *Symbolic and Structural Archaeology*, 1–16. Cambridge: Cambridge University Press.

Hodder, I. 1982b. *Symbols in Action*. Cambridge: Cambridge University Press.

Hodder, I. 1982c. Sequences of structural change in the Dutch Neolithic. In I. Hodder (ed.) *Symbolic and Structural Archaeology*, 162–178. Cambridge: Cambridge University Press.

Hodder, I. 1991a. Interpretive archaeology and its role. *American Antiquity*, 56.1, 7–18.

Hodder, I. 1991b. *Reading the Past*. Cambridge: Cambridge University Press (2nd edition).

Hodder, I. 1993a. Bridging the divide: a commentary on theoretical Roman archaeology. In E. Scott (ed.) *Theoretical Roman Archaeology: first conference proceedings*, xiii-xix. Aldershot: Avebury (Worldwide Archaeology Series 4).

Hodder, I. 1993b. The narrative and rhetoric of material culture sequences. *World Archaeology*, 25.2, 268–282.

Hodder, I. 1995a. Material culture in time. In I. Hodder, M. Shanks, A. Alexandri, V. Buchli, J. Carman, J. Last, and G. Lucas (eds.) 1995. *Interpreting Archaeology: finding meaning in the past*, 164–168. London: Routledge.

Hodder, I. 1995b. *Theory and Practice in Archaeology*. London: Routledge.

Hodder, I. 1999. *The Archaeological Process: an introduction*. Oxford: Blackwell.

Hodder, I. and Hutson, S. 2003. *Reading the Past*. Cambridge: Cambridge University Press (3rd edition).

Hodder, I., Shanks, M., Alexandri, A., Buchli, V., Carman, J., Last, J., and Lucas, G. (eds.) 1995. *Interpreting Archaeology: finding meaning in the past*. London: Routledge.

Hodgson, N. 1991. The *Notitia Dignitatum* and the later Roman garrison of Britain. In V.A. Maxfield and M.J. Dobson (eds.) *Roman Frontier Studies 1989*, 84–92. Proceedings of the 15th International Congress of Roman Frontier Studies. Exeter: University of Exeter Press.

Hodgson, N. 1994a. Courtyard house [period 7]. In P. Bidwell and S. Speak, *Excavations at South Shields Roman Fort: volume 1*, 35–39. Newcastle: Tyne and Wear Museums/Society of Antiquaries of Newcastle upon Tyne (Monograph Series 4).

Hodgson, N. 1994b. Courtyard house [period 8]. In P. Bidwell and S. Speak, *Excavations at South Shields Roman Fort: volume 1*, 44. Newcastle: Tyne and Wear Museums/Society of Antiquaries of Newcastle upon Tyne (Monograph Series 4).

Hodgson, N. 1996. A late Roman courtyard house at South Shields and its parallels. In P. Johnson with I. Haynes (eds.) *Architecture in Roman Britain*, 135–151. York: C.B.A. Research Report 94.

Hodgson, N. 1999. Wallsend—*Segedunum*. In P. Bidwell (ed.) *Hadrian's Wall 1989–1999*, 83–94. Handbook of the 12th Pilgrimage of Hadrian's Wall,

14–21 August 1999. Carlisle: Cumberland and Westmorland Antiquarian and Archaeological Society/Society of Antiquaries of Newcastle upon Tyne.

Hodgson, N. and Bidwell, P.T. 2004. Auxiliary barracks in a new light: recent discoveries on Hadrian's Wall. *Britannia*, 35, 121–57.

Hoffmann, B. 1995. The quarters of legionary centurions of the Principate. *Britannia*, 26, 107–151.

Hogarth, D.G. 1899. Prefatory. In D.G. Hogarth (ed.) *Authority and Archaeology: sacred and profane*, v–xiv. London: John Murray.

Holbrook, N. (ed.) 1998. *Cirencester: the Roman town defences, public buildings and shops*. Cirencester: Cotswold Archaeological Trust (Cirencester Excavations V).

Holbrook, N. and Salvatore, P. 1998. The street system. In N. Holbrook (ed.) *Cirencester: the Roman town defences, public buildings and shops*, 19–34. Cirencester: Cotswold Archaeological Trust (Cirencester Excavations V).

Holbrook, N. and Timby, J. 1998a. The basilica and forum. In N. Holbrook (ed.) *Cirencester: the Roman town defences, public buildings and shops*, 99–121. Cirencester: Cotswold Archaeological Trust (Cirencester Excavations V).

Holbrook, N. and Timby, J. 1998b. Shops and houses in insula VI. In N. Holbrook (ed.) *Cirencester: the Roman town defences, public buildings and shops*, 230–245. Cirencester: Cotswold Archaeological Trust (Cirencester Excavations V).

Hooppell, R.E. 1878. The results of the recent exploration of the Roman station at South Shields. *Journal of the British Archaeological Association*, 34, 373–383.

Isaac, B. 1992. *The Limits of Empire*. Oxford: Clarendon Press (revised edition).

James, S. 1999a. The community of the soldiers: a major identity and centre of power in the Roman empire. In P. Baker, C. Forcey, S. Jundi, and R. Witcher (eds.) *TRAC 98: proceedings of the eighth annual Theoretical Roman Archaeology Conference, Leicester 1998*, 14–25. Oxford: Oxbow Books.

James, S. 1999b. *The Atlantic Celts: ancient people or modern invention?* London: British Museum Press.

James, S. 2001. 'Romanization' and the peoples of Britain. In S. Keay and N. Terrenato (eds.) *Italy and the West: comparative issues in Romanization*, 77–89. Oxford: Oxbow Books.

James, S. 2002. Writing the legions: the development and future of Roman military studies in Britain. *Archaeological Journal*, 159, 1–58.

James, S. 2003. Roman archaeology: crisis and revolution. *Antiquity*, 77 (295), 178–184.

James, S. and Millett, M. (eds.) 2001a. *Britons and Romans: advancing an archaeological agenda*. York: Council for British Archaeology (Research Report 125).

James, S. and Millett, M. 2001b. Introduction. In S. James and M. Millett (eds.) *Britons and Romans: advancing an archaeological agenda*, 1–3. York: Council for British Archaeology (Research Report 125).

James, W. 2001 [1892]. *Psychology: the briefer course*. Mineola, NY: Dover Publications.

James, W. 1995 [1907]. *Pragmatism*. Mineola, NY: Dover Publications.

Jenkins, K. 1991. *Re-thinking History*. London: Routledge.

Jenkins, R. 1992. *Pierre Bourdieu*. London: Routledge.

Jenkins, R. 1996. *Social Identity*. London: Routledge.

Jenkins, R. 1997. *Rethinking Ethnicity: arguments and explorations*. London: Sage Publications.

Jenkins, R. 2002. *Foundations of Sociology: towards a better understanding of the human world*. Houndmills: Palgrave Macmillan.

Jenkins, R. 2004. *Social Identity*. London: Routledge (2nd edition).

Jobey, G. 1959. Excavations on the native settlement at Huckhoe, Northumberland. *Archaeologia Aeliana*, Series 4, 37, 217–278.

Jobey, I. 1979. Housesteads ware—a Frisian tradition on Hadrian's Wall. *Archaeologia Aeliana*, Series 5, 7, 127–143.

Johnsen, H. and Olsen, B. 1992. Hermeneutics and archaeology: on the philosophy of contextual archaeology. *American Antiquity*, 57.3, 419–436.

Johnson, A. 1983. *Roman Forts of the 1st and 2nd Centuries A.D. in Britain and the German Provinces*. London: A&C Black.

Johnson, M.H. 1999a. Rethinking historical archaeology. In P.P.A. Funari, M. Hall, and S. Jones (eds.) *Historical Archaeology: back from the edge*, 23–36. London: Routledge (One World Archaeology Series 31).

Johnson, M. 1999b. *Archaeological Theory: an introduction*. Oxford: Blackwell.

Johnson, S. 1980. *Later Roman Britain*. London: Book Club Associates.

Jones, A. 2002. *Archaeological Theory and Scientific Practice*. Cambridge: Cambridge University Press.

Jones, A.H.M. 1964. *The Later Roman Empire, 284–602: volume II*. Oxford: Blackwell.

Jones, N. 1993. Brecon Gaer. *Archaeology in Wales*, 33, 57.

Jones, M.E. 1996. *The End of Roman Britain*. Ithaca, NY: Cornell University Press.

Jones, S. 1997. *The Archaeology of Ethnicity*. London: Routledge.

Jones, S. 1999. Historical categories and the praxis of identity: the interpretation of ethnicity in historical archaeology. In P.P.A. Funari, M. Hall, and S. Jones (eds.) *Historical Archaeology: back from the edge*, 219–232. London: Routledge (One World Archaeology Series 31).

Kenyon, K.M. 1980. Excavations at Viroconium in insula 9, 1952–3. *Transactions of the Shropshire Archaeological Society*, 60 (1975–76), 5–73.

Keppie, L. 1991. *Understanding Roman Inscriptions*. London: Batsford.

King, A.C. 1984. Animal bones and the dietary identity of military and civilian groups in Roman Britain, Germany and Gaul. In T.F.C. Blagg and A.C. King (eds.) *Military and Civilian in Roman Britain: cultural relationships in a frontier province*, 187–217. Oxford: B.A.R. British Series 136.

King, A. 1990. *Roman Gaul and Germany*. London: British Museum Publications.

King, A.C. 1999a. Animals and the Roman army: the evidence of the animal bones. In A. Goldsworthy and I. Haynes (eds.) *The Roman Army as a Community*, 139–149. Papers of a conference held at Birkbeck College, University of London, 11–12 January 1997. Portsmouth, RI: Journal of Roman Archaeology, Supplementary Series 34.

King, A. 1999b. Diet in the Roman world: a regional inter-site comparison of the mammal bones. *Journal of Roman Archaeology*, 12, 168–202.

King, A. and Millett, M. 1993. Samian ware. In P.J. Casey, J.L. Davies, and J. Evans (eds.) *Excavations at* Segontium *(Caernarfon) Roman Fort, 1975–1979*, 234–249. London: C.B.A. Research Report 90.

King, C.E. 1986. Coins. In D. Miles (ed.), *Archaeology at Barton Court Farm, Abingdon, Oxon*, mf.5/B7-C5. London/Oxford: C.B.A. Research Report 50/Oxford Archaeological Unit Report 3.

King, J. 1996. The animal bones. In D.F. Mackreth, Orton Hall Farm: a Roman and early Anglo-Saxon farmstead, 216–218/mf.9. *East Anglian Archaeology*, 76 (Manchester: Nene Valley Archaeological Trust).

Knappett, C. 2002. Photographs, skeuomorphs and marionettes: some thoughts on mind, agency and object. *Journal of Material Culture*, 7.1, 97–117.

Knight, J.K. 1964. Excavations at Cold Bath Road, Caerleon. *Archaeologia Cambrensis*, 113, 41–46.

Knight, J.K. 1988. *Caerleon Roman Fortress*. Cardiff: Cadw.

Koerner, S. 2001. Archaeology, nationalism, and problems posed by science/values and epistemology/ontology dichotomies. *World Archaeology Bulletin*, 14, 57–96.

Koerner, S. 2003. Breaking ground or treading water? Roman archaeology and constructive implications of the critique of meta-narratives. In G. Carr, E. Swift, and J. Weekes (eds.) *TRAC 2002: proceedings of the twelfth annual Theoretical Roman Archaeology Conference, Canterbury 2002*, 126–139. Oxford: Oxbow Books.

Koerner, S. 2004. Agency and views beyond meta-narratives that privatise ethics and globalise indifference. In A. Gardner (ed.) *Agency Uncovered: archaeological perspectives on social agency, power, and being human*, 211–238. London: UCL Press.

Kopytoff, I. 1986. The cultural biography of things: commoditization as process. In A. Appadurai (ed.) *The Social Life of Things*, 64–91. Cambridge: Cambridge University Press.

Kosso, P. 1995. Epistemic independence between textual and material evidence. In D.B. Small (ed.) *Methods in the Mediterranean: historical and archaeological views on texts and archaeology*, 177–196. Leiden: E.J. Brill.

Langouët, L. 1977. The Gallic evidence: the 4th century Gallo-Roman site at Alet (Saint-Malo). In D.E. Johnston (ed.) *The Saxon Shore*, 38–45. London: C.B.A. Research Report 18.

Latour, B. 1999. *Pandora's Hope: essays on the reality of science studies*. Cambridge, MA: Harvard University Press.

Laurence, R. 1994. *Roman Pompeii: space and society*. London: Routledge.

Laurence, R. 2000. Metaphors, monuments and texts: the life course in Roman culture. *World Archaeology*, 31.3, 442–455.

Lavan, L. and Bowden, W. (eds.) 2003. *Theory and Practice in Late Antique Archaeology*. Leiden: Brill.

le Bohec, Y. 1994. *The Imperial Roman Army*. London: Batsford (English translation).

Leach, J. and Wilkes, J. 1962. Excavations in the Roman fort at Housesteads, 1961. *Archaeologia Aeliana*, Series 4, 40, 83–96.

Lindenlauf, A. 2004. Dirt, cleanliness, and social structure in ancient Greece. In A. Gardner (ed.) *Agency Uncovered: archaeological perspectives on social agency, power, and being human*, 81–105. London: UCL Press.

Lockyear, K. 2000. Site finds in Roman Britain: a comparison of techniques. *Oxford Journal of Archaeology*, 19.4, 397–423.

Loyal, S. 2003. *The Sociology of Anthony Giddens*. London: Pluto Press.

Lucas, G. 2005. *The Archaeology of Time*. London: Routledge.

Lucy, S.J. 1997. Housewives, warriors and slaves? Sex and gender in Anglo-Saxon burials. In J. Moore and E. Scott (eds.) *Invisible People and Processes*, 150–168. London: Leicester University Press.

Lucy, S.J. 1998. *The Early Anglo-Saxon Cemeteries of East Yorkshire: an analysis and reinterpretation*. Oxford: B.A.R. British Series 272.

Luttwak, E.N. 1976. *The Grand Strategy of the Roman Empire from the First Century AD to the Third*. Baltimore: John Hopkins University Press.

MacGregor, G. 1994. Post-processual archaeology: the hidden agenda of the secret agent. In I.M. Mackenzie (ed.) *Archaeological Theory: progress or posture?*, 79–91. Aldershot: Avebury (Worldwide Archaeology Series, 11).

Mackreth, D.F. 1996. Orton Hall Farm: a Roman and early Anglo-Saxon farmstead. *East Anglian Archaeology*, 76 (Manchester: Nene Valley Archaeological Trust).

MacMullen, R. 1963. *Soldier and Civilian in the Later Roman Empire*. Cambridge, MA: Harvard University Press.

MacMullen, R. 1982. The epigraphic habit in the Roman empire. *American Journal of Philology*, 103, 233–246.

MacMullen, R. 1984. The legion as a society. *Historia*, 33, 440–456. (Reprinted in R. MacMullen, 1990, *Changes in the Roman Empire: essays in the ordinary*, 225–235. Princeton, NJ: Princeton University Press).

Macmurray, J. 1957. *The Self as Agent (Volume I of the Form of the Personal)*. London: Faber and Faber.

Mann, J.C. 1985. Epigraphic consciousness. *Journal of Roman Studies*, 75, 204–206.

Marcus, J. and Flannery, K.V. 1994. Ancient Zapotec ritual and religion: an application of the direct historical approach. In C. Renfrew and E.B.W. Zubrow (eds.) *The Ancient Mind: elements of cognitive archaeology*, 55–74. Cambridge: Cambridge University Press.

Marx, K. 1983 [1852]. The eighteenth brumaire of Louis Bonaparte, In E. Kamenka (ed.) *The Portable Karl Marx*, 287–323. Harmondsworth: Penguin.

Mason, D.J.P. 1980. *Excavations at Chester: 11–15 Castle Street and Neighbouring Sites 1974–8: a possible Roman posting-house* (mansio*)*. Chester: Chester City Council/Grosvenor Museum (Grosvenor Museum Archaeological Excavation and Survey Reports 2).

Mason, D.J.P. 1996. An elliptical peristyle building in the fortress of Deva. In P. Johnson with I. Haynes (eds.) *Architecture in Roman Britain*, 77–92. York: C.B.A. Research Report 94.

Mathisen, R.W. and Sivan, H.S. (eds.) 1996. *Shifting Frontiers in Late Antiquity*. Papers from the First Interdisciplinary Conference on Late Antiquity, University of Kansas, March 1995. Aldershot: Variorum.

Matthews, K. 1995. *Excavations at Chester: the evolution of the heart of the city. Investigations at 3–15 Eastgate Street 1990/1*. Chester: Chester City Council (Archaeological Service Excavation and Survey Reports 8).

Matthews, K.J. 1999. Britannus/Britto: Roman ethnographies, native identities, labels, and folk devils. In A. Leslie (ed.) *Theoretical Roman Archaeology and Architecture (the Third Conference Proceedings)*, 14–32. Glasgow: Cruithne Press.

Mattingly, D. 2002. Vulgar and weak 'Romanization', or time for a paradigm shift? Review of *Italy and the West: comparative issues in Romanization* edited by S. Keay and N. Terrenato (2001). *Journal of Roman Archaeology*, 15, 536–540.

Mattingly, D. 2004. Being Roman: expressing identity in a provincial setting. *Journal of Roman Archaeology*, 17*, 5–25.

Maxfield, V.A. and Dobson, M.J. (eds.) 1991. *Roman Frontier Studies 1989*. Proceedings of the 15th International Congress of Roman Frontier Studies. Exeter: University of Exeter Press.

McCarthy, E.D. 1984. Toward a sociology of the physical world: George Herbert Mead on physical objects. *Studies in Symbolic Interaction*, 5, 105–121.

McCarthy, M.R. 1990. *A Roman, Anglian and Medieval Site at Blackfriars Street*. Kendal: Cumberland and Westmorland Antiquarian and Archaeological Society/Carlisle Archaeological Unit (C.W.A.A.S. Research Series 4).

McCarthy, M.R. 1991. *Roman Waterlogged Remains at Castle Street*. Kendal: Cumberland and Westmorland Antiquarian and Archaeological Society/ Carlisle Archaeological Unit (C.W.A.A.S. Research Series 5).

McGuire, R.H. 2002 [1992]. *A Marxist Archaeology*. Clinton Corners, NY: Percheron Press/Eliot Werner Publications.

McPeake, J. 1978. The end of the affair. In T.J. Strickland and P.J. Davey (eds.) *New Evidence for Roman Chester*, 41–45. Material from the Chester Conference, November 1977. Liverpool: Institute of Extensions Studies, University of Liverpool.

McWhirr, A. 1986. *Houses in Roman Cirencester*. Cirencester: Cirencester Excavation Committee (Cirencester Excavations III).

McWhirr, A., Viner, L., and Wells, C. 1982. *Romano-British Cemeteries at Cirencester*. Cirencester: Cirencester Excavation Committee (Cirencester Excavations II).

Mead, G.H. 1934. *Mind, Self and Society, from the standpoint of a social behaviorist*. Edited and with an Introduction by C.W. Morris. Chicago: University of Chicago Press.

Mead, G.H. 2002 [1932]. *The Philosophy of the Present*. Amherst, NY: Prometheus Books.

Meadows, K. 1994. You are what you eat: diet, identity and Romanisation. In S. Cottam, D. Dungworth, S. Scott, and J. Taylor (eds.) *TRAC 94: proceedings of the fourth annual Theoretical Roman Archaeology Conference, Durham 1994*, 133–140. Oxford: Oxbow Books.

Merleau-Ponty, M. 2002 [1962]. *Phenomenology of Perception*. London: Routledge.

Mertens, J. 1964. *Laat-Romeins Graf te Oudenburg*. Brussels: Archaeologia Belgica 80.

Mertens, J. 1972. *Oudenburg, Romeinse Legerbasis aan de Noordzeekust*. Brussels: Archaeologicum Belgii Speculum, IV.

Mertens, J. 1977. Oudenburg and the northern sector of the continental *Litus Saxonicum*. In D.E. Johnston (ed.) *The Saxon Shore*, 51–62. London: C.B.A. Research Report 18.

Mertens, J. and van Impe, L. 1971a. *Het Laat-Romeins Grafveld van Oudenburg. Deel I: Tekst*. Brussels: Archaeologia Belgica 135.

Mertens, J. and van Impe, L. 1971b. *Het Laat-Romeins Grafveld van Oudenburg. Deel II: Platen*. Brussels: Archaeologia Belgica 135.

Meskell, L. 1999. *Archaeologies of Social Life*. Oxford: Blackwell.

Meskell, L. 2004. *Object Worlds in Ancient Egypt: material biographies past and present*. Oxford: Berg.

Miles, D. (ed.) 1986. *Archaeology at Barton Court Farm, Abingdon, Oxon*. London/Oxford: C.B.A. Research Report 50/Oxford Archaeological Unit Report 3.

Miller, D. 1994. Artefacts and the meaning of things. In T. Ingold (ed.) *Companion Encyclopedia of Anthropology: humanity, culture and social life*, 396–419. London: Routledge.

Miller, D. 1998. Why some things matter. In D. Miller (ed.) *Material Cultures: why some things matter*, 3–21. London: UCL Press.

Miller, S.N. 1928. Roman York: excavations of 1926–1927. *Journal of Roman Studies*, 18, 61–99.

Millett, M. 1981. Whose crisis? The archaeology of the third century: a warning. In A. King and M. Henig (eds.) *The Roman West in the Third Century: contributions from archaeology and history (vol. II)*, 525–530. Oxford: B.A.R. International Series 109(ii).

Millett, M. 1990. *The Romanization of Britain*. Cambridge: Cambridge University Press.

Millett, M. 1995. Strategies for Roman small towns. In A.E. Brown (ed.) *Roman Small Towns in Eastern England and Beyond*, 29–37. Oxford: Oxbow Books (Oxbow Monograph 52).

Milner, N.P. 1993. Introduction. In Vegetius, *Epitome of Military Science (Epitoma Rei Militaris)*, xiii–xxx. Translated by N.P. Milner. Liverpool: Liverpool University Press.

Mithen, S.J. 1990. *Thoughtful Foragers: a study of prehistoric decision-making.* Cambridge: Cambridge University Press.

Mommsen, T. 1958 [1854–6]. *The History of Rome.* New York: Meridian Books (new edition of works of 1854–6, by D. A. Saunders and J.H. Collins).

Monaghan, J. 1997. *Roman Pottery from York.* York: York Archaeological Trust/ Council for British Archaeology (The Archaeology of York: The Pottery, 16/8).

Moore, H.L. 1986. *Space, Text and Gender: an anthropological study of the Marakwet of Kenya.* Cambridge: Cambridge University Press.

Moran, D. 2000. *Introduction to Phenomenology.* London: Routledge.

Moreland, J. 2001. *Archaeology and Text.* London: Duckworth.

Morris, B. 1991. *Western Conceptions of the Individual.* Oxford: Berg.

Morris, I. 1997. Archaeology as cultural history. *Archaeological Review from Cambridge*, 14.1, 3–16.

Mouzelis, N. 1995. *Sociological Theory: what went wrong? Diagnosis and remedies.* London: Routledge.

Munslow, A. 1997. *Deconstructing History.* London: Routledge.

Munslow, A. 2000. *The Routledge Companion to Historical Studies.* London: Routledge.

Musolf, G.R. 2003. *Structure and Agency in Everyday Life: an introduction to social psychology.* Lanham, MD: Rowman and Littlefield.

Nash-Williams, V.E. 1929. The Roman legionary fortress at Caerleon in Monmouthshire: report on the excavations carried out in 1926. *Archaeologia Cambrensis*, 84, 237–307 (reprinted Cardiff: National Museum of Wales c.1941).

Nash-Williams, V.E. 1954. The forum-and-basilica and public baths of the Roman town of *Venta Silurum* at Caerwent in Monmouthshire. *Bulletin of the Board of Celtic Studies*, 15.2 (May 1953), 159–168.

Nash-Williams, V.E. and Grimes, W.F. 1952. The coins found during the 1925 (south wall) excavations at Caerwent (Venta Silurum) Monmouthshire. *Bulletin of the Board of Celtic Studies*, 14.3, 242–249.

Newstead, R. and Droop, J.P. 1932. The Roman amphitheatre at Chester. *Journal of the Chester and North Wales Architectural, Archaeological and Historic Society*, 29, 5–40.

Newstead, R. and Droop, J.P. 1939. Excavations at Chester 1939: the Princess Street clearance area. *Journal of the Chester and North Wales Architectural, Archaeological and Historic Society*, 34.1, 5–47.

Nicasie, M.J. 1998. *Twilight of Empire: the Roman army from the reign of Diocletian until the battle of Adrianople.* Amsterdam: J.C. Gieben.

Noddle, B. 1993. Bones of larger mammals. In P.J. Casey, J.L. Davies, and J. Evans (eds.) *Excavations at* Segontium *(Caernarfon) Roman Fort, 1975–1979*, 97–118. London: C.B.A. Research Report 90.

Notitia Dignitatum. 1876. Edited by O. Seeck. Berlin: Apud Weidmannos.

O'Connor, T.P. 1986. The animal bones. In J.D. Zienkiewicz, *The Legionary Fortress Baths at Caerleon, II: the finds*, 225–248. Cardiff: National Museum of Wales/Cadw.

Orton, C., Tyers, P., and Vince, A. 1993. *Pottery in Archaeology*. Cambridge: Cambridge University Press.

Ottaway, P. 1992. *Archaeology in British Towns from the Emperor Claudius to the Black Death*. London: Routledge.

Ottaway, P. 1996. *Excavations and Observations on the Defences and Adjacent Sites, 1971–90*. York: York Archaeological Trust/Council for British Archaeology (The Archaeology of York: The Legionary Fortress, 3/3).

Ottaway, P. 1997. Recent excavations of the late Roman signal station at Filey, North Yorkshire. In W. Groenman-van Waateringe, B.L. van Beek, W.J.H. Willems, and S.L. Wynia (eds.) *Roman Frontier Studies 1995*, 135–141. Proceedings of the 16th International Congress of Roman Frontier Studies. Oxford: Oxbow Books (Oxbow Monograph 91).

Owen-John, H.S. 1988. Llandough—the rescue excavation of a multi-period site near Cardiff, South Glamorgan. In D.M. Robinson (ed.) *Biglis, Caldicot and Llandough: three Late Iron Age and Romano-British sites in south-east Wales, excavations 1977–79*, 123–78. Oxford: B.A.R. British Series 188.

Parker, J. 2000. *Structuration*. Buckingham: Open University Press.

Parkhouse, J. 1988. Excavations at Biglis, South Glamorgan. In D.M. Robinson (ed.) *Biglis, Caldicot and Llandough: three Late Iron Age and Romano-British sites in south-east Wales, excavations 1977–79*, 1–64. Oxford: B.A.R. British Series 188.

Peacock, D.P.S. 1982. *Pottery in the Roman World: an ethnoarchaeological approach*. London: Longman.

Pearson, A. 2002. *The Roman Shore Forts: coastal defences of southern Britain*. Stroud: Tempus Publishing.

Peddie, J. 1987. *Invasion: the Roman conquest of Britain*. Stroud: Alan Sutton.

Peddie, J. 1994. *The Roman War Machine*. Stroud: Alan Sutton.

Pegler, A. 2000. Social organisations within the Roman Army. In G. Fincham, G. Harrison, R.R. Holland, and L. Revell (eds.) *TRAC 99: proceedings of the ninth annual Theoretical Roman Archaeology Conference, Durham 1999*, 37–43. Oxford: Oxbow Books.

Perrin, J.R. (with F. Wild and K.F. Hartley) 1996. The Roman pottery. In D.F. Mackreth, Orton Hall Farm: a Roman and early Anglo-Saxon farmstead, 114–204. *East Anglian Archaeology*, 76 (Manchester: Nene Valley Archaeological Trust).

Perring, D. 1991. *Roman London*. London: Seaby.

Perring, D. 2002. *The Roman House in Britain*. London: Routledge.

Petch, D.F. 1978. The major buildings of the fortress. In T.J. Strickland and P.J. Davey (eds.) *New Evidence for Roman Chester*, 17–24. Material from the Chester Conference, November 1977. Liverpool: Institute of Extensions Studies, University of Liverpool.

Petch, D.F. and Thompson, F.H. 1959. Excavations in Commonhall Street, Chester, 1954–6: the granaries of the legionary fortress of Deva. *Journal of the Chester and North Wales Architectural, Archaeological and Historic Society*, 46, 33–62.

Petts, D. 2003. *Christianity in Roman Britain*. Stroud: Tempus Publishing.

Pharr, C. 1952. *The Theodosian Code and Novels and the Sirmondian Constitution.* Translation, commentary, glossary, and bibliography by C. Pharr with T.S. Davidson and M.B. Pharr; Introduction by C. Dickerman Williams. Princeton, NJ: Princeton University Press.

Phillips, D. and Heywood, B. 1995a. *Excavations at York Minster, Volume I: Roman to Norman: the Roman legionary fortress at York and its exploitation in the early Middle Ages A.D. 71–1070. Part 1: the site.* Swindon: Royal Commission on the Historical Monuments of England (edited by M.O.H. Carver).

Phillips, D. and Heywood, B. 1995b. *Excavations at York Minster, Volume I: Roman to Norman: the Roman legionary fortress at York and its exploitation in the early Middle Ages A.D. 71–1070. Part 2: the finds.* Swindon: Royal Commission on the Historical Monuments of England (edited by M.O.H. Carver).

Philpott, R. 1991. *Burial Practices in Roman Britain: a survey of grave treatment and furnishing, A.D. 43–410.* Oxford: Tempus Reparatum/B.A.R. British Series 219.

Philpott, R. and Reece, R. 1993. Sépultures rurales en Bretagne romaine. In Ferdière, A. (ed.) *Monde des Morts, Monde des Vivants en Gaule Rurale,* 417–423. Actes du Colloque ARCHEA/AGER. Tours: FERACF/La Simarre.

Pilet, C. 1980a. *La Nécropole de Frénouville: i, essai de synthèse.* Oxford: B.A.R. International Series 83(i).

Pilet, C. 1980b. *La Nécropole de Frénouville: ii, inventaire des sépultures et catalogue des monnaies.* Oxford: B.A.R. International Series 83(ii).

Pilet, C. 1980c. *La Nécropole de Frénouville: iii, planches.* Oxford: B.A.R. International Series 83(iii).

Pilet, C. (ed.) 1994. *La Nécropole de Saint-Martin-de-Fontenay (Calvados).* Paris: C.N.R.S. Editions (Gallia Supplément 54).

Pohl, W. 1997. Ethnic names and identities in the British Isles: a comparative perspective. In J. Hines (ed.) *The Anglo-Saxons from the Migration Period to the Eighth Century,* 7–40. San Marino: Boydell Press.

Pollard, N. 1996. The Roman army as 'total institution' in the Near East? Dura-Europos as a case study. In D.L. Kennedy (ed.) *The Roman Army in the East,* 211–227. Ann Arbor, MI: Journal of Roman Archaeology Supplementary Series 18.

Pollard, N. 2000. *Soldiers, Cities, and Civilians in Roman Syria.* Ann Arbor: University of Michigan Press.

Potter, D.S. 1999. *Literary Texts and the Roman Historian.* London: Routledge.

Poulton, R. and Scott, E. 1993. The hoarding, deposition and use of pewter in Roman Britain. In E. Scott (ed.) *Theoretical Roman Archaeology: first conference proceedings,* 115–132. Aldershot: Avebury (Worldwide Archaeology Series 4).

Preucel, R.W. 1991. The philosophy of archaeology. In R.W. Preucel (ed.) *Processual and Post-processual Archaeologies: multiple ways of knowing the past,*

294 ■ AN ARCHAEOLOGY OF IDENTITY

17–29. Carbondale: Center for Archaeological Investigations, Southern Illinois University.

Pretty, K. 1997. Small finds. In P. Barker, R. White, K. Pretty, H. Bird, and M. Corbishley, *The Baths Basilica Wroxeter: excavations 1966–90*, 249–258. London: English Heritage (Archaeological Report 8).

Price, J., Henig, M., Manning, W.H., Lloyd-Morgan, G., Butcher, S.A., MacGregor, A.S., and Walton, P. 1995. Small finds reports. In D. Phillips and B. Heywood, *Excavations at York Minster, Volume I: Roman to Norman: the Roman legionary fortress at York and its exploitation in the early Middle Ages A.D. 71–1070. Part 2: the finds*, 346–432. Swindon: Royal Commission on the Historical Monuments of England (edited by M.O.H. Carver).

Randsborg, K. 1995. *Hjortspring: warfare and sacrifice in early Europe*. Aarhus: Aarhus University Press.

Rathje, W.L. 1992. *Rubbish! the archaeology of garbage*. New York: Harper Collins.

Reece, R. 1968. The Roman coins found in 1931–8/Summary of the Roman coins from Richborough. In B. Cunliffe (ed.) *Fifth Report on the Excavations of the Roman Fort at Richborough, Kent*, 188–217. Oxford: Oxford University Press/London: Society of Antiquaries (Reports of the Research Committee of the Society of Antiquaries of London, XXIII).

Reece, R. 1977. Coins and frontiers—or supply and demand. In J. Fitz (ed.) *Limes: Akten des XI. Internationalen Limeskongresses*, 643–645. Budapest: Akadémiai Kiadó (Hungarian Academy of Sciences).

Reece, R. 1979. Military pots or calibrated assemblages? In M. Millett (ed.) *Pottery and the Archaeologist*, 81–85. London: Institute of Archaeology (Occasional Publication 4).

Reece, R. 1980. Town and country: the end of Roman Britain. *World Archaeology*, 12.1, 77–92.

Reece, R. 1982. Bones, bodies and disease. *Oxford Journal of Archaeology*, 1.3, 347–358.

Reece, R. 1987. *Coinage in Roman Britain*. London: Seaby.

Reece, R. 1988. *My Roman Britain*. Cirencester: Cotswold Studies III.

Reece, R. 1989. Models of continuity. *Oxford Journal of Archaeology*, 8.2, 231–236.

Reece, R. 1991. *Roman Coins from 140 Sites in Britain*. Cirencester: Cotswold Studies IV.

Reece, R. 1993a. Theory and Roman archaeology. In E. Scott (ed.) *Theoretical Roman Archaeology: first conference proceedings*, 29–38. Aldershot: Avebury (Worldwide Archaeology Series 4).

Reece, R. 1993b. British sites and their Roman coins. *Antiquity*, 67 (257), 863–869.

Reece, R. 1993c. Roman coins. In W.J. Rodwell and K.A. Rodwell, *Rivenhall: investigations of a villa, church and village, 1950–1977. Volume 2: specialist studies and index to volumes 1 and 2*, 50–51. London: C.B.A. Research Report 80/Chelmsford Museums Service (Chelmsford Archaeological Trust Report 4.2).

Reece, R. 1995. Site-finds in Roman Britain. *Britannia*, 26, 179–206.

Reece, R. 1996. The interpretation of site finds—a review. In C.E. King and D.G. Wigg (eds.) *Coin Finds and Coin Use in the Roman World*, 341–355. Papers from the 13th Oxford Symposium on Coinage and Monetary History, 25–27/3/1993. Berlin: Gebr. Mann Verlag (Studien zu Fundmünzen der Antike, Band 10).

Reece, R. 1997. *The Future of Roman Military Archaeology*. Cardiff: National Museums & Galleries of Wales (10th Annual Caerleon Lecture).

Reece, R. 1999a. *The Later Roman Empire: an archaeology AD 150–600*. Stroud: Tempus Publishing.

Reece, R. 1999b. Two late Roman cemeteries in Italy: questions of interpretation. *Journal of Roman Archaeology*, 12**, 793–797.

Reece, R. 2002. *The Coinage of Roman Britain*. Stroud: Tempus Publishing.

Reece, R. and James, S. 1986. *Identifying Roman Coins*. London: Seaby.

Renfrew, C. 1979. Systems collapse as social transformation: catastrophe and anastrophe in early state societies. In C. Renfrew and K.L. Cooke (eds.) *Transformations: mathematical approaches to culture change*, 481–506. New York: Academic Press.

Renfrew, C. 1994. Towards a cognitive archaeology. In C. Renfrew and E.B.W. Zubrow (eds.) *The Ancient Mind: elements of cognitive archaeology*, 3–12. Cambridge: Cambridge University Press.

Rennie, D.M. 1971. Excavations in the Parsonage Field, Cirencester, 1958. *Transactions of the Bristol and Gloucestershire Archaeological Society*, 90, 64–94.

Richmond, I.A. and Birley, E.B. 1930. Excavations on Hadrian's Wall in the Birdoswald-Pike Hill sector, 1929. *Transactions of the Cumberland and Westmorland Antiquarian and Archaeological Society*, Series 2, 30, 169–205.

Ridley, R.T. 1982. Introduction. In Zosimus, *New History (Nea Historia)*, xi–xv. Translated by R.T. Ridley. Sydney: Australian Association for Byzantine Studies.

Rodwell, W.J. and Rodwell, K.A. 1985. *Rivenhall: investigations of a villa, church and village, 1950–1977*. London: C.B.A. Research Report 55 (Chelmsford Archaeological Trust Report 4).

Rogers, A. 2005. Metalworking and late Roman power: a study of towns in later Roman Britain. In J. Bruhn, B. Croxford, and D. Grigoropoulos (eds.) *TRAC 2004: proceedings of the fourteenth annual Theoretical Roman Archaeology Conference, Durham 2004*, 27–38. Oxford: Oxbow Books.

Rosenthal, S.B. and Bourgeois, P.L. 1991. *Mead and Merleau-Ponty: toward a common vision*. Albany: State University of New York Press.

Rush, P. 1997. Symbols, pottery and trade. In K. Meadows, C. Lemke, and J. Heron (eds.) *TRAC 96: proceedings of the sixth annual Theoretical Roman Archaeology Conference, Sheffield 1996*, 55–64. Oxford: Oxbow Books.

Russell Robinson, H. 1975. *The Armour of Imperial Rome*. London: Arms and Armour Press.

Ryan, N.S. 1988. *Fourth Century Coin Finds from Roman Britain: a computer analysis*. Oxford: B.A.R. British Series 183.

296 ■ An Archaeology of Identity

Sackett, J.R. 1982. Approaches to style in lithic archaeology. *Journal of Anthropological Archaeology*, 1, 59–112.

Salway, P. 1993. *The Oxford Illustrated History of Roman Britain*. Oxford: Oxford University Press.

Salzman, M.R. 1990. *On Roman Time: the codex-calendar of 354 and the rhythms of urban life in late antiquity*. Berkeley: University of California Press.

Schiffer, M.B. 1972. Archaeological context and systemic context. *American Antiquity*, 37.2, 156–165.

Schiffer, M.B. 1999. *The Material Life of Human Beings: artifacts, behavior, and communication*. London: Routledge.

Schutz, A. 1967. *The Phenomenology of the Social World*. Translated by G. Walsh and F. Lehnert. Evanston, IL: Northwestern University Press.

Scott, E. (ed.) 1993a. *Theoretical Roman Archaeology: first conference proceedings*. Aldershot: Avebury (Worldwide Archaeology Series 4).

Scott, E. 1993b. Writing the Roman empire. In E. Scott (ed.) *Theoretical Roman Archaeology: first conference proceedings*, 5–22. Aldershot: Avebury (Worldwide Archaeology Series 4).

Scott, E. 1995. Women and gender relations in the Roman empire. In P. Rush (ed.) *Theoretical Roman Archaeology: second conference proceedings*, 174–189. Aldershot: Avebury (Worldwide Archaeology Series 14).

Scull, C. 1995. Approaches to material culture and social dynamics of the migration period of eastern England. In J. Bintliff and H. Hamerow (eds.) *Europe Between Late Antiquity and the Middle Ages*, 71–83. Oxford: Tempus Reparatum/B.A.R. International Series 617.

Shalin, D.M. 2000. George Herbert Mead. In G. Ritzer (ed.) *The Blackwell Companion to Major Social Theorists*, 302–344. Oxford: Blackwell.

Shanks, M. and Tilley, C. 1987. *Social Theory and Archaeology*. Cambridge: Polity Press.

Shanks, M. and Tilley, C. 1992. *Re-Constructing Archaeology: theory and practice*. London: Routledge (2nd edition).

Shaw, B.D. 1983. Soldiers and society: the army in Numidia. *Opus*, 2, 133–159.

Shennan, S.J. 1989. Introduction: archaeological approaches to cultural identity. In S.J. Shennan (ed.) *Archaeological Approaches to Cultural Identity*, 1–32. London: Routledge (One World Archaeology 10).

Simpson, F.G. 1976. *Watermills and Military Works on Hadrian's Wall: excavations in Northumberland 1907–1913*. Edited by G. Simpson. Kendal: Titus Wilson & Son.

Smith, E.A. 1983. Anthropological applications of optimal foraging theory: a critical review. *Current Anthropology*, 24.5, 625–651.

Smith, D.J. 1977. Mythological figures and scenes in Romano-British mosaics. In J. Munby and M. Henig (eds.) *Roman Life and Art in Britain: part I*, 105–193. Oxford: B.A.R. British Series 41(i).

Smith, J.T. 1997. *Roman Villas: a study in social structure*. London: Routledge.

Snape, M. 1994. The southwest gate, intervallum street, and fort ditches. In P. Bidwell and S. Speak, *Excavations at South Shields Roman Fort: volume 1*,

107–144. Newcastle: Tyne and Wear Museums/Society of Antiquaries of Newcastle upon Tyne (Monograph Series 4).

Snyder, C.A. 1998. *An Age of Tyrants*. Stroud: Sutton Publishing.

Southern, P. and Dixon, K.R. 1996. *The Late Roman Army*. London: Batsford.

Spector, J. 1991. What this awl means. In J. Gero and M. Conkey (eds.) *Engendering Archaeology: women and prehistory*, 388–406. Oxford: Blackwell.

Stallibrass, S. 1995. Review of the vertebrate remains. In J.P. Huntley and S. Stallibrass, *Plant and Vertebrate Remains from Archaeological Sites in Northern England: data reviews and future directions*, 84–198. Durham: Architectural and Archaeological Society of Durham and Northumberland (Research Report 4).

Stallibrass, S. 2000. Cattle, culture, status and soldiers in northern England. In G. Fincham, G. Harrison, R.R. Holland, and L. Revell (eds.) *TRAC 99: proceedings of the ninth annual Theoretical Roman Archaeology Conference, Durham 1999*, 64–73. Oxford: Oxbow Books.

Stanford, S.C. 1968. The Roman forts at Leintwardine and Buckton. *Transactions of the Woolhope Naturalists' Field Club*, 39.2 (1967–9), 222–326.

Stark, M.T. (ed.) 1998. *The Archaeology of Social Boundaries*. Washington, DC: Smithsonian Institution Press.

Stephenson, I.P. 1999. *Roman Infantry Equipment: the later empire*. Stroud: Tempus Publishing.

Stephenson, I.P., and Dixon, K.R. 2003. *Roman Cavalry Equipment*. Stroud: Tempus Publishing.

Storey, G.R. 1999. Archaeology and Roman society: integrating textual and archaeological data. *Journal of Archaeological Research*, 7.3, 203–248.

Strickland, T.J. 1982. Chester: excavations in the Princess Street/Hunter Street area, 1978–1982. A first report on discoveries of the Roman period. *Journal of the Chester Archaeological Society*, 65, 5–24.

Strickland, T.J. 1994. An overview. In S. Ward et al. *Excavations at Chester: Saxon occupation within the Roman fortress, sites excavated 1971–1981*, 5–17. Chester: Chester City Council (Archaeological Service Excavation and Survey Reports 7).

Summerfield, J. (with contributions by L. Allason-Jones, J. Bayley, J.C.N. Coulston, J. Davies, G. Edwards, M. Henig, G. Lloyd-Morgan, Q. Mould, J. Price, S. Cottam, I. Riddler, and R.S.O. Tomlin) 1997. The small finds. In T. Wilmott, *Birdoswald: excavations of a Roman fort on Hadrian's Wall and its successor settlements: 1987–92*, 269–361. London: English Heritage (Archaeological Report 14).

Swift, E. 2000. *The End of the Western Roman Empire: an archaeological investigation*. Stroud: Tempus Publishing.

Tainter, J.A. 1988. *The Collapse of Complex Societies*. Cambridge: Cambridge University Press.

Tait, J. 1963. An excavation at Housesteads, 1962. *Archaeologia Aeliana*, Series 4, 41, 37–44.

Tarlow, S. and West, S. (eds.) 1999. *The Familiar Past? archaeologies of later historical Britain*. London: Routledge.

Thayer, H.S. 1981. *Meaning and Action: a critical history of pragmatism.* Indianapolis, IN: Hackett Publishing Co. (2nd edition).

Thomas, J. 1996. *Time, Culture and Identity: an interpretive archaeology.* London: Routledge.

Thomas, J. 2000. Reconfiguring the social, reconfiguring the material. In M.B. Schiffer (ed.) *Social Theory in Archaeology*, 143–155. Salt Lake City, UT: University of Utah Press.

Thomas, J. 2004. *Archaeology and Modernity.* London: Routledge.

Thompson, E.A. 1977. Britain, A.D. 406–410. *Britannia*, 8, 303–318.

Thompson, E.A. 1983. Fifth-century facts? *Britannia*, 14, 272–274.

Thompson, J.B. 1989. The theory of structuration. In D. Held and J.B. Thompson (eds.) *Social Theory of Modern Societies: Anthony Giddens and his critics*, 56–76. Cambridge: Cambridge University Press.

Thompson, J.B. 1990. *Ideology and Modern Culture.* Cambridge: Polity Press.

Thompson, M. 1979. *Rubbish Theory: the creation and destruction of value.* Oxford: Oxford University Press.

Tilley, C. 1984. Ideology and the legitimation of power in the middle Neolithic of southern Sweden. In D. Miller and C. Tilley (eds.) *Ideology, Power and Prehistory*, 111–146. Cambridge: Cambridge University Press.

Tilley, C. 1989a. Archaeology as socio-political action in the present. In V. Pinsky and A. Wylie (eds.) *Critical Traditions in Contemporary Archaeology*, 114–116. Cambridge: Cambridge University Press.

Tilley, C. 1989b. Interpreting material culture. In I. Hodder (ed.) *The Meanings of Things: material culture and symbolic expression*, 185–194. London: Harper Collins (One World Archaeology 6).

Tilley, C. 1991. *Material Culture and Text: the art of ambiguity.* London: Routledge.

Tilley, C. 1999. *Metaphor and Material Culture.* Oxford: Blackwell.

Timby, J., Darvill, T., and Holbrook, N. 1998. The public building in insula VI. In N. Holbrook (ed.) *Cirencester: the Roman town defences, public buildings and shops*, 122–141. Cirencester: Cotswold Archaeological Trust (Cirencester Excavations V).

Todd, M. 1981. *Roman Britain, 55 BC–AD 400.* London: Fontana Press.

Todd, M. 2005. Baths or baptisteries? Holcombe, Lufton and their analogues. *Oxford Journal of Archaeology*, 24.3, 307–311.

Tomlin, R.S.O. 1976. Notitia dignitatum omnium, tam civilium quam militarium. In R. Goodburn and P. Bartholomew (eds.) *Aspects of the* Notitia Dignitatum, 189–209. Papers presented to the conference in Oxford, 13–15 December 1974. Oxford: B.A.R. Supplementary Series 15.

Tomlin, R.S.O. 1988. The curse tablets. In B. Cunliffe (ed.) *The Temple of Sulis Minerva at Bath: vol. 2, the finds from the sacred spring*, 59–277. Oxford: Oxford University Committee for Archaeology, Monograph No. 16.

Tonkin, E., McDonald, M., and Chapman, M. 1996. History and ethnicity. In J. Hutchinson and A.D. Smith (eds.) *Ethnicity*, 18–24. Oxford: Oxford University Press.

Treherne, P. 1995. The warrior's beauty: the masculine body and self-identity in Bronze Age Europe. *Journal of European Archaeology*, 3.1, 105–144.

Trigger, B.G. 1984. Alternative archaeologies: nationalist, colonialist, imperialist. *Man*, 19, 355–370.

Trigger, B.G. 1989. *A History of Archaeological Thought*. Cambridge: Cambridge University Press.

Tyers, P.A. 1996. *Roman Pottery in Britain*. London: Batsford.

Urry, J. 1991. Time and space in Giddens' social theory. In C.G.A. Bryant and D. Jary (eds.) *Giddens' Theory of Structuration: a critical appreciation*, 160–175. London: Routledge.

Urry, J. 2000a. *Sociology Beyond Societies: mobilities for the twenty-first century*. London: Routledge.

Urry, J. 2000b. Sociology of time and space. In B.S. Turner (ed.) *The Blackwell Companion to Social Theory*, 416–443. Oxford: Blackwell.

Varien, M.D. and Mills, B.J. 1997. Accumulations research: problems and prospects for estimating site occupation span. *Journal of Archaeological Method and Theory*, 4.2, 141–174.

Vegetius. *Epitome of Military Science* (*Epitoma Rei Militaris*). 1993. Translated by N.P. Milner. Liverpool: Liverpool University Press.

Vyner, B.E. and Allen, D.W.H. 1988. A Romano-British settlement at Caldicot, Gwent. In D.M. Robinson (ed.) *Biglis, Caldicot and Llandough: three Late Iron Age and Romano-British sites in south-east Wales, excavations 1977–79*, 65–122. Oxford: B.A.R. British Series 188.

Wacher, J.S. 1964. Cirencester, 1963. Fourth interim report. *The Antiquaries Journal*, 44, 9–18.

Wacher, J.S. 1965. Cirencester, 1964. Fifth interim report. *The Antiquaries Journal*, 45, 97–110.

Wacher, J.S. 1989. Cities from the second to fourth centuries. In M. Todd (ed.) *Research on Roman Britain: 1960–89*, 91–114. London: Society for the Promotion of Roman Studies (Britannia Monograph 11).

Wallace-Hadrill, A. 1986. Introduction. In Ammianus Marcellinus, *The Later Roman Empire (A.D. 354–378)*, 13–35. Translated by W. Hamilton. Harmondsworth: Penguin Books (Penguin Classics).

Walthew, C.V. 1981. Possible standard units of measurement in Roman military planning. *Britannia*, 12, 15–35.

Ward, T. and Strickland, T.J. 1978. *Chester Excavations: Northgate Brewery 1974–5. A Roman centurion's quarters and barrack*. Chester: Chester City Council/Grosvenor Museum.

Watson, G.R. 1969. *The Roman Soldier*. London: Thames and Hudson.

Webster, G. 1985. *The Roman Imperial Army*. London: A&C Black (3rd edition).

Webster, J. (with M. Guido, M. Henig, T. Ambrose, and D. Peacock) 1975. The finds. In B. Cunliffe, *Excavations at Portchester Castle, Volume I: Roman*, 198–269. London: Society of Antiquaries (Reports of the Research Committee of the Society of Antiquaries of London, XXXII).

Webster, J. 1988. Bronze and silver objects. In J. Parkhouse, Excavations at Biglis, South Glamorgan, 53–56. In D.M. Robinson (ed.) *Biglis, Caldicot and Llandough: three Late Iron Age and Romano-British sites in south-east Wales, excavations 1977–79*, 1–64. Oxford: B.A.R. British Series 188.

Webster, J., Scott, I.R., Evans, D.R., Allen, D., Greep, S.J., Parkhouse, J., Henig, M., and Barford, P.M. 1992. Small finds reports. In D.R. Evans and V.M. Metcalf, *Roman Gates Caerleon*, 103–196. Oxford: Oxbow Books.

Webster, J. and Cooper, N. (eds.) 1996. *Roman Imperialism: post-colonial Perspectives*. Leicester: University of Leicester, School of Archaeological Studies (Leicester Archaeology Monographs 3).

Webster, L. and Brown, M. (eds.) 1997. *The Transformation of the Roman World, AD 400–900*. London: British Museum Press.

Webster, P.V. 1988. Coarse pottery. In H.S. Owen-John, Llandough—the rescue excavation of a multi-period site near Cardiff, South Glamorgan, 161–170. In D.M. Robinson (ed.) *Biglis, Caldicot and Llandough: three Late Iron Age and Romano-British sites in south-east Wales, excavations 1977–79*, 123–178. Oxford: B.A.R. British Series 188.

Webster, P. 1993. Coarse pottery. In P.J. Casey, J.L. Davies, and J. Evans (eds.) *Excavations at* Segontium *(Caernarfon) Roman Fort, 1975–1979*, 250–316. London: C.B.A. Research Report 90.

Wells, P.S. 1999. *The Barbarians Speak*. Princeton, NJ: Princeton University Press.

Welsby, D.A. 1982. *The Roman Military Defence of the British Provinces in its Later Phases*. Oxford: B.A.R. British Series 101.

Wenger, E. 1998. *Communities of Practice: learning, meaning and identity*. Cambridge: Cambridge University Press.

Wenham, L.P. 1968. *The Romano-British Cemetery at Trentholme Drive, York*. London: H.M.S.O./Ministry of Public Building and Works (Archaeological Reports No. 5).

Wheeler, R.E.M. 1924. *Segontium and the Roman Occupation of Wales*. London: The Honourable Society of Cymmrodorion.

Wheeler, R.E.M. 1926. The Roman fort near Brecon. *Y Cymmrodor*, 37.

White, H. 1973. *Metahistory: the historical imagination in nineteenth-century Europe*. Baltimore: John Hopkins University Press.

Whittaker, C.R. 1994. *Frontiers of the Roman Empire: a social and economic study*. Baltimore: John Hopkins University Press.

Wiessner, P. 1989. Style and changing relations between the individual and society. In I. Hodder (ed.) *The Meanings of Things: material culture and symbolic expression*, 56–63. London: Harper Collins (One World Archaeology 6).

Wiessner, P. 1990. Is there a unity to style? In M. Conkey and C. Hastorf (eds.) *The Uses of Style in Archaeology*, 105–112. Cambridge: Cambridge University Press.

Wilkes, J. 1960. Excavations at Housesteads in 1959. *Archaeologia Aeliana*, Series 4, 38, 61–71.

Wilkes, J. 1961. Excavations in Housesteads fort, 1960. *Archaeologia Aeliana*, Series 4, 39, 279–301.

Wilkinson, P. 2001. *What the Romans did for us*. London: Boxtree.

Williams, A. and Frere, S. 1949. *Roman Canterbury: an account of the excavations in Butchery Lane, Christmas 1945 and Easter 1946*. London: Medici Society (Roman Canterbury IV).

Wilmott, T. 1993. The Roman cremation cemetery in New Field, Birdoswald. *Transactions of the Cumberland and Westmorland Antiquarian and Archaeological Society*, Series 2, 93, 79–86.

Wilmott, T. 1995. Collapse theory and the end of Birdoswald. In P. Rush (ed.) *Theoretical Roman Archaeology: second conference proceedings*, 59–69. Aldershot: Avebury (Worldwide Archaeology Series 14).

Wilmott, T. 1997. *Birdoswald: excavations of a Roman fort on Hadrian's Wall and its successor settlements: 1987–92*. London: English Heritage (Archaeological Report 14).

Wilson, R. 1980. *Roman Forts: an illustrated introduction to the garrison posts of Roman Britain*. London: Bergström and Boyle Books.

Wobst, H.M. 1977. Stylistic behavior and information exchange. *University of Michigan, Museum of Anthropology Anthropological Papers*, 61, 317–342.

Wood, I.N. 1992. Continuity or calamity? The constraints of literary models. In J. Drinkwater and H. Elton (eds.) *Fifth-Century Gaul: a crisis of identity?* 9–18. Cambridge: Cambridge University Press.

Woodward, K. 2002. *Understanding Identity*. London: Arnold.

Woolf, G. 1995. The formation of Roman provincial cultures. In J. Metzler, M. Millett, N. Roymans, and J. Slofstra (eds.) *Integration in the Early Roman West: the role of culture and ideology*, 9–18. Luxembourg: Musée National d'Histoire et d'Art.

Woolf, G. 1998. *Becoming Roman*. Cambridge: Cambridge University Press.

Woolf, G. 2004. The present state and future state of Roman archaeology: a comment. *American Journal of Archaeology*, 108, 417–428.

Wright, T. 1872. *Uriconium: a historical account of the ancient Roman city, and of the excavations made upon its site at Wroxeter, in Shropshire, forming a sketch of the condition and history of the Welsh border during the Roman period*. London: Longmans, Green & Co.

Wylie, A. 1992. The interplay of evidential constraints and political interests: recent archaeological research on gender. *American Antiquity*, 57.1, 15–35.

Yoffee, N. 1988. Orienting collapse. In N. Yoffee and G.L. Cowgill (eds.) *The Collapse of Ancient States and Civilizations*, 1–19. Tucson: University of Arizona Press.

Zienkiewicz, J.D. 1986a. *The Legionary Fortress Baths at Caerleon, I: the buildings*. Cardiff: National Museum of Wales/Cadw.

Zienkiewicz, J.D. 1986b. *The Legionary Fortress Baths at Caerleon, II: the finds*. Cardiff: National Museum of Wales/Cadw.

Zienkiewicz, J.D. 1988. British Telecom site, Museum Street, Caerleon. *G-GAT Annual Review 1987–88*, 8–9.

Zienkiewicz, J.D. 1993. Excavations in the *scamnum tribunorum* at Caerleon: the Legionary Museum site 1983–5. *Britannia*, 24, 27–140.

Zosimus. *New History (Nea Historia)*. 1982. Translated by R.T. Ridley. Sydney: Australian Association for Byzantine Studies.

INDEX

Abinnaeus Archive
  as collection of correspondence, 127, 210
  on masculinity, 231
  on military-civilian distinction, 218, 219, 225, 226
  on religion, 234
  and scribes, 124
  on violence by soldiers, 213
affective mode, 19
age
  as identity category, 202, 239
  in 21st century Roman studies, 32
agency. *See also* structuration theory
  as active involvement, 130
  conceptual role of, 18–19
  defined, 43
  in structuration theory, 43–45
  vs. structure, 40–43
Aldborough, 144
Allectus, 53
Alston, Richard, 231, 259
Ammianus Marcellinus
  on aggression by soldiers, 213
  on masculinity, 231
  on military-civilian distinction, 218–19, 220, 226
  military focus of, 28
  perspective of, 127, 187–89
  on religion, 234
analytical dualism, 45–46
Anglo-Saxon period, 28
animal bone, 94–97, 160–64
Antonine Wall, 53
Archer, Margaret, 45–46
architecture
  building plans, 114–19
  construction technologies, 119–22
  fortress plans, 105–7
  fort-type plans, 99–105
  structuration and space, 97–99
  town plans, 107–14
army, in traditional narrative, 55–56
army studies, 29–31
artefacts. *See* material culture; texts

barbarians. *See* ethnicity
barbarisation, perceived, 213–14
Barnsley Park, 149
barracks
  architecture of, 117–19
  at Caernarfon, 120
  at Housesteads, 171
  patterns of change in, 169–70
  at South Shields, 171–72
Barth, Fredrik, 198
Barton Court, 149
Bath, 124
baths
  architecture of, 115–16
  at Canterbury, 120
  changes over time, 194
  modifications to, 168
  structural changes to, in Canterbury, 172
  subdivision of, in Binchester, 171
BB1 (Black-Burnished Ware category 1), 91, 93, 157, 158, 160, 163
Biglis, 144, 149
Binchester
  changes over time, 169
  coin deposition history at, 144, 146
  modifications to baths, 168, 171
  modifications to *praetorium*, 194, 206
  rubbish deposits, 175
Binford, Lewis, 21
biographies of assemblages
  animal bone, 160–64
  coins: discussion, 150–51; methods of study, 139–43; regional comparisons, 143–46; site type comparisons, 145–50
  pottery, 157–60
  small finds, 151–57
biographies of built spaces
  administrative buildings, 167–69
  discussion, 171–72, 183–86
  domestic architecture, 169–71
  public vs. private spaces, 166–67
Birdoswald
  building inscriptions, 122

304 ■ INDEX

Birdoswald (*Continued*)
burials, 232
changes over time, 168, 192–93, 206
construction technologies, 119–20
deposits: coins, 71–73, 144, 146; pottery,
157–58; rubbish, 174, 175; small
finds, 84–85
and norms of military practice, 184
structures
barracks, 118
western gate area, 72
Black-Burnished Ware category 1 (BB1),
91, 93, 157, 158, 160, 163
bone, animal, 94–97, 160–64
Boudican revolt, 52
boundaries, ethnic, 199
Braintree, 148
Brecon Gaer
coin deposition history, 142, 144, 146
earthwork defences, 120
rubbish deposits, 173
British Empire (modern), 15, 16, 17,
26–27
British Empire (of 3rd century), 53
British Mean, 140–43
brooches
crossbow, 157, 206, 214, 215
penannular, 156
building plans, 114–19
Burgh Castle
barracks architecture, 119
coin deposition history at, 146
coin loss patterns, 145
burials
age-related practices, 239
changes in, 258–59
cremation *vs.* inhumation, 232–33
sexing of, 230
small finds in, 88–89

Cadw, 69
Caerhun
coin deposition history, 142, 144, 146
small finds, 81
Caerleon
changes over time, 227
construction materials, 120
deposits: animal bone, 160–61; coins,
140–42, 144, 146; pottery, 158;
rubbish, 173–76, *177*; small finds,
81

'Roman Gates' depositional chronology,
151, 152
structures: amphitheatre, 169; barracks,
119, 167–68; baths, 115–16, 168;
fortress, 16, 105–7
Caernarfon
changes over time, 168, 191–92
deposits: animal bone, 96, 161, 162;
coins, 69–71, 142, 144, 150;
crossbow brooches, 215; pottery,
92–93; rubbish, 175; small finds,
83–84, 151, 153
layout, *100–101*, 115
structures: barracks, 119, 120; baths,
116; southwestern corner, *70*;
temple, 233; timber gate tower, 120
Caerwent
changes over time, 227
deposits: coins, 142, 144, 148; rubbish,
175
layout, 107, 109–10, 115
structures: courtyard buildings, 170;
temples, 168, 234
calcite-gritted ware, 94
Caldicot, 144, 149
calendars, 136
Camerton, 146, 148
Canterbury
changes over time: baths, 168, 172;
prevalence of, 194; public buildings,
169
deposits: coins, 146, 147, 148; rubbish,
175, *180*, 182
layout, 110–11, 227
structures: baths, 120; houses, 170;
market stalls, 205; temple, 234
timber construction, 120
Carausius, 53, 123–24
Carlisle
deposits: coins, 144, 148; rubbish, 156:
small finds, 151–52, 154
domestic architecture, 170
timber construction, 120
categories of materials, 67
Catsgore, 149
chalet layout, 118–19
change as structured transformation,
247–53
chauvinism, temporal, 47
Chedworth, 146, 149
Chelmsford, 148

INDEX ■ 305

Chester
 barracks, 118
 changes over time, 169, 171
 construction materials: sill walls, 121;
  timber, 120
 deposits: coins, 146; rubbish, 174,
  176–77, *178*
 layout, 105–7
Christianity, 57, 232, 234
chronology of Roman Britain
 problems of interpretation, 55–59
 traditional narrative, 52–55
Cirencester
 changes over time: basilica, 171; central
  building, 168; forum, 226; public
  buildings, 169
 deposits: coins, 146, 147, 148; pottery,
  159; rubbish, 173, 175, *181*, 182;
  small finds, 81
 layout, 111, *112*
 practices: burials, 230; eating, 227
 structures: houses, 117, 170; urban farm,
  170
civitas capitals
 Canterbury as, 110
 coin deposition, 146–47
 in traditional narrative, 57
classical sources. *See also* historical writing,
  Roman; texts
 as focus for Roman studies, 24
 and Late Antique studies, 27–28
 and military identity, 210–11
classification of material, 67, 92
Claudius, 52, 104
clothing, 214–15
coin deposition
 trends in, 250–51
coins
 biographies of assemblages: discussion,
  150–51; methods of study, 139–43;
  regional comparisons, 143–46; site
  type comparisons, 145–50
 use of, 68
 general observations, 76–79
 inscriptions on, 123–24
 and military identity, 215–16
 patterns of supply, 69
 presence-availability and distanciation, 205
 at specific sites: Birdoswald, 71–73;
  Caernarfon, 69–71; South Shields,
  74–76; York, 76

collapse. *See* 'decline and fall' narratives
collective agency, 47
coloniae, 57, 110
commonalities, human, 15, 17, 22–23
complexity of soldiers' lives, 19–20
consciousness, 130, 202–3
conscription, 56
Constitution of Society, The (Giddens), 48
construction technologies, 119–22
context
 and archaeological methods, 48–51
 and artefacts, 65
 and spaces, 97
contubernia, 117
Cool, Hilary, 156
co-presence, 97, 126
courtyard houses, 117
cremation, 232–33
critical threshold, early 5th century as,
  253–57
crossbow brooches, 157, 206, 214, 215
cultural ideal, ancient Rome as, 24, 25
curse tablets, 124, 125

data, inter-relation with theories, 20
'decline and fall' narratives. *See also* Late
  Antique studies
 and Christianity, 59
 discourse of, in Roman studies, 25–26,
  27
 role of agency and identity, 20
 role of army in, 56
 and transition as historical category,
  137–38
Dewey, John, 42
diet, 31, 94–97, 160–64
differentness of Romans, 15, 17
Diocletian, 56
discursive consciousness, 46, 130, 202–3
distanciation, 97–98, 126, 204–5
domestic space
 building architecture, 116–19
 in Caerwent, 109–10
 patterns of change in, 166–67, 169–71
drystone construction, 120
dualism
 of agency vs. structure, 40–43 (*See also*
  structuration theory)
 analytical, 45–46
 generalist–particularist, 20–23
 and understandings of time, 134

306 ■ INDEX

duality (vs. dualism), 43, 44
dwelling practices
    and identity, 206–7
    and military identity, 211–12

earthworks, 120
eating practices
    and identity, 207–8
    institutionalisation of, 227
    and military identity, 216
elites, as focus of research, 24
embodiment, 42, 47
emotional dimensions of action, 130
empiricism, 36–37
English Heritage, 71
epigraphic habit, 123
Epitoma Rei Militaris (Vegetius), 127, 190
equipment, military, 29, 30
ethnicity
    and identity, 197–201, 234–36
    as theme of Late Antique studies, 26

familiarity, perception of, 15–16
farms
    coin deposition history at, 147, 149
    urban, 170–71
faunal remains, 94–97
Fel Temp Reparatio coin issues, 124, 150
Feriale Duranum, 136
Filey, 175
flooring materials, 120
fora, 115, 167–68
Forden Gaer, 107, *108*
fortresses
    at Caerleon, 16
    coin deposition histories at, 145–46
forts
    coin deposition histories at, 145–46
    layout of, 99–105
framing, 201
Frere, Sheppard, 35–36
frontier
    location of, 52–53
    studies of, 30–31
functionalism, 41
    material culture in, 63
    and style, 64

Gallic Empire, 53
garrison, in traditional narrative, 55–56
gender

and identity, 202, 229–31
and small finds, 80
in 21st century Roman studies, 32
and traditional research agenda, 24, 25
gendering of artefacts, 118, 119, 230
generalist–particularist dualism, 20–23
Germanisation, 58
Giddens, Anthony. *See also* structuration
    theory
    on conceptions of time, 134–36, 135
    on context, 129
    on hermeneutics and archaeology, 48
    on presence-availability, 97
Gloria Exercitus coin issues, 124, 216
Goffman, Erving, 42, 198, 201
golden age, 4th century as, 20
Greatchesters, 118
Guest, Peter, 147

habitual mode, 19
Hadrian's Wall, 53. *See also* Birdoswald;
    South Shields
Hägerstrand, Torsten, 134
Hall, Jonathan, 200
hall structures, 120
Haverfield, Francis, 26, 27
head-associated objects, 233
Heidegger, Martin, 42
hermeneutics
    archaeology, 48–49
    material culture, 64–65
    small- and large-scale analysis, 22
    theory and data, 37
Hingley, Richard, 26
historical theory
    and postmodernism, 36–39
    and post-processual movement, 25
historical writing, Roman
    Epitoma Rei Militaris (Vegetius), 127,
        190
    on military-civilian distinction, 218–19
    and military identity, 210–11
    Nea Historia (Zosimus), 127, 189–90
    Res Gestae (Ammianus), 127, 187–89
    truthfulness in, 125–27
Hodder, Ian, 21, 37
horrea, 168–69
hot and cold societies, 134–35
houses, 116–19, 170–71
Housesteads
    building inscriptions at, 122

changes over time: barracks, 169, 171, 194–95; building XV, 168; *principia*, 168

deposits: coins, 144, 146, 150; rubbish, 177–78, *179*

layout, 102

and military identity, 221–23

and norms of military practice, 184

stone roofing materials at, 120

structures: barracks: 118, 119, *222*; *principia*, 234

humanism, 22–23

hypocausts, 171–72

identity. *See also* military identity; nominal-virtual identity relationship

complexity of, 239–42, 261–64

conceptual role of, 18–19

and consciousness, 202–3

dimensions of: age, 202, 239; ethnicity, 197–201, 234–36; gender, 202, 229–31; kinship, 202; occupation, 201, 238–39; regionalism, 236–38; religion, 202, 231–34; social status, 238

and practice, 203–8

questions about, 59–60

understandings of: post-colonial, 32; in 21st century Roman studies, 31–32; in traditional research agenda, 24

individual, nature of, 41, 46–47

inhumation, 232–33

institutionalisation, 209–10, 227

instrumentalism, 198

intramural infant burials, 232–33

isochrestic style, 64

James, William, 42

Jenkins, Richard, 197, 199

Johnson, Matthew, 65

Jones, Siân, 198, 200

Julian, 188

Julius Caesar, 52, 125, 126

Kelvedon, 148

Kenchester, 148

kinship, 202

Lankhills, 88

Late Antique studies

and 'decline and fall' discourse, 26

within Roman studies, 27–29

Leicester

alterations to *forum*, 168

Christian cemetery, 232

coin deposition history, 146, 148

domestic architecture, 170

Leintwardine

coin deposition history, 148

layout, 107, *108*

Lévi-Strauss, Claude, 47, 134

Lincoln

deposits: animal bone, 96, 161, 162; rubbish, 175

domestic architecture, 170, 172

eating practices, 227

layout, *111*

literacy, 123–24

literary writing, 125–28

Llandough, 158, 159

Llantwit, 144

locales, 97–98

Lydney, 149

map of Roman Britain, *54*

Marlowe, 194

married quarters, 118, 119

Marxism

agency *vs.* structure in, 41

and classification of societies, 47

and late Roman Britain, 28

Maryport, 144

masculinity, 231

material culture. *See also* animal bone; architecture; coins; pottery; small finds; texts

approaches to interpretation, 63–67

and identity, 128–31

language-like meanings of, 38

materiality

conceptual role of, 18–19

in Roman studies, 32–33

and structuration theory, 51, 52

Mead, George Herbert, 42

mentality, 47

Merleau-Ponty, Maurice, 42

milestones, 122

military identity. *See also* identity; nominal-virtual identity relationship

as abstraction, 223–24

and institutionalisation, 209–10

and military-civilian distinction: in
Roman historical sources, 210–11,
218–19; and Roman state,
224–29
and practice contexts: coin use, 215–16;
eating, 216; fort architecture,
211–12; fort-based community, 212;
organised violence, 213–14;
personal appearance, 214–15
Miller, Danny, 66
Millett, Martin, 27
Mithraism, 58, 232–33
modern influences, 15, 33
modes of engagement, 19
monumental inscriptions, 122–23
mosaics, 122
Mouzelis, Nicos, 46
multi-vocality, 28–29
municipia, 57

Nazi Germany, 225
Nea Historia (Zosimus), 25, 127, 189–90
Nene Valley ware, 93, 94
Nettleton, 149
New Archaeology
artefacts in, 63
Binford on, 21
style in, 64
views of identity, 198
nominal-virtual identity relationship
general comments, 217–20
and identity categories: age, 239;
ethnicity, 234–36; gender, 229–31;
occupation, 238–39; regionalism,
236–38; religion, 231–34; social
status, 238
and military-civilian distinction, 223
at specific sites: Housesteads, 221–23;
South Shields, 220–21
Notitia Dignitatum
on ethnicity, 236
on Housesteads, 220
military focus of, 28
on military vs. civilian authority, 218–19,
220
production and copying, 128, 210

occupational identity, 32, 201, 213–14,
238–39
origin myths. *See* political ideal, ancient
Rome as

Orton Hall
animal bone, 96, 163
coins, 146, 149
pottery, 94
small finds, 81, 152–56
Oudenburg, 88–89, 157, 215

penannular brooches, 156
performative processes, 199
personal objects
and barbarianism, 235
and gender identity, 230–31
presence-availability and distanciation,
205–6
phenomenology, 41–42, 66
political ideal, ancient Rome as, 15–17,
24–27
Pollard, Nigel, 259
Portchester
barracks architecture, 119
changes over time, 194–95
deposits: coins, 146; rubbish, 175,
178–82; small finds, 81
layout, 104
timber construction, 120
postmodernism, 36–39, 65
post-processual archaeology
and gender and cultural biases, 25
and generalist–particularist dualism,
21–22
and interpretation of texts, 37
on material culture, 64–66
and postmodern history, 38–39
post-structuralism, 64–65
Potter, David, 126
pottery, 90–94, 157–60
practical consciousness, 130, 202–3
practice and identity, 203–8
praetoria, 169–71
pragmatism, 42–43, 66
presence-availability, 97–98, 204–5
principia, 115, 167–68, 171
private space. *See* domestic space
processual archaeology
and context, 50
and gender and cultural biases, 25
and generalist–particularist dualism,
21–22
material culture in, 63
and *The Romanization of Britain* (Millett)
and texts, 37

INDEX ■ 309

rational choice theory, 40–41
reality of social structure, 46, 47
reflective mode, 19
regionalisation
    and building plans, 114–15
    and presence-availability, 97–98
    at town sites, 110
regionalism, 236–38
relativism
    and artefacts as texts, 65
    vs. empiricism, 36–37
religion
    and identity, 202, 231–34
    in 21st century Roman studies, 32
    in traditional narrative, 57–58
rescript of Honorius, 190
Res Gestae. See Ammianus Marcellinus
resolution, degrees of
    in archaeological vs. historical data, 37
    and context, 49
    as defining problem of sociology, 40
    and 'Romanisation' narrative, 59
reversible and irreversible time,
    134–35
Richborough
    barracks architecture, 119
    coin deposition history, 146
    layout, 104–5
    possible timber construction in, 120
Rivenhall, 117, 149
'Roman Gates' excavation, 151, 152
Roman Imperial Army (Webster), 30
Romanisation paradigm
    and beef consumption, 161
    collapse of, 33, 34
    as dominant historical narrative, 58
    and modern imperialism, 27, 28
    and pottery, 90
    as theory of identity, 31, 32
    in towns vs. forts, 112
Romanization of Britain, The (Millett), 27
Roman studies
    Britain in, 26–29
    broadening of perspective in, 24–25
    and Late Antiquity, 25–26
    military in, 29–31
    21st century agenda, 31–34
roofing materials, 120
routinisation, 202–3
rubbish disposal
    and coins, 70–71, 73–75, 147

and cultural attitudes to waste, 172–73,
    184, 185
    discussion, 182–83
    fortress sites, 176–82
    spatial location of, 173–76
    town sites, 182–83
Rudston, 149

Sackett, James, 64
Samian pottery
    absence of, at Birdoswald, 157
    copies of, 160
    deposits over time, 163
    as index of cultural change, 90
Saxon Shore, 53, 119. *See also* Portchester
    Castle; Richborough
Schutz, Alfred, 42
self-identity, 43
Shanks, Michael, 22
shell-tempered pottery, 160, 163
Shennan, Stephen, 198
Silchester, 147, 148
sill walls, 120, 121
small finds
    in barracks, 118
    in burials, 88–89
    comparative deposition patterns,
        81–82
    defined, 79–80
    examples, *82*
    functional categorizing of, 80–82
    at Orton Hall Farm, 81
    patterns over time, 151–57
    at specific sites: Birdoswald, 84–85;
        Caerhun, 81; Caerleon, 81, 151,
        152; Caernarfon, 83–84, 151, *153*;
        Carlisle, 151–52, *154*; Cirencester,
        81; Orton Hall, 152–56, *155*;
        Portchester Castle, 81; South
        Shields, 81, 85–86; York, 85–88
Smith, J. T., 117
social constructionism, 37
social histories, 29, 31
sociality
    conceptual role of, 18–19
    and structuration theory, 51, 52
social status, 32, 238
source criticism, 25, 37
South Shields
    changes over time, 193–94, 206
    construction technologies, 119–20

310 ■ INDEX

South Shields (*Continued*)
  deposits: coins, 74–76, 144; pottery, 158;
      rubbish, 175; small finds, 81, 85–86
  layout, 102–4
  and military identity, 212, 220–21
  and norms of military practice, 184
  structures: barracks, 118, 119, 169–72;
      central building, 168, 233–34;
      horrea, 168; officer's house, *221*;
      southwestern gate, *74*
spolia, 120
squatters, 16
stall structures, 120
stone construction, 120, 121
Strabo, 125
structural anthropology, 134
structuralism, 41
structuration theory
  and archaeological interpretation, 47–51
  and architecture, 97–99
  criticisms of, 45–47
  and identity, 199–200
  and materiality, temporality, sociality,
      51, 52
  outline of theory, 43–45
  and problem of dualism, 39–43
structure. *See also* structuration theory
  conceptual role of, 18–19
  in structuration theory, 43–45
  vs. agency, 40–43
style, artefactual, 63–64
sub-Roman studies, 28
symbolic interactionism, 42

Tacitus, 125, 126
taxation, 56
taxonomies of materials, 67
temples
  changes in, 234
  coin deposition history at, 147, 149
temporal chauvinism, 47
temporality. *See also* biographies of
      assemblages; biographies of built
      spaces; rubbish disposal
  and artefacts, 164–66
  conceptual role of, 18–19
  and Roman historical texts, 186–90
  and structuration theory, 51, 52, 191–95
  theoretical background, 133–39
tetrarchic system, 53, 56
texts

as artefacts, 37–38, 65
dearth of, 122–23
and literacy, 123–24
and literary writing, 125–28
postmodern view of, 36–37
relation to theoretical framework,
    35–36, 38
Theodosian Code, 127–28, 218, 219, 225,
    226
theories, inter-relation with data, 20
Thomas, Julian, 22, 37
Tilley, Christopher, 22
timber construction, 120, 121
time. *See* temporality
time-geography, 134, 135
tombstones, 123
total institutions, 201
townhouses, 170, 172
transformation processes, 33, 50
transition, as historical category,
    137–38
translation, archaeological interpretation
    as, 17

Uley, 149
urban farms, 170–71
utilitarianism, 42

Vegetius, 127, 190
Verulamium, 148
villas
  coin deposition history at, 147, 149
  internal spaces in, 117
  as spending focus, 57
  in traditional narrative, 52
Vindolanda, 122, 210
violence, 213–14

Wallsend, 118, 119
war machine, 19
Wheeler, Mortimer, 69
Whitton, 149
Wiessner, Polly, 64
Winchester, 148
Wobst, Martin, 64
women, Roman view of, 229
working practices
  and identity, 207
  and military identity, 213–14
Wroxeter
  changes over time, 169, 227

Index ■ 311

construction technologies, 119
deposits: coins, 146, 147, 148; crossbow
    brooches, 157
layout, 110, *113*
post-Roman construction, 121
structures: baths, 168; *forum*, 168;
    halls, 120; houses, 170; temple,
    234

York
    changes over time, 119, 168, 171,
        193–94, 226
    deposits: coins, 76, 77, 144, 150;
        rubbish, 175, 176; small finds,
        85–88, *87*

Zosimus, 25, 127, 189–90

ABOUT THE AUTHOR

Andrew Gardner is Lecturer in the Archaeology of the Roman Empire at the Institute of Archaeology, University College London. He has worked previously at the University of Reading, the University of Leicester, and Cardiff University. His publications include the edited volume *Agency Uncovered: Archaeological Perspectives on Social Agency, Power, and Being Human* (Left Coast Press), and his research interests centre upon the social dynamics of Roman imperialism, the role of material culture in the expression of cultural identity, and the ways in which people in different societies understand time.